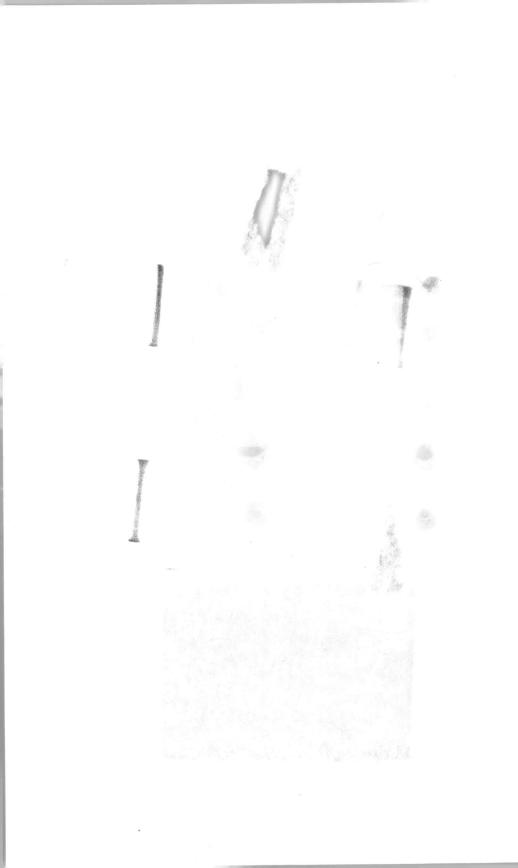

BAYREUTH:

THE EARLY YEARS

BAYREUTH:

THE EARLY YEARS

An account of the Early Decades of the Wagner Festival as seen by the Celebrated Visitors & Participants

Compiled, edited and introduced by

ROBERT HARTFORD

CAMBRIDGE UNIVERSITY PRESS
Cambridge
London   New York   New Rochelle
Melbourne   Sydney

Published by the Press Syndicate of the
University of Cambridge
32 East 57th Street, New York, NY 10022, USA

Selection and original material © Robert Hartford 1980

Library of Congress Catalog Number: 80–67459
ISBN 0 521 23822 6

ACKNOWLEDGMENTS

For permission to use copyright material, acknowledgment is due to:

Boosey & Hawkes Music Publishers Ltd for *Recollections and Reflections* by Richard Strauss
Calder & Boyars Ltd and Weissberger and Harris (NY) for *Chronicle of My Life: An Auto-biography* by Igor Stravinsky
Curtis Brown Ltd for *My Life of Music* by Sir Henry Wood
Faber & Faber Ltd for *Béla Bartók Letters* edited by Janos Démény
John Farquharson Ltd for *Music Criticisms 1846–1899* by Eduard Hanslick, in the translation by Henry Pleasants III
Hamish Hamilton Ltd for *My Own Trumpet* by Sir Adrian Boult
The Hutchinson Publishing Group Ltd for *Buffets and Rewards* by Felix Weingartner and *A Mingled Chime* by Sir Thomas Beecham
The Society of Authors on behalf of the Bernard Shaw Estate and The Bodley Head, publishers of *Shaw's Music, the Complete Musical Criticism*, 3 volumes, edited by Dan H. Laurence
Mr Hallam Tennyson for the radio broadcast *Memories of Bayreuth* by his late father, Sir Charles Tennyson
The Hogarth Press, Quentin Bell, Angelica Garnett and Harcourt Brace Jovanovich Inc., New York, for Virginia Woolf's article, 'Impressions at Bayreuth'
Faber & Faber Ltd and the St Martin's Press Inc., New York, for *Alban Berg, Letters to his Wife* edited by Bernard Grun

Printed in Great Britain at
The Camelot Press Ltd, Southampton

CONTENTS

LIST OF ILLUSTRATIONS

Between pages 192 and 193
(all photographs by Sidney Loeb)

FIGURES IN THE TEXT

PREFACE

I SEE THIS book as serving to entertain, divert or instruct those with idle moments between the serious business of attending the Wagner performances at Bayreuth; I hope it will appeal to those who have already been to the Festival as well as those who intend some day to go there. In addition, those who have no wish to set foot within a hundred miles of the place may find many good reasons for staying away, even though the commentators who give them were writing as much as a century ago.

The Bayreuth visitor will today find a town of 70,000 inhabitants with a new University, a fine concert hall and conference centre, a certain amount of light industry and the general air of prosperity common to all of modern West Germany. The main point of interest in Bayreuth, however, remains its association with Richard Wagner and the yearly Festivals devoted to his works.

The town suffered needlessly in the later stages of the Second World War, but narrowly escaped being encapsulated in the German Democratic Republic; the frontier is only a few kilometres away. The bombing in 1945 destroyed the rear section of Wagner's house, Wahnfried, including the *Saal*; the Festspielhaus, a magnificent target up on its hill, was spared.

In 1949 Wahnfried was repaired in a rather utilitarian way to make it habitable for Wieland Wagner and his family; it also housed the Archive that had been collected by Siegfried Wagner and Otto Strobel. In 1973 the Richard Wagner Foundation was set up, largely at the instigation of Winifred Wagner; until then the entire Wagner apparatus at Bayreuth – Wahnfried, the Festspielhaus and all the material in the Archive – had been the private property of the Wagner family. The funds for the Foundation came from the Federal Government, the State of Bavaria, the City of Bayreuth and the Friends of Bayreuth, as well as private individuals. Wahnfried was given by Winifred and Wolfgang Wagner to be arranged as a Wagner Museum.

Before this could be done essential repairs to the fabric of the building had to be carried out, the two main rooms, the *Halle* and the *Saal*, had to be restored to their original state and the other rooms prepared for exhibition purposes. Wolfgang Wagner directed the restoration work, and he and his mother were of considerable help in matters such as the colour of the walls and woodwork and the general layout of the house, for they had both lived there for many years before it was damaged and when it had been kept just as it had been in the Master's time.

Despite the many experts who were brought in to deal with the restoration there were unavoidable delays and it was only on the morning of the opening ceremony, when the official speeches were being made outside in the garden, that the last display cases were installed and the final exhibits placed in them.

The opening took place on 24 July 1976, the centenary year of the Festival.

As it now stands the Wahnfried Museum is a record of the life and achievements of its builder and owner; in this it is a model of its kind, neither pompous nor stuffy and showing an awareness of some of the absurdities that have accrued over the years to the names of Wagner and Bayreuth. The vaults are a house of rare treasure for here are kept the autograph scores of *Der fliegende Holländer*, *Tristan und Isolde*, *Siegfried*, *Götterdämmerung* and *Parsifal*.

On the other side of the town, the Festspielhaus is the busy scene of the Festivals held every year from the end of July to the end of August. Visitors flock from many lands, and the demand for tickets is sufficient to fill the theatre several times over. Opinions as to the musical and dramatic values of the productions vary a great deal, but the Festival Director, Wolfgang Wagner, grandson of the founder, has fortunately not allowed the Festival to rest entirely on tradition. He has encouraged experiment in the staging of the operas and kept the interest of the audiences; today Bayreuth is full of life, excitement and controversy, and that surely would have pleased Richard Wagner more than anything.

In the first part of this book I have attempted to show that for Wagner and his novel works Bayreuth was a necessity and not, as has often been said, a temple he erected for self-aggrandisement. Whatever its qualities, theatres on the Bayreuth pattern have not proliferated, the single exception being the Munich Prinzregententheater built in 1901, and Wagner's operas are given with great success in traditional opera houses. However, Wagner's concept of the Festival in the manner of Ancient Greece has proved an enduring one, as the many annual events now flourishing all over the world show.

In 'Interlude' I have drawn together, under their national headings, various groups of visitors to Bayreuth and related their varied reactions to Wagner and his Festival. For the rest, I have allowed them to speak for themselves. To the best of my knowledge a number of the extracts appear in English for the first time. For help in translating Saint-Saëns I am indebted to Alain Royer, for similar assistance with Grieg to Bente Marcussen; in both cases the final version is my own. The translations of Lilli Lehmann, Humperdinck and the Brockhaus letter are mine; the Romain Rolland piece was given to me several years ago by Dr Joachim Bergfeld of Bayreuth in an uncredited German version – not being able to discover the original, I have translated the translation.

Some of the previously published material has had very small editorial alterations made to achieve a consistency of style. Bernard Shaw's idiosyncratic spelling and punctuation has been retained; he disliked the mixing of Roman and Italic letters and refused to use quotation marks ('I want none of those bacilli infecting my pages') to distinguish, say, Lohengrin the man from *Lohengrin* the work. I am pleased to note that *The Perfect Wagnerite* and Shaw's other writings on music are to be re-issued in 1980 by The Bodley Head, London.

My thanks also to Dr O. G. Bauer of Bayreuth for allowing me to reproduce the plans of the Festspielhaus, and to Reginald Coleman for drawing the ground plan of Wahnfried. Sylvia Loeb, who lives in Chelsea, and who is the granddaughter of no less a figure than Hans Richter, very kindly provided me with photographs taken by her father, of the celebrities around Bayreuth at the turn of the century; many of these are published for the first time. Margot Levy of Victor Gollancz made many helpful suggestions when preparing the manuscript for publication. Sonia Crutchlow was of invaluable assistance in scrutinizing the page proofs and making the Index.

LONDON   R.H.
1980

PART I

Introduction

Richard Wagner and the Idea of the Festival

RICHARD WAGNER'S TURBULENT life spanned seventy years of a century of momentous political, social and artistic change. By the middle of the century, his part in the revolutionary movement then threatening the established order all over the continent of Europe had forced Wagner to flee his native Saxony for exile in Switzerland. During his years there Wagner began to conceive a new art form for the musical theatre. In 1848 he had completed the romantic opera *Lohengrin*, and from that time on he was to insist that the works he planned to succeed it would not be 'operas' but 'dramas' (the term 'music drama', in the Wagnerian sense as opposed to the antique Italian *dramma per musica*, came later and Wagner himself never used it). The distinction was to prove a revolutionary one.

It was probably inevitable that Wagner would become involved in the theatre in one form or another, for he was born (in Leipzig in 1813) into a family with many theatrical connections. His father, who died when Richard was only six months old, was a passionate theatre-goer and amateur actor, and three of his older children took up singing or acting as a career. Ludwig Geyer, Wagner's stepfather, was a professional actor of some standing, and by the age of twelve Richard had already written several juvenile dramas and sketches for plays. His musical education was not a conventional one: Leipzig and Dresden, where he spent his formative years, were musical centres of importance out of all proportion to their size and, although he did receive some formal tuition there, in later years he liked to give the impression that he had largely taught himself by studying important scores, such as Beethoven's Ninth Symphony, then a novel and much misunderstood work. When dictating his autobiography many years later, Wagner gave a vivid account of an event that he claimed set him on his path as innovator in the opera house. When he was just sixteen, he saw Wilhelmine Schröder-Devrient as Leonore in *Fidelio*; this dramatic singing actress had so impressed Beethoven in his opera in 1822 that he promised to write another one for her. Wagner could not contain his excitement after her performance and wrote to tell her that '. . . from that moment my life had acquired its true significance, and that if in days to come she should ever hear my name praised in the world of Art, she must remember that she had that evening made me what I swore it was my destiny to become.'

The state of music and the condition of the musician in Central Europe in the first half of the nineteenth century are described by Ernest Newman in Volume I of his *Life of Richard Wagner*. Weber, Spohr, Lortzing, Berlioz, Schumann and the two Englishmen, Henry Chorley and Edward Holmes, all wrote about the music-making of their day and from their accounts it appears conditions were wretched. Even in Germany, concerts were a haphazard affair, with small incompetent orchestras led (more often than not) by a conductor who could read no more than the first violin part of the score. Little wonder that the 'new' music of Beethoven was not comprehended, for it was rarely given an adequate performance. Concert programmes demonstrate that the public appetite was fed with what satisfied it most easily; a symphony was more readily digested if the gaps between the movements were filled with sugary songs or trivial display pieces. The condition of the performing musician was a miserable one too: the changes in the social order had virtually destroyed aristocratic patronage, and if he was unable to lead the life of the travelling virtuoso – like Chopin, Paganini or Liszt – he was doomed to a life of drudgery in an opera house. Italian opera was in demand all over Europe, and where the Italians went they took the standards of Italy with them. Berlioz described an opera house in Milan 'full of people talking at the tops of their voices with their backs to the stage,' and Schumann wrote that 'music in Italy is hardly to be tolerated, you have no idea of the slovenliness'. For their part, audiences demanded an endless succession of novelties; anything substantial or designed to last was out of favour, and the composer was compelled to produce new operas of this order or starve. As Gerald Abraham points out,* it is astonishing that against this background works as fine as *Il Barbiere, Norma* and *Don Pasquale* came to be written.

In 1833 Wagner began his career as a professional musician when he went to Würzburg as chorus-master and *répétiteur*. His brother Albert already held a post at this theatre and Wagner was able to avoid military service by moving there. During the next six years he worked, first as musical assistant and eventually as conductor, on the preparation of operas and other stage works for the modest provincial theatres at Würzburg, Magdeburg and Riga. He also worked for a short time at Königsberg. It is interesting to note that Wagner actually visited Bayreuth for the first time in 1835 when he was sent by the theatre at Magdeburg on a search for promising young singers; he was then twenty-two years old, and not yet married to Minna. He arrived in Bayreuth after travelling through the Fichtelgebirge on his way to Nuremberg and in his autobiography, *Mein Leben*, he recorded that happy memories of the little town, 'gloriously illumined by the setting sun', remained long in his mind.

Wagner's first biographer, Carl Friedrich Glasenapp, who knew the Master and who became an acolyte of Wahnfried, provides a list of the operas with which the young musician was involved between 1833 and 1839.† The list shows the influences that played to varying degrees on Wagner in the years he wrote *Die Feen* and *Das Liebesverbot*, and made a start on *Rienzi*. It shows too the repertoire of a typical small opera house; there is a surprising preference for 'modern' works, but rather than this indicating advanced public taste, it is more likely that the provincial audiences merely craved what was currently fashionable in the larger centres.

The opera house at Riga, where Wagner worked for two years from August 1837, was not built like the old Italian-style opera houses with their tiers of showy boxes, their gilded ornamentation, plush furnishings and brilliant chandeliers, where the audience was more interested in displaying itself than in what was happening on the stage. The Riga house was built of wood, and the seating in the auditorium was deeply raked, with the orchestra and conductor out of sight in a deep pit under the stage, in contrast to the traditional theatres where they often formed a visible barrier between audience and performer. Furthermore, during a performance the house lights were lowered – a most unusual practice at this time. Wagner found all these things kept the audience's attention on the stage and added greatly to the effectiveness of what was taking place there, and it is possible to see how these elements were incorporated in his concept of an ideal theatre, and later developed for the one he built in Bayreuth.

Another episode too may be considered in this context. In 1839, during his first visit to Paris, Wagner went to a performance of Beethoven's Ninth Symphony. This was in fact a public rehearsal at the Conservatoire taken by the Director, François Habeneck. Wagner found himself seated in a part of the hall which was screened off from the rest; he could hear the orchestra perfectly even though he was denied sight of it. To Wagner the effect was magical; the music 'came to the ear in a compact and ethereal unity' and the eye was spared the distraction of the players' efforts and contortions. Here, without doubt, is the genesis of the invisible orchestra, that unique feature of the Bayreuth Festspielhaus.

The succeeding phase of what might be described as Wagner's theatrical enlightenment came when he took up the post of assistant conductor in the opera house at Dresden in 1842. Wagner now had two new works of his own awaiting performance and a very disparate pair they were: *Rienzi* and *Der fliegende Holländer*, one a traditional 'grand opera' in the Parisian style, and the other what may be termed 'proto-music-drama'. Weber and E. T. A. Hoffmann had already tried to unify the content of the opera and do away with the regime of set numbers, and this had been Wagner's aim too when he wrote the *Holländer*. To his dismay it was the older 'primitive' opera which succeeded, while the other piece was received with reserve and lack of understanding. By now Wagner was aware that his future output would be along the lines of the *Holländer* and if the public wanted more *Rienzi*s it would have to look elsewhere. Likewise, he himself would have to look elsewhere than the opera houses if he wanted his new works produced in anything like accordance with his wishes.

In his present condition of poorly-paid musical assistant, there was little Wagner could do about this state of affairs except write the articles, essays and polemics that were to be a regular feature of his life until the very day he died. In 1849 he pieced together some of his complaints and misgivings in 'A Project for the Organisation of a German National Theatre' in which he made a plea for, amongst other things, fewer performances but of a superior quality. There had been rumours that the Court officials were intending to reduce the amount of money made available to the Dresden Opera House: Wagner's riposte, that in the theatre the people should not take second place to the Court, went too far. It was even seen as a challenge to the throne of Saxony and when there was a revolutionary uprising in Dresden in 1849 and Wagner was to be found at the barricades with Michael Bakunin, Auguste Röckel and Theodor Uhlig the outcome was certain – a price on his head and flight and exile in Switzerland.

During the first years of his exile Wagner was not actually engaged in writing music; instead he was attempting to consolidate his artistic principles and present these lofty concepts to his friends and to the general public (or such of it as cared) in letters and lengthy essays, the most important of which were 'Das Kunstwerk der Zukunft' ('The Artwork of the Future') in 1850, and 'Oper und Drama' ('Opera and Drama') in 1851, outlining the dramatic and musical principles subsequently embodied in the *Ring*.

From this time too stems the autobiographical article 'Eine Mitteilung an meine Freunde' ('A Communication to my Friends'), and it shows Wagner was beginning to change his mind about reforming the condition of the existing opera houses. If he had been unable to do much about it when in Dresden there was even less he could do about it now so, being the man he was, Wagner set his sights on a still higher target. Before the development of the *Ring* called forth its special requirements, Wagner had written to Uhlig in 1850 defining the concept of a totally new kind of theatre, one quite different from the conventional Italian opera house favoured by so many Courts. Wagner was to develop this idea in his treatise 'A Theatre in Zurich' of 1851 and again much later in 'The Vienna Royal Opera' of 1863 and 'A German School of Music' of 1865. However, the real germ of the idea is connected with the creation of the *Ring* and the problems of staging such a work. In 1850 Wagner wrote to Ferdinand Heine, an old family friend from Leipzig who now worked as stage designer at the Dresden Opera:

> I am now thinking of writing the music to *Siegfried*. In order to be able to produce it properly some day, I am cherishing all sorts of bold and unusual plans, for the realisation of which nothing further is necessary than that some rich old uncle or other should take it into his head to die.

Siegfried at this stage was *Siegfried's Tod* [sic] which Wagner later revised as the final drama of the *Ring*. He had been offered 500 thalers by Liszt, then in charge of the Court Theatre at Weimar (where he had given the first performance of *Lohengrin* in 1848), for the production there of this new work. Nothing came of it, however, and Wagner wrote to his friend Theodor Uhlig, who played the violin in the Dresden Opera Orchestra, on 30 September 1850:

> I should like to send *Siegfried* into the world in a different fashion from that which would be possible to the good people of Weimar. With this in mind, I am occupied with plans which appear chimerical at the first glance, and yet it is this alone which gives me heart to finish *Siegfried*. In order to carry into execution my plans in regard to the best, the most important and significant work which I am able to produce under any circumstances – in short to accomplish the conscious mission of my life – would mean a matter of 10,000 thalers. If I could command such a sum, I should proceed as follows:

Here, in Zurich, where I now chance to be, and where many conditions are far from unfavourable, I should erect a rough theatre of planks and beams, according to my own plans, in a beautiful meadow near the city, and furnish it merely with the scenery and machinery necessary for *Siegfried*. Then I would select the best available artists and invite them to come to Zurich. I should go about selecting my orchestra in the same way. At the new year a notification of the event would be made through the leading newspapers of Germany to all friends of the musical drama, with an invitation to be present at the proposed music festival; anyone giving due notice and coming to Zurich for the purpose would be assured admission, gratis of course, as would be all admissions.

The invitation would be further extended to the young people of Zurich and to the University students and to members of the various choral societies.

When everything was in order, I should give three performances of *Siegfried* in the course of a week; after the third, the theatre would be pulled down and the score burned.

To those who had been pleased with the thing, I should say – Now let me see you do the same!

If, however, they wished to hear something more from my pen, I should say – You furnish the money!

Well, do I seem quite mad to you? It may be, but I assure you that to be able to do this is the end and aim of my life, and the only prospect which could tempt me to commence a new work of art.

In 1852 Wagner wrote to Liszt and once more indicated what he had in mind:

I can only imagine my audience as being composed of friends who have assembled in some place for the sole purpose of becoming familiar with my works – preferably, in some beautiful retreat far from the smoke and industrial odours of city civilisation: as such a retreat, I should at the most consider Weimar, but certainly no larger city.

By 1852 the *Ring* poem was cast in its final four-part form and Wagner had a few copies printed privately; not a note of the music had been written, and he had no idea how, when and where the colossal work would be performed. Nevertheless, he gave his friends wildly optimistic dates for completion: in 1854 he said it would be 1856, but by March of that year he had progressed no further than the end of *Die Walküre*. Failure to keep to a schedule, albeit a self-imposed one, was to become a way of life for Wagner as far as the *Ring* was concerned. It is true he was compelled to earn a living, and the giving of concerts, which also did something to promote his music, was one way that he found not too uncongenial, even if it took him away from his creative work for long intervals.

It was during one such concert tour, in London in 1855, that Wagner came across an old friend and fellow-revolutionary from his Dresden days, Gottfried Semper. Semper, also an exile, was an architect with a passionate interest in music. He was responsible for the design of the Dresden Opera House and the

South Kensington Museums in London, and with him Wagner saw a way of getting his ideal theatre designed if not actually built. He persuaded Semper to return to Switzerland with him, but although they were there together for three years, nothing in the shape of a new theatre building came of the collaboration.

When the poem *Der Ring des Nibelungen* was published in 1862, Wagner's Preface to this first edition showed that the idea of a festival in a secluded small town, with a theatre specially built for the performances, was now firmly established in his mind:

> With me the chief thing is to imagine such a performance as entirely free from the influence of the repertory system in vogue in our permanent theatres. Accordingly, I have in mind one of the smaller German cities, favourably located and adapted to the entertainment of distinguished guests, and particularly a city in which there would be no collision with a larger permanent theatre, and where, consequently, a strictly metropolitan theatrical public with its well-known customs would not present itself. Here a provisionary theatre would be erected, as simple as possible, perhaps only of wood, and with the interior designed only for artistic purposes. I should confer with an experienced and intelligent architect as to a plan for such a house, with amphitheatrical arrangement of the seats, and the decided advantage of an invisible orchestra. Here then, in the early spring months, the leading dramatic singers, chosen from the ensemble of the German opera houses, would be assembled, in order to study the various parts of my stage work, entirely uninterrupted by any other claims upon their artistic abilities.
>
> On the days appointed for the performance – of which I have in mind three in all – the German public would be invited to be present, as these performances, like those of our large music festivals, are to be made accessible, not only to the partial public of any one city, but to all friends of art, far and near.
>
> A complete performance of the dramatic poem in question would take place in midsummer – on a fore-evening *Das Rheingold* and on the three following evenings the chief dramas *Die Walküre*, *Siegfried* and *Götterdämmerung*.
>
> To complete the impression of such a performance, I should lay great stress upon an invisible orchestra, which it would be possible to effect by the architectural illusion of an amphitheatrical arrangement of the auditorium.
>
> The importance of this will be clear to anyone who attends any of our present operatic performances for the purpose of gaining any genuine impression of the dramatic art work, and finds himself made the involuntary witness of the mechanical movements made by the players and conductor. These should be as carefully concealed as the wires, roped canvas and boards of the stage machinery, the sight of which, as everyone must know, creates a most disturbing impression and one calculated to destroy all illusions.
>
> After having experienced what a pure, etherealised tone the orchestra gains by being heard through an acoustic sounding-board which has the effect of eliminating all the non-musical but inevitable sounds which the instrumentalist is obliged to make in producing the notes; after having realised the ad-

vantageous position in which the singer is set before his listeners, by being able to stand, as it were, directly before them – no one could arrive at other than a favourable conclusion as to the effectiveness of my plan for an acoustic-architectural arrangement.

The building of a theatre for the performance of his own works would also ensure that the *Ring* was produced in a manner which Wagner alone could control, and he had in this respect the example of Berlioz who, in Wagner's Paris days, used to assemble a special orchestra to play his music. Furthermore, Wagner might with his own theatre be able to prevent the performance of his new works without the payment of royalties to the composer, as had happened in the case of his earlier operas.

The next stage in Wagner's progress to Bayreuth is marked by one of the most remarkable and dramatic events in a life rarely free from such things. In 1864 he was summoned to Munich by King Ludwig II of Bavaria, who at once told him that his theatre would be built in that city and his works performed there without delay.

This young king had come to the throne in 1864 at the age of eighteen; he was of an unusually intellectual disposition, having no use for royal pursuits such as soldiering or hunting, nor much tolerance for his courtiers, his subjects or the trappings of the Church. His entourage found it impossible to accommodate him to the more conservative notion of kingship, and conveniently dismissed him as 'mad' (something he was certainly not – either clinically or legally). Discovering *Lohengrin* as a boy, Ludwig had plunged into as many of the works of Wagner as he could find; to escape from the uncongenial world around him he sought to dwell in a mental world of myth and legend. In the pursuit of these fantasies he had acquired a copy of a poem of *Der Ring des Nibelungen*, and its spirit had fired his romantic imagination.

When Wagner prepared this verse drama for publication in 1862, he had introduced it by stating that the realisation of the work in accordance with his wishes would only be possible through the support of a group of wealthy art-lovers, or by the patronage of a German prince. 'But where,' wrote Wagner, 'would this prince be found?' Just two years later it was the prince who sought out, and eventually found, the composer. It seemed that Wagner, now the object of the King's indulgence, was set for the most spectacular success that any musician had ever known. At their first effusive meetings in Munich it was decided that Wagner would complete the music for the *Ring* cycle while the King, with the Wittelsbachs' zeal for building, would erect a monumental stone theatre with a ceremonial approach and a new bridge over the Isar. In addition, the first performances of *Tristan und Isolde* and *Die Meistersinger von Nürnberg* would be given at the Munich Court Theatre under the composer's direction.

Wagner at once sent for Gottfried Semper to help him with the designs for the special theatre, and together they showed the King their plans. To avoid delay, a simple wooden auditorium with steeply-raked seating and a deep pit for the orchestra was to be built inside the shell of the existing building, such as an exhibition hall. After the performances of the *Ring* planned for 1867 or 1868, this auditorium would be transferred to the more imposing structure favoured by the King. Semper produced a splendidly detailed model that could not fail to appeal to Ludwig's taste for the grandiose; Wagner, for his part, was quite prepared to settle for the more modest wooden theatre.

This scheme for a Wagner theatre in Munich came to nothing for a variety of reasons. There was political intrigue against Wagner by those who resented the sums of money the King was ready to spend on the composer and his extravagant works; Wagner himself crossed powerful and influential persons at Court and, to crown it all, there was the affair with Cosima von Bülow, daughter of Liszt and the wife of the highly-respected Hofkapellmeister, Hans von Bülow. Everything Wagner did or said – or was reputed to have done or said – was seized upon by the Munich press and subjected to ridicule. Things eventually became so inflamed that the throne itself was threatened and so in 1865, with the King's agreement, Wagner went into exile in Switzerland once more.

Over the next couple of years he gradually lost interest in the Munich project, and was probably not greatly disappointed when in 1867 the King wrote to tell him there was no money for the grandiose scheme. Semper, however, took the decision differently, and was embittered by the King's action; there had been other setbacks for the architect in Munich, and when the question arose of who should pay for all his drawings and models, the architect and composer fell out over the bill.

Exile in Switzerland was no hardship for Wagner. In 1866 he took up residence at Tribschen (Wagner spelled it 'Triebschen' and others have followed his example) near Lucerne, a beautiful spot on a promontory overlooking the lake. He counted the years there amongst the happiest of his life. In 1868 Cosima came to live with him there, after a succession of visits, and in June 1869 their son Siegfried was born. The following year, after her divorce, Cosima and Richard Wagner were married and they lived at Tribschen with the other children until they moved to Bayreuth in 1872.

Not all the days there were idyllic; Wagner was being pressed by the King to complete the *Ring* so that it could be performed at the Court Theatre in Munich. When the composer deliberately delayed the completion of the work to thwart him, Ludwig decided to have performed what was already written, namely *Das Rheingold* and *Die Walküre*. This was defying the composer's wishes in no uncertain fashion, and Wagner did all he could to prevent the performances taking place. In the event he failed, and the first two parts of the *Ring* were given in Munich in 1869 and 1870 with little success. For all his artistic ideals and protestations, Ludwig had shown himself to be a prince like any other, determined that what his whim ordained be carried out. Wagner did not attend these performances; much had taken place since the triumph of *Die Meistersinger* just over a year or so before. He was aware that the King had not taken kindly to the deception which he and Cosima had played out behind his back, day after day. However, for Wagner (and for Bayreuth too) the arrival of Cosima as a permanent feature of the composer's life was a most decisive event: as long as he lived she encouraged and protected him, clearing all possible obstacles from his path, defending his aims and ideals against all comers and, after his death, preserving them in the form of the Bayreuth Festival.*

The events of 1870 convinced Wagner that the complete *Ring* cycle would have to be staged somewhere other than Munich, by his own efforts and in a way that was not yet clear to him. To this end he began to consider which small town might be suitable for his purpose.

*   *   *

The little North Bavarian town of Bayreuth lies almost at the geographical centre of Germany. The name ('Baireuth' in the old spelling) is mentioned in documents as early as the twelfth century and is said to originate from the stem 'reuth' which means a clearing in a forest. In Karl Baedeker's *Southern Germany and Austria* of 1873 it merits an entry of rather more than a page. The town then had 17,837 inhabitants of whom only some 3,000 were of the Roman faith – Bayreuth thus stands as a Protestant enclave in the largely Catholic State of Bavaria. Baedeker mentions the Residenz, the Neues Schloss and one or two churches as worthy of note as well as the Bürgerreuth eminence with its restaurant; excursions to the Eremitage and Schloss Fantasie at Donndorf are recommended.

The town had a period of modest splendour in the middle of the eighteenth century when Wilhelmine, the favourite sister of Frederick the Great, married the Margrave Frederick and took up residence there; it was a transient period of glory, for after the Margrave's death the provincial court returned to Anspach. It is to the Margravine Wilhelmine that Bayreuth owes the Neues Schloss, the Eremitage and the Margräfliches Opernhaus, which was completed in 1748. Like the Neues Schloss, the Opernhaus was built by Joseph St Pierre, and the interior, with its richly carved and gilded boxes and magnificent painted ceiling, was decorated by the celebrated Bibiena.

Richard Wagner was not the first artistic figure to become closely associated with Bayreuth, for Jean Paul, the writer and humanist, was born at nearby Wunsiedel in 1763 and lived in the town at 384 Friedrichstrasse until his death in 1825. Jean Paul, whose real name was Johan Paul Friedrich Richter, was one of the group of writers (E. T. A. Hoffmann, the Schlegels and Novalis were others) which exercised considerable influence over the new school of 'Romantic' composers such as Liszt, Berlioz and Schumann, who took an interest in the literary movement of their time. It is usually said that the writings of Jean Paul do not translate well and for this reason he is not much known outside his native land. Nevertheless, he received honours in his own country, indeed his own town, where a bronze statue was erected in his honour by King Ludwig I of Bavaria.

* Cosima's connections with that event extend for almost sixty years; after she relinquished control to Siegfried Wagner in 1910 she remained an influence in the background until she died in 1930 at the age of ninety-two.

Cosima Wagner recorded 5 March 1870 as 'the birth of Bayreuth'; on that date she looked up, and read out to Richard Wagner, the entry on the town in the *Brockhaus Lexikon*. The Baroque theatre was reputed to possess the largest stage of any theatre in Germany, and this was reason enough for the Wagners to make the journey to inspect it in April 1871. They saw at once that the little theatre was too small. 'The theatre is entirely unsuited to our purpose,' Cosima wrote, 'so we shall have to build, which is all the better.' On this informal visit Wagner was well received by the local men of standing who, perhaps thinking that he would put their town on the map once again, seemed to understand what he wanted, and were sympathetic from the start to his plans for a festival there.

Two men who played a particularly active part in encouraging Wagner to settle in Bayreuth were the Bürgermeister Theodor Muncker and Friedrich Feustel, a banker and local politician. Wagner had long ago decided his theatre would be best built in a small town – being a big fish in a small pond was not something he found entirely uncongenial – and in November 1871 he outlined his plans in a long letter to Feustel:

The place must not be a large city with a permanent theatre, nor one of the larger summer resorts, where during the season an absolutely undesirable public would offer itself; it must be centrally located in Germany, and moreover be a Bavarian city, as I also intend to take up permanent residence in the place, and consider that I could do this only in Bavaria, if I hope to enjoy the continued patronage of the King of Bavaria. Apart from these factors, this pleasant old city, and its surroundings, made an indelible impression upon me years ago and so the fact that I am an utter stranger to the citizens of Bayreuth gives me no cause for alarm. . . .

It is to be taken for granted that the city of Bayreuth is in no way to be called upon in collecting the funds for my undertaking. . . . The chief thing to me seems to be whether the city of Bayreuth, in consideration of the advantages accruing to the city from my undertaking (both as regards her reputation as well as the increased intercourse with strangers), is in a position to promise, or feels herself moved to offer me, free of charge a piece of ground for the erection of my theatre. I will not say that my undertaking is absolutely dependent upon such support; but it must be clear to anyone that such concessions will tend to establish from the very outset pleasant relations between the city and my undertaking. In the event that such willingness is shown, there can be no question of a choice of place on my part. . . .

I have further to mention the chief objection which has been made against Bayreuth on the part of my patrons, and that is their anxiety that sufficient accommodation for the guests cannot be found. It will be necessary to ensure satisfactory entertainment for a personnel of 200 persons – in the height of the season.

As my experience furnishes me with no suggestion, I leave this point with you for your kind consideration, and should be very pleased if you could put me in possession of information which would serve to quiet the anxieties of my patrons. It would also be a comfort to me to feel assured that there would be no lack of workmen for the rapid erection of the building, and that we should not find ourselves crippled by a strike. . . .

It would be well to keep in mind the fact that this undertaking has nothing to do with a money-making theatrical enterprise; the performances will be attended only by invited guests and the patrons of the undertaking; no one will be allowed to pay for admission. One the other hand, I have already provided for a sufficient number of seats to be placed at the disposal of the citizens of Bayreuth – these to be distributed free of charge.

The people of Bayreuth responded by providing Wagner with the site for his theatre, and on hearing the news he wrote to Feustel, 'Bayreuth and the Festival are now inseparable.'

In 1871 Wagner wrote to the King's secretary in Munich asking for the plans and architect's drawings which he and the still-estranged Semper had prepared for the King. It is at this point that some writers have confused the Munich Wagner Theatre project with the Bayreuth Festival Theatre – they state that because Wagner could not build his theatre in the Bavarian capital he had the building that had been planned erected in Bayreuth. This is not the case; the Munich project and the Bayreuth theatre were separate concepts. It is true they were aspects of the same idea, but Wagner's letters make it clear that in Bayreuth he wanted to use only those parts of Semper's plans that had been his own original innovation.

At first Wagner had hoped to build his theatre in the Hofgarten, on a site just behind the one he had acquired for his house, but the land there was swampy, and for the theatre deep foundations were essential. A more suitable site on the Stückberg, near St Georgen, was lost because of a dispute amongst its owners, and it was not until January 1872 that the Town Council of Bayreuth obtained the present site of the Festspielhaus on the Bürgerreuth hill, for 14,000 guilders; this is the plot they presented to Wagner, free of charge.

In April 1872 Wagner and his family left Tribschen and made the journey to Bayreuth; even though they had no home to go to and had to stay at the Hotel Fantasie at Donndorf, Wagner was determined to make this gesture of commitment to the little town at the earliest possible moment – also, he wished to be on hand to supervise the building work. In September the family moved into a convenient and comfortable house in the Dammallee, and lived there until their own house was finished.

Wagner described the sequence of events in an essay on Bayreuth in 1873:

Already in the spring of 1871 I had chosen Bayreuth for my goal, after a quiet visit of inspection: all idea of using the famous opera house of the Margraves I abandoned as soon as I had seen its interior; but the character and situation of the kindly city were all that I had wished for. So I repeated my visit in the winterly late autumn of that year; this time to open negotiations with the

Bayreuth town authorities themselves. I have no need here to reiterate the earnest thanks I owe those true and honest men; in excess of every expectation, their courteous hospitality now gave my daring enterprise the friendly soil whereon to thrive in common with my lifelong home. An unrivalledly beautiful and extensive freehold, hard by the town itself, was bestowed upon me for the erection of the theatre I had in mind. Having arranged the structural scheme with a man of eminent experience and proved inventiveness in the internal disposition of theatres, I agreed with him to commit to an equally practised architect the preparation of the further plans and execution of the provisional building. And thus, despite the many difficulties occasioned by the unusual nature of our task, we were able to announce to our friends and patrons the 22nd of May in the year 1872 as the date for laying the foundation stone.

For this event I conceived the notion of giving my supporters an artistic reward for their trouble of meeting at Bayreuth, in the shape of as perfect a performance as possible of Beethoven's great Ninth Symphony. The simple invitation which I addressed to our best orchestras, choirs and famous soloists sufficed to procure me a body of such admirable executants as scarcely ever can have been assembled for a similar purpose.

This first success was of most encouraging augury for the future prospering of the grand theatrical performances themselves. It set all concerned in so excellent a temper that even the drenching rain storm which maimed the rites of laying the foundation stone was unable to damp our spirits. In the capsule to be buried in that stone we placed a message from the illustrious defender of my best endeavours, together with various records and a verse indicted by myself:

Hier schliess' ich ein Geheimnis ein,	A secret here I deep have lain,
da ruh' es viele hundert Jahr':	for centuries there may it rest:
so lange es verwahrt der Stein,	while e'er the stone shall this contain,
macht es der Welt sich offenbar.	its meaning may the world attest!

Friedrich Nietzsche, at that time a great admirer of Wagner, was present at the ceremony and wrote the following impression:

On that day in May when the foundation stone was laid on the hill in Bayreuth, Wagner drove together with some of us back to the town – he was silent and for a long time remained with a look of introspection which was not to be described in words. He was entering on his sixtieth year; everything up to now had been in preparation for this moment. It is known that at a time of unusual danger or indeed of an important decision in life, one is able, by means of an infinitely accelerated inward vision, to compress all past experiences and to recognise with rare clarity both the furthest and nearest events. . . . What Wagner saw in his inward vision on that day – his past development, what he is, what he will be – we who are closest to him can follow to a certain degree:

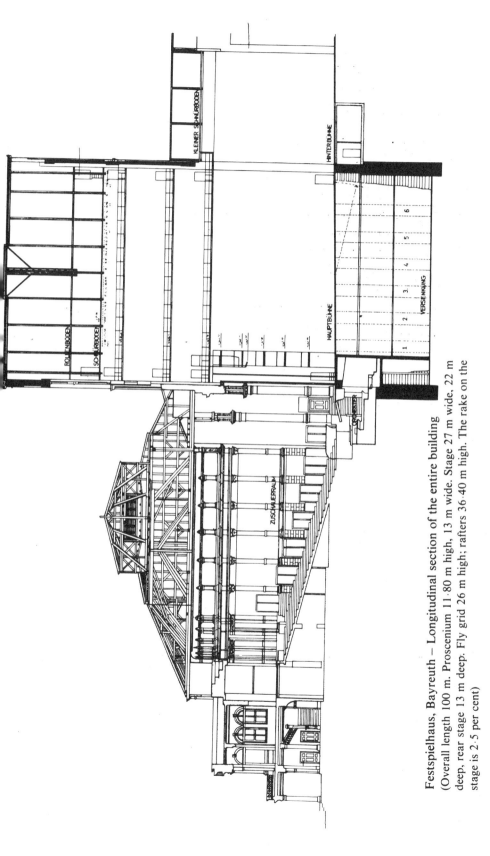

Festspielhaus, Bayreuth – Longitudinal section of the entire building
(Overall length 100 m. Proscenium 11·80 m high, 13 m wide. Stage 27 m wide, 22 m
deep, rear stage 13 m deep. Fly grid 26 m high; rafters 36·40 m high. The rake on the
stage is 2·5 per cent)

and only with this vision of Wagner's shall we ourselves be able to understand his great work, and with this understanding vouch for its fruitfulness.

While building of the theatre progressed Wagner was expounding the thoughts that lay behind it in the essay 'Bayreuth':

To explain the plan of the Festival Theatre now in course of erection at Bayreuth I believe I cannot do better than to begin with the need I felt the first, that of rendering the mechanical source of the music invisible, to wit the orchestra; for this one requirement led step by step to a total transformation of the auditorium of our neo-European theatre.

The reader of my previous essays already knows my views about the concealment of the orchestra, and, even should he not have felt as much before, I hope that a subsequent visit to the opera will have convinced him of my rightness in condemning the constant visibility of the mechanism for tone production as an aggressive nuisance. In my essay on Beethoven I explained how fine performances of ideal works of music may make this evil imperceptible at last, through our eyesight being neutralised, as it were, by the rapt subversion of the whole sensorium. With a dramatic representation, on the contrary, it is a matter of focusing the eye itself upon a picture: and that can be done only by leading it away from any sight of bodies lying in between, such as the technical apparatus for projecting the picture.

Without being actually covered in, the orchestra was therefore to be sunk so deep that the spectator would look right over it, immediately upon the stage; this at once applied the principle that the seats for the audience must be ranged in gradually ascending rows, their ultimate height to be governed solely by the possibility of a distinct view of the scenic picture. Our whole system of tiers of boxes was accordingly excluded; beginning at the walls beside the stage itself, their very height would have made it impossible to prevent their occupants looking straight down into the orchestra. Thus the arrangement of our rows of seats acquired the character obtaining in the antique amphitheatre: yet the latter's actual form, with arms stretched out on either side beyond the full half-circle, could not be seriously thought of; for the object to be plainly set in sight was no longer the chorus in the orchestra, surrounded for the greater part by that ellipse, but the 'scene' itself; and that 'scene', displayed to the Greek spectator in the merest low relief, was to be used by us in all its depth.

Hence we were strictly bound by the laws of *Perspective*, according to which the rows of seats might widen as they mounted higher, but must always keep their front toward the stage. From the latter forward the *Proscenium*, the actual framing of the scenic picture, thus necessarily became the starting point of all further arrangements. My demand that the orchestra should be made invisible had at once inspired the genius of the famous architect Gottfried Semper whom I was first privileged to consult in the matter with a scheme for the empty space between the proscenium and the first row of seats: this space – which we called the 'mystic gulf', because it had to part reality from ideality

– the master framed in a second, a wider proscenium, from whose relation to the narrower proscenium proper he anticipated the singular illusion of an apparent throwing-back of the scene itself, making the spectator imagine it quite far away, though he still beholds it in all the clearness of its actual proximity; while this in turn gives rise to the illusion that the persons figuring upon the stage are of larger, superhuman stature.

The success of this arrangement would alone suffice to give an idea of the spectator's completely changed relation to the scenic picture. His seat once taken, he finds himself in an actual 'theatron', that is, a room made ready for no purpose other than his looking in, and that for looking straight in front of him. Between him and the picture to be looked at there is nothing plainly visible, merely a floating atmosphere of distance, resulting from the architectural adjustment of the two proscenia; whereby the scene is removed as it were to the unapproachable world of dreams, while the spectral music sounding from the 'mystic gulf', like vapours arising from the holy womb of Gaia beneath the tripod of Pythia, inspires him with the clairvoyance in which the scenic picture melts into the truest effigy of life itself.

A difficulty arose in respect of the side walls of the auditorium: unbroken by any tiers of boxes, they presented a flat expanse, to be brought into no plausible agreement with the rows of seats. The famous architect at first entrusted with the task of building the theatre in monumental fashion had all the resources of his art to draw upon, and made so admirable a use of the noblest renaissance ornament that the bare surface was transformed into a perpetual feast for the eye. For our provisional theatre at Bayreuth we had to renounce all idea of a like adornment, which has no meaning unless the material itself be precious, and were once more faced with the question how to treat these walls that stood at variance with the actual space for holding the audience.

A glance at the first of the plans . . . shows an oblong narrowing toward the stage, as the space to be employed for the spectators, bounded by two unsightly wedges that widen as they approach the proscenium. While the side walls flanking these wedges were obliged to be rectangular because of the structural requirements of the building, and although the space left on either hand could be conveniently utilised for stairways giving access to the seats, the visual effect of the whole would have been ruined by those two empty corners. Now, to mask the blanks immediately in front of our double proscenium, the ingenuity of my present adviser had already hit on the plan of throwing out a third and still broader proscenium.

Seized with the excellence of this thought, we soon went further in the same direction, and found that, to do full justice to the idea of an auditorium narrowing in true perspective toward the stage, we must extend the process to the whole interior, adding proscenium after proscenium until they reached their climax in the crowning gallery, and thus enclosing the entire audience in the vista, no matter where it took its place. For this we devised a system of columns, answering to the first proscenium and broadening with the blocks of seats they bounded; at once they cheated us of the square walls behind them, and admirably hid the intervening doors and steps. With that we had settled our internal arrangements.

As we were building a provisional theatre, and therefore had only to keep in view its inner fitness for its end, we might congratulate ourselves on being relieved, for the present, of the task of furnishing our edifice with a beautiful exterior in architectural harmony with the inner idea. Had we even been supplied with nobler material than our estimates allowed of, we should have shrunk in terror from the task of erecting a monumental pile, and been obliged to look around us for assistance such as we could scarcely anywhere have found just now, for here presènted itself the newest, the most individual problem, and, since it could never yet have been attempted, the most difficult for the architect of the present (or future) day.

Our very poverty of means, however, compelled us to think of nothing but the sheer objective fitness of our building, the absolutely essential for our aim: and aim and object here resided in the inner relation of the auditorium to a stage of the largest dimensions necessary for mounting perfect scenery. Such a stage requires to be of three times the height it presents to the spectator, since its scenery must be able to be raised alike and lowered in its full extent. Thus from floor to roof the stage needs twice the height required by the auditorium. If one consults this utilitarian need alone, the outcome is a conglomerate of two buildings of totally different form and size. To mask the disproportion of these two buildings as much as possible, most architects of our newer theatres have considerably increased the height of the auditorium, and above that, again, have added rooms for scene painting and sundry managerial purposes – though such rooms have generally been found so inconvenient that they are very seldom used. Moreover, one could always fall back on the expedient of adding another tier or two of boxes, even allowing the topmost gallery to lose itself high up above the opening of the stage, since it was meant only for the poorer classes, upon whom one thought nothing of inflicting the inconveni- ence of a bird's-eye view of the goings-on below them in the parterre. But these tiers are banished from our theatre, nor can an architectural need dictate that we should lift our gaze on high, above blank walls, as in the Christian dome.

Now, by treating in the very baldest way our task of erecting an outwardly artless and simply provisional theatre, to be placed on a high and open site, I believe we have at like time reduced the problem itself to its plainest terms. It now lies naked and distinct before us, the tangible diagram, so to speak, of what a theatrical structure should outwardly express if it have no common, but an altogether ideal purpose to reveal. The main body of this structure thus represents the infinitely complex apparatus for scenic performances of the greatest possible perfection of technique: its annexe, on the other hand, consists of little more than a covered forecourt, in which to accommodate those persons for whom the performance is to become a visual play.

There it may stand, on the fair hill by Bayreuth.

Wagner's insistence that the theatre building was to be regarded as merely temporary is a striking feature of his views at this time, although he had given up the early idea that after the performances it should be burned to the ground! He wrote to Feustel in April 1872:

The theatre building is to be considered absolutely provisional; it would please me if it were entirely of wood, like the gymnasiums and Sängerfest halls: no further solidity than what is necessary to ensure it does not collapse. Therefore economise – no ornamentation. In this building we are only giving the outline of the idea, and handing it over to the nation to perpetuate it as a monumental structure.

The machinery and stage decor all to be ideal, and in relation to the inner nature of the artwork – absolutely perfect. Here no economy – everything designed for permanency – nothing temporary.

The singers and musicians to receive only compensation, but no payment as salary. He who does not come to me from glory and enthusiasm can stay where he is. A lot of use to me a singer would be who came to me only for the sake of a silly salary! Such a person would never satisfy my artistic demands. This, my dear friend, is one of *my* miracles, by which I show to the world how a personnel is secured for the performance of my work – my friends must believe in this.

I need about twenty leading and secondary persons; they must not cost me more than 30,000 thalers for the two months, or otherwise I can have nothing to do with them. About a hundred musicians, at a monthly compensation of 50 thalers, would make at the most 10,000 thalers. I *vouch* for this, for this is *my* field.

It is quite different when one has to deal with builders, carpenters, wood, canvas, lead, brushes and machinery; here I have no power but am able only to arrange and give instructions. Here only *money* is able to accomplish anything.

He wrote to Feustel again a few days later:

The dimensions of the auditorium as well as of the stage must be so estimated that they may serve as the foundation of the future massive structure, for I wish to present my patrons at once with the ultimate ideal plan in a clear and distinct form. The material for the provisional building, on the contrary, must be so selected as to meet only the most necessary requirements in regard to safety. I consent to an entire structure of wood, however much this will vex my dear Bayreuth fellow citizens, who would very much like to see a building of stately exterior.

On the provisional nature of his theatre building Wagner remained constant. Equally firm were his views on the conditions under which the public were to be admitted and the artists recompensed. In December 1873 Wagner wrote to Joseph Hoffmann about the designs for the *Ring* and also informed him:

> The performances at the Festival Theatre at Bayreuth are never to be access-ible by an admission fee, nor are they to be given for the financial profit of any person. On the contrary, they are to take place, once for all, only when the costs of the same – that is, the necessary outlay and the compensation of the assisting personnel – shall be covered by the voluntary subscriptions of the patrons, but never is there to be a question of recompense for the author.

*   *   *

The Bayreuth Festspielhaus took four years to build and they were not easy ones for Wagner. As Gottfried Semper was no longer available, he obtained the services of the Berlin architect Wilhelm Neumann. To attend to the stage machinery and the specifically theatrical appointments, the brilliant young innovator Karl Brandt came from Darmstadt. The latter was a particularly for-tunate choice for Wagner and Bayreuth, the former less so. After tolerating protracted and unnecessary delays on the part of his architect, Wagner could eventually take no more, and so dismissed Neumann. On Brandt's advice he was replaced by Otto Brückwald of Leipzig. Wagner was happy with his new man, and their collaboration was soon augmented by Carl Runkwitz, from Altenburg, who acted as assistant and attended to the more mundane aspects of the work. Bayreuth too played its part in the construction, for the master mason Carl Wölfel and the master carpenters Hans Weiss and Christian Vogl were local men.

In spite of the now harmonious collaboration, there were problems such as attend any sort of building project, and Wagner's project was of a new and unusual kind. It was, for a start, the largest free-standing timber-framed building ever undertaken and its unique feature, the sunken orchestra pit, called for the digging of unusually deep foundations. These were prone to regular flooding, and progress was further impeded. By the time of the 'topping-out' ceremony on 2 August 1873 there were financial problems to add to the constructional ones. The public subscriptions on which Wagner depended had been slow in arriving and by this date only about one-third had been taken up. It began to look as if the whole bold venture would have to be abandoned. Eventually, Wagner turned to the only person who was able to help him and, on 20 February 1874, he received a very substantial contribution from King Ludwig. Work continued.

During these anxious days the Wagners, comfortably installed in their tem-porary home, made regular visits to the site of the theatre. It was after one such visit, on 5 July 1873, that Cosima wrote in her diary how the sight of the building had terrified her with the huge size of the auditorium and the realisation of what they had undertaken; as long as it had been a remote idea and not, as was now manifest, 'an overweening reality', it had seemed worth striving for. Now it rose up like some great tomb – the Pyramids! Cosima, however, loyally kept these thoughts to herself. On 23 September 1873 a workman fell from the scaffolding and, as might be expected, Cosima took it as a sign of foreboding; but the visits went on as before and, weather permitting, became a feature to entertain the increasing number of guests being received by the Wagners.

Wagner was very concerned to prevent the funds of the Festival being wasted on things he considered unnecessary – as his letter to Feustel in May 1875 shows:

> I wish to return to the city the entire piece of land reaching from the Theatre terrace to the extreme front entrance, with the serious suggestion that this large piece of land be used entirely according to the wisdom of the City Council. If needs be, the *chaussée* already built can be used profitably as a street.
>
> I shall content myself, then, with the still very considerable space which now forms a plateau surrounding the theatre; the entrance and exit can take place by way of the *chaussée* leading to Bürgerreuth. I found yesterday, in a conversation . . . that this could be easily accomplished.

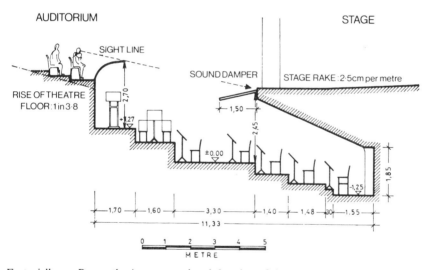

Festspielhaus, Bayreuth. A cross-sectional drawing of the orchestra pit to show the relationship between pit, auditorium and stage. In the orchestra the strings sit at the highest level, the woodwind in the middle and the brass and percussion at the lowest level.

Later in the same letter Wagner returns to the point. He indicates too that he had the cost of the preliminary rehearsals, planned for August 1875, in mind. Although the artists were giving their services, Wagner felt obliged to pay their out-of-pocket expenses, and wrote: 'It shall now be my chief concern to hold this fund intact for these rehearsals; on the one hand, the fact that the city of Bayreuth will have to transform a large piece of ground into a park for the Sunday promenades of its citizens, cannot be laid to my ambition.'

When the rehearsals began on 1 August 1875 the auditorium was still full of scaffolding and builders' props with only a few wooden benches, boxes and beams to seat such spectators as were admitted. However, the theatre was found to have a very resonant acoustic, with a reverberation period of no less than ten seconds, and to test it properly and achieve a satisfactory orchestral layout, it was necessary to fill it with people. Soldiers from the local garrison were brought in to squat on the floor and Wagner was moved to describe them as the ideal audience on three counts:

1. They were all in their places before the music began
2. They did not talk or fidget while it was being played
3. When it was over they made no pretence of having understood anything of what they had seen or heard and so refrained from airing their opinions about it.

At the close of the rehearsals Wagner bade farewell to the participants with these words:

The first difficulties have been overcome. Within a short time we must bring to perfection a genuine heroic deed. If we bring it off in such a manner as I now distinctly see that we shall do, then we may well say with justice – we have done something truly great!

The Festspielhaus was finished only a few months before the opening of the Festival of 1876, when a huge ceiling of painted sailcloth, made by the Brückner brothers, was hauled up into place.

The interior of the theatre in 1876 looked very much as it does today – the broad amphitheatre of seats, flanked on either side by a series of pillared but-tresses that serves to continue the perspective set by the double proscenium arches, the absence of overhanging balconies and protruding boxes that elsewhere interfere with the view of the stage and distract the spectator's eye, the orchestra out of sight in the concealed pit. Whatever the shortcomings of that first production of the *Ring* cycle – and there were many, as Wagner himself was ready to admit – not one of his critics could deny, as they denied the dramas, that Wagner's ideal theatre, embodying as it did a lifetime's experience and delibera-tion, was anything but a complete and unqualified success.

Successive generations of participants and visitors have thought the same, and everything possible has been done, for more than a hundred years, to preserve in its original form the theatre that Wagner put up as a temporary measure. This, it must be said, is not out of some misplaced piety, to create a shrine for pilgrims, but is due to the fact that this old theatre with its wooden auditorium possesses the most marvellous acoustics and, as has been discovered many times, good acoustics are a nebulous attribute and one, it seems, that can be arrived at only by chance. Designs based on the most involved calculations have resulted in many of the most modern halls and theatres having the most unappealing sound qualities. So, although there have been many essential alterations, renovations and modernisations carried out at the Bayreuth Festspielhaus over the years these have all been done with regard to the special qualities of the unique auditorium.

The first addition was by Wagner himself – in 1882 he had the portico and reception rooms built expressly for King Ludwig by Otto Brückwald, at a cost of 27,000 marks, so that he could attend the *Parsifal* performances that year in something like privacy. To Wagner's great annoyance the King did not come.

In 1876, gas lighting had been installed at the very last minute; electric arc lamps were also used for spots and magic lantern projections. In 1888 full electric lighting was introduced, and a generator set up in a shed behind the theatre (it took several teams of horses all day to drag it up the hill); when in operation it could be heard for miles around.

Bayreuth has always had the most up-to-date lighting system even if, as in Wieland Wagner's day, a modification had to be made to the ceiling to get it in. In 1973 the latest electronically-controlled 'Sitralux' system was installed.

In 1924 and 1925 Siegfried Wagner extended the storage area behind and to the side of the stage to accommodate the massive monumental stage sets then in favour. In 1931 the various administrative offices, up to that time located down the hill in the town, were housed in a new wing on the west side of the theatre. New boxes, now known as the Balcony, originally designed for the press, were built into the back wall of the auditorium above the so-called Princes' Gallery.

Between 1961 and 1973 the wooden beams that made up the timber frame of the building were gradually replaced by ferro-concrete in an ingenious bit of 'invisible mending', the brickwork was restored and, inside, the old wooden panels were similarly made good. It was about this time that new restaurants for both public and participants began to appear and, if some of the old atmosphere and dignity had to be sacrificed in the process, the gain in convenience was considerable.

In 1968 the old cane-bottomed seats were replaced by bentwood ones; these are fortunately free from the tiresome creaks that used to erupt at the slightest movement and as there are more of them to the row, the capacity of the theatre has been increased to 1,925.

A glance at any old engraving of the Bayreuth Festival hill will show just how much the exterior of the Festspielhaus has changed over the years – just as a glance at an old photograph of the interior will show how much has remained the same. Wagner, of course, when he put up the 'old barn', was thinking of a temporary theatre; it was his wish, often expressed, that if his works and the Festival survived, future generations would replace it with a more permanent structure. That they have not seen fit to do so is entirely due to Wagner who, after years of planning, got it exactly right in the end.

*   *   *

Wagner has been censured over and over again by his biographers for the way in which he handled his financial affairs; when in 1871 he settled on Bayreuth for

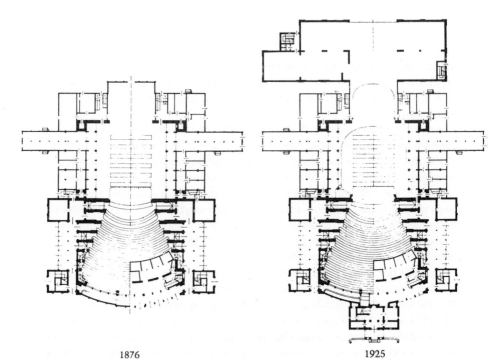

1876   1925

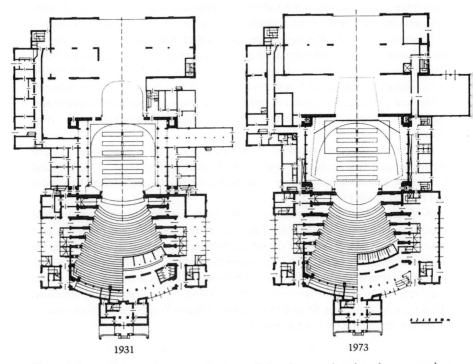

1931   1973

Festspielhaus, Bayreuth. Ground plans of the theatre showing the successive additions and modifications to the building. The portico was added in 1882.

his Festival he not only had no site for his theatre but no money to pay for it. To Wagner, however, this was less a deterrent than a temporary inconvenience. As his prince had failed him, he would take up his other scheme and appeal to the art-loving public for support – it was as easy and straightforward as that. To deal with the practical side of the money-raising Wagner obtained the help of two friends from Berlin, Karl Tausig, a young and gifted pianist, and the Countess Marie von Schleinitz. They proposed to issue, for a subscription, a *Patronatschein* (Certificate of Patronage) which would entitle the subscriber to a seat at the forthcoming performances of the *Ring* – admission could be gained in no other way. Wagner reckoned that a total of 300,000 thalers (900,000 marks) would be needed for his venture, so 1,000 *Patronatscheine* of 300 thalers each had to be sold; the other two organisers concurred and, with a touch of Wagner's optimism, considered that this large amount would both be adequate and forthcoming.

There was a problem, nevertheless. According to Wagner's long-vaunted ideal, the theatre, to his mind a social necessity, should be open, free of charge to all who wished to enter. It was obvious that *Patronatscheine* at 300 thalers apiece were a betrayal of this ideal and Wagner must surely have been glad to hear of a suggestion made by Emil Heckel, a book- and music-seller from Mannheim, that the subscription scheme be taken a stage further – those of modest means banding together to buy one of the *Patronatscheine* and distribute its privileges amongst themselves. As it was Wagner and his cause they were supporting, and supporting it in the best possible way, what better than to declare this by calling each group a *Wagnerverein* or Wagner Society? Every city or town of any importance in the artistic world was not to be without one, and indeed, such a Wagner Society was founded in London in 1874 by Edward Dannreuther. Liszt, Nietzsche and von Bülow offered their various services and Wagner recognised that he himself could raise money by a concert tour of the major musical centres. With this backing Wagner went ahead with his building. By the time of the 1873–4 crisis the following money had been received (just what thalers, marks and guilders of a century ago are worth today is anybody's guess, but the figures do show what the relative contributions amounted to):*

Berlin (1872)	75,000
Mannheim Wagner Society	51,000
Richard Wagner (concerts)	47,000
Hans von Bülow (concerts)	40,000
Vienna	30,000
Berlin (1873)	18,000
Khedive of Egypt	10,000
Sultan of Abdul Asis	9,000
Duke of Mecklenburg	5,400
Pesth	1,600
	287,000 marks

* One authority gives one mark, *ca.* 1880 = ten marks, *ca.* 1980.

Between 1874 and 1875 additional sums came in:

Loan from King Ludwig	300,000
Countess von Schleinitz	30,000
Frau Betty Schott (Mainz)	6,000
	336,000 marks

From his own resources and efforts Wagner contributed:

Private resources of Cosima and Richard Wagner	50,000
American Centennial March 1876	20,000
From concert tours:	
Berlin and Hamburg 1872	36,000
Vienna 1875	33,000
Berlin 1875	18,000
Cologne 1873	9,000
Pesth 1875	8,700
Vienna	2,400
	177,100 marks

To set against this income there is the total cost of the first Festival of 1876: the final figure was not available until as late as August 1878 when 1,272,876·09 marks, a staggering sum, was arrived at as the final reckoning. The deficit was 147,851·99 marks and to help to pay this King Ludwig granted yet another loan of almost 100,000 marks.

Was this, in the end, one more example of Wagner's profligacy and his readiness to squander other people's money? The answer is provided by two facts: the amount paid to artists, singers and musicians (177,823·99 marks) corresponds almost exactly to the amount of Wagner's own personal contribution, and the 400,000 marks loaned by the King were paid back by Wagner and his heirs from royalties on his works and the proceeds of later Bayreuth Festivals. There can be little for censure in that.

Wahnfried, Wagner's house in Bayreuth, the first home he ever owned, is worth considering in some detail not only because it was the home of an artist of standing but because it became the model for many another house built by successful writers and artists, and by persons with artistic pretensions amongst the developing bourgeoisie of the late nineteenth century.

The site for the house, between the Hofgarten and what was then the Rennweg, was secured by Wagner as early as April 1871, even before he had obtained the plot for his theatre. In February of the following year Wagner paid out 12,000 guilders for the land and, shortly afterwards, when he came to build, he was sent the sum of 25,000 thalers by King Ludwig. To describe this gift as marking a reconciliation is to allow there had been a breach between them – that would be less than the truth, for no matter how cool their relationship had at times become the King still wished above all to see the performance of the *Ring* and that now meant having Wagner well-established in Bayreuth.

Wagner himself supervised the design of his house and the overall Italianate aspect of the villa reflects his visits to that country. His first architect was Wilhelm Neumann, and his plans included such features as a sweeping staircase in the entrance hall. Wagner, however, would have none of this and, together with Carl Wölfel (who was acting as contractor), he changed the layout to the simpler plan to be seen today, where concealed spiral stairways lead to the upper floors.

Work on the house went on for two years, and Wagner's problems in getting it finished as he wanted it will demonstrate to anyone who has had dealings with builders that in some things a century brings but little change. There were seemingly inevitable delays, poor workmanship and endless frustrating details calling for correction. In her diary Cosima recorded their visits to the site and the depressed state of mind in which they came back from them. Long before he gave his house its more familiar name Wagner, in despair, called it 'Ärgersheim' ('The Home of Vexations').

When Wagner gave the name 'Wahnfried' to his house he was clearly not thinking how it would translate into English. 'Yearning's Rest' and 'Peace from Delusion' are examples of how it has been rendered. Three plaques on the front of the house declare 'Hier, wo mein Wähnen Frieden fand / Wahnfried / sei dieses Haus von mir benannt' ('This house, where finally my quest is fulfilled, shall be named by me Wahnfried'). It is not unlike a couple of lines from the *Ring*.

The pictorial panel on the centre wall above the entrance was put there after the house was completed, at Cosima's instigation, to relieve the rather dull façade the house presented to the street. It is an allegory, done in *sgraffito*, and tells how the various aspects of drama and music are united in the art of Richard Wagner; his son, Siegfried, represents the future.

The bust of King Ludwig that stands in front of the house was made by Caspar David Zumbusch and was given by the monarch in 1875. The main entrance has a pair of doors with carved panels decorated with the letter 'W' (based on a motif by Albrecht Dürer) and above these a glass panel that Wagner designed to show his family's history; the Pleiades represents Wagner and the vulture (in German, 'Geier') his stepfather, Ludwig Geyer. Inside the entrance is a small vestibule with a door leading directly into the *Halle*, the hall or music room, which rises the full height of the house to a skylight in the roof. A gallery runs round at the level of the upper storey. A number of marble busts stand around the walls: there were six by Zumbusch representing Wagnerian characters (Lohengrin has now disappeared); Richard and Cosima by Gustav Adolf Kietz, and King Ludwig and Liszt, also by Zumbusch. The great black Ibach grand piano stood in the centre of the flagstone floor, and there used to be an organ too, a gift from America. Between 1874 and about 1930 the Festival soloists were regularly coached in the *Halle*, and it was here that the Prelude to *Parsifal* was heard for the first time at the end of 1878.

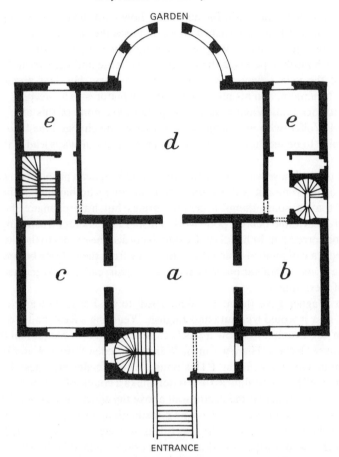

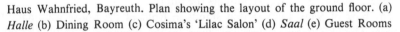

Haus Wahnfried, Bayreuth. Plan showing the layout of the ground floor. (a) *Halle* (b) Dining Room (c) Cosima's 'Lilac Salon' (d) *Saal* (e) Guest Rooms

Doors to the side of the hall lead to smaller rooms, a modest dining room on the right, and Cosima's drawing room, the 'Lilac Salon', on the left. In the centre another door leads to the *Saal*, the main room of the house, part drawing room, part library – the show-place of the establishment, it takes up more than one-third of the floor area and, in addition, has a large round bay window overlooking the garden and the grave of Richard and Cosima. Here, in the *Saal*, Wagner kept his collection of books (2,310 in number), scores, manuscripts and paintings, and the Steinway grand piano, a gift in 1876 from the New York firm in honour of the first Festival. The books lined the walls and the binding of them was enough to keep the Bayreuth bookbinder, Christian Senfft, in work for years. Not that the finely-bound volumes were there just to decorate the room, for Cosima's diaries tell of the considerable amount of reading that took place as part of the evening's relaxation. Visitors too have told how the Master, caught up in an argument or dispute with someone, would dart around the shelves pulling out one book after another to verify a point he wished to make, with the unhesitating aim that comes only from complete familiarity: 'just like playing the organ', was how one of them described it. Above the bookcases were portraits of King Ludwig, of Wagner's mother and his stepfather, as well as those of Schiller, Beethoven, Liszt and Goethe. The coffered ceiling of the *Saal*, designed, like the bookcases and the chandeliers, by Lorenz Gedon, a Munich sculptor, contained the coats-of-arms of the first towns to set up Wagner Societies, with one plaque to each of the thirty recesses. This room was the centre of the artistic life of Wahnfried, and it features in the many paintings and photographs of gatherings there from Wagner's own day and from the decades after his death, when Cosima held court there.

These rooms apart, Wagner's house is remarkably simple; there is no grand entrance, and the bedrooms are neither large nor ornate. As to the decoration, many visitors of Wagner's time have commented on the good taste displayed; in this they were reflecting the fashion of the day, but times change and fashion with them, and although it looks pleasant enough today it is seen without the dark draperies, the cluttering of bric-à-brac and impedimenta that the old photographs show, and which were rather more prized then than now.

Wagner was at last, at the age of sixty, settled in a home of his own, surrounded by all he held dear: his family, his dogs, and his treasured possessions. However, to his great regret, he was forced to leave his home for longer and longer periods; there were the concert tours to raise money, and the searches for artists for the forthcoming Festival, but worst of all was the wretched winter weather of Upper Bavaria. Even while it was being built a workman had told him, 'You will have a damp house here, Herr Wagner.' The area where Wahnfried stands had never been popular with the local people for this reason. As he grew older Wagner craved the sun more and more, and was compelled to pass the winters away from home, south of the Alps in Italy.

Nevertheless, his satisfaction in his house and home was no small one. Wagner moved into his house on 28 April 1874, and when, after more than twenty years' work, he completed the *Ring*, he wrote at the foot of the score of *Götterdämmerung*, 'Completed at Wahnfried on the 21st of November 1874. Need I say more!! R.W.'

PART II

The First Bayreuth Festival, 1876

Lilli Lehmann

The first Bayreuth Festival took place in August 1876 but long before then Wagner had gathered around him a band of artists wholeheartedly devoted to his cause. Lilli Lehmann (1848–1929), the German soprano, described those days at Bayreuth and what it was like to be directed by Richard Wagner. She first went to Wahnfried in 1875 with her mother, the singer Marie Loew, who was already known to Wagner, to study with him the small parts of Woglinde and Helmwige, and she returned to sing these in the first performances of the Ring the following year. The passages which follow are from her memoirs, which were published some forty years later.

We went to see Wagner one afternoon (early in 1875) and he greeted us like old friends. He received us in his large library which was reached by a hall and which was lined with shelves full of costly books in elaborate bindings. Above these were portraits, in oils, of King Ludwig and the Countess d'Agoult, Frau Cosima's mother (also known by her pen name, Daniel Stern) and, by the left of the door, a picture of Schopenhauer faced Wagner's large desk. To the right stood the piano – and a bust of Wilhelmine Schröder-Devrient whom Wagner admired so much. All around there were souvenirs set out on precious fabrics. Comfortable chairs and stools in many styles were distributed about the room. Outside the window, across the lawn, there lay a slab of marble, shaded by shrubs – the future resting place of Richard Wagner.

After we had met Frau Cosima, who greeted us graciously, and Wagner had made some preliminary comments, he opened the score of *Rheingold* and played and sang the first scene to us. Scarcely had he played the first few bars than I felt myself compelled to sing the part of Woglinde at sight – I could see the scene before me and, within these few bars, I grasped all three roles mentally. When we had finished the scene I said, 'I shall sing Woglinde, my sister Marie, Wellgunde, and Fräulein Lammert, Flosshilde – you do not need to trouble yourself any more about Rhine-maidens, Herr Wagner.'

We stayed for a meal with the Wagners and he talked a lot about vegetarianism. Wagner wished to take it up completely but his doctor would not allow it. Knowing what I do now, after my own experience, I am sure that Wagner, without going to extremes, would have found in vegetarianism a means of prolonging his life.

Lilli Lehmann returned to her post at the Berlin Opera and there recruited her fellow Rhine-maidens. They began to prepare their parts, after persuading the Director to release them for Bayreuth.

The *Rheingold* we soon mastered but when we received our parts for *Götter-dämmerung* we had great difficulty in even reading them for they were written in tiny characters and so hard to make out. I spent many hours over them and came to the conclusion they were wrongly copied. But when the printed parts arrived I saw that the harmonies were correct – and how hard we were now going to have to work at them to get up to scratch!

After *Rheingold* and *Götterdämmerung* came *Walküre* in which I was to sing Helmwige, my sister, Ortlinde, and Minna Lammert, Rossweise – and for me, in addition, there was the Woodbird in *Siegfried*. I wanted all this prepared and ready by the spring of 1875.

The first great period of Bayreuth, 1875–1876, is for me surrounded by an aura which the passing of years has failed to diminish and, in spite of later developments on the operatic stage, the proof of its power remains. The concept was wholly that of Richard Wagner, he alone urged and led the efforts needed, and yet numerous diverse talents were involved in the final production – and the success that would have eluded a single person can thus be attributed to a combination of them all. There was a spiritual bond between all concerned and this produced great artistic results; all took delight in unprecedented efforts to surmount the musical and intellectual problems, as a tribute to the Master. This individual artistic spirit was of the greatest value to Wagner for without its greater or lesser genius he would not have achieved his mighty goal. He was aware of his debt to stagecraft, what he could take from his artists and those who participated creatively in his work. Therefore he was able to liberate all those emotions that no score, scenery or stage apparatus, however glorious, can by themselves indicate.

So these days were, in their way, unique and never to be repeated – Wagner in his full creative power, the splendidly liberating ambience and those particular artistic and stimulating performances that are gone forever. There was the sound of the orchestra, made up of only the greatest players; and the music itself which lifted us up to the great Genius – all combined to produce a state of inspired exaltation. It was a powerful and strange magic spell that remains in my memory and, all pettiness gone, still works on my emotions.

Wagner was kindness and consideration itself to all the artists – and especially to me, even though his penetrating eye often gazed searchingly upon me as if it would pierce me right through. Others would often trouble him over trivialities and it was not surprising that he sometimes flew into a temper. Few realised the extent of his labours. Had he reached his goal by trampling over bodies, who could have blamed him for it? But this Wagner did not do – his exertions were honest, patient and just and he sought to resolve the most distasteful happenings in a beneficial manner. I never felt any of his 'ingratitude' nor saw it towards others. To create Bayreuth he had to be self-confident and to demand sacrifices from people who could help him – he had cares in plenty which we did not, at that time, suspect. Money which was needed for the colossal expenses was not forthcoming and just how bad the prospect was, even in his own house, I did not discover until Frau Cosima told me, twenty years later.

At the end of June 1875 we were installed again in the 'Sonne' at Bayreuth. This time we were not alone. The inns were beginning to fill up with many other artists and suddenly an unusual degree of life began to animate the dead little town. Bayreuth was taken over by the artists in 1875, they had it to themselves and they turned it upside down; they used it as their playground and the narrow-minded Bayreuthers knew not what to make of it. After our work was over, in the evenings, it became very lively at the 'Sonne' – Scaria had a little monkey which constantly was scampering about the window-sills. Also, when his wife, who was tiny, annoyed him, he used to pick her up and sit her on top of the high stove from where she could not get down. Gura and some other fellows dressed up in linen sheets and did wild dances outside the front of the inn. Amalie Materna would sit in the empty hotel carriage that stood at the door, without its horses, and my sister and I would perch up on the box, whip in hand, while Friedrich and Scaria dragged it through the streets – all in broad daylight! We used to serenade each other every evening too. Every morning all the boots and shoes outside the doors were mixed up. And so it went on – parties and picnics to 'Rollwenzel' (made famous by Jean-Paul) or 'Fantasie', or up to the theatre where the builders had struck water, resulting in the need to alter the whole of the stage foundations – in short, it was a truly mad existence such as will never be recaptured.

We were the first to turn up for rehearsals. We sang our Rhine-maidens' trio for Wagner, by heart and without a single mistake, and I remember well the tears of joy rolling down his cheeks as he listened to us. We were very moved and, at the same time, very proud. We were the first to learn our roles and were called upon to give our song every morning and every evening. As we sang it to Liszt for the first time, and brought off the very difficult passages in *Götter-dämmerung*, he laughed and shook his head as if he could not believe his ears.

I was present at all the rehearsals, even when I had no part to play, and ob-served, listened and learned. Even so it was quite bewildering to gain acquaint-ance with the work by hearing fragments and there were many of the artists who found it incomprehensible – until Wagner went through their parts with them. But as we learned so our enthusiasm grew.

Two scenes, especially, show how Wagner worked. Sieglinde was Fräulein Scheffsky from Munich, believed to be a friend of King Ludwig. She was big and powerful and had a big, powerful voice. She lacked poetry (and the brains to contrive to express what she lacked) and in her first scene, where Sieglinde, overcome by her wretched lot, calls back Siegmund to her, she failed totally. Her Sieglinde had no suggestion of great sorrow or inner longing. Wagner was very dissatisfied and acted the scene out for her – 'his' Sieglinde stood transfixed at the broad stone table as Siegmund leaves the hearth to rush off 'fort wend' ich Fuss und Schritt'. Something beyond control stirs in her breast, her face is grief-stricken and shows her fear that this man, whom she does not know but feels belongs to her, will abandon her to her misery. She turns her face and body, only slightly, as if to run after him as she cries, 'So bleibe hier!' – then she adopts her former stance and at the phrase 'wo Unheil im Hause wohnt' she is supporting herself with both hands behind her, grasping the table. There she remains, almost crushed by agony, head back, eyes closed, until startled by Hunding's foot-fall. This she follows with eye and ear before going to open the door to him. Wagner, no feminine figure, played all this with an overwhelmingly touching expression. Never since has any Sieglinde, in my experience, come near to matching him, even remotely.

Fräulein Scheffsky used to sing for King Ludwig but, as he could not bear to have ugly people about him, he had the lady concealed behind plants and shrubbery. A story told about one of these song recitals has the singer contriving to fall into an ornamental pond, hoping to be rescued by the King. But Ludwig, telling her to keep away from him, rang for his servant to help her out.

The other scene is also concerned with Sieglinde, in the third act of *Walküre* at the point where Brünnhilde announces to her 'ein Wälsung wächst Dir im Schoss'. Sieglinde, who has just been kneeling before Brünnhilde passionately imploring her for death, springs up in consternation and remains transfixed for a moment. Suddenly her face becomes transfigured and a wave of joy surges through her body as she now begs as passionately for the rescue of herself and her unborn child as she had previously begged for death.

Wagner himself expressed this transformation, for the spectator as well as for the singer, with masterly clearness. Only somebody totally lacking in talent could fail – if they did not feel it in themselves, the least they could do was to imitate the Master. However, there was a lot of trouble over this and Wagner was quite beside himself. Even as late as the last rehearsals in 1876 he asked me if it would not be better for me to sing Sieglinde. But who could have taken over Helmwige at such short notice? It was much too late and I begged Wagner not to press it further. . . .

Wagner was consumed by his task but in the evening, after the labours of the day, he gathered the artists at Wahnfried where lavish refreshments were laid out in the garden for them. In this garden, then still quite new, I strolled arm in arm with Wagner himself, while he talked of his plans for Bayreuth and how he was intending to perform not just the *Ring* and his own works but those of other masters – such as *Fidelio* and *Don Giovanni*.

At one of these gatherings Frau Jaide (our Waltraute and Erda) was standing, with a plateful of food, next to Niemann whom she had known well for many years. She was playfully feeding him from her plate – Frau Cosima, observing this little scene, took exception and gave the singer a severe reprimand, whereupon Niemann packed his bags and left! He was, of course, coaxed back but he was not the last to refuse to submit to the tyranny of Wahnfried.

Of course, we had the most of Wagner when our circle was at its smallest. When Bayreuth opened its gates to the public in 1876 there were many calls on Wagner's attention and all intimate contact with him was over. Much against his will, his house became the gathering place for the aristocratic and influential. This was Frau Cosima's world and she made the most of it, but Wagner, as an artist, felt as little at ease as the rest of us did in such unsympathetic surroundings.

It was on 3 June 1876 that we saw the Rhine-maidens' swimming apparatus for the very first time – this was a sort of cradle stuck on a pole at least twenty feet high and mounted on a little wagon with four wheels. We were to be strapped in this to sing! Now, I had been suffering from attacks of giddiness (due to extended sessions of sitting for my portrait in oils) and for this reason declined to perform in this contraption – until, that is, after much coaxing and pleading, I was put to shame and I climbed up the ladder and allowed myself to be buckled in place. I found myself delighted with the sensation and when Minna Lammert joined me we sang and swam so freely up aloft that it was a pleasure not to be missed. But it was dangerous – for the first scene in *Rheingold* we were pushed about on a high platform that stood on wooden supports which wobbled back and forth. My machine was directed by Anton Seidl and Lammert's by Felix Mottl. As soon as our scene was over we were pushed into the wings and Fricka and Wotan were already well into their duet before anybody gave a thought to releasing us poor creatures. At the very last rehearsals someone had the dreadful idea of fastening a tail to our supporting cradles. This set up a constant quivering motion in the machine which was transmitted back to us. I can hear, even now, the voice of Flosshilde calling out 'Mottl, if you don't hold me still, I'll spit on your head!'

During rehearsals Wagner sat on the stage, his legs crossed and the score on his lap. He conducted away to himself while Richter led the orchestra in the pit. They started off together but Wagner became so absorbed in the score that he did not keep with the orchestra and they went on ahead of him. Then, when he chanced to look up, he perceived for the first time that it was playing something quite different from what he was inwardly hearing. In this respect it is interesting to note his comments on keeping to a strict time beat – something he frequently repeated to all artists who had solo passages – 'That is your business, do it as you like.'

The singers on the stage saw almost nothing of the conductor. A black sheet was nailed up behind him against the sounding-board, so that Richter in his shirt-sleeves could be made out. He always conducted in his shirt-sleeves (and indeed he usually came up to the theatre for rehearsals sitting in a cart drawn by a pair of oxen). Everything was novel at Bayreuth – there was no prompt box, for example. We Rhine-maidens had no need of one but there were others who seemed to need one just because it was not there. So an army of prompters arose behind every bit of scenery and in every corner of the wings. I myself prompted Siegmund from behind Hunding's fireplace! Siegmund was Albert Niemann – never since have I heard a Siegmund to equal him. He had intellect, vocal power and incomparable expression at his command. His singing, his acting and his stage presence took possession of everyone – this Siegmund was unique and will no more come again than will another Wagner.

Frau Cosima, indebted as she was to Amalie Materna, arranged for her birthday a delightful garden party on 9 July 1876.* Each participant was asked

---

* Amalie Materna sang Brünnhilde at Bayreuth in 1876.

to bring a rose for 'Mali' and she, having accepted them all, ended up on a veritable throne of roses. First came a group of children, then the artists and, finally, Wagner with the entire orchestra. There were lanterns and fireworks in the moonlit garden, Angermann's beer on tap and food laid out for the guests. The Rhine-maidens' song brought the happy celebrations to a close. The next day (the birthday) more celebrations took place in the evening at the 'Sonne' and a small booth was set up in the garden to act as a stage, lit by smoky lanterns and draped with hotel linen. There was a varied programme – the orchestra consisting of a piano and bass drum on which Mottl and Levi accompanied the performers. I danced with the ballet-master Fricke from Dessau, a 'Pas de bouquet' which caused a sensation despite my becoming inhibited by the presence of the audience – we had a thousand times more fun when we were rehearsing it! More than forty turned up but Wagner was too tired to attend. How right he was when he said that artists like us were an unruly lot – such an evening would never be understood by others, outsiders would only get the wrong impression. So it was best to keep to ourselves. And this is what we did.

Supper at the "Sonne' was, it seems, always a lively affair and Lilli Lehmann tells how the meals often ended with Mottl, dressed in Mali's gown, hat and veil, going across the street to purchase chocolate cakes which he brought back for the guests' dessert. Doubtless the stolid Bayreuthers shook their heads over the singers' passion for pets:

Had it not caused so many tragedies, the results of the newly-imposed dog tax would have been amusing. But it was sad to see so many animals falling into the hands of coarse dealers – whole cart-loads of these best of man's friends. Dear Wilhelmj, who loved all men and beasts, bought many from the flayers and distributed them amongst the singers, chorus and orchestra – everybody had to take one and new ones turned up by the hour. He paid three marks for each one and, taking into account those he set free, it must have cost him a fortune. The result was thirty or forty dogs tied up outside the Festspielhaus during rehearsals and one can well imagine the noise when each owner came and let his dog off for a run. I too bought 'Mime' for three marks from Wilhelmj as company for my 'Petze Lehmann'. Mali had a Pintscher which accompanied her on all her travels for many years – once, on a picnic, Mottl had to plunge into the Rote Main to rescue the poor fellow and then my 'Petze' hurt his leg jumping from a first-floor window when he heard me call 'Ho-jo-to-ho' in the street.

So there was much in 1876 that could never be repeated – Wagner, of course, in his full creative power and the splendid setting of Bayreuth that gave us such freedom for expression. As Rhine-maidens we played our part to the full – gay and capricious of mood at the beginning of *Rheingold* and grave in our solemn warning to Siegfried in the last act of *Götterdämmerung*. And here I must mention that I always sang in my part in *Rheingold* – 'Nur wer der Minne Macht entsagt' never 'versagt' as I always heard it sung later. I drew Levi's attention to this in 1884 at Munich, when he wanted me to sing 'versagt' instead of 'entsagt' –

Wagner, who heard me sing it hundreds of times would surely have corrected me if he wanted it otherwise. The scene itself goes to demonstrate this too, for the quaver rest comes before 'entsagt' and not before 'Macht' as it would do if the meaning was different. Another detail too, in *Götterdämmerung*, is that we never sang the phrase 'Sag'es, Siegfried, sag'es uns' in unison under Wagner's own direction. I would like to know who made the alteration.

Looking back after all these years I recall nothing ever made my heart beat so much as hearing the first sounds of *Rheingold* when the orchestra began to stir in the depths below and I was called upon to make my voice ring out above it – the first tones of the human voice in the magic realm of the *Ring*. For me it was a glorious moment even at the cost of much anxiety and nervous apprehension.

Others have written about the performances and judged them from their various viewpoints – as listener or spectator – but what I have related here about Bayreuth is purely personal and describes how it affected me to work there with Richard Wagner.

Lilli Lehmann ends her account of Bayreuth in 1876 with an undated letter, received by her some time afterwards, in which Wagner expresses his gratitude:

Oh, Lilli, Lilli!
You were the most beautiful of all – and you are right, dear child – it will never come again. That was the magic of it all – my Rhine-maidens! Fidi sings their song all the time – 'Gebt uns das Reine zurück – '
Greetings to Marie, she is so good. Great God how good both of you were. And now you are really engaged – my congratulations!
Farewell, dear, good child! Lilli!

Richard Wagner

Lillie Lehmann had become engaged to Fritz Brandt, son of Karl Brandt, Wagner's stage manager. It was, apparently, an unhappy affair (she hints at Brandt's 'unusual behaviour') and was soon broken off, but the episode prevented her from returning to sing at Bayreuth until 1896.

Before the opening performances of the Ring *in August of that year Wagner put up notices behind the scenes for the participants:*

Last Request to my Faithful Artists!
Distinctness! The big notes will take care of themselves; the little notes and the text are the chief things. Do not address the audience, but always each other – in monologues look either up or down but not directly in front of you!
Last wish! Be good to me, you dear children!

For the orchestra, this admonition:
Piano, pianissimo and all will be well!

*   *   *

*Among the celebrated visitors who attended the Bayreuth Festival in 1876 were
three famous composers – Saint-Saëns, Tchaikovsky and Grieg – in an unfamiliar capacity as music critics. Their reports show the very different responses
which the* Ring *evoked on first hearing, and Tchaikovsky's notices describe the
problems of the little town in its attempts to cope with the influx of sophisticated
visitors. This was a problem Wagner himself had been well aware of, as a letter
to Feustel as early as May 1875 indicates:*

I shall refrain from having anything further to do with the agitation concerning
the hotel question. In response to my very first enquiry in regard to the accommodation of the visitors, I received the assurance of the city that this question
would be satisfactorily solved, and it was only upon receiving this promise that I
decided on Bayreuth as the home for my Festival. . . .

In any case I shall present my work in three successive performances; as to
whether out of this a permanent institution will be formed for the benefit of
Bayreuth will depend largely on what Bayreuth does in the summer in the matter.

Tchaikovsky

*Peter Ilyich Tchaikovsky (1840–93) went to Bayreuth in 1876 from Vichy,
where he had been taking the cure. He was engaged as correspondent for* Russky
Viedomosty *and, in addition to his writings for this paper, there are a number of
letters containing his observations on the Festival.*

The dates have been transposed from the old-style Russian ones.

To Modeste Tchaikovsky   Bayreuth, August 14th

I arrived here on August 12th, the day before the performance. Klindworth met
me. I found a number of well-known people here, and plunged straightaway into
the vortex of the Festival, in which I whirl all day long like one possessed. I have
also made the acquaintance of Liszt, who received me amiably. I called on
Wagner who no longer sees anyone. Yesterday the performance of *Rheingold*
took place. From the scenic point of view it interested me greatly, and I was also
much impressed by the truly marvellous staging of the work. Musically, it is in-
conceivable nonsense, in which here and there occur beautiful, and even captivating, moments. Among the people here who are known to you are Nikolai
Rubinstein – with whom I am staying – Laroche and Cui. Bayreuth is a tiny
town in which, at the present moment, several thousand people are con-
gregated. . . . I am not bored at all, although I cannot say I enjoy my visit here,
so that all my thoughts and efforts are directed to getting away to Russia, via
Vienna, as soon as possible. I hope to accomplish this by Thursday.

To the *Russky Viedomosty*

I reached Bayreuth on August 12th and found the town in a state of great excitement. Crowds of people, natives and strangers, gathered literally from the ends of the earth, were rushing to the railway station to see the arrival of the Emperor. I witnessed the spectacle from the window of a neighbouring house. First some brilliant uniforms passed by, then the musicians of the Wagner Theatre, in procession with Hans Richter, their conductor, at their head; next followed the interesting figure of the 'Abbé' Liszt, with the fine characteristic head I have so often admired in pictures; and, lastly, in a sumptuous carriage, the serene old man, Richard Wagner, with his aquiline nose and the delicately ironical smile which give such a characteristic expression to the face of the creator of this cosmopolitan and artistic Festival. A rousing 'Hurrah' resounded from the thousands of throats as the train entered the station. The old Emperor stepped into the carriage awaiting him and drove to the Palace. Wagner, who followed in his wake, was greeted by the crowds with as much enthusiasm as the Emperor. What pride, what overflowing emotions must have filled at this moment the heart of that little man who, by his energetic will and great talent, has defied all obstacles to the final realisation of his artistic ideals and audacious views.

I made a little excursion through the streets of the town. They swarmed with people of all nationalities, who looked very much preoccupied and as if in search of something. The reason for this anxious search I discovered only too soon, as I myself had to share it. All these restless people, wandering through the town, were seeking to satisfy the pangs of hunger, which even the fullness of artistic enjoyment could not entirely assuage. The little town offers, it is true, sufficient shelter to the strangers, but it is not able to feed all its guests. So it happened on the very day of my arrival, I learnt the meaning of the words 'struggle for existence'. There are very few hotels in Bayreuth, and the greater part of the visitors find accommodation in private houses. The tables d'hôte prepared in the inns are not sufficient to satisfy all the hungry people; one can only obtain a piece of bread, or a glass of beer, with immense difficulty, by dire struggle, or cunning stratagem or iron endurance. Even a modest place at a table, when it has been obtained, is not the end – it is then necessary to wait an eternity before the long-desired meal is served. Anarchy reigns at these meals; everyone is calling and shrieking, and the exhausted waiters pay no heed to the rightful claims of an individual. Only by the merest chance does one get a taste of any of the dishes. In the neighbourhood of the Theatre is a restaurant which advertises a good dinner at two o'clock. But to get inside it and lay hold of anything in that throng of hungry creatures is a feat worthy of a hero. I have dwelt on this matter at some length with the design of calling the attention of my readers to this prominent feature of the Bayreuth melomania. As a matter of fact, throughout the whole duration of the Festival, food forms the chief interest of the public; the artistic representations take a secondary place. Cutlets, baked potatoes, omelettes – all are discussed much more eagerly than Wagner's music.

I have already mentioned that the musical representatives of all civilised nations were assembled in Bayreuth. In fact, even on the day of my arrival, I perceived in the crowd many leaders of the musical world in Europe and America. But the greatest of them, the most famous, were conspicuous by their absence. Verdi, Gounod, Thomas, Brahms, Anton Rubinstein, Raff, Joachim and von Bülow had not come to Bayreuth.

The performance of the *Rheingold* took place on August 13th at 7 p.m. It lasted without a break two hours and a half. The other three parts will be given with an hour's interval between their Acts – and will last from 4 p.m. to 10 p.m. In consequence of the indisposition of the singer Betz, *Siegfried* was postponed from Tuesday to Wednesday, so that the first cycle lasted fully five days.

At three o'clock we make our way to the Theatre, which stands on a little hill rather distant from the town. That is the most trying part of the day, even for those who have managed to fortify themselves with a good meal. The road lies uphill, with absolutely no shade, so that one is exposed to the scorching rays of the sun. While waiting for the performance to begin, the motley troop encamps on the grass near the Theatre. Some sit over a glass of beer in the restaurant. Here acquaintances are made and renewed. From all sides one hears complaints of hunger and thirst, mingled with comments on present or past performances. At four o'clock to the minute, the fanfare sounds and the crowd streams into the Theatre. Five minutes later all the seats are occupied. The fanfare sounds again and the buzz of conversation is stilled, the lights are turned down and darkness reigns in the auditorium. From the depths – invisible to the audience – in which the orchestra is sunk float the strains of the beautiful prelude; the curtain parts in the middle, and the performance begins. Each of the Acts lasts an hour and a half; then comes an interval, but a very disagreeable one, for the sun is still far from setting and it is difficult to find a place in the shade. The second interval, on the contrary, is the most beautiful part of the day. The sun is already near the horizon; in the air one feels the coolness of the evening, the wooded hills around, and the charming little town in the distance, are lovely.

Towards 10 p.m. the performance ends and now begins the most bitter struggle for life – that is, a battle for a place in the Theatre restaurant. Those visitors who have no luck there stream back into the town only to experience an even more terrible disappointment. In the inns every seat is taken – one thanks God if one is able to find a piece of cold meat and a bottle of wine or beer. I saw a woman in Bayreuth, the wife of one of Russia's most influential men, who had not eaten one meal during the whole of her sojourn in Bayreuth. Coffee was her sole succour.

Some readers, who perhaps feel that I have already related too much about Bayreuth itself and my stay there, may expect that I will now turn to the essential subject of my task – that is, the critical discussion of the artistic merits (or otherwise) of Wagner's creativity. I must, however, apologise to my readers and promise them a detailed analysis of the *Nibelungenring* only in the distant future. After I had made myself familiar with that extensive work last winter, I was of the naïve opinion that it would suffice to hear it but once to become quite familiar with it. I found myself bitterly disappointed in this expectation. Wagner's tetralogy is so complicated and so finely detailed that much time is necessary for a study of it – and it really ought to be heard often. It is only after repeated hearing that the merits or deficiencies of a piece of music become clear. Very often one is suddenly seized and fascinated by a section one did not notice on first hearing and on the other hand it often happens that another section which seemed at first so delightful will fade into the background in the face of newly-discovered material. Repeated listening alone is not sufficient to become familiar with new music – the score too must be studied, for only after that can one attempt to make a sound assessment. I will follow this path later on. I will, at present, make only a few general observations with regard to the music of the *Ring* and the stage presentation of the work.

Anyone who believes in the civilising power of Art must take away from Bayreuth a very refreshing impression of this great artistic endeavour which will form a milestone in the history of Art. In the face of this building erected for artistic enjoyment; in the face of the mass of people who have come from all over to a corner of Europe in the name of an unprecedented musico-dramatic Festival; in the face of all this how wretched and ridiculous appear all those prophets who, in their blindness, regard our age as the age of total decay of pure Art. At the same time the Bayreuth Festival is a lesson for those hidden persecutors of Art – those who haughtily believe that progressive people ought to occupy themselves with nothing other than that which is of immediate and utilitarian value. In respect of the welfare of mankind the Bayreuth Festival is of no importance whatsoever. There is, however, an even greater and more eternal meaning – in the sense of a striving towards an artistic ideal. Whether Richard Wagner was right in serving his idea to the extent he has done, whether he neglected the principles of artistic and aesthetic balance and whether Art will now progress from his work as a point of departure or whether the *Ring* will mark a point at which a reaction will set in – who would wish to pronounce on that today? One thing is certain, that something has happened at Bayreuth, something which our grandchildren and great-grandchildren will remember.

If I, as a professional musician, had the feeling of total mental and physical exhaustion after the performance of each of the parts of the *Ring* – how great must be the fatigue of the amateurs! It is true that the latter concern themselves far more with the wonders which take place on the stage than with the orchestra or the singers – but one must assume that Wagner wrote the music for it to be listened to and not to be secondary to the drama. The musician, then, judges the actual music whereas the amateur-dilletante enjoys the scenery and transformations, the dragon and the snakes, the swimming Rhine-maidens and the rest. Since he is, in my opinion, totally incapable of extracting any musical enjoyment out of this sea of sound, he takes his pleasure from the spectacular production. This pleasure he confuses with musical pleasure and he attempts to convince himself and others that he has completely grasped all the beauties of the music of Wagner.

I made the acquaintance of a Russian business man who assured me that he acknowledges Wagner alone in the field of music. 'But are you familiar with all the others?' I asked him. It turned out that my dear fellow-countryman had no idea about music but had the fortune to be personally acquainted with the Master and had been invited to his receptions. He was very flattered by this and felt it his duty to deny everything which Wagner himself did not recognise. The impression made by these many admirers of Wagner is most unfortunate. Wagner has, of course, a great many sincere and enthusiastic devotees amongst professional musicians. These, however, came to a conscious enthusiasm by means of study and if Wagner is to get any moral support in seeking out his Ideal it will be through the warm-hearted devotion of these people. It would be interesting to discover if Wagner is able to differentiate them from the horde of false admirers – the women in particular – who from their standpoint of ignorance are impatiently against all those who do not share their opinions.

I repeat that I had the opportunity at Bayreuth of meeting many musicians of the first rank who were completely devoted to the Wagner muse and whose sincerity I have no reason to doubt. I do admit that through my own short-comings I have not yet reached a full understanding of the music of Wagner and that after industrious study of it I will, at some later date, join the circle of true Wagnerians. For the present I say quite honestly that the *Ring* made an overwhelming impression on me not so much through its musical beauty (which it possesses in perhaps too great an abundance) but rather through its gigantic proportions.

I brought away the impression that the *Ring* contains many passages of extra-ordinary beauty, especially symphonic beauty, which is remarkable, as Wagner has no stated intention of writing an opera in the style of a symphony. I feel a respectful admiration for the immense talents of the composer and his wealth of technique, such as has never been heard before. I will, however, continue the study of the music – the most complicated which has hitherto been composed. Yet if the *Ring* bores one in places, if much of it is incomprehensible and vague, if Wagner's harmonies are at times open to objection as being too complicated and artificial, and his theories false, even if the results of his immense work should eventually fall into oblivion, and the Bayreuth Theatre drop into an eternal slumber, yet the *Nibelungenring* is an event of the greatest importance to the world, an epoch-making work of art.

*   *   *

To Modeste Tchaikovsky   Vienna, August 20th

Bayreuth has left me with disagreeable recollections, although my artistic ambition was flattered more than once. It appears I am by no means as unknown in Western Europe as I had believed. The disagreeable recollections are raised by the uninterrupted bustle in which I was obliged to take part. After the last notes of the *Ring*, I felt as though I had been let out of prison. The *Nibelungenring* may be actually a magnificent work, but it is certain that there never was anything so endlessly and wearisomely spun out. . . .

If Tchaikovsky was in two minds about the worth of the Ring *in 1876 he did at least pursue his interest in Wagner. In his correspondence with Nadezhda von Meck he refers, in 1879, to his study of* Lohengrin *('the crown of Wagner's work'), to seeing* Tristan *in 1883 ('an endless void, without movement, without life') and, a year later, to reading the* Parsifal *score ('we are dealing with a great master, a genius, even if he has gone somewhat astray . . . to my mind Wagner has killed his colossal creative genius with theories'). The impression remains that Tchaikovsky (like Debussy later) fought off the Wagnerian influence to guard his own individual style.*

Saint-Saëns

Camille Saint-Saëns (1835–1921), the French composer, also attended the second cycle of the Ring *at Bayreuth in 1876 as a newspaper correspondent. He went to visit Liszt at Wahnfried and there met Wagner, whom he chided for the unpleasant anti-French attitude he had adopted, the consequences of which are described later on in this book. The reviews which Saint-Saëns sent back to France caused an uproar when they were published, and this was renewed in 1885 when they were reprinted in* Harmonie et Mélodie. *The following passages illustrate his views on Wagnerism, and give an assessment of Wagner's innovations in the theatre.*

From the outset let us avoid any confusion between nationalism and art. Richard Wagner hates France – but does this matter in considering the quality of his works? Those writers who have been insulting him in the crudest fashion for fifteen years now think him ungrateful – in this they may well be right, because nothing gave him greater publicity than their ceaseless attacks. However, Wagner's hatred for France has become almost pleasantly tolerable since the time he wrote that strange document called *Eine Kapitulation* – a revolting parody no German theatre would consider staging and which will only bring harm to the author. Let us, however, forget the author of this work and deal solely with the *Nibelungenring* – that poem was written out and published in 1863 and has nothing to do with the difficulties between France and Germany since that date.

This celebrated Tetralogy can be considered the most thorough expression of the Wagnerian method – its performance the best way to study this method and to convey the ideas in it.

By way of preface I would like to give some details of Wagnerians and anti-Wagnerians which will not be out of place.

I myself have studied the works of Richard Wagner for a long time. I have given myself completely to this study and all the performances I have attended have left me with a profound impression that all the theories in the world will never succeed in making me forget. Because of this I have been accused of being a Wagnerian. Indeed, for a while, I believed myself to be one. What a mistake and how far from the truth! I had only to meet some true Wagnerians to realise that I was not one of them and never could be!

For the Wagnerian, music did not exist before Wagner, or rather it was still in embryo – Wagner raised it to the level of Art. Bach, Beethoven and occasionally Weber, announced that the Messiah would come and thus have their importance as prophets. The rest are of no importance. Handel, Haydn, Mozart, Mendelssohn, none has written a single bearable note. The French school and the Italian school have never existed. If a Wagnerian should hear music other than Wagner's his face shows profound disdain. Any of the Master's works, be it the ballet music from *Rienzi*, plunges him into an indescribable state of ecstasy.

I once witnessed a very curious scene between the Master and a charming young lady, a talented writer and a Wagnerian of the first rank. This lady was imploring the Master to play her on the piano this unparalleled, indescribable chord she had discovered in the score of *Siegfried*.

'Oh, Master, this chord!'

'But my dear child, it is simply the chord of E minor, you can play it quite as well as I can.'

'Oh, Master, Master, please, this CHORD!'

The Master, in the end, went to the piano and played E G B – whereupon the lady fell back on a couch with a cry. It was more than she could bear!

On the other hand, I have seen a musician, a man of some talent and experience turn red, then blue, then purple on hearing the 'Entry of the Gods into Valhalla' at the end of *Rhinegold*. This consists of a slow progression of perfect major chords. At the sixth chord he began to froth and his eyes bulged from their sockets to such an extent that I was unable to finish playing the passage he himself had requested.

What is there to be said about those who feel their sense of patriotism outraged at the very thought of Wagner having his Tetralogy performed in a small Bavarian town? Truly it is possible to impute much to this patriotism and it might be more sensible not to so misuse one of the finest of mankind's sentiments but to preserve it carefully as a weapon to be drawn only on special occasions. But each one should be his own judge in these matters.

Others, true and proven Frenchmen, would gladly immolate themselves on their idol's altar if it took his fancy to ask for human sacrifices.

I regret I am not able to share any of these feelings, I merely respect them. In any case, I much prefer those who give themselves to such evident superiority, even if they do take it on trust, to those who deliberately run down and pretend to see nothing in these works, who fail to see that there are many others who do understand and that they could do likewise if they took the trouble.

Saint-Saëns quotes the French scholar Choron on the state of opera in the first part of the nineteenth century: 'everything is devoted to display and feats of vocalisation . . . and opposed to the true aims of art'. Originating in Italy, this florid style flourished in France, then paramount in the music of the theatre; but the opposing style, in which music and words go together 'so that one talks while singing and sings while talking' – this was no new thing, and not confined to the Wagnerian method; it was present in opera from the beginning.

It must be mentioned in passing, that France shows a special fondness for the lyric drama. Here it is not difficult to see the fact that stage realism, fine presentation, beautiful verse were as nothing compared with a graceful song ornamented with a pause like a hat ornamented with an ostrich feather. It was not without difficulty that the work which began with Rameau and ended with Gluck was destroyed. The struggle was harsh and basically it was the same struggle then as it is now. Pergolesi was opposed to Rameau, Piccini to Gluck. The enemies of these celebrated masters used the same weapon as is used today – melody. This word 'melody' was always brought out to oppose the loftiest arguments and to challenge the most obvious of the beauties . . . critics have been harping on the concept of 'melody' for the past one hundred and fifty years.

There was one man, in these last few years, who did notice that modern opera, despite its greatness and its beauties, was built upon a system opposed to the simultaneous development of poetry, music and drama. This man conceived a new form of lyric drama in which the music would not be forced on the verse in an arbitrary fashion, it would not conflict with the action – but symphonic development, with all its modern innovations, would bring back to the music all that which it had lost in the theatre. From this the drama itself would benefit greatly and would withstand presentation to an intelligent and educated public.

It was for no other reason that this man was hated, for no other reason he has, in his own country, for the last twenty years been called a maniac, an idiot, and a raving lunatic as well as a tin-can musician – in fact, insulted in every way. Thus are treated musicians who take their art too seriously and who believe that music in the theatre should be at one with the words and the drama – not merely provide a vehicle for singers to show off their doubtful talents.

Let us now consider for a moment – is this man pursuing a mere fantasy? Certainly it is a noble fantasy, it does not seek after easy fame or money but after the respect of an art-loving public. Nothing in that to undermine the foundations of civilisation! Why then should it provoke reactions other than sympathetic interest? Why then these impediments in the way of art which, by its very nature, must stand as one of the greatest achievements of mankind? Why then do writers, whose lives are spent demanding the freedom of the press, freedom of trade, freedom of public meeting and association, refuse to a musician the freedom to compose as he chooses? Why all this fury?

There are two reasons – the first of which is inertia. Every work of art is based on a convention; but when this convention is a new one, the public, in some strange way, is not aware of it. Both artist and public imagine what they are experiencing is reality. This will last for a while, until such time as the convention loses prestige and fades away and a new one becomes necessary. Thus does art progress — and here the word 'progress' has the meaning of simple movement. Without this the existence of art would be an impossibility.

Great artists who use their powerful imaginations wear them out as any craftsman wears out his tools. They soon discover everything about the convention as they use it to express their ideas. They then create another one, adapted to their needs — thus art has taken a step forwards, even before the public has become aware of the necessity for the change. Therefore the public puts up a furious resistance. That is what happened to Rameau and later to both Gluck and Beethoven and it is what is happening to Richard Wagner. This alone, however, is not enough to explain the degree of harshness which marks the opposition.

There is a second emotion added to it — a hatred of art. This is a secondary cause, albeit a mighty one, of the persecution that all bold and innovating artists have to suffer. It is not openly expressed; it uses any pretext or any mask. It is this hatred which is the basis of all these protestations about 'melody' — it is in the name of 'melody' that symphonic music is kept out of the theatre in favour of the most undramatic Italian operas — in its name praise is heaped on singers with no voice and who cannot sing in tune. These same people are destroying art in all its forms — simple peasant costume, old carved furniture and glass — all of these are being done away with. They press the priest to have the church painted over, the council to pull down old houses — they encourage bourgeois ideas and taste — small minds against great feelings and sentiments.

But how does all this hatred come about? For myself, I do not know and do not wish to know. It is enough to realise that it does exist and to strive against it.

Thus the new style of opera, shorn of all elements of mere display, is not to be blamed on Wagner after all. Nor, apparently, is the concept of the concealed orchestra.

Out of the many new ideas for which Richard Wagner was duly reproached mention must now be made of the newly-built Theatre — a theatre in a new form, a theatre with a different type of seating arrangement and with an orchestra pit closed to the eyes of the audience.

Strangely enough this idea is to be found in the musical essays of Grétry — here is what he was writing in 1797:

I would like to see a hall which is rather small, seating not more than a thousand persons, with only one kind of seat throughout, with no boxes, neither large nor small. I would like the orchestra to be out of sight so that neither the musicians nor the lights of the music desks can be seen by the audience. This would create a magical effect as no one would expect the orchestra to be there.

The same idea of the invisible orchestra is to be found in the manual of music by Choron: 'The presence of the orchestra amongst the audience, playing in full view of them, is every bit as disturbing as would be the sight of the back-stage machinery and the stage-hands working away on it.'

To hide the orchestra away is indeed a good idea, but how? Wagner found a way, by placing it in a deep pit beneath the stage. Adolphe Sax showed his plan for a theatre some time ago. The seating differed from Grétry's and Wagner's but the orchestra was placed as in this latest one. Sax's theatre was on the verge of being built for the 1867 Exhibition but the bureaucrats withheld their permission. It was left to Richard Wagner to achieve the dream of Grétry.

In the Preface to the poem, published in 1863, Wagner laid down the requirements for the fulfilment of his ideas – a theatre to be specially constructed in a small country town, a company of artists of exceptional merit, and he added, 'the will of a Prince would be needed; will this Prince be found?'

The answer by the King of Bavaria is well known.

This venture should not appear as strange here in Bavaria as it would elsewhere, for there is a long tradition of attending performances which are deliberately out of the ordinary. Every ten years, the town of Oberammergau, in its open-air theatre, puts on its Passion Play for a three-month period. It is performed every Sunday and lasts from eight in the morning to five in the evening. The public, who often come from far away after difficult and tiring journeys, sit listening to the performance as if it were a sermon.

One can understand, therefore, in a country where such performances are common that the people are not more dismayed by the *Nibelungenring* with its *ad hoc* Theatre and its four long consecutive evenings.

Grieg

Edvard Hagerup Grieg (1843–1907), the Norwegian composer and pianist, became interested in Wagner at an early age. In a letter to Gerd Schjelderup on 11 May 1904, he wrote that in 1858 he had seen Tannhäuser *in Leipzig and recalled, 'I was so taken by it that I heard it fourteen times in a row.' Some months before setting out for Bayreuth, Grieg wrote to his friend Bjørnsen of the Ring, 'this strange work, summing up the whole of our present culture, has an added strangeness in being so far in advance of our time.'*

Grieg went to the Bayreuth Festival of 1876 as correspondent of the journal Bergensposten, *in which his reviews appeared between 20 August and 3 September.*

6 August 1876

Dear Editor,

Well, here I am – keeping my promise and trying my hand at something new – musical correspondent! And if the irresponsible ones tear me to pieces, what of that? I am used to it.

But it is with a feeling of personal responsibility, indeed duty, that I shall attempt to give my fellow-countrymen an account of the unprecedented events taking place here and try to expand the knowledge of those in my homeland who have an interest in the world of our old legends and their gods. If I can show how these have been brought to life by means of the modern music drama I will consider my mission fulfilled. I will try to express myself as clearly and concisely as I can, but if I do get carried away, then put that down to the musician (or artist) in me.

I think the best way will be for me to give my views in the form of a diary of events. Even though the performance of Wagner's trilogy of the *Ring* does not begin for eight days I came here yesterday in order to see the dress rehearsals which start this afternoon at six o'clock. I have been promised admission to these but, after hearing the King of Bavaria arrived last night (travelling, in his romantic way, by night), and wishes to have the theatre all to himself, this may not be possible. Owing to his great shyness he does not want to attend the public performances and, Wagner being greatly in his debt, it looks as if he will have to yield to his wishes in this matter. So I shall have to wait and see. But, whatever happens, I am determined to see the dress rehearsal – I have not come all the way from Norway to let the opportunity pass me by without some struggle.

Grieg continues with his description of the theatre and its arrangements. He approves of these and would like to see the National Theatre proposed for Kristiana (Oslo) built in the amphitheatre style like Bayreuth.

I would now like to get down to the subject of the sources Wagner has used for his *Ring* stories – for us Norwegians these have special significance in that Wagner has taken the Volsunga Saga and the Older Edda as well as the German Nibelungenlied and, with poetic licence, has interwoven these elements all together for his drama. Wagner must be given credit for having kept to Nordic sources and, above all, to those of the older period, untainted as these are by the Christian outlook and ethic. Because of this we now have the myth in its true and original greatness. That is why this work is of importance to the Scandinavian.

Wagner has taken the characters' names from the Edda but, in place of the Nordic forms, he has given them a Germanic tone; thus, not Sigurd but Siegfried; not Gunnar but Gunther; not Odin but Wotan and not Loki but Loge, and so on. In writing his poetry he has followed the Edda in employing alliteration rather than rhyme. . . . I shall not pass judgment on this text but point out one thing that is strange – the Prologue takes the form of a drama played out on the stage; this is not really necessary because in Norse epics there was always something which went before. Also, it is difficult to become involved with these mermaids, giants, gods and goddesses – one can observe them, one can admire their display on the stage but one can not, as a human being, respond to and share their emotions.

About the music I shall write tomorrow, I am off now to the dress rehearsal, after all.

7 August 1876

Yesterday, I came face to face with the greatest that the music drama of our century has given to us. I can now understand Liszt's assessment of the great work of Wagner when he says it rises above all of our epoch's art like Mont Blanc over the Alps.

As I had feared, the King wished to be rid of any audience in the theatre and nobody, not even those closest to the composer, was allowed inside. But I was on my mark and slipped in with the orchestra. The orchestra pit was a complete world of its own – here I found that I was known to many of the celebrated musicians and was thus given a good seat from which I was able to see the action up above on the stage.

There are about one hundred and twenty-five in the orchestra and what tremendous artists they all are! All of the very first rank. And with their magnificent fullness of tone each one sounds like two – so this orchestra could be taken for one of two hundred ordinary players!

As they gather in the pit it comes to resemble a huge ant-hill of players and instruments. Then the conductor of genius, Hans Richter, comes to take his place. A silence falls on the pit – it is said the King is on his way – and then Wagner's voice roars out from the principal box 'Begin!'

Now the celebrated prelude to *Rheingold* sets out on its one hundred and thirty-six bars of E flat major, beginning on a pedal note of thirty-two foot organ pedal, plus contrabass tuba and string basses specially tuned down. It is impossible to imagine the depths of the waters of the Rhine portrayed to better effect than in this veritable sea of tone – the greenest of green one could call it. And then when the curtain parts the song of the Rhine-maidens adds to the effects of nature. . . .

Wagner's special ability to describe scenes such as occur in *Rheingold* causes the spectator to be carried away by the effect and to forget the lack of drama in them. Long dialogues such as the gods have cannot be consistently interesting; no matter how much the music sustains them, they still become quite tedious. Again, Wagner writes better for the giants and dwarfs than he does for the gods and goddesses – he does not have the elevated serenity and noble simplicity that the character of Wotan demands.

Returning to my lodging after the rehearsal I tell myself that, in spite of much there is to criticise, the inadequate characterisation of the gods, the ceaseless modulations and wearying chromaticism of the harmonies and the end result of leaving the listener totally exhausted, this music drama is the creation of a true giant in the history of art, comparable in his innovation only to Michelangelo. In music there is nobody to approach Wagner.

That the rehearsal performance itself was outstanding I do not need to assure you – I shall describe all that later, after the scheduled performance. Today it is said that Wagner has persuaded the King that to have the theatre filled with people will greatly enhance the sound of the music and accordingly free tickets have been issued. Tonight is the dress rehearsal of *Die Walküre*. From what I know of this work I expect more of it than *Rheingold* – it contains more life, more drama and more lyrical passages of great beauty; one can identify with Siegmund and Sieglinde largely because of the music Wagner has created for them. The love relationship between brother and sister seems to me to be normally quite wrong but that is how the myth tells it and Wagner here gives us music of the greatest beauty to enlist our sympathy and overcome our objections.

12 August 1876

As you see by the date I have been compelled to make a break in my reports – by now I have heard the dress rehearsals of the whole gigantic work but have not had a spare moment when I could take up my pen. There are large numbers of musicians, writers and artists of all types, from all parts of the world, all mingling together and it is impossible to avoid them, wherever one goes. All the great names of Europe and even America have gathered here. Such an excess of art and artists would be unbearable for any length of time. I am not lodged in an hotel but chose to stay in a private house. But no, on the stairs and in the passages, I am constantly meeting famous people. In the flat next to me there lives a composer of operas, across the corridor a famous singer, below me a celebrated music director and above me a wellknown critic. Sitting here I can hear all around me Wagnerian themes being hummed, sung, yodelled and shouted up from the garden. Going to the window I can see Valkyries, Rhine-maidens, giants and dwarfs, gods and mortals, all disporting themselves under the shade of the trees. To get a bit of peace I shut the windows and draw the curtains but Erda's mighty contralto voice pierces the thick walls. No wonder I am sitting here quite disconcerted.

To return to the *Ring*. As I have said, I expected the utmost of *Walküre* and when I tell you that I was not disappointed by it, that is to understate the case.

Grieg describes the rehearsal of Die Walküre; *he found the action of the first act acceptable after all, on account of the glorious music, and in the 'Ride of the Valkyries' there was, for him, a real ancient Nordic spirit. 'Wotan's Farewell' moved him greatly and the use of the orchestra he found constantly fascinating. With* Siegfried *Grieg was less happy, but he was nevertheless intrigued by the music associated with Mime, and he makes an interesting observation on the ending of the first act:*

Overjoyed with his success at forging the sword Siegfried splits the anvil with Nothung and the orchestra rejoices with a pulse very much like the Scherzo of Beethoven's Ninth Symphony, rewritten in a Wagnerian mode.

The second act is one of those endless dialogues that cannot help being tiresome; the pity is that the action is not of much interest and the words meaningless. Such dialogues embody the principles of Wagner's dramatic composition and he is always ready to defend them passionately – they do need a champion of genius for they have little to say for themselves. Even the music, I am sorry to say, cannot give form to these passages, for Wagner has overestimated its ability to underline and characterise the spoken word. His dialogues are indeed put together like the long dialogues of Schiller or Goethe – with the difference that in the plays of these authors the listener can at least hear every word. Wagner's passages of dialogue, I have realised, were added at a late stage of composition and are lacking in real inspiration when compared with the scenes full of action which they link together.

I must not forget the wonderful nature music in this second act where Siegfried is in the forest and listening to the songs of the birds. The audience is held rapt too for never before has the atmosphere of the deep forest been so well captured; how unbelievably well done is the orchestration and how well it was played; it demonstrates just how the invisible orchestra can create an illusion. To conjure up Fafner may seem beyond the capability of musical art; but what does Wagner do? He employs simple low notes on the tuba and organ pedal tones and with these rising and falling he manages to get the proper effect.

The beginning of the third act, where Wotan conjures up Erda from the womb of the earth, is mostly based on the Vegtamskvida of the Edda; the music is tragic in style but far removed from the tone of the saga. The concluding scene between Siegfried and Brünnhilde has beautiful moments but cannot be compared with the first act of *Die Walküre*.

13 August 1876

I now come to the last of the four dramas, *Götterdämmerung*, which the composer first called *Siegfried's Tod* but subsequently altered it to the more imposing title. Our forebears, in days of old, expressed in *Ragnarok* the conflict between light and darkness – they thought it would end in a battle as evil seemed in the ascendant – in particular, due to the misdemeanours of the gods. This is the fundamental source of Wagner's work and, as a wellknown German critic says, it is of universal interest to an audience, for its psychological conflicts and moral values are, so to speak, part of every human being.

Wagner does not only let Siegfried, together with all who have betrayed him, die – but also the gods, who seem to have failed themselves. If they, in the first place, had not stolen the gold and later refused to return it, mankind would never have learned of its power and fallen under its curse.

There is no doubt that *Götterdämmerung* is the most effective of the dramas and the one with the most compelling action. In it all that has gone before is resolved and the fates of the gods and of men are fulfilled. The use of a chorus seems to involve all of mankind – and what an effect it makes! By allowing the Rhine-maidens to recover the gold in the end Wagner underlines the message that, in the hands of man, it is a force for evil and intrigue. It further shows that *Der Ring des Nibelungen* is the only possible title for the cycle.

I cannot say that any part of the music is better than any other for it is all divinely composed and to pick out any one passage at random is to pick out a pearl.

I want to start by considering the opening scene with the three Norns where the orchestra spins out the rope of fate for them – I once heard this piece played at a concert in Berlin, with no voices, and it seemed just as effective as it was here with them. I mention this because I think that the voice parts play only a secondary part in the *Ring* – the orchestra is all – and of primary importance. Why then is it that Wagner does not make more use of the voices and why, when he does use them, do they not convey more of the text? The human voice must have an opportunity to express everything going on in the innermost soul of the character – failing which it should not be used at all. It is a pity Wagner has got such peculiar concepts about the employment of the human voice because he does prevent his works becoming coherent and lucid – and thereby expressing his ideas properly. Beethoven was not the most accomplished writer for the voice but even so he chose to use them to heighten the climaxes in his music – who could possibly tolerate a performance of his Ninth Symphony without the vocal and choral parts? Nevertheless, I do not wish to disparage the work of Wagner – I merely express how it all appears to me.

It is the mortals in the *Ring* that interest us and move us. Wagner's portrayal of these characters is more sympathetic than that of the gods. We identify with them from start to finish. I marvel at the differences in the portrayals of the two characters, Hagen and Siegfried. When Hagen summons his vassals I can detect, in this powerful music, a fundamental Nordic force – and remember, I am now hearing it for the very first time, too. But most enchanting of all, to me, is the song of the Rhine-maidens. And then there is Siegfried's Funeral March – I do not think there is anything to measure up to it other than Beethoven's 'Eroica', it is simply incredible.

My impression of the whole work is so great I can hardly express it properly – it is difficult for me to give you an overall view of the music so I will therefore relate only the events of the Festival, the audiences and the productions.

14 August 1876

To be a music critic and journalist in this weather is a tall order. The heat is killing. But, as you will agree, now I have started the job I must proceed to finish it. I will now tell you about the fantastic Festival itself and the occasion of the first public performance of *Rheingold*.

The day is fine and the town all decorated with flags to welcome the German Kaiser who has just turned up; it appears his arrival is to crown the occasion, which we must not forget is the bringing forth of the first real drama festival since the days of the Greek tragedies, or so the Wagner-fanatics would have it. King Ludwig, however, as everyone who knows him feared, has run away from all the tumult; this is odd since he himself invited the Kaiser to Bavaria.

Thank God that the performance is now to begin two hours later at seven o'clock instead of five; the heat in the Festspielhaus at that hour is impossible, it would have been like a Turkish bath. It is now just four o'clock and people have already started to walk up the hill to the theatre. To judge from their clothes there are people here from all social classes, the gentry in all their grand attire and jewels, young fanatical intellectuals and hundreds of artists and musicians of all kinds, all united by the excitement of the unique occasion.

Everybody is in his place in the theatre. Suddenly a silence. The Kaiser has arrived. In comes one prince of the blood after another and, at the end, the Kaiser who greets his people, in his warm human way, as he passes through them.

The performance begins. The theatre is hot and packed with people and this makes the tone of the orchestra subdued, compared with the rehearsals, and it also affects the pitch of some of the singers. But it is really wonderful. Of the singers the most impressive are Vogl as Loge and Schlosser as Mime who is actually applauded after his 'numbers' and not even Jaides's fantastic Erda receives such recognition. Though I can tell the audience gets tired of the long monologues, when the curtain falls it is a riot of enthusiasm throughout the auditorium. People stand up to applaud and call for Wagner to appear, even the Kaiser is waiting for him, but the Master is not to be seen. There are differing opinions about this episode – the Wagner-fanatics say it is because he is annoyed with the technical staff for all the little mistakes that crept into the production; the Wagner-enemies say that it is because Wagner, since his Munich days, has become used to taking his calls from the royal box and will not condescend to appear on the stage, something beneath an artist of his calibre. Well, I leave all that for the Germans to fight about. Yes, they actually do come to blows – in the local inns, and with beer-mugs for weapons (anybody being hit on the head with a 'Töpfchen' is *hors-de-combat!*).

If Wagner has been annoyed by the imperfect scene-changes and sloppy stage management then he has every right to be, for they all left a lot to be desired. Things like the rainbow on the wrong side of the stage and scene-changing so tardy that the orchestra had to slow down to match up with the action – these are hardly what the Master wanted. Considering the fact that Wagner and his circle have been publicly criticising performances elsewhere (performances generally liked and praised) it must be rather embarrassing for them to have such mistakes at Bayreuth.

Well, I think that, with exceptions such as Valhalla, which looks more like a royal castle than the abode of the gods, these sets, on the whole, were good. Nevertheless, I had expected something more of this *Rheingold* performance – perhaps my trouble was that I had already been to the dress rehearsals of the *Ring*; *Rheingold* is, of course, a masterpiece, but ought not to be seen immediately following *Götterdämmerung*. It is thus like comparing the Scottish Highlands with the Swiss Alps – even big things are diminished when compared with even greater ones.

15 August 1876

Wagner has arranged for placards to be put up to tell the audience not to interrupt the performance with applause while it is still under way as this spoils the balance and the continuity of the work. And here we go, once again, with the old factions and fresh rows and new beer-mug battles. Some say Wagner is jealous of Vogl's success last night and the rumour is that Wagner never appreciated his skills as a performer – if he had wanted to have no applause during the performances he should have sent out his 'rules for conduct in the theatre' well before it all started, for he must have known people would break in with their appreciation.

The first night of *Die Walküre* was, in short, a success. Niemann as Siegmund was overwhelmingly good, so successful in combining his vocal and acting abilities on the stage that he represents the very best I have seen. Even in passages where Wagner relies on the orchestra alone to express the inner sense of the drama Niemann acts with conviction and sensibility.

Scheffsky as Sieglinde was convincing too although her acting ability is not to be compared with that of Niemann. Betz as Wotan was actually disappointing – perhaps because expectations were high and the part so difficult to bring off. A funny sort of a god he is – so weak, so ready to yield to the provocations of his wife. Even if Materna as Brünnhilde does not give as much as later in *Götterdämmerung*, she is, nevertheless, impressive vocally. Her cries of 'Ho-jo-to-ho!' were impeccable – faultless pitch in the difficult intervals and with flawless trills all the way through. The 'Ride of the Valkyries', one of the most inspired scenes Wagner has ever written, was quite realistic and overwhelmingly beautiful – I left the Festspielhaus feeling that I had witnessed the true genius of Richard Wagner.

17 August 1876

Today a few lines about *Siegfried*. The performance was delayed one day because of the bass, Betz, who was creating trouble. Not that any of the audience grumbled about it for all of us needed the extra day's rest. Every performance is so exhausting emotionally that it leaves one quite worn out. The four o'clock starts and the late finishes are physically very tiring, in spite of the lengthy intervals – and these intervals are usually hard enough to get through, what with fighting to get out of the Festspielhaus and then fighting to get back in again, it is no easy struggle.

Once again it is Schlosser as Mime who strikes me as a special sort of artist – he declaims more than he sings, which brings out the words of the text more distinctly. This is maybe the answer to music-drama. Unger as Siegfried is not much to talk about, although he does not actually spoil anything. It is said Wagner chose him for his fine appearance rather than his talent and I dare say he regretted it afterwards. Betz as the Wanderer made a good impression as the god on earth, meddling with the mortals' destinies. However, here again the stage properties jeopardise the drama by being so realistic; it is almost impossible to construct a dragon that does not look a bit ridiculous – and this one certainly did that. When Wagner puts so much emphasis on these properties and highlights them as he does, he poses some difficult problems; even if he has them constructed by the best people (in London) the question remains, why make them so realistic and so obvious? In, for example, *Don Giovanni*, a lot is left to the onlookers' imaginations instead of being openly displayed on the stage – this makes the audience use its imagination to create devil and demons within its own mind.

After every act there is tremendous applause, especially the second with its 'Forest Murmurs' in which Wagner surpassed himself. He is, however, hard on his singers in the scenes, for they have nothing to sing for long periods and have to act out their part to the music of the orchestra alone – it always surprises me how well they manage it. Once again Materna sang Brünnhilde like a true goddess.

18 August 1876

Today Bayreuth has left off its festive garb. Many hundreds left the town last night and there is now a refreshing air of tranquillity about the place which will enable me to put the final touches to my last report on these memorable Festival days.

Yesterday's performance of *Götterdämmerung* made a great and profound impression – just as in the case of *Die Walküre* with its great uses of the forces of nature, so in the case of the final work of the *Ring*, so *Götterdämmerung* impresses by its tragic power and thus becomes equally moving.

I do not have anything to add to my previous report, on the dress rehearsal, the performance was, as a whole, on a very high level. The Brünnhilde of Materna, especially in the closing pages of the work, was completely above any sort of criticism; Niering as Hagen had the character darkly and sharply drawn, as it should be and Gura brought great depth and power to his part of Gunther. Such a melting ensemble as these Rhine-maidens is rarely to be encountered; when they sang there were murmurings among the audience, a sign of the highest ecstasy. Siegfried's Funeral March and the stage procession that accompanied it made another indescribable and totally overwhelming impression.

When the final curtain came down, at the end of the last act, in which the Master had demonstrated his great creative abilities, I thought the theatre would come down too, so great was the outbreak of cheering! The whole house resounded with the call – Wagner! Finally, he came out in front of the curtain and gave his thanks for the ovation but, unfortunately, I could not hear what he had to say, merely that he was moved by the approval of his 'friends' and the fine spirit of self-sacrifice of his fellow artists. Then he said something like 'Now we have shown that we can have an art; now it is up to you, and your will, to decide if our future will have its art.' Words like these have again stirred up the passions – they were certainly not without self-esteem, but Wagner does deserve much credit.

Whatever the shortcomings of detail, one thing is certain – Wagner has created a great work, full of audacious originality and dramatic merit. He has, in his new lively way, brought out old material, little known in Germany, and by means of his clever musical-dramatic treatment has breathed new life into it. Many of these profound legends, for most people a closed book, will be opened up and made popular by Wagner's work – just like a child's picture-book, the eye comes to the assistance of the mind. It may also be a good tonic for people nowadays, when parties and factions rule, to witness these great heroes and personalities with their strong passions, selfless actions and complete lives.

The ethical background that Wagner has given the material, one that is in harmony with current philosophies, may also be of importance for the future of the work outside its own sphere of music theatre. This may be whatever it will – the result of this occasion is boundless in its range. An important new chapter in the history of the arts has been written by Wagner. The thousands who have taken part in this Festival will be able to tell the world that German art at Bayreuth has celebrated a triumph that is unique of its kind.

Angelo Neumann

An idea of what the German-speaking visitors made of Bayreuth can be seen from the memoirs of Angelo Neumann, a director of the Leipzig Opera, and from the writings of Eduard Hanslick, the famous Viennese musicologist. Angelo Neumann (1837–1909) studied singing in Vienna and was present when Wagner took rehearsals of Tannhäuser *and* Lohengrin *at the Vienna Opera House in 1875. When he took up his post at Leipzig the following year, he resolved to go to Bayreuth. His co-director, who attended the first cycle of the* Ring, *put him off, as did others whose opinions he valued; they assured him it was 'not worthwhile'. However, another friend insisted that it was Neumann's duty, holding the position he did, to see the new work, and gave him a ticket for the second cycle. Neumann left for Bayreuth in haste:*

It was then about eleven o'clock, and the last train for Bayreuth left at twelve; the last possible chance of getting there in time for the opening of the second cycle the next day. I rushed home, just across the street, ordered my things to be packed, drove to the station, which was some distance off, and barely catching the train, I arrived in Bayreuth the following morning. The second cycle was to begin with the *Rhinegold* that afternoon, August 20th 1876, at five o'clock.

I shall not attempt to describe the excitement that prevailed in Bayreuth in those days. I shall simply say that if impressions could be weighed, the predominant element of public opinion would have proved strongly adverse to the performances.

Under these circumstances I first entered the Bayreuth theatre. My seat was in the centre of the front row and commanded an uninterrupted view of the stage. From the moment of the introduction with that long-drawn chord of E major, when the green gauze curtains rolled gradually away to reveal the swimming Rhine-maidens, I was under a spell that lasted till the final note – a spell of dissolving pictures on the stage, and the incomparable magic of the orchestra. I was particularly entranced by the trio of Rhine-daughters, and heaved a sigh of devout satisfaction at the close, while Wotan and the other gods are striding towards the rainbow bridge, their beautiful song is repeated from the distance.

I still fail to understand why it was that portion of the opera that provoked the most savage criticism.

At the close of that performance of *Rhinegold* I was incapable of speaking to a soul, so deeply sunk was I in all that I had seen and heard. To be sure, I had known Richard Wagner as a producer in Vienna, and admired his methods; but in this performance I realised that a new field had been opened by the greatest of the world's stage directors; that it was an epoch-making performance, and from now on all our work lay along altogether different lines.

I went back to my hotel and looked for a quiet corner to eat my supper alone, then directly to bed – to lie half-waking and half-dreaming, wrapped in the delicious melodies of the *Rhinegold*. Early next morning I awoke refreshed, and waited impatiently through the day for four o'clock – the time set for the opening of the *Valkyrie*.

While all the elect, and most of the non-elect, felt it their duty to cavil and jeer at the artistic impossibilities of *Rhinegold*, the *Valkyrie*, on the contrary, seemed to be more suited to their comprehension. It is unnecessary to record the deep effect that this first performance had upon me. I shall simply say that, great though my enthusiasm was for all these splendid artists, Vogl as Loge, Schlosser as Mime, Hill as Alberich and especially Betz as Wotan – Albert Niemann's performance of Siegmund transcended them all, and I was moved to the very depths of my being. Also I think no one who had the good fortune to hear Franz Betz as Wotan and Amalie Materna as Brünnhilde will ever forget their great scene together in the third Act.

As far as the mere scenic effects go I must admit that the great tableau of the fire-music was absolutely unconvincing; but, on the other hand, I shall never again see a more beautiful setting than the scene in Hunding's hut, as it was given that summer of 1876 in Bayreuth.

One can readily understand how eagerly I looked forward to the last two days. *Siegfried* seemed like a clear fresh spring on a parching summer day. Though Georg Unger was not to my mind an ideal Siegfried, yet he was not enough of a disturbing element to mar the beauty of the whole. Technically, the fire-scene in the third Act of this production was a marvellous achievement.

After this Ring *cycle, Neumann conceived the idea of taking the whole thing back to Leipzig and staging it there. Contriving to meet Liszt, he made his way into* Wahnfried *to see what Wagner would have to say:*

Promptly at the given hour I appeared at Wahnfried. Liszt received me with his well-known gentleness and talked with me a while, discussing the plan in a tone that fell in exactly with my views. Then he wrote a few hasty words on a scrap of paper and sent the note up to Wagner who was still in his bedroom. Presently the servant came down with the answer. Liszt looked at it a moment, smiled, then frowned and seemed to hesitate, but finally decided to let me see what Wagner had written. On one side I read in Liszt's handwriting, 'Incomprehensible man Neumann is here, come down and talk it over with him' – on the reverse Richard Wagner had written, 'Still more incomprehensible one – I have nothing on but my shirt, hence I cannot come down. Have considered Neumann's proposition, but still cling to the hope of repeating the *Ring* at Bayreuth next season.'

However, events proved otherwise and – as will be described later – Neumann did in fact tour with the Ring *from 1881.*

Eduard Hanslick

Eduard Hanslick (1825–1904), Viennese lawyer and music critic, met Wagner at Marienbad in 1845 and was invited to attend a performance of Tannhäuser *in Dresden the following year. His enthusiastic reviews of this work gave him his first success as a critic. He obtained his Doctorate in Law in 1849, and held an official post until 1861, when he resigned to take up an appointment in the music department of the University of Vienna. He wrote on music for the* Weiner Zeitung *until 1855, when he moved to the more influential* Presse; *in 1864 he was among those who left that paper due to a pay dispute and formed the* Neue Freie Presse, *with which he was associated until his retirement in 1895.*

Hanslick, regarded as a bête-noire. *by Wagnerians and caricatured as Beckmesser in* Meistersinger, *nevertheless wrote an account of the first Festival which is notably impartial and reasoned.*

Bayreuth, 12th August 1876

'If the theatre at Bayreuth, built at the direction of Richard Wagner solely for the production of his works, and financed by private contributions, should become a reality, as now seems likely, that fact alone may be counted one of the most remarkable events in the whole history of art and the greatest personal success of which any composer ever dreamed.'

How well I recalled those words (with which I closed a study of *Rheingold* many years ago) when I first saw Wagner's completed Theatre on the eve of the first Festival performance of the *Ring* (13th to 17th August). An extraordinary theatrical experience, and much more! This four-evening-long music drama is a remarkable development in cultural history, not to mention the construction of a special theatre solely for its production, and the pilgrimage of thousands of persons from half of Europe to this remote, half-forgotten little town whose name is now indelibly recorded in the history of art. Whether or not the work meets the expectations of the Bayreuth pilgrims, there is one thing in which all will be of one mind: in admiration of the extraordinary energy and capacity for work and agitation of the man who, on his own, conceived this phenomenon and carried it through to fulfilment.

The *Ring* represents almost twenty-five years' work, an undertaking to which Wagner returned with redoubled enthusiasm after each interruption (*Meistersinger* and *Tristan*). As long ago as 1848 he sketched the draft of a 'Nibelungen

Drama' – shortly thereafter he began working out the poem of *Siegfried's Tod* – it was completed in 1853 and consisted of four separate dramas, and in the same year he began composition of the music. Twenty-two years later, in the summer of 1875, he directed the first rehearsals in Bayreuth. And now, a year later, we are witnessing the first complete production.

This section continues with a lengthy discussion on the poem and its sources; there is a commentary on the drama in which Hanslick misses no opportunity to point out absurdities.

Bayreuth, 14th August 1876

And why of all places, Bayreuth?

Wagner had not originally intended the construction of a new theatre in this town. He thought first of using the old Bayreuth opera house, a stately monument of former feudal magnificence. But the more he considered the necessary alterations, the less did it seem that the house could suffice. Wagner soon recognised that, reforming from scratch, he would have to build from scratch, and that a new operatic genre would require a new theatre. But he stuck to tiny, out of the way Bayreuth in order that listeners might not be distracted from his work by urban disturbances. In this he counted upon the festive mood of an audience predisposed in his favour. According to the unanimous statements of numerous festival guests he appears to have miscalculated.

A little town like Bayreuth is in no way prepared for the reception of so many visitors. Not only are there no luxuries; often enough there are not even the necessities. I doubt that the enjoyment of art is furthered by being uncomfortably housed for a week, sleeping badly, eating wretchedly, and after a strenuous five or six hours' performance of opera, being uncertain of securing a modest snack. Even yesterday I saw many who had arrived in the flush of enthusiasm crawling up the hot dusty street to the distant Wagner Theatre in a considerably more sober frame of mind. The participating artists, too, have expressed fully justified reservations. How easily, they say, could many a deficiency, which came to light only at the dress rehearsals (inadequate casting of minor roles) have been corrected in a big city, while here a change is no longer possible. A distinguished member of the orchestra arrived with a cello half-ruined on the journey. In any larger city it could have easily been repaired; Bayreuth, however, has no instrument maker. There is no need to go any further with this chapter . . . I only wish to state my increased conviction that a major artistic undertaking belongs in a major city.

Hanslick goes on to ask whether the Bay-euth Theatre was for the Ring *alone, and whether the* Ring *was to be exclusive to Bayreuth. He concluded that the* Ring *would not be fully tested until it had survived presentation on the ordinary stages of ordinary opera houses.*

The Wagner Theatre itself is one of the most interesting and instructive of curiosities, not for its exterior, which is rather meagre, and impressive only because of its situation, but rather because of the ingenious novelties of its interior arrangement. Even the entrance to the auditorium is surprising: rows of seats rising in the style of an amphitheatre in a semi-circle, behind them a low gallery, the Royal Box. Otherwise there are no boxes in the entire house; in their place are columns right and left. There is no chandelier, no prompter's box. Vision is equally good from every seat. One sees the proceedings on the stage without obstruction – and nothing else. At the beginning of a performance the auditorium is completely darkened; the brightly lighted stage, with neither spotlights nor footlights in evidence, appears like a brilliantly coloured picture in a dark frame. Many of the scenes have almost the effect of transparent pictures or views in a diorama. Wagner claims that 'the scenic picture should appear to the spectator with the inapproachability of an apparition in a dream.'

Most noteworthy of all is the invisible orchestra, the 'mystical abyss' as Wagner called it, 'because its mission is to separate the real from the ideal.' The orchestra is set so deep that one is reminded of the engine room of a steamship. It is moreover almost entirely hidden by a kind of tin roof. The musicians have not the slightest view of the stage or the public; only the conductor can see the singers, and not even he can see the audience. Wagner's inspired idea of sparing us the disturbing spectacle of the musicians' fiddling and puffing and pounding is something to which I gave my blessing long ago and for which, following the Munich example, I have even campaigned. The lowering of the orchestra is one of the most reasonable and enduring of Wagner's reforms; it has already taken hold of the legitimate theatres (where its necessity is even more obvious), and it has become a blessing of our Burgtheater. And yet, it seems to me that Wagner has gone too far, or to put it better, gone too deep; for in the whole of *Rheingold* I missed, if not the precision, at least the brilliance of the orchestra. Even the stormy passages sound muffled and dampened. This is, of course, a boon for the singers, but at some cost to the role of the instruments, to which, especially in this work, is assigned much of the most significant sound and the most beautiful. From this muffled sound hardly anyone would have guessed the numerical strength of the orchestra, whose eight harps sounded like two or three. But not only in important matters, such as the position of the orchestra, but also in secondary matters, Wagner has been at pains to rearrange things so as to avoid as much as possible any resemblance to our 'opera houses'. Thus, the signal at the beginning of each piece and each act is given not by a bell but by a fanfare of trumpets; the curtain, instead of being rung up and down, is parted in the middle, etc.

Bayreuth, 18th August 1876

Yesterday we had *Götterdämmerung* as the finale of the whole cycle. With the Bayreuth programme now completed, the music of the future has become a force of the present – outwardly, at least, and for the moment. The critic indulges in prophecies about art with as little eagerness as the serious astronomer about the weather. But this much is highly probable: the style of Wagner's *Ring* will not be the music of the future; it will be, at best, one style among many, possibly only a yeast for the fermentation of new developments harking back to the old. Wagner's most recent reform does not represent an enrichment, an extension, a renewal of music in the sense that the art of Mozart, Beethoven, Weber and Schumann did; it is on the contrary a style alien to the nature of human hearing and feeling. One could say this of tone poetry: there is music in it, but it is not music.

To raise one point for the temporary orientation of the reader: through four evenings we hear singing upon the stage without independent, distinct melodies, without a single duet, trio, ensemble, chorus or finale. The exceptions vanish as fleeting moments in the whole. This alone demonstrates that the knife is applied not to an outward form but to the living roots of dramatic music. Opera lovers who do not know *Tristan* and the *Ring* are prone to suspect that the opponents of these late works are opponents of Wagner altogether. They think only in terms of *Holländer* or *Tannhäuser*, which are as different from this newest music as two things can be within the same art. One can regard *Tannhäuser* as one of the most beautiful of operas and think the opposite of the *Ring*; and, indeed, one must. For what made the fortune of Wagner's earlier operas, and continues to make it, is the firm bond of the descriptive, specifically dramatic element with the charm of the comprehensible melody, the alternation of dialogue with ensembles, choruses and finales. In the *Ring* Wagner has removed all trace of anything reminiscent of these virtues. Even *Meistersinger*, in which separate vocal melody occurs less frequently but, for all that, in certain magnificent examples, seems by comparison a musically charming and popularly comprehensible work.

The *Ring* is, in fact, something entirely new, something essentially different from all that has gone before, a thing alone and apart. As such, as an imaginative experiment, inexhaustibly instructive for the musician, it has enduring significance. That it will ever become popular in the way that Mozart's or Weber's operas are popular appears improbable. Three main considerations distinguish this music in principle from all previous operas, including Wagner's – first, the absence of independent, separate vocal lines, replaced here by a kind of exalted recitative with the 'endless melody' in the orchestra as a basis; second, the dissolution of all form, not just the usual forms (arias and duets, etc.) but of symmetry, of musical logic developed in accordance with laws; third, the exclusion of multiple-voiced pieces, of duets, trios, choruses and finales, not counting a few passing entrances.

Let us hear the Master's own words on his new musical method. He has, says Wagner,

elevated the dramatic dialogue itself as the main substance of the musical production, whereas in the real 'opera' the moments of lyrical dalliance imposed upon the action specifically for this purpose have been regarded as sufficient for the only kind of musical production heretofore considered possible. It is music which, while independently awakening our sensibilities to the motives of the action in their widest ramifications, makes it possible to present just this action with drastic precision; since the protagonists do not, in the sense of conscious reflection, have to inform us of their motivations, the dialogue gains a naïve precision which constitutes the life of the drama.

It reads well enough, but Wagner's objective has, in the implementation, in no way been attained, and the complete amalgamation of opera and drama remains an illusion. The ostensible equality of word and tone renders impossible the full effectiveness of either. It is natural to tone that it broadens out and extends the duration of the word. That is why continuous dialogue belongs to the drama, and sung melody to the opera. The separation of the two is not unnatural; on the contrary it is Wagner's method of uniting them that is unnatural. The artificial *singsprechen* or *sprechsingen* of the *Ring* is an adequate substitute neither for the spoken word of the drama nor for the sung word of the opera, if only because with most singers one does not understand the text anyway, and even with the best only here and there. And, since the auditorium of the Festival Theatre is entirely darkened, there is not even the possibility of consulting the libretto. Thus we sit there, helpless and bored, amid these endless dialogues, thirsting equally for articulate speech and intelligible melody. And what dialogue! Never have human beings spoken to one another in this fashion, probably not even gods. Jumping here and there in awkward intervals, always slow, always glum, exaggerated, one dialogue is essentially like another!

Since, in the music drama, the people involved are not distinguished from one another by the character of the vocal melodies assigned them, as in the old-fashioned opera (Leporello and Don Giovanni – Zelina and Donna Anna – Max and Caspar) but are identical in the physiognomy of their *sprechton*, Wagner has sought to fill the gap with the so-called leitmotives in the orchestra. He had already employed this musico-psychological aid rather extensively in *Tannhäuser* and *Lohengrin*; he overdid it in *Meistersinger*. In the *Ring* he has carried it to the point where it becomes an actual arithmetical problem. It is easy to retain the few melodically and rhythmically pregnant leitmotives of *Tannhäuser* and *Lohengrin* – but how does one proceed in the *Ring*? The answer is given in a brochure by Hans von Wolzogen (a 'Thematic Guide'), a musical Baedeker without which no respectable tourist here dares to be seen and which is on sale everywhere in Bayreuth. Anywhere but in Bayreuth one might well find such a book funny. The serious and sad thing about it is simply that it is necessary. Wolzogen cites no fewer than ninety separate and distinct leitmotives which the hapless Festival visitor should impress upon his memory and recognise wherever they turn up in the tonal mass of the four evenings. Not only persons but also inanimate objects have their leit- or leib-motives, which bob up here there and everywhere, and in the most mysterious relationships. Thus we have the 'ring' motive, the motives of 'subjugation', of the 'threat', of the 'gold of the Rhine', of the 'tired Siegmund', of the 'sword', of the 'giants', of the 'dwarf', of the 'curse', of the 'dragon', and of 'revenge'; the motives of Alberich, Siegfried, Wotan, and so on to No. 90. This rich musical wardrobe in which the heroes share is changed, however, only at their feet, in the orchestra; on the stage they have no melodic finery whatsoever.

The leitmotives are, with few exceptions ('the Ride of the Valkyries', the 'Valhalla' motive, the 'arrival' motive and Siegfried's horn call) of meagre melodic and rhythmic substance, made up of only a few notes, and often very much alike. Only an extraordinary ear and memory can retain them all. And supposing that one has actually accomplished it and has recognised that the orchestra is alluding here to the giants, there to the gods, and somewhere else to the giants and gods together, has anything really great been achieved? It is simply a matter of comprehension, a conscious process of comparison and association. Full enjoyment and reception are impossible when understanding and memory must be ever on the alert to catch the wary allusion. This mystico-allegoric tendency in the *Ring* is reminiscent in many respects of Part II of Goethe's *Faust*, whose poetic effect is diminished by just this habit on the part of the poet of indulging in 'hidden inner meanings' which torture the reader as riddles. Whether a given composition derives from the depths of musical sensibility or from the result of imaginative contrivance cannot – as evident as it may appear to the individual – be proved scientifically.

In the old pre-Nibelungen opera, the composer followed the universal rules of musical logic, fashioned by a succession of individual organisms, each intelligible in itself. In 'opera' the masters gave us music understandable in its unity, pleasurable in its beauty, and dramatic in its inner identification with the action. They have demonstrated a hundred times that the 'absolute melody' so despised by Wagner, can also be eminently dramatic and, in multiple-voiced pieces, particularly in finales, can energetically compress and complete the progress of the action. To abolish the multiple-voiced song, duet, trio and chorus as ostensibly 'undramatic' is to ignore the most valuable accomplishments of the art of music and to go back two hundred years to the musical kindergarten. It is the most beautiful property of music, its most characteristic charm, its greatest advantage over the drama, that it permits two and more persons, even whole masses, to speak out at once. This treasure, for which the poet must envy the musician, Wagner heaves out of the window as superfluous. In the *Ring* there may be two, three or six persons standing together on the stage, but, aside from insignificant and fleeting exceptions, they never sing together; they speak, instead, as in court proceedings, one after the other. Only he who has experienced it can fully appreciate what a torture it is to follow this musical goose-step set-up for a whole evening. But since Wagner continues the tyranny of this monodic style through four evenings in a row, he compels us, with almost suicidal pointedness, to attack the nonsense of his method and to long for the much-abused old-fashioned 'opera'.

On top of that is the incredible and iniquitous length of the individual scenes and conversations. I do not overlook the new element of greatness and exaltation which Wagner gives to his work by limiting each act to only two or three episodes, each unfolding in serene breadth, often appearing, like plastic pictures, to stand still. The *Ring* is most advantageously distinguished from the restless change and surplus action in our 'grand opera' precisely through this simplicity. But an epic breadth must not be permitted to jeopardise the whole drama. It is hard to understand how so theatre-wise a dramatic composer should lose all sense of proportion and fail to sense that conversations such as Wotan's with Fricka, with Brünnhilde, with Mime, etc., try the listener's patience to the utmost. One seeks in vain a dramatic or musical justification for the unheard-of length of the 'Valhalla' scene in *Rheingold*, of the dialogues in the second act of *Walküre*, of the six questions in *Siegfried*, etc.

An eloquent and imaginative advocate of Wagner's, Ludwig Ehlert, suggests in his critique of *Tristan und Isolde* that in order to ensure the opera's survival every episode might be considerably shortened. Now one may well ask: where has there ever been a real dramatic composer in whose operas any piece may be cut at will without damage? But in listening to the *Ring* I felt that every scene could stand not only the most extensive cuts but also the most extensive expansion. The new method of 'dialogue music drama' does, indeed, reject every thought of musical proportion; it is the formless infinite. Wagner, to be sure, protests that his stage plays should not be criticised from the standpoint of music. But then why does he write music, and a lot of music at that – four whole evenings of it?

In many places, indeed, one is confronted with musical beauties, brilliantly effective, strong as well as tender. It is as if the new Wagner were recalling the old. It is hardly necessary to cite these fine moments specifically – the song of the Rhine-maidens in the first and last works, Siegmund's Spring song, the Magic Fire Music', the 'Ride of the Valkyries' and the 'Forest Murmurs' among others. In the Bayreuth performances, one could note how each of these was remarked with visible pleasure by the listeners and literally pressed to their hearts. When, after two hours of monodic steppe, there appears a bit of multiple-voiced song – the closing chords of the three Rhine-maidens, the group singing of the Valkyries, the few triads at the close of the love duet in *Siegfried* – one can see in the faces of the listeners a joyous thrill, as if they had been released from long imprisonment. These are noteworthy symptoms. They bear eloquent witness to the fact that the musical nature of human beings cannot be denied or suppressed, that Wagner's new methods are not a reform of outlived traditions but an assault upon musical sensibilities inherent within us and cultivated by centuries of education. Let the assault be undertaken with the most brilliant weapons of the intellect – nature resists it and throws the besieger back at will with a few roses and violets.

The descriptive powers of Wagner's fantasy, the astonishing mastery of his orchestral technique, and many musical beauties, exert a magic force to which we surrender readily and gratefully. These beautiful details, which somehow sneak in behind the back of the system, do not prevent the system itself, the tyranny of the word, the tuneless dialogue, the dreary monotony, from poisoning the whole. The strange colouristic splendour of the *Ring*, the fascinating fragrance of the orchestra, surround us with a demoniac charm. But as Tannhäuser longed for the familiar and loved sound of the bells of the earth, so we soon long with all our hearts for the melodic blessing of the old music.

Hanslick, having dealt with the drama and music of the Ring, *now goes on to give his impressions of the actual performances and the production.*

Bayreuth, 19th August 1876

Were the impression which Wagner's *Ring* made upon the audience predominantly concerned with the music, it would have to be described as depressing. But Wagner's versatility, certainly the most brilliant aspect of his talent, allows him to work simultaneously with the special talents of the musician, the painter, the librettist and the stage director, and he often achieves through the last three that which the first could not have effected alone. The painter's fantasy is inexhaustibly at work in the *Ring*, and from it appears to have stemmed the initial impulse for many scenes. If one studies the photographs of the sets so poetically devised by Joseph Hoffmann, one cannot escape the thought that such scenes must have first appeared in Wagner's imagination and inspired the appropriate music.

Thus it is with the first scene of *Rheingold*. The Rhine-maidens, singing and swimming in the Rhine, encompassed for 136 bars by no more than the diffused chord of E flat major, provide a tableau which achieves a predominantly visual effect. But in this scene, unquestionably the best of *Rheingold*, the concept is essentially a musical one. From that point on, the musical charm of the work declines rapidly, and since, at the same time, the listener's sensibility, taxed for almost three hours without interruption, wears thin, he leaves the theatre with the impression of utter monotony. I shall waste no words on the indigestible German stammered in *Rheingold* and offered as poetry. It would, indeed, be a misfortune if familiarity with this Nibelungen style, together with indiscriminate admiration for everything that comes from Wagner, were gradually to so dull public perception as to render it impervious to the ugliness of such diction.

The second drama *Die Walküre* begins very impressively with the entrance of the fugitive Siegmund into Hunding's house. The tedious breadth of the scene at the table (Siegmund, Hunding and Sieglinde) is compensated for, gradually, in the course of the love duet between Siegmund and Sieglinde, in which the B flat major episode, 'Winterstürme wichen dem Wonnemond', enters like long-missed sunlight. Here we are revived by a ray of melodious sustained song.

The second Act is an abyss of boredom. Wotan appears, holds a long conversation with his wife, and then, turning to Brünnhilde, gives an autobiographical lecture covering eight full pages of text. This utterly tuneless, plodding narrative, in a slow tempo, engulfs us like an inconsolable broad sea from which only the meagre crumbs of a few leitmotives come floating towards us out of the orchestra. Scenes like this recall the medieval torture of waking a sleeping prisoner by stabbing him with a needle at every nod. We have heard even Wagnerites characterise this second Act as a disaster. It is entirely unnecessary, since with two cuts both episodes could be done away with, painlessly. *Die Walküre* has, indeed, a very loose relationship with the action of the whole; it tells nothing of the fateful ring which we have not already learned in *Rheingold*, and only Brünnhilde's punishment is important for the purpose of the drama.

In the third Act, there is a return to music of significant force and fullness, first through the Valkyries, whose wild and disordered ensemble enlivens the scene advantageously. The 'Ride of the Valkyries' and the 'Magic Fire Music' are two brilliantly conceived specimens of tone painting, abundantly familiar from concert performances. Taking their dramatic connotation into consideration, I had, in my reviews of them, predicted a much greater effect than they actually seemed to have had in Bayreuth. There are two possible explanations: first, the 'mystic abyss' of the Bayreuth Theatre offered nothing like the brilliance and verve of a freely exposed concert orchestra; second, both pieces occur towards the end of the opera and are thus heard by an audience exhausted and dulled by what has gone before.

Contrary to all expectations *Siegfried* had a greater effect than *Die Walküre*. It was not an entirely inexplicable surprise. A fresh tone is felt in the first Act, something realistic, a boyish naturalness. This is dissipated, to be sure, in the disproportionate length of the scenes and musical episodes, but the effect is refreshing after the stilted progress of the first two evenings. But what can one say of Wotan's long scene with the dwarf? Each gives the other three questions, and each answers with the detailed precision of a well-tutored candidate at a school examination. The whole scene, utterly superfluous from the dramatic point of view, is an oppressive bore. The listeners are abandoned to the diversion of hunting hidden leitmotives in the orchestra (where is the cat? where is the bear?). Generally speaking, one can be certain that with the appearance of so much as the point of Wotan's spear, a half-hour of emphatic boredom is in store. Should this exalted 'god' who never knows what is needed or who does the right thing, who yields in the first drama to a stupid giant, in the second to his domineering wife and in the third to an impudent youth – should this unctuous pedant be revered as the godly ideal of the German people?

For the illustration of the forging of the sword, the orchestra provides admirable tone painting. Siegfried's much-praised 'Forging Song' is more funereal than joyous. Wagner simply is not acquainted with naïve, natural joyousness. He has just as little knack for the comical, as we know from Beckmesser. In the characterisation of Mime he has been totally unable to distinguish between the comical and the tedious.

The second Act introduces us to a forest near the cavern of the *Lindwurm*. Following a scene between Alberich and Wotan, a model of forced anti-lingual declamation, comes the high point of the whole score, the 'Forest Murmurs'. Siegfried reclines under a tree, listening to the rustling of the leaves and the song of the birds. Here Wagner's virtuosity as a tone painter enjoys its most genuine triumph – derived, as it is, from natural materials and imbued with purely human impressions. Here, as in his concert-piece, the *Siegfried Idyll*, he portrays the song of the birds with a fidelity to nature achieved neither by Haydn in *The Creation* nor by Beethoven in the 'Pastoral' Symphony.

Now Siegfried comes face to face with the giant Fafner as the *Lindwurm*, roaring and spitting fire. Wagner has composed the scene in deadly earnest, but the effect is comical, particularly at the end, when the croaking *Lindwurm* becomes sentimental and offers his murderer confidential information. A woodland bird, whose language Siegfried now understands, shows him the way to Brünnhilde. The song of the bird is an illuminating example of how much better Wagner can make an orchestra sing than he can the human voice.

The third Act brings Siegfried to Brünnhilde. First, however, we have two

A view of Bayreuth about 1870

Gottfried Semper's model for the Wagner Theatre in Munich

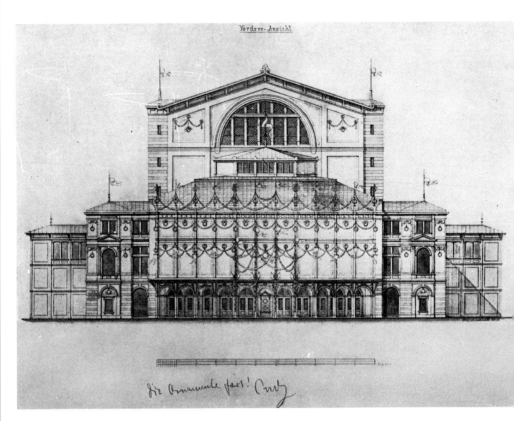

Drawing by Otto Brückwald of his design for the Festspielhaus.
At the bottom is Wagner's instruction: 'The decoration will have to go!'

The Festspielhaus on 2 August 1873, the day of the 'topping-out' ceremony

Certificate of Patronage entitling the subscriber to a seat for the *Ring* in 1876

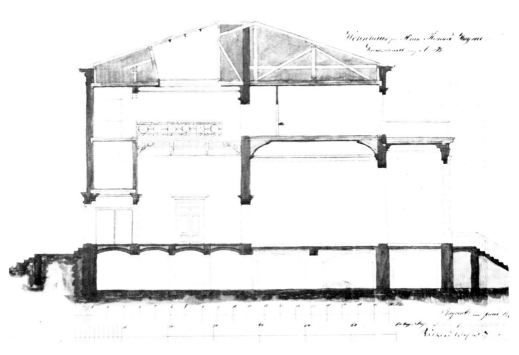

PATRONAT-SCHEIN

Nro.

Der Inhaber dieses Scheines

hat durch die hiemit quittirte Einzahlung von **300 Thalern** die Rechte eines Patrones der in

Bayreuth

zu bewerkstelligenden drei vollständigen Aufführungen des Bühnenfestspiels

DER RING DES NIBELUNGEN

erworben, als welche Rechte ihm die unbedingte Verfügung über einen bequemen Sitz-platz für jeden der zwölf Abende, in denen die dreimalige Aufführung des viertheiligen Werkes bestehen wird, sowie ferner die Betheiligung an der Bildung einer Patronat-Commission zuerkannt sind, welcher die Verfügung über 500 Freiplätze für jede der durch die Beisteuer der Patrone ermöglichten Festaufführungen zustehen soll, und in welcher der Inhaber dieses Scheines sich für eine Patronat-stimme durch Delegirung vertreten lassen wird.

BAYREUTH,

1 Februar 1872.

Als Bevollmächtigte und Verwalter:

'A dwelling-house for Herr Richard Wagner', Carl Wölfel's drawing of Wahnfried. The front entrance is to the left

Wahnfried: the *Saal* as
it was in Wagner's day

Orchester=Probe.

Wagner on the stage of the Festspielhaus during the Ring rehearsals of 1875. Drawing by Adolph von Menzel (*left*)

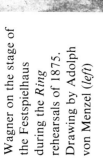

Wagner on the stage of the Festspielhaus addressing Hans Richter in the orchestra pit during the *Ring* rehearsals of 1876

The Bayreuth Festival, 1876: a contemporary drawing
(some of the architectural features of the Festspielhaus
are the invention of the artist)

The view of Bayreuth from the Festspielhaus at the time of the first Festival
in 1876

The Festspielhaus auditorium, 1876

The orchestra pit during the *Parsifal* rehearsals of 1882.
Wagner talks to Hermann Levi through a little trap-door in the cover

Lilli Lehmann, Marie Lehmann and Minna Lammert: the Rhine-maidens in the first *Ring*, 1876

The 'swimming apparatus' for the Rhine-maidens

heavy scenes to survive. Wotan appears in a rocky cleft and summons Erda from below. He asks her weighty questions, but she, the fountain of knowledge, knows absolutely nothing and disappears. It seems unlikely that ten persons in the theatre were quite in the clear about this Erda. I was not among them. Enter Siegfried. A dispute, expressed in rather uninhibited language, develops between him and Wotan, who attempts to bar his way to Brünnhilde. Finally Siegfried smashes Wotan's spear, whereupon this divine nightwatchman slinks away, more helpless than ever. An orchestral interlude of tumultuous forces, conjuring up the motives of the 'Ride of the Valkyries' and the 'Magic Fire Music' conducts us at once through fire and smoke to Brünnhilde's resting place. The scene between Siegfried and Brünnhilde is of exhausting length. Brünnhilde's awakening is tenderly depicted, and in the E major section of the love duet 'Ewig bin ich' the melody blossoms more freely and expressively. The duet falls off lamentably towards the end through the inexplicable introduction of a stiff theme in descending fourth (in C major, *alla breve*). These exalted accents, of which Wagner is so proud – passionate groaning and moaning, crying out and collapsing – border offensively on the ultimate limits of a flaming, insatiable sensuality. The textual excesses become sheer nonsense – 'godlike repose is plunged into tempest' – the poet and composer of this scene has a fine right to poke fun at the 'high-flown' Schumann.

Götterdämmerung strikes me as the most successful, dramatically, of the cycle; here we move about again on our own earth and among our flesh and blood fellows. We even have a real plot, although the intrusion of the draught of forgetfulness, which affected me so unpleasantly in prospect, proved even more repulsive and incomprehensible in performance. Executed with truly bee-like industry, even more carefully than in the preceding dramas, the music of *Götterdämmerung* is noticeably inferior. The first three dramas may seem sterile and unnatural in their musical method, sometimes violent and abstruse, but they are animated by quicker, warmer blood and a more original invention. This is possibly due to their earlier origin. *Götterdämmerung*, on the other hand, is oppressed by a singular exhaustion and fatigue, something like the approaching affliction of middle age.

Someone has said – and not unjustly – that the action in *Götterdämmerung* is distinct from the other three dramas, while the music, on the whole, is the same. The music is constructed predominantly upon the leitmotives of the first three: thus, from the same material and according to the same method. The essential musical distinction consists in the presence – albeit sporadic – of multiple-voiced song. The unexpected concession of a real male chorus, in particular, must come as a pleasant surprise to listeners so long subjected to monodic discipline. I attribute the pleasure afforded by the mad merriment of Gunther's men to simple delight in the long-denied sound of men's voices in concert. Of incomparably more beautiful invention is the charming glimmer of the song of the Rhinemaidens in the third Act. Neither the first nor second Act is without beautiful melodious moments, but they all possess, like Siegfried, a Tarnhelm under which they quickly disappear or change at will into something else.

In the first Act, the parting of Siegfried and Brünnhilde makes the deepest impression. Studying single phrases of the great duet individually and separately, one finds them full of substance and passion; taken as a whole, the declamatory song, continually goading itself on to ecstasy, resembles a succession of expressive interjections, making no cohesive speech. At first excited, the listener gradually gives way to fatigue and finally to distraction; with the best of intentions he can no longer remain attentive. The subsequent orchestral postlude, with the horn fanfare of the departing Siegfried, makes a nice effect. The piece has the utmost musical charm and cohesiveness, particularly by virtue of the attractive contrapuntal ornamentation surrounding that vigorous horn call. Siegfried's death is much less satisfactory. What the dying man sings with astonishing lung power seems almost superfluous in the dazzling fluctuation of the orchestra, which with four harps, trombones, kettle-drums and the most piercing high notes of the violins, excites acute nervous irritation. More significant and more gripping than Siegfried's death song is the funeral march now intoned for the departing hero. It is an instrumental necrologue assembled from earlier Siegfried motives, and rather a work of imaginative reflection than of immediate creative force. Brünnhilde's monologue at Siegfried's bier is simply colossal. She sends the ravens home and hurls the torch into the pyre. The way in which the croaking birds and their upward flight are pictured by the muted trumpets and whirling figurations in the violins, and the way in which the crackling of the flames is represented by the most delicate and ingenious handling of the brass and percussion – all this belongs among the most distinguished accomplishments of a master unrivalled in this kind of painting. Brünnhilde's song rises to the height of exaltation, continuously in the extreme upper range and under the most violent strain, soaring above the hurricane of the orchestra. Then, for a moment, the orchestra subsides in deference to a tender passage for Brünnhilde, and we are touched as by a supernatural revelation. Now, following Brünnhilde's death, comes the *Götterdämmerung* – the end of the world; with a mighty crash Wagner releases all the demons of the orchestra and so overwhelms us that we are hardly capable even of admiring the technique with which it is all accomplished.

The best things in *Götterdämmerung* made an uncommon, intellectually stimulating, sensuously dazzling impression, but not a profound or enduring one. The music has, at best, the fascination of a magic charm; it does not have the faculty of making the heart rejoice, which is the essential characteristic of a work of art. One must certainly admit its incomparable objectivity and its dazzling richness of colour. One has only to read the text to admire Wagner's painter's eye and his genius for theatrical effect. How wonderful it is all thought out and how vividly it is all seen! How Siegfried rides through the flames to the Rhine after taking leave of Brünnhilde! How the latter, at Siegfried's bier, springs upon her horse and leaps into the flaming pyre! These are pictures such as have never before been offered upon the stage. In keeping with this mission, Wagner's music is first and foremost graphic and decorative. The orchestra, in the utmost refinement of sound, is the essential element. The singing voices alternate between monotonous declamation and explosive outbursts of unbounded passion. One can listen to this incoherent ardour amidst the fluctuations of deafening and nerve-racking orchestral effects for only a short time without relaxation. The majority of listeners were already more or less exhausted after the second Act. Who could endure four consecutive evenings of this exaltation?

The musical style is familiar from the preceding parts; it is completely stereotyped. Wagner is mannered; an inspired genius, but still a mannerist. His eccentricities of declamation, modulation and harmonisation are imposed on every kind of material. In this style he could probably write ten more operas without undue effort or inspiration. Although the element of passionate exaltation never seems to achieve satiety, it is often difficult to believe in its truth and necessity. It is reminiscent of many of Victor Hugo's poems, products of inner coldness which imagine themselves glowing and inspired. The music to *Götterdämmerung* characterises its author anew as a brilliant specialist, rather adjacent to music than of it. It is unthinkable that his method shall be, as he contends, the only valid opera style from now on, the absolute 'art-work of the future'. When an art arrives at a period of utmost luxury, it is already on the decline. Wagner's opera style recognises only superlatives; but a superlative has no future. It is the end, not the beginning. From *Lohengrin* on, Wagner broke a new path, dangerous to life and limb; and this path is for him alone. He who follows will break his neck, and the public will contemplate the disaster with indifference.

I have given here only a fleeting impression of the four 'Nibelungen' dramas; there can be no thought of an intensive analysis. Nor can there be any thought, as I have said before, of a purely musical impression. Wagner felt, indeed, that the pleasure of listening would be insufficient for so long a period of incarceration in the theatre, and he has provided much to occupy the eye as well. Never before has such an accumulation of scenic wonders been offered in an opera. Devices heretofore held impossible or, more accurately, unthought of, follow one on top of another: the Rhine-maidens swimming deep in the water; the gods strolling over a rainbow; the transformation of Alberich, first into a serpent, then a toad; the magic fire; the twilight of the gods, etc. In all this the poet has given the composer the widest possible scope for his brilliant virtuosity – tone painting. But it should be the highest ambition of the dramatic composer to make music for a succession of magic contrivances – or should it?

Actually, the *Ring* has much in common with the genre of magic tricks and fairy tales. These utterly material effects are in direct contradiction to the pure idealism which Wagner claims for his works. He strives everywhere for the strongest sensual impression, and with every available means. The mysterious heaving of the invisible orchestra gives the listener a mild opium jag even before the rise of the curtain; he is subjected to the enduring impression of a magically-lighted fairy-tale scene before anyone on the stage has opened his mouth. In the numerous night scenes, a dazzling electric light plays upon the figure of the principal character, while tinted steam undulates upon and above the stage. This steam, which in *Rheingold* even takes the place of a change-of-scene curtain, constitutes the most powerful weapon in Wagner's new dramatic arsenal. As a formless, fantastic, sensually fascinating element it has a special affinity with

Wagner's musical principles. He himself compares the music emanating from the invisible orchestra with the 'steam rising up from under Pythia's tripod which introduces the listener to an exalted condition of clairvoyance.' From here it is only a step to the artful employment of certain smells and odours – Psychology does recognise them, indeed, as particularly stimulating and exciting. We are quite in earnest. Who does not know from children's fairy tales that fairies are encompassed by a sweet smell of roses, while the devil regularly makes off in a stink of sulphur? The principle of allowing all atmosphere-promoting stimulants to co-operate in the heightening of certain sensations and images should draw upon the sympathetic and pleasurable faculties of the olfactory nerves. Wagner has utilised all the modern advances of applied science. We have seen in astonishment the colossal machinery, the gas apparatus, the steam machines above and below the stage at Bayreuth. Wagner could have as little composed the *Ring* before the invention of the electric light as without the harp and bass tuba. Thus it is that the element of colour in the broadest sense disguises the paltry design in his newest works and usurps for itself an unheard-of self-sufficiency. It is through its sensually fascinating magic that this music, as a direct nervous stimulant, works so powerfully on the audience and on the female audience particularly. The professional musician's part in this highly advanced orchestral technique has rather to do with how it is all accomplished. I underestimate neither the one nor the other; but neither is entitled to violent domination. Neither the conductor's technical gourmet's interest, nor the hashish dream of the ecstatic female, fulfills the nature and benediction of genuine musical composition; both can, and often do, exist independently of the soul of music.

With whatever hopes and fears one may have made the pilgrimage to Bayreuth, we were all united at least in our anticipation of an extraordinary theatrical event. But even this expectation was only partially fulfilled. I have duly acknowledged Wagner's imaginative innovations in the arrangement of his theatre, including, as regards the mechanical side, the scene of the swimming Rhine-maidens in *Rheingold*. From there on there is a gradual descent. That the very first change of scene failed mechanically, that everything went generally awry, is not something to which I can attach much importance. That sort of thing can happen in any theatre, although it would have been better had it not happened in this widely heralded and elaborately prepared 'model production' at Bayreuth. There were examples aplenty of incorrect and deficient mounting, and in decisive places. The rainbow, over which the gods proceed to Valhalla, was set so low that one could have taken it for a painted bridge in a flower garden. The struggle between Siegmund and Hunding, and Wotan's intervention, took place in such remote darkness that none of the listeners got any idea of what was going on. The Valkyries never appeared on horseback – they simply moved across the horizon in ineffective and indistinct dissolving views. In Munich they had young stable boys dressed as Valkyries jumping back and forth on thick carpets; their riding, uncannily rapid and noiseless, was remarkably effective. What was possible for such a humble court theatre should certainly be possible for the model stage at Bayreuth. The wall of fire which should surround Brünnhilde was visible only behind her; on three sides she was perfectly free and approachable. The Munich Theatre, years ago, showed how this too should be done. I shall pass over Fricka's ludicrous team of rams and the ageing nag which Brünnhilde did not ride but which was led by the bridle and held fast by a cord beneath the stage; likewise the many unsuccessful scenic effects. I shall mention only the final scene of *Götterdämmerung* in which the scenic art of the Wagner Theatre should have reached its height. Who could not have looked forward eagerly to the moment when Brünnhilde, according to the explicit assurance of the libretto, would 'leap impetuously upon the steed and with one impulse vault into the flaming fire.' Instead of this she led her miserable Rosinante calmly off into the wings. There was no thought of leaping or vaulting. Hagen, who should throw himself as if crazed into the river, strolled into the wings on the right and turned up a few seconds later in the middle of the Rhine. And finally, the Rhine, which should 'burst its banks in a mighty flood', wobbled – with its badly daubed and visibly sewn-up waves – like the Red Sea in a provincial production of Rossini's *Moses*. If in such a principal scene a performance cannot achieve what Wagner expressly prescribes in the libretto and promises to the spectator, then there is little further occasion to speak of a 'model production'. By far the most successful were the sets by Joseph Hoffmann, as well painted as they were original in conception; with faithful execution and more purposeful lighting they could have been even more effective. The painter of the scenery can only account for a half of the total effect; the other half rests with the lighting, which corresponds to the instrumentation of a musical idea. This second half was not fully carried out in Bayreuth, and Hoffmann's ideas appear more melodiously conceived in the photographs than they sounded in the Festival Theatre.

That the vast majority of the Bayreuth pilgrims broke into jubilant applause after each of the four dramas was to be expected; they came for that purpose. The conviction I expressed in my first report, that the durability of Wagner's newest works and their effect on the public will be definitively proved only on other stages, still stands.

Clemens Brockhaus

A different view of the Festival of 1876 comes from Wagner's nephew Clemens Brockhaus whose father, Friedrich Arnold Brockhaus, founder of the Leipzig publishing house, had married Richard Wagner's sister Ottolie in 1828. Clemens Brockhaus wrote to his wife about the Bayreuth Festival in 1876:

The interior of the theatre, where I had a very good seat, is very simple. A row of doors leads to the raked amphitheatre. At the back is the Princes' Gallery; the seats there are by no means the best, they are too far away. Above are places for the music students, where they cannot see the orchestra.

I saw Cosima, she has become really ugly and faded. She goes around in white silk with a *Mozartzopf*.* She told me, in a friendly way, she simply had no time to receive me as they were too busy, which I can understand.

A trumpet fanfare announces the arrival of the Emperor and Princes and, at the same time, the start of *Rheingold*. It was pitch black in the theatre and impossible to see one's neighbour.

The curtain went up and the Rhine-maidens began to play. The musical effect was wonderful, with all the magic of Uncle Richard's work, but the most striking thing about the stage apparatus was its shortcomings; I have seen much better in Berlin and Paris. The lighting of the water was so dim the nixies were almost invisible and it was obvious they were in a machine – their swimming movements were just like a roundabout. A few curtains rose and fell at the wrong time and the effect of the transformation from the bottom of the Rhine to the upper ground was lost. The Rhine gold was a feeble glimmer on the rock and had no real glow. The steam curtain came at the wrong time and failed to conceal what was behind it. The dragon with a child working its jaws was just as ridiculous as in *Zauberflöte*.

The impression was one of cost-cutting where money should have been spent. It was effective but, in view of the amount of publicity beforehand, nothing should have been lacking. . . .

To find Uncle Richard was impossible, mainly because the performance yesterday had no interval; I hope it will be possible today at *Walküre*. . . .

In the evening the town was fresh and cool and there were fireworks and illuminations – as beautiful and artistic as I have seen in Leipzig. Uncle Richard's house and garden were lit up with little lanterns. . . . It must be very strange for Uncle to see this multitude of people, for thousands are gathered here.

The Emperor has installed himself, with half a dozen Princes too, and this brings a certain pomp to the little town. He is surrounded by admirers but seems to have no real friends. . . .

It is all very fine and doubtless will become finer still but I would not have liked to pay out 100 thalers for the *Ring* when there is so much else I could do with the money.

I am here on my own but know several families; just as well, for to be here quite alone, amongst all these ladies – that would be terribly embarrassing.

The most elegant of ladies are having to force themselves into low pubs and even sit on the doorsteps in the alleyways – and still get nothing. The three Rhine-maidens have just managed to make their midday meal in this fashion, one of them getting sausages, another bread, and the third beer.

* A way of dressing the hair.

Joseph Bennett

The three leading English newspapers sent their critics to the Ring *in 1876, and the man from the* Daily Telegraph *was Joseph Bennett (1831–1911), whose reviews were later published under the title* Letters from Bayreuth *(1877). Bennett was also editor of the* Musical Times, *and drew the scorn of Bernard Shaw for writing 'doggerel' for a series of oratorios published by Novello. However, Shaw acknowledged Bennett's enormous power as a music critic, power he used to demonstrate the objectionable character of Wagner's music. These extracts from Bennett's reviews include another amusing pen-portrait of Bayreuth trying to cope with its first Festival.*

Bayreuth, August 12 [1876]

Bayreuth is, of itself, a negation; a stranger may wander long about its streets without coming into contact with anything suggestive of the living, active, and positive world, unless, indeed, he encounter a big Bavarian soldier. Of all dull towns I imagine Bayreuth, in its normal state, to be the dullest. Moreover, the utter sluggishness of the place has its impression heightened by plentiful signs that, once on a time, there was life here. In the fine old days when Germany grew princes wholesale, Bayreuth had its little court and was a little capital. The potentate whose sway it owned called himself, I believe, a Margrave, and contrived, somehow or other, to keep up a considerable state. He built palaces, whereof two stand in the town, and, though used for a variety of purposes, are decaying with a fit air of dignity. The third, some two miles off, serves to perpetuate the memory of its builders, much as the Brighton Pavilion immortalises our own George the Fourth. But these edifices are by no means the only signs of Bayreuth's dead-and-gone grandeur. The place abounds in fine old houses; its streets are adorned with some very respectable statues – that, among others, of Jean Paul Richter, who lived and died here – while numerous fountains are continually pouring out streams of clear water. These fountains, by the way, are a distinctive feature of the town which they serve to ornament as well as to bless. Of course they trace their origin to the Margraves, and the question at once arises why it was that the tyrannous old German princes expiated their bad ways by providing so much water. Once on a time they built churches, but the logic of that course is clear enough, and, unless they saw in the 'pure element' a symbol of the 'mystical washing away of sin' I can not account for the fountains. The Bayreuth churches, let me add, are not remarkable, and it is to be feared that the Margraves cared very little about them. On the whole, the town has a stately and dignified look, but is woefully faded. It is a tenth-rate Versailles, crossed with a sleepy provincial borough. Sleepy! I should think so, indeed! Even now, when the place has been galvanised into prodigious activity, one can easily distinguish

Bayreuthers from the strangers. The native and his favourite beast of draught, the ox, are well matched, both going dreamily through life at the slowest possible pace, and with a constant disposition to lie down and ruminate.

Just now, as I have said, Bayreuth is uncommonly alert, having actually two things on its mind at once – making money in abundance out of the strangers within its gates, and spending a little economically in decoration. The first of these operations Bayreuth will certainly carry out with success, and, as regards the second, a convenient decision has been arrived at to the effect that there is something exhilarating in the appearance of the fir which chances to abound on the neighbouring hills. The result is that Bayreuth has a fir eruption all over it. Great branches, stuck in the ground to resemble trees, line the pavements – or rather the space where the pavements should be – festoons of fir cover the fronts of the houses, and wreaths of the same cheerful material, made more lively by paper flowers, are stuck wherever room can be found for them. Adding to this a crowd of poles, from which in due time – for the Bayreuther is careful of his bunting – flags will fly, and it must be granted that the inhabitants, considering their normal sleepiness, have bestirred themselves to some purpose, even though, like John Gilpin's spouse, they do not overlook the value of 'a frugal mind'.

The most conspicuous figure in Bayreuth life just now is made by strangers who swarm all over the town and are contemplated by the natives with placid wonderment. They are certainly worth contemplating, as being a remarkable crowd of curious people. Let me frankly say that never before did I see so many short-sighted folk, with long hair and 'loud' hats, gathered together in one place. The ambitious literary youth of England used to imagine an intimate connection between genius and the Byron collar, but they had a model which these Wagnerites lack. Why, then, is it that faith in the 'Art Work of the Future' goes in company with spectacles, long hair, and funny head-gear? I confess I cannot tell. There must be a reason, else hardly would the phenomenon manifest itself in men who have come from all points of the compass and have nothing in common save their faith. An eager race are they, and a splendid contrast to the slow Bayreuther. You may see them flying along the road that conducts to the Wagner Theatre, 'larding the lean earth' à la Falstaff, as they go. Or you may see them racing about the streets, stopping suddenly whenever some fresh manifestation of Wagner is made by a shop window, which means stopping every few yards, for upon the man who has given Bayreuth fame Bayreuth, in turn, bestows whatever it can of honour. The whole town is, so to speak, given up to him, and you see him everywhere. In photographs and statuary, on pipe-bowls and tobacco-boxes, on toilet ornaments and album covers – on countless things, indeed, appear the well-known face and form. Nor is this all. Wagner's music floats about the streets. Here a soprano may be heard declaiming at the top of her voice some passage from the *Nibelungen*; here a tenor, and there a bass, labour hard and lustily; or, perhaps, a violinist has got up among the harmonics, or a pianist is hammering out a succession of 'diminished sevenths' which clash against each other in their search for a key never to be found. I declare to you that I have not yet heard in Bayreuth a single quiet melodic phrase. Music, here and now, is nothing if not 'sound and fury'; nor do musicians deserve the name unless they rave and roar. Well, these are times when the world lives fast and has sharp emotions.

Wagner's house – 'an eligible residence standing in its own grounds' – points to the fact that a musician 'of the future' need not be prepared, as a matter of necessity, to sacrifice the present. Let me confess to looking upon this, the master's chosen home, with anything but complacency. One is glad, of course, when genius meets with the reward of life's good things. It rarely does so, because, perhaps, adversity supplies better nourishment; but in the exception we recognize that which is fitting. There is, however, about Wagner's state a pretentious, theatrical air such as a man of taste must regret to see. A house decorated with gaudy frescoes and mottoes, bearing a fantastic name, and surmounted, as now, by three tall poles, from the top of which stream three large flags – such a place I can associate with genius only by a severe wrench. But Wagner was never chargeable with failing to exhibit his light in all sorts of ways and places. He strives to keep himself before the world, and if he attracts passing attention by decorating his house, he is, at least, consistent. Though the house and the theatre be wide apart, in this respect they are very close together indeed. Pass we, then, at a step, to the edifice in which, for three weeks to come, Wagner will exhibit his perfected music-drama. The site has been well chosen, some half a mile beyond the skirt of the town, and on top of a gentle eminence which itself is backed by a wooded hill, crowned with a round tower. Rather a pretty way runs thither, the tree-shaded road being flanked by corn-fields and gardens, while the little terrace in front of the building commands an interesting view of the quaint old town and the hills beyond – a view none the less German because the most prominent object in the foreground, next to the lunatic asylum, is a big brewery. Some attempt has been made to lay out the meadow through which the carriage way passes to the theatre as a pleasaunce, but at present the trees are small, the walks ill-kept, and the grass rough. Roughness, indeed, is characteristic of the whole affair, for, to say nothing of the wooden houses flanking the main building, and devoted to refreshment, the theatre itself seems to have been hastily thrown up, and its courses of red brick left innocent of pointing. Of architectural beauty the exterior has none whatever. The object was utility, and, this gained, nothing beyond was sought. In time to come, perhaps, when funds are plentiful, the artist as well as the builder will have to do with the place, and succeed in making it less of a disappointment than it is now. As with the exterior, so elsewhere.

Bennett goes on to describe the auditorium of the Festspielhaus, commenting on how apparently small it is and how few gas lamps there are to light it – a darkened house was then considered worthy of comment. He was favourably impressed by the working of the stage apparatus, how smooth and quiet the scene changes and how effective the sunken orchestra pit. This all before the 'première'; Bennett says he went to a 'rehearsal' – in fact this was King Ludwig's private performance, to which the public had been admitted in order to enhance the sound in the theatre.

Bayreuth, August 13 [1876]

A Kaiser does not come to Bayreuth every day, and it must cheerfully be granted that the inhabitants made very respectable, and unwonted, exertions to give Emperor William a fitting welcome. Not only did they dress their streets and houses with the plentiful fir, but managed to achieve a display of flags. The Bavarian colours – blue and white – were, of course, plentiful, and so were the black, white and red of the German Reich. Of other national flags I saw none, not even the Union Jack, which, considering the swarm of English now here, might have been shown, if only as a matter of courtesy to stranger guests. The Emperor arrived on Saturday afternoon, and his progress through the town to the fantastic place called the Hermitage was a triumph. I am not sure that it is needful to give minute particulars of an event which, if memorable for the Bayreuthers, was not in itself remarkable, nor shall I inflict upon you a list of the Royal and other dignitaries who came with or immediately after their Imperial chief: Enough that the distinguished visitors were so numerous that the officials, whose full evening dress grew more and more dusty as the day progressed, were kept on the alert till a late hour. As a matter of course, the Emperor was serenaded by torchlight, but, as the Hermitage is some miles away, you must take the imposing effect of that ceremony upon trust, and not from my description. This I can answer for – that Bayreuth did not go to bed till eleven o'clock; and, as it is usually fast asleep by ten, the sense of dissipation and of 'making a night of it' which generally prevailed may be imagined. But, if Saturday was a great day, what shall I say for Sunday, when, at an early hour, the population, strengthened by crowds from all the country around, descended into the streets, and kept those usually deserted thoroughfares in a state of commotion till midnight? Bayreuth, like Marguerite decked with the jewels, must have doubted its own identity, and asked with puzzled surprise, 'Can this be I?' But the day was one of puzzles all round. The provincial folk from the hills and plains walked about in wonderment, staring hard at Wagner's painted villa. Bands of youths in wonderful braided caps, and decked with mysterious insignia, furnished strangers with matters of curious inquiry; while, as train after train brought hundreds of fresh arrivals, the question of what was to be done about food and lodging became more and more a riddle. The spare house-room in a town of 18,000 inhabitants is necessarily limited – and limited, I am obliged to say, most of us found the commissariat yesterday. At hotels people begged a meal in vain, and it was only after a hot dusty walk to the huge restaurant adjoining the Wagner Theatre that a reasonable prospect of restoring exhausted nature opened out. However, the day wore on, and, as the blinding brilliant sun dropped in the west, all Bayreuth poured itself along the road to the ugly temple from which is to shine a new light upon German Art.

The scene in the neighbourhood of the building became really animated and picturesque towards seven o'clock, at which hour the performance of *Das Rheingold* was announced to begin. From the terrace the eye commanded a long stretch of the thronged highway, and of the flag-decked town beyond, while near at hand were assembling the component parts of such a gathering as the art world rarely sees. A polyglot gathering it was, and to move about amongst it gave one an idea of the confusion that must have prevailed at the foot of Babel. English, French, German, and Italian were mixed up in jabbering confusion, but in the minds of all, I will venture to say, there was often a single thought: 'This is a great day for Wagner.' A great day, verily – so great that it is easy to imagine the master looking back incredulously upon the time when, as he somewhere says, with a self-humorous sense of degradation, he 'made pianoforte arrangements of Halévy's operas'. Let us think what we will about Wagner's theories, let us detest his music as we may, and entertain what opinions we choose as to the means he has adopted to assert both, there is no getting away from the fact that through long years of opposition or indifference – laughed at by some, treated with silent scorn by others – he has persevered, till now a great nation, headed by its emperor, sits at his feet, and the whole civilised world, moved by curiosity or admiration, gathers round. The qualities necessary for such a career are no ordinary ones, and I am very sure that the most hearty opponent of Wagner's principles was yesterday generous enough to sympathise with his amazing triumph.

But while we are gossiping thus on the terrace, the gaily-dressed crowd is moving quickly into the theatre, and the road yonder has become lined with people waiting to see the Emperor and his companions pass. Now, too, a trumpeter advances, and blows a phrase from the *Götterdämmerung* by way of signal that places should be taken. Let us obey. When at length Emperor, Princes and Mightinesses of various orders have also seated themselves, what an audience is gathered in front of that mysterious curtain! Were there at our elbow some timely informant who knows all, he might say, passing over the exalted personages with whom everybody is acquainted, 'Yonder is Liszt, as the representative of modern German music, and around him are hundreds of his fellow-countrymen, who are also his fellow-artists. It is true we do not see Heller, or Brahms, or Raff, or Volckmann, or Joachim; but German art is here in mass, if some of its heads are wanting. America has sent Laing from cultivated Boston. Yonder is Hanslick, of Vienna, most terrible of thrusters at the joints in Wagner's harness. Filippi, of Milan, is not far off; Albert Wolff, of Paris, sharpens his pencil above us; from England have come Benedict, Randegger, Davison and a score of others.' But we do not want to be told this. We are assured, without such details, that Wagner is now to be tried by a very special jury indeed – men of eminence gathered from every land, to command whose notice is in itself an honour. There is little time for personal observation. Hardly have the occupants of the Princes' Gallery taken their places before the gas is turned down, sounds are heard from the concealed orchestra, and a peremptory command for silence runs round the house.

Bennett's Letters from Bayreuth *continue with an account of the story of the* Ring, *at considerable length: like other writers on the 1876 Festival, he provides little comment on the degree of success that Wagner and his artists achieved in bringing off the epic.*

In an appendix, however, Bennett gives an account of how he came to attend 'A Supper with Wagner':

Had the Bayreuth Festival taken place in England it is tolerably certain that the official arrangements would have comprised a dinner – but as the Festival happened in Germany, the idea of a feast other than that of reason, and a flow other than that of soul, was left about for any one to pick up who chose. Naturally the proprietor of the restaurant attached to the Wagner Theatre seized upon it, with a tradesmanlike view to profit, as well as, no doubt, a commendable desire to unite the master and his disciples under pleasant circumstances. Wagner agreeing that this should be, the theatre was one day bespotted with handbills emanating from the spirited caterer, who desired all and sundry to note that for five marks of the realm the honour of a supper with the great man could be obtained. I paid five marks and enjoyed the distinction, which was certainly cheap at the price.

It was an 'off-day' of the Festival, when one might have been excused for lolling in the shade of a Biergarten, trying to clear one's throat of accumulated dust, or anticipating the delight of the happy hour when next the eye would rest upon a well-spread English dinner-table – food in Bayreuth was only to be had by skilful foraging. But one could not yield to this temptation and also sup with Wagner – so once more I dragged wearily along the blinding choking road that led to the scene of operations, passing as I did so the squirt upon wheels which the corporate intellect of Bayreuth had previously determined was a watering-cart of sufficient dimensions. A motley throng gradually whitened themselves with me along that via dolorosa – enthusiastic Yankee ladies, in a chronic state of ecstasy about 'darling Liszt' whose shadow they hoped would fall upon them by-and-by; wild-looking Germans of various types, bound by the common bond of long hair and spectacles; unbelieving Frenchmen, always keeping together, as though for mutual assistance, and always meditating epigrams of a withering character; and English pilgrims not a few, looking at one another askance. One after another, or in straggling groups, we gained the Wagnerian inclosure, pulled ourselves up the gentle ascent, and sank to rest in the open balconies of the refreshment buildings. Inside preparations were making for many guests; but the resources of the establishment were not taxed to the degree one might have expected. The sanguine eye had seen visions of the whole town-full of visitors, to say nothing of the town itself, rushing pell-mell to the supper-tables. But the reality came short of the dream, and only some four or five hundred thought the honour worth its cost. The rest were wrong.

A blazing sun, like that in the 'Ancient Mariner', drooped over the distant town as we were permitted to enter the supper room and seek our places. Let me here describe the arrangement of the tables, asking the reader to imagine the nave of a church, having at one end a transept sunk six feet or more below the level. The transept was the place of honour. There, at tables seating some dozen guests each, were placed the visitors of distinction, and indeed most of those who had come from foreign lands. On the higher floor of the nave were ranged other tables stretching along its whole length, the centre one devoted to artists and persons connected with the theatre. It followed, of course, that the guests in the nave were for the most part out of sight of those in the transept, and vice versa; but the arrangement quite harmonised with proceedings marked generally by a delightful absence of rule and order. The chief place of honour was at the table immediately facing the steps leading down from nave to transept, and round this soon gathered a group amid which the striking figure of Liszt was prominent. Madame Wagner, too, was there, and naturally the 'Master' also: but he had taken a resolution. Rejecting the distinguished place assigned to him, and preferring to be with his artists, he mounted the steps and moved to the head of the centre table in the nave, amid loud applause. The coup met with the success it deserved, and the American ladies near me had such an aggravation of ecstasy as could only be relieved by copious notes in dainty pocket-books. At length all was ready, and at the sound of a bell out filed a little army of waiters with the first of the curious courses that make up a German repast. Englishmen who are unacquainted with the fashions of their Teutonic relatives on such occasions, and who know only that among themselves the feeding process is solemn enough to go undisturbed, will scarcely be prepared for the information that at Bayreuth we took bodily and mental refreshment in alternate layers. Sandwichlike, a speech came between two dishes, and a dish between two speeches. The effect upon our supper, I am bound to add, was not happy. With such hunger as characterised life in Bayreuth only half appeased, it was provoking – I put it feelingly to the average Englishman – to see dishes cooling in the hands of waiters, who dared not serve them till some long-winded orator chose to sit down. But worse still remains to be told. As at a Quakers' meeting, those who were moved to speak spoke, when they could get the chance; and it was simply owing to the modesty or self-restraint of the guests that a score were not haranguing their neighbours at the same moment. How much of the proceedings therefore was either comical or aggravating, according as the unaccustomed spectator chose to regard it, I need not stop to tell.

Bennett describes the tributes paid to Wagner, including one likening him to his hero, Siegfried ('awakening the Brynhild of Art') and how, on being crowned with a wreath, the Master laughingly made fun of the whole incident, romping about like a boy, the absurd object on his head the while.

But the 'game', using the term without irreverence, had only just begun. The big guns were yet to come into action, only the biggest of all was the first to open fire. Wagner, posing on the top of the steps, with his body-guard around him, delivered a speech. He is no orator. His manner lacks grace, and his words do not flow freely. Yet there is something about him that would dispose one to listen, even if his claim upon attention were unknown. His words on this occasion were not offensively marked by the assumption of superiority which necessarily belongs to a man who pretends to reform where others think no reform necessary. He even condescended to explain a previous utterance, which, having been misinterpreted, had given offence. 'You now have an art,' said Wagner to the Germans in the theatre. The words naturally wrankled into wounds, and men began sorely to cry out, 'What, had we no art before the Ring?' At the supper we learned that Wagner really intended to say, 'You have now a new art,' and the explanation, coming from such a quarter, was no doubt a condescension to be prized. But Wagner, gracious beyond himself, actually spoke of the national opera of France and Italy without a sneer; not only so, he admitted that the forms of art in question were suited to the genius of their respective nations. This was not Siegfried luring the dragon from his hole but rather Siegfried in the gentle shepherd mood, making a pipe to imitate the little birds. Wagner was all that evening in the gentle shepherd mood.

The crowning incident of the whole evening was the Wagner–Liszt episode. Here let me speak in terms of studied respect. To English eyes the sight of two elderly gentlemen embracing and mingling their tears in public seems odd – however, the males of the Germanic race have no objection to kiss each other, and on German ground there was not the smallest reason why Liszt and Wagner, after sounding each other's praises with ten-trumpet power, should not fall on each other's bosom. At all events they did it, and twice. First Wagner, from the eminence of the steps, spoke to Liszt, who rose and faced the orator. Embrace No. 1 followed. Next, having given his son-in-law time to remount the steps, Liszt spoke of Wagner; after which came embrace No. 2, the lively assembly meanwhile expressing the liveliest satisfaction. Very funny to the British eye was all this, but no possessor of the optic in question had a right to utter his favourite ejaculation, 'humbug!' The distinguished actors were doubtless perfectly sincere. During long years, through evil and through good, they had remained true to a common friendship, based on mutual admiration and sympathy, and both had now reached the goal of many hopes, the end of arduous labour, the consummation of many wishes. The occasion was therefore one of extraordinary interest, and before all who cared to look on they showed how deeply it touched them. But such a high-strung condition of things could not last long, and Wagner ended it by exclaiming, 'Now let us have no more serious business!'

Here the interest of my story ends, for the reader would probably fail to appreciate the heavy forms of humour in which merry-minded Germans indulge. Enough that the festivity went on, and that the feasters – some of them – might have been seen and heard at the principal Bierhalle of the town – well, perhaps I had better not say how many hours afterwards.

The Manchester Guardian

The Manchester Guardian *was at Bayreuth in 1876; this review was not signed, but the paper's music critic from 1867–95 was George Freemantle, to whom it may perhaps be attributed.*

Bayreuth August 9 |1876|

Portraits of the composer and the singers who are to take part in the approaching festival adorn every shop. From each window frame his characteristic features stare one in the face. The cigar shops are selling but one form of pipe, meerschaum carved with the heroic features of Bayreuth's present idol; wine, cigars, hats, collars, cravats, etc., are all of the Wagner brand; and from the windows float snatches of Nibelungen music.

Wagner has laboured for very nearly thirty years upon the work he is now producing, slowly approaching his ideal; much of the music was composed more than a quarter of a century ago. For the Bayreuth festival is the legitimate out-growth of two desires on the part of its originator: viz. to found a distinctively national type of opera (i.e. dramatic music) and then to produce this opera free from the trammels which have been created and fostered during a century and a half by the nonsensical *libretti* and the 'machine music' that marks much of the work of the Italian and French schools. The German musician, as Wagner says, looking down from his own field – that of instrumental and choral (i.e. symphonic) music – saw no finished and imposing form in the operatic *genre*, for which Gluck, Mozart, Beethoven and Weber had only introduced partial reform such as cropped characteristically out of their nature and gave most satisfaction to their individual poetic sensibilities. Whilst the oratorio and symphony presented him a nobly finished form, the opera only offered a disconnected mass of undeveloped, illogical, and inartistically arbitrary rules, encumbered by con-ventionalities quite incomprehensible and most inimical to freedom of develop-ment. Further, Wagner had been deeply impressed with the fact that an ideal perfection of the opera such as so many men of genius had dreamed of could in the first instance only be attained by means of a total revolution in the character of the poet's participation in the work. Building on these ideas, he has produced his musical dramas, which bid fair to fulfil the first of his desires and certainly have accomplished the second.

A pleasant stroll brought me to the 'terraced' front of the great theatre building; a rambling, no-style building, resembling rather two buildings, large and small, joined together, stood before me and a single glance sufficed to show that all fancy form had fled in the face of stage demands. Entering one of the ample portals, we find ourselves in an exceedingly plain auditorium. The cane-seated chairs, large and comfortable, rise in 30 rows one above the other as in an ancient amphitheatre, and are 1,350 in number. The rear wall – that opposite the stage – is semicircular in form, and at each side is a granite stairway to the sole gallery the house contains, a gallery given up to those entitled to free seats, wives of artists, singers, etc. Below this gallery are the the royal boxes. . . .

Herr Brandt, the master machinist, from the Royal Theatre at Darmstadt, offered politely to explain the mysteries of the stage apparatus. The roof above my head was composed apparently of a hazy myriad of ropes, sticks, pulleys and canvases, and I could see the sides of some snow-clad hill in what seemed sad juxtaposition with the glowing interiors of princely palaces. In fact, above me were the pieces and sections of many a wonderland Herr Brandt will produce in the coming festival. There is a height of 108 ft from the stage to the flies, and the sides are occupied by five machine galleries, the first being 45 ft from the boards. The bowels of the stage have a depth of 40 ft, a descent to which discovered a most distressing labyrinth of ropes and traps and awkward elbowed joists that resembled a section of some universal motor. There were, in addition, two immense long wooden drums for working the machinery by means of steam, a steam pump, and other requisites for the production of vapour, which in some portions of the Nibelungen drama covers the scene from sight, so that while the fleecy clouds are radiant with reflected coloured lights the transformation necessary to the story will take place. The nymphs who swim from rock to rock in the Rhine do so with the most perfect of motions apparently without support from above or below. In fact the Lehmann sisters and Fräulein Lammert, who personate the Rhine-daughters, refused at first to submit themselves to the clasp of the dreadful device; but Wagner was imperative, and now they are said to like the motion. Their movements are guided by an accomplished musician in time to the music's rhythm. The dwarf Prince Alberich who climbs with positively frightening rapidity from ledge to ledge, on a base of machinery, in and out, here and there, like a flash, is in pursuit of the evading Rhine-daughters.

The first grand dress rehearsal took place on Sunday night. Joining the band of profound-looking music lovers, I groped my way to my seat in the gallery. The anxieties of a nervous spectacled gentleman, who was afraid that sufficient support had not been placed beneath the gallery, were hushed at the appearance of Herr Wagner. A curt bow, a few immaterial words in a low monotone, hardly audible from where I sat, a pause, then a rap, and the wonderful waves of un-dulating music which introduce the prologue to the trilogy, *Das Rheingold*, came floating up from the mysterious depths beneath the stage, without in the least diminishing the volume or dulling the tone. It seemed to flow and follow, growing fuller and grander, like the current of some mighty stream, until the curtain parted and the realistic effect of the scenery was added to the impressive power of the music, and one thought he saw the lonely depth of the Rhine, each crested wave lit with a golden light. Of course there were inevitable hitches and pauses consequent on any rehearsal, yet they were few and far between and everything went most smoothly.

Wagner, as stage director, sat normally in a chair at the side of the stage. He was dressed in light clothes and wore his velvet cap. Suddenly he would shuffle across the stage with his hands beneath his coat tails, gesticulate violently to put more force into the orchestra, or rush up to a singer in the midst of his or her part and say, in a light sharp voice, 'No, no, no; not so; sing it so,' and, suiting the action to the direction, would sing the part as it should be, or throw the necessary dramatic fire into the action. All of his directions were given with the aim of pro-ducing the greatest naturalness and through this, the most perfect power.

The delighted audience sat in silence, and as they streamed out of the theatre on to the terrace and into the beer-room in their festal dress, the only word to be heard was 'Herrlich'.

J. W. Davison

James William Davison (1813–1885), music critic and musicologist, was attached to The Times *from 1846 to 1876 and went to the first Bayreuth Festival to report the event for the readers of that newspaper. His account, although of less value today than some of his fellow critics', does, nevertheless, contain valuable points of interest. The story of the* Ring *is given at inordinate length and in great detail (but not repeated here), and goes to show that some of these critics, even if not sympathetic to Wagner, were at least prepared to study his work.*

THE WAGNER FESTIVAL AT BAYREUTH

The rehearsals for this long-talked-of and un-exampled celebration are over; and, we have reason to believe, the result is eminently satisfactory to Richard Wagner himself. What has hitherto been disclosed it is the privilege of very few to take note of inasmuch as with the exception of the singers, players, decorators, machinists and, etc., engaged in the performances, only some of the most intimate friends of the poet-musician were admitted. Among these must have been a privileged contributor to a local journal, who, under the signature of Heinrich Porges, has contributed glowing accounts of the rehearsals one after another as they occurred, and when descriptions of his have been perused they have enlightened not only the inhabitants of Bayreuth in particular and Bavaria in general, but have penetrated through various channels to other and more remote corners of the earth. Herr Porges, comparing his demi-god to Aeschylus and Shakespeare, with Beethoven thrown in, leads us to expect much, and if but a fourth part of what he affirms be accepted as gospel, an exhibition without precedent is really in store for us.

Heinrich Porges, a young musician who had been associated with Wagner for a number of years, was acting as musical assistant, and he was also charged with writing down all the many stage directions given by Wagner. These he published, in three volumes, some years later. In Cosima's hands, when she produced the Ring *in 1896, they became responsible for many authoritative directions that 'that was the way the Master did it' and led, ultimately, to the ossification of style that discredited the Festival around the turn of the century.*

Having advanced half-way, we are in possession of tolerably fair grounds for estimating the results, more or less probable, of Richard Wagner's colossal undertaking – we mean with regard to its general influence upon the 'art-work of the future'. Our own impression after hearing *Rheingold* and the *Walküre*, is that the art of music, not in its trivial manifestations, which are of small consequence, but as it is understood and practised by the 'great masters', stands in no danger from the gods and giants, dwarfs and heaven-descended heroes, that people the scenarium of the Nibelungen Ring. Opera, in the legitimate acceptance of the term, will rest precisely where it was; and operatic composers worthy of the name, to say nothing of the 'piping operatic singing birds' who give noise to their melody, can rest in quietude with arms enfolded. In strict truth the Tetralogy (or Trilogy with *Vorspiel*), is no opera at all. It is a play, the speeches in which are declaimed, rather than sung, to orchestral accompaniment; if that may be called accompaniment which has nearly all the business to itself, and to which the development of the melodies, such as they are, is chiefly assigned; if that may be called accompaniment which, caring nothing for the physical stamina of the stage declaimer, pursues its independent course, in all measures and modifications of measures, the totality ever shifting from key to key, careless of the hitherto recognised laws of modulation, from the pulling aside of the curtains even to the pulling to thereof, and after. The fact that the Tetralogy is not opera may bring consolation to those who persist in liking what Herr Wagner styles 'that doubtful kind of entertainment'. Opera being safe, it is no less pleasant to be informed by Mr Dannreuther, one of the master's zealous apostles, that while drama (Wagnerian drama) must in future be 'the height of man's musical ambition', the 'various beautiful forms of instrumental music now current' will not 'cease to be cultivated'; so that the further hearing of symphonies, quartets, sonatas and trios still lies within the pale of orthodoxy. Fortified by such assurances, a brief survey of what has already been witnessed of this memorable week's proceedings may be entered upon with more equanimity than might have otherwise been the case.

The 'brief survey' runs to quite a few thousand words and relates the story fully, adding a number of comments on the success, or lack of it, in the stage realisation. There are observations on the audience and celebrities that are familiar from other sources. Several days later Davison wrote the first of a series of 'summings-up' of the cycle:

In musical, not less than dramatic merit, *Die Walküre* and *Siegfried* are very nearly equal, the first act of the former and the second act of the latter standing out with conspicuous prominence among the finest parts of the *Ring des Nibelungen*. As a whole, perhaps, *Siegfried* makes the quickest appeal to the understanding. But these considerations for a general survey must take into account *Götterdämmerung*, the longest drama of the trilogy, and, despite many fine passages – among others the superb slow march which accompanies the body of the murdered Siegfried to the hall of the Gibichungs – perhaps the least well-balanced of the three. The execution last night of this concluding section of the *Ring* was remarkable not only for the fine acting and singing of Amalie Materna, but for the magnificent performance of the orchestra, conducted by Hans Richter and led by the eminent violinist Auguste Wilhelmj. To these 120 musicians, who labour as diligently as though they were above instead of below ground – 'gods' rather than 'niblungs' – no small share of the success of the Bayreuth stage-play is due.

After attending the complete second cycle Davison wrote another 'summing-up' of the Ring:

The performances of the second series are a great improvement on the first. The orchestra, playing louder, is more effective; and the scenic transformations now work properly. The volume of steam is diminished; the illusion is not weakened, and the nuisance is abated. *Siegfried* has been heard with increasing satisfaction. It is generally thought the best of the four dramas. . . . The scene with the birds in the forest when Siegfried kills the dragon causes as great a sensation as before. Wilhelmj's violin solos are admirable. . . . Large sale of tickets for the third series of performances.

That a dramatic poem like the *Ring des Nibelungen* could not possibly be set to music in the received operatic fashion will be apparent to any one who has attentively perused the three dramas with their prologue. Every word placed in the mouth of every character must be distinctly conveyed, while the dramatic action is carried on from end to end without interruption. Thus, it may be argued, the thing itself is complete without the music; and the argument would hold good for ordinary intelligences. Wagner's, however, is not an ordinary intelligence; and his scheme for making the drama a combination of the arts includes music as a very essential element. True, it is the poet who rules – and from what the poet thinks and speaks the musician must obediently take his cue. Happily, Wagner, in his dramas, plays the part both of poet and musician; while composing his music he is in much the same position as an accompanist following a singer whom he cannot naturally control. We consider it barely practicable for any musician except Wagner himself to furnish music for one of Wagner's dramas – that is, of course, in the perfected shape revealed, as he insists, in *Tristan* or the *Ring*. He might, doubtless, set the whole to recitative – either *parlante*, or with accompaniment; but, forbidden all the hitherto accepted varieties of musical form in the way of airs, duets, trios and, etc. – even choruses and concerted finales, as they are generally understood, being outside Wagner – he would find himself at a loss to make the characters declaim or the orchestra play in exact accordance with the poet's innermost promptings. How could he indeed? The orchestra must be forever doing something – like a wind that is always blowing, or a stream that is always flowing, or trees that are always bending in obedience to the swayings of the breeze; but what that something shall be the poet alone can decide. Thus, in concocting the drama of the future, that poet and musician must be one and inseparable would seem to follow as a Wagnerian deduction. It is hardly too much to say that apart from the drama to which it is allied, the orchestral music of the *Ring* would signify slightly more at the best than a succession of chords, scales (frequently chromatic), figures and snatches of tunes, distributed capriciously among the instruments, *tremulandos* (*ad infinitum*), strange unheard-of combinations, perpetual changes of key and, etc. – a chaos of sounds in short, now more or less agreeable, now more or less the opposite, and – deprived of the weird and singular fascination that attends it when obviously explained by what is being said and done upon the stage – almost unmeaning. Wagner's symphony may be likened to an omni-coloured kaleidoscope, where the same bits of painted glass incessantly appear and disappear, yielding prominence to others that have been seen before, and puzzling the eye of the examiner, as the Wagner orchestra puzzles, while it frequently enchants, the ear. Without being distinguished by anything affording evidence of uncommon contrapuntal skill, it is crowded with details, many of which, till after repeated hearings, would elude detection, however closely scrutinised. These may possibly be typified by the 'multitudinous forest voices' and 'countless hosts of stars' referred to in Wagner's famous comparison of his own symphonic music with the effect produced upon a solitary visitor by 'a fine forest on a summer evening' and the 'ever-growing eloquence of the forest melody', the many melodies in one, that, while never ceasing to haunt the memory, cannot be repeated or hummed, and to hear which again a return to the woods, on a summer night, is indispensable (a tolerably plain hint that the Wagnerian music cannot be heard too often). We have no pretension to decide but simply feel that in a majority of instances it is perplexing. Wagner cannot be likened to the wild minstrel who sweeps or twangs the strings of his lyre, while giving voice to a lay of war or love; but his music – we mean the orchestral part of it – not infrequently suggests the idea of an Aeolian harp, under the influence of shifting currents, now generating one, now another wayward melody, as the case may be.

But to leave speculation – Wagner's general way of procedure, in adding the music to his art-drama, may be analysed without many words. It differs widely, as may be guessed, from the ways of Mozart, Beethoven *et hoc genus omne*; nor does it at all resemble that of Gluck, to which it has frequently been likened. The way being one of Wagner's own invention, quite original, owing nothing whatever to foregoing models, he has a perfect right to it provided that he allows others, not of his own opinion, to possess a right to theirs. (It may be added here, parenthetically, that the comparison insisted upon by sundry of his disciples, between Wagner's treatment of the orchestra with that of Beethoven in the Ninth Symphony, does not by any means hold.) Taking his system for what it is intended, nothing can be more logical, nothing more consistently exemplified.

There follows a dissertation on the use of the leitmotive: not as novel a feature as Davison makes out when he describes it as solely Wagner's method of composition. He ends with the comment that 'Wagner recalls all these motives in Götterdämmerung; *themes, characteristic orchestral figures, even chords and special combinations being summoned back by the composer, one after another or one with another to suit his plan; the treatment, though long-drawn-out, being imposingly fine.'*

The second series of representations, if we may judge from the three that have already been given, seems likely to form a fairer opportunity of estimating what

Wagner has accomplished in the *Ring* than the first. It also serves to confirm a general impression that the work can never again be seen and heard under similarly favourable conditions. The bringing together of an orchestra of 130 in number, composed of the eminent performers from all parts of Germany, who, without remuneration, and for simple love of the task, all cheerfully undertook the indispensable toil and trouble attendant on endless rehearsals, to be followed up by twelve grand performances, the latter extending over three weeks, was alone a feat to be achieved by no other man than Wagner, and by the aid of no other means than those he found expedient to adopt. Still more surprising is the magnetic influence he must have exercised over the highly-paid singers whom he compelled to serve his purpose, and with whose proverbial jealousies and consequent squabbles he had to deal, and dealt successfully, in the matter of distribution of parts. Every tenor was a Siegfried or Siegmund, every soprano a Brünnhilde or Sieglinde, every bass a Wotan or Hagen, every character singer an Alberich or Loge, every comic a Mime, and so on. The remaining characters . . . Wagner must have occasionally been at no small pains to fill up as he desired. Nevertheless, he overcame all obstacles, and gathered around him artists of recognised standing from the most reputed German Opera Houses, ready to make a similar abnegation of their claims and assist gratuitously in the furtherance of his great life-object. The magic watchword that enabled him to effect all this, and more besides that need not be specified, was simply 'A National Art for Germany'. The precise significance attached to his idea to which now – armed and, as he judged, invulnerable at all points – he was about to show.

The experience derived from the more familiar acquaintance with the great stage-play as represented in the Wagner Theatre, leaves rather the impression of a nearly perfect *ensemble* than of distinguishing excellence in particulars. About one feature only is opinion quite unanimous. That feature is the orchestra. A company of executive musicians . . . more admirably balanced, or in every respect more competent, in all probability never before assembled together. Their playing from first to last has been little short of marvellous – as marvellous, indeed, as the task set before them by the uncompromising master who allows but few intervals for rest, and these intervals as brief as they are rare. Their consignment to a sort of abyss, out of sight from the audience, even were the theatre lighted in the ordinary manner, instead of being thrown into semi-obscurity by the lowering of the lamps, would allow them no means of observing how heartily their efforts are appreciated.

During the first series of performances, remembering their numerical strength, the members, by common consent, played in a more subdued tone than under more conventional circumstances they would have done; and, though their execution was faultless, it was not infrequently accompanied by a *quasi* sense of dullness, which their subsequent assumption of a bolder, general tone – their ordinary tone, in fact – during the second series successfully dissipated. The sufferings undergone by these estimable professors through daily confinement for long hours in a steam-invaded pit, a glance at which brought with it the uncomfortable suspicion that there was scarcely room for them to breathe freely, must, in such terribly hot weather, have been intense; and no wonder that, almost to a man, they played in their shirt-sleeves. No considerations whatever, it is stated, will induce them again to submit to similar torture; so that it looks as though the orchestra in a pit is now destined, after all, not to be the orchestra of the future.

Davison continues with his estimation of the singers. He also apologises to the readers of The Times *for the way in which his reports are, of necessity, broken up into fragments. Like Shaw at a later date, he blames the hours when the Bayreuth mail is collected, and his having to terminate his reviews in mid-performance to catch it. This report ends:*

Today has been, for a wonder, wet; and a passing thunderstorm gives pleasant warning of an approaching change in the weather which, up to now has, under the exceptional circumstances been, for the most part, scarcely tolerable.

The final review, written after this critic had been to all three cycles of the Ring, *yet again takes the form of a general summing-up of the work and the stage representation in particular:*

As part and parcel of the combination of the Arts in his 'drama of the future', Wagner includes all that relates to scenic appliance. In consideration of the general result we have, therefore, to take this into account. Curiosity had been raised to an extravagantly high pitch; and even those whom long habit has spoilt for such things looked forward to a spectacular display, equal, if not superior, to all they had previously experienced – a display, in short, which, in startling novelty and characteristic splendour should truly justify whatever had been said and written about it in advance. Those who looked forward so much – travellers from Vienna, Paris and London in particular – were in a great measure doomed to disappointment, their anticipations not being half realised. Had less been predicted, less might have given satisfaction, with criticism less suspiciously on the alert. A great deal of the scenery is, doubtless, beautiful and the picturesque element has been happily resorted to where rocks, huge crevices, overhanging trees, winding pathways and subterranean caverns are in request, which is oftener the case than otherwise. But the water is a comparative failure, whether seen as in the *Rheingold*, with the Naiads sporting in the depths of the river, or as in *Götterdämmerung* when Siegfried lands from his boat at the hall of the Gibichungs. Under the new conditions of darkening the auditorium every object on the stage comes out so sharply that the lines of division are plainly detected, and the illusion thus to a great extent imperilled. The fire that encircles Brünnhilde's home upon the Valkyrie rock, exhibited successively in the *Walküre, Siegfried* and *Götterdämmerung*, is dexterously managed, and the effect imposing in proportion; but the employment of the new steam apparatus in the transformation scenes was at the outset found excessive – somewhat of a nuisance, moreover, to the audience, not to speak of those unhappy dwellers in the orchestra who had to play like demons in a cavern choked with vaporous exhalations. This has happily been subdued; and the descent of Wotan to the deep recesses of Nibelheim has lost nothing of its cloud-wrapped mystery. The rainbow bridge, moreover, by which the gods walk leisurely to Valhalla . . . is poor and clumsy. It would excite the derision of the audiences at transpontine London theatres. . . . As for the long-bodied snake into which Alberich transforms himself . . . the bear with which Siegfried terrifies Mime and the dragon which he kills, if it be true that they came from London, they can only have been selected from among the useless lumber of some forgotten Christmas pantomime.

But, nevertheless, with some other incongruities allowed for, there is enough originality of conception and arrangement, to say nothing of the several manifestations of pictorial beauty and suggestiveness distinguishing the *mise en scène* of the great Tetralogy to show that, with the unlimited stage appliances of Wagner's theatre, still more can be done, and will be done when, next year, the projected representations of the first and second parts of Goethe's *Faust*, with music by Wagner himself, are given.

This surprising intelligence is unique. No mention of such a project occurs elsewhere, and it was clearly no more than a Bayreuth rumour.

Greater things by way of decoration might have been accomplished for the *Ring*, and greater things were expected; but Rome was not built in a day and such performances as those at Bayreuth are unlikely to be of regular periodical occurrence. And now that the *Ring* is an accomplished fact, that before the third series is over it will have been heard by thousands of more or less intelligent people . . . the question arises what may be the future result of such an unprecedented expenditure of preparation, such an extraordinary combination of intelligence with hard labour.

Those who were absent from the performances have missed an opportunity which may never again present itself under similar circumstances for neither the earnest discourses of Wagner's disciples, nor the personal authority which the chief has learnt by incessant practice to assume, as, in a certain way, the leading energetic spirit of his period, can, except in the opinion of blind enthusiasts, help much towards again bringing together such a company of able and devoted artists, or such a host of visitors, in the majority of instances of more or less distinction, from all parts of Europe and America, curious to witness the result of an undertaking which has been incessantly talked about for upwards of quarter of a century.

Sir Charles Villiers Stanford

Sir Charles Villiers Stanford (1852–1924), Irish composer, who became Professor of Composition at the Royal College of Music. He was at the first Bayreuth Festival, and returned there in 1883. He wrote his impressions of these visits in Pages from an Unwritten Diary *(1914) and* Records and Reflections *(1922). The following passages are drawn from both these sets of recollections.*

In the same summer (1876) I went to the long-expected performance of the *Nibelungen-Ring* at Baireuth [*sic*]. I had secured places for the second cycle, which was a fortunate choice as it was, by all accounts, superior in every way to the first. To visit the head-centre of modernity was in those days a perilous business. Partisanship ran to such fever-heat that even friendships were broken, and the friction was almost intolerable. Macfarren, the successor to Sterndale Bennett in the Cambridge Professorship, roundly and loudly rated me in a music-shop in Bond Street, when I informed him of my approaching journey – ending with an expression of contemptuous pity for my having to sit through an opera consisting wholly of the chord of E flat on a pedal; a criticism which suggested that he did not know much of it beyond the opening pages of the *Rheingold*. He and many others of his kidney looked upon a pilgrim to the Wagnerian shrine as a brazen-faced traitor to musical art. If feeling was so strained in this country, it was a thousand times more so in Germany itself. France, still rankling under the insult of the Aristophanic farce, *Die Kapitulation*, which Wagner had published at the moment of her greatest troubles, kept sternly aloof. There was but a sprinkling of English and Americans. The mass of the public consisted of the theatrical world, and of such professional musicians as were identified with Wagnerismus to the exclusion of every other contemporary writer.

The atmosphere was not sympathetic, and gave a feeling of polemic prejudice which militated against whole-hearted appreciation or valuable discrimination. 'He that is not with me is against me' was the motto of the whole Festival. (*1914*)

A pilgrimage to Baireuth in 1876 was no easy matter. Of railway facilities there were, practically, none: of local assistance there was but little. The theatre still had its name to make, and the presence of its creator only succeeded in attracting . . . the 'faithful' of the Wagner cult. His own polemic pen was his worst enemy. He did not appeal to music generally, but to that part of it which was in un-doubted sympathy with himself. That the Festival and its theatre survived its first experience was due, not to the personal attractions of the Master, but rather to his disappearance from the field. It was only after his lamented death in Venice . . . that the greater world began to journey to this remote Bavarian town, and to reckon its performances as an experience not to be missed, or to be neglected. . . .

The Wagner Theatre was perched upon a hill which in 1876 was only attainable by trudging up a very hot, or very muddy road, according as the weather pleased. The Theatre had at this time no front entrance or even cover for the traveller, save the Theatre itself. Shanties on each side were supposed to fill the functions of a beer-establishment and a restaurant, the latter of which was more remarkable for its unsightliness of exterior than for the sufficiency of its contents. . . . Beer, it is true, was in sufficient quantities, but the human being cannot exist upon it, and the complaints of the crowds at the restaurants in the town were pitiable to hear, and easy to substantiate. (*1922*)

Stanford describes the interior of the Theatre and approves of the sunken orchestra pit – but for Wagner's music only – especially because 'a gesticulating conductor had no chance of calling attention to himself'.

The orchestra, of which the backbone came from Meiningen, was admirable. Richter, then a young fair-haired Viking, was in command. The stage effects were, with a few exceptions, in advance of most theatres. Steam was used, I believe for the first time, for stage purposes; but the noise of its escape was so great that it often nearly drowned the music. The close of the *Rheingold* and the *Walkürenritt* were, scenically speaking, failures, as was the end of the *Götterdämmerung*. The dragon, which was made by 'Dykwynkyn', the property man of Drury Lane, was a gruesome beast, redolent of the English pantomime. The best sets were the depths of the Rhine, the first two acts of the *Walküre*, the second act of *Siegfried*, and the third act of *Götterdämmerung*. It seemed to me then, as it does still, far too long for the enjoyment of average human nature. The theatre seats have not yet been devised which will insure the hearer against overmastering bodily fatigue, and certainly the cane-bottomed stalls of Baireuth did not mitigate suffering. (*1914*)

Hercules Macdonnell of Dublin, the friend of Costa and of all the great singers of bygone days . . . expressed to me one view which the lapse of years has only strengthened: that it is a pity that Wagner was his own librettist – for there was no librettist to check the length of the composer, and no composer to curtail the librettist. This is truer than the fabled story of Rossini, who is supposed to have said that Wagner had beautiful moments, and bad quarters of an hour. (That Rossini angrily denied this, Richter told me himself, from his own experience.) (*1922*)

Concerning all the failings, I preserved a stony silence and felt even inclined to champion them when I heard the fulminations of Davison, Joseph Bennett and others of the ultra-Tory battalions, on a terrace outside between the acts. It was as good as a play to see this little band of malcontents, defending themselves as best they could against the onslaughts of broad-minded George Osborne, as he brought his best Limerick brogue to bear on them. (*1914*)

A German conductor of eminence afterwards said to me that he was sure that the world would live to see the *Nibelungen* compressed from four into two operas, of decent length. The Grand Opera of Paris has already moved in this direction, by giving the *Walküre* with all the long and dull portions omitted. A relief to hear, but *anathema* to the true Wagnerite. (*1922*)

I sat in the theatre behind Liszt and noted with some amusement the contrariness which showed itself in his obvious admiration (real or feigned, who shall say?) of the duller and uglier passages. I could not but smile at the amount of time which he spent at these moments in the arms of Morpheus. He walked up and down afterwards under my window, speaking with enthusiasm of these very moments which I knew he had not heard, or which came to him from reading the score, or from – dreams, nightmares perhaps. (*1914, 1922*)

The performances in 1876 were on the whole excellent. The best available singers had come forward to help. Materna, Lilli Lehmann, Brandt were chief among the women; the first masterly, the second winning, the third a genius of the first order.... The most amazing feat at the performance was due to her. The singer of the solitary Valkyrie at the close of the first act of the *Götterdämmerung*, a long and exacting scene, fell ill. Brandt, at a moment's notice, sang the complicated part, and so well that not a trace of unfamiliarity or insufficient rehearsal was discernible. The average ability of the women singers was good throughout.

The same cannot be said of the men. Their ranks contained some great, some passable, and some inferior specimens. Amongst the tenors Vogl was easily pre-eminent, but he was unfortunately heard too seldom. Niemann was a great actor, but his voice was nearly gone; he was but a shadow of his former great self. Unger, the Siegfried, who was popularly supposed to be Wagner's especial choice, was unequal to the part, and did not show the ability, either vocal or histrionic, necessary for it. Of the character parts, Mime and Alberich were supremely well filled. Amongst basses, Betz was admirable; so was Gura, in a provokingly small part. But many others were rough, though large of voice. The older singers were well trained; the younger not.

As a principle Wagner seemed to me to differ from his predecessors by portraying ugly characters by ugly music ... looking back at the work over forty-five years has not changed my opinion. The criminal colouring which Beethoven gave to Pizarro without a note of ugliness, was not there. The Rhine-daughters were beautiful, but Alberich was ugly. It may be a matter of temperament, but I dislike it, as I should the inferior painting of a hateful subject. Verdi has proved, in his characterisation of Iago, that it is possible to combine villainy with beautiful music. I did not note this, however, in the *Nibelungen*. The theory of leitmotives was, to my mind, carried too far, even to annoyance. The motives were so interwoven that they were often of no avail. Less of them would have effected more, and would have heightened their value. As it is, the plethora of over-done phrases of similitude, so valuable in themselves when used with economy, is threatening to destroy what is inherent in opera and which, properly used, is essential to characterisation and to situation. Piled as they are in the

Nibelungen they may give satisfaction to curious porers over the score, but they fail to grip the listener, and often to attract his attention, or to give characterisation when it is most needed. In lesser quantities, as Wagner used them in the *Dutchman* and even in the *Meistersinger* they carry a fuller conviction to the hearer. (*1922*)

Wagner appeared on the stage at the close of the cycle, but happily did not make one of his unfortunate speeches. I regretted seeing him in the flesh. The music was the music of Jekyll, but the face was the face of Hyde. Whatever magnetism there was in the man, his physiognomy did its best to counteract. The brow and head was most impressive, the mouth and chin equally repulsive. Together they made a most curious combination of genius and meanness which exactly correspond to the Wagner of the Liszt letters, and the autobiography. In one respect opera at Baireuth in the lifetime of the composer had a virtue which has gradually tended to disappear since his death. The composer did not permit his conductor to exaggerate slowness of pace. This was especially noticeable, when Levi directed *Parsifal* in 1883 – Dannreuther, who stayed at Wahnfried for the rehearsals in 1882, told me that Wagner frequently called out from the stalls, 'Schneller! Schneller! Die Leute werden sich langweilen' (Quicker, quicker, the people will be bored). With the advent of Mottl, every movement became slower and slower. His playing of the prelude was, by my watch, five minutes slower than Levi's. The *Ring* suffered in the same way, unless Richter was at the helm. The disease of exaggerated Adagios spread to an alarming extent, and Mottl's fad became a cult. (*1914*)

Oscar Browning

After the famous and celebrated visitors' complaints of the hardships they suffered in 1876, this letter from an ordinary music lover makes a nice contrast. It was written by Mr Oscar Browning and appeared in The Times *on 22 August 1876:*

While every nation in Europe has sent its contingent to this place, England has been chiefly represented by musical critics and professional musicians, and the crowd of music lovers who swell the triumphs of a Joachim or Rubinstein at St James's Hall have been conspicuous by their absence. I hope, therefore, that I am doing a service to those who would be sorry to have missed this unrivalled performance in advising them to lose no time in obtaining tickets for the third representation of the *Ring des Nibelungen*, many of which remain unsold. The third series of representations begins on Sunday, the 27th of this month and continues during the three following days. Tickets may be obtained from Herr Feustel, banker, Bayreuth. The price (£15 for the four performances) is large, but not excessive when everything is taken into account. Bayreuth is easily accessible from every part of the Continent, and comfortable rooms may be secured by application to Herr Feustel for four, five, or six shillings a day. Carriages, the want of which was at first much felt, have now been supplied. The theatre restaurant offers an excellent *table d'hôte* for 5s a head and breakfast and supper can be secured easily and cheaply at the different hotels in the town. Nothing can exceed the courtesy and kindness of the inhabitants of Bayreuth to their guests. . . .

I hope this letter may induce some English lovers of music not to neglect an opportunity of hearing the perfect execution of a work of art such as will not occur again in the present generation.

PART III

The Festival of 1882
and *Parsifal*

The Re-opening of the Festival

At the close of the Festival of 1876 Wagner had gathered his artists about him and addressed them with the following words:

The Festival is now at an end, and I do not know whether it will take place again! I have called this work with its years of preparation a Festival Music Drama – with what right I cannot say as the annals do not record a feast-day at this time of the year. It was designed with confidence in the German spirit, and completed to the glory of its exalted patron, His Majesty the King of Bavaria, who has been not only its patron and promoter, but also a co-creator of the work.

Wagner had hoped to repeat the Ring *performances in 1877 and to continue the Festival in succeeding years – and to correct all the things that had gone wrong the first time. The colossal financial losses sustained in 1876 put an end to this, and the Festspielhaus was to stand silent for the next six years. While at Bayreuth in 1876, Angelo Neumann, as has been already noted,* had approached Wagner with a view to staging the* Ring *in Leipzig. Although unenthusiastic at first, Wagner later agreed and Neumann took the* Ring *not only to Leipzig but on an extensive tour as well. It was given in Berlin in May 1881 before Kaiser Wilhelm I and Bismarck, and the Wagner family travelled there for the event (Wagner even sanctioned an interval in* Das Rheingold!*). In May 1882 it was performed for the first time in London, at Her Majesty's Theatre, where Neumann found he had to provide the carpets and furnishings for the auditorium and foyers. The Prince of Wales was persuaded to attend, and was so enthusiastic that he went to eleven of the performances. Much taken with the Rhine-maidens, the Prince went backstage to see them at close quarters. He was very disappointed to find that, in place of the pretty young girl he had seen singing on the stage, there was a male stage-hand strapped in the harness for demonstration. It was during these London performances that Emil Scaria, who was singing the part of Wotan, first showed signs of the madness which later took him over completely. In the third act of* Die Walküre *he crept on to the stage, and transposed all his notes – yet remembered nothing of his lapse afterwards.*

    Neumann's touring company took the Bayreuth Ring *to Italy, France and all over Germany, and ended in St Petersburg in 1889. The tour not only enhanced Wagner's reputation throughout Europe but brought in much-needed money in royalties. These sums were all given by Wagner and his heirs to pay off the Bayreuth Festival deficit; they took nothing for themselves. While on tour the* Ring *was staged in the Court Theatres found in major cities – theatres built in*

* See page 71 above.

the old Italian style. Many cycles have been given since, in such theatres, which suggests that the Ring *and the Bayreuth Festspielhaus are by no means inseparable. The comments of Richard Strauss on this subject are noteworthy.**

Wagner's relationship with Neumann had always been a happy one; 'if anything on this earth could astonish me, it would be you!' he once wrote, concerning the impresario's efforts on his behalf. During the 1882 Festival, Wagner rashly promised Neumann the right to take Parsifal *on tour, but when the contract was presented for his signature the composer begged to withdraw; Neumann magnanimously agreed to this, counting Wagner's gratitude a greater reward than money.*

Throughout the years when Bayreuth was closed, Wagner was actively working on Parsifal *and giving concerts to augment the royalties from the* Ring *tour. He realised that if he was to open his Festival again he would need a new work to attract the public, and the idea for a drama on the* Parsifal *subject had been in his mind for a long time – since 1857, he recorded in* Mein Leben. *In June 1881 Wagner wrote from Naples to Friedrich Feustel:*

I can see no other possibility of meeting your wishes than by – as you think – endeavouring to give a fresh impulse to the interest we failed to arouse with the Festival of 1876, by presenting *Parsifal* at the earliest possible moment.

This plan seems feasible for the year 1882, provided I can remain perfectly quiet until that time; but this only, as far as the material possibilities are concerned, in the event that I can lay claim to the assistance of the King of Bavaria.

Under such assured conditions I intend to present, in addition to *Parsifal,* one of my older works each year at Bayreuth, in turn, to make these model performances my artistic testament to my friends. As I am now in my sixty-eighth year, I can count upon a ripe and vigorous old age for the realisation of this plan, and I think I shall then have done enough to be released from the performance of *Zauberflöte, Freischütz* and *Fidelio,* etc.

If with each performance of my works I do not leave behind me my 'school' then I have nothing whatsoever to do with such a 'school'. . . .

Another letter to Feustel, from Venice in July 1881, touches on the subject of the Parsifal *copyright; this controversy was to rage for thirty years:*

Parsifal I retain solely and exclusively for Bayreuth – at least I think so – even the King renounces it for Munich, but will send me every year his chorus and orchestra.

Yearly performances open to everyone – admission price *high!*

The last remark stands in contrast to the idealism of 1876 – Wagner had learned a financial lesson during the past five years.

* See page 163 below.

Engelbert Humperdinck

Wagner spent most of 1880 in Italy, for his health's sake. For part of the time he established himself at the Villa Angri, a superb house on the hillside overlooking the Bay of Naples. He paid out a colossal rent for the privilege. Here Engelbert Humperdinck (1854–1921), who later wrote the children's opera Hänsel und Gretel *in the 'Wagnerian' style, made the acquaintance of Wagner and became involved in the preparations for the first performance of* Parsifal. *Humperdinck described his years with Wagner in these personal recollections, which appeared many years later:*

'The Master is receiving nobody – '
I doffed my cap, handed over to the servant, who had received me with this less than endearing greeting, my card, on which I had added to my name the re-sounding title, 'Member of the Order of the Grail'. I then strolled down through the gardens of the Villa Angri to the crowded via Posilipo, feeling as if I had just escaped some great danger. It was unprecedented audacity which had led me, on chance and unbidden, to approach the ornate villa on the Posilipo hill in which, as I knew, Richard Wagner had been living for some weeks in quiet seclusion with his family, putting the finishing touches to *Parsifal*.
As a hopeful music undergraduate with a primer on composition in my pocket, I had set out in the winter of 1879–80 from Munich for Italy 'in order to further my musical studies', as my Mendelssohn travelling scholarship had it. And also (with open eyes – unlike Tannhäuser) to get to know the Italian country. In Rome I had joined a small group of fellow artists and archaeologists who were making a New Year trip to Naples and Sicily.
At that time I had not quite come out of a period of infatuation with the work of the Bayreuth master. Developed in a western German Conservatory, where to mention the very name of Wagner was still a hazardous undertaking, I had had little opportunity to get to know his work. Also, my period at the Munich High School for Music, where a similar spirit prevailed, would have done little to alter this state of affairs, had I not joined a group of young people there who, sworn to the cause of Richard Wagner, had banded together to form the 'Knights of the Order of the Grail', to further the understanding and promote the reforms and artistic endeavours of Bayreuth. I was thus indebted to this young society (which in the course of time produced many famous artists and writers) for my deep familiarity with the Bayreuth concept. So, prepared in this way, I believed I could without too much apprehension set about seeking out in person the Master I had venerated from afar.
'Nun, Alberich, das schlug fehl' I said to myself with a sigh of relief as I arrived

below, letting my yearning gaze wander once more over the blue splendour of the Bay of Naples. As I set about opening the iron gate of the villa I perceived hasty footsteps and gentle breathing behind me, 'If you please, the Master has sent for you – ' In half a minute I was back up again and another half a minute later I was standing in a spacious, semi-dark apartment and from the twilight glow two large serious eyes were gazing at me. I bowed in the formal fashion of the Munich High School for Music and the severity of the Master's features gave way to a good-natured laugh.

'What are you doing here in Naples, Knight of the Grail? Why have you come so far, to Italy?'

I explained briefly the object and purpose of my being in Italy and the arrangements of the travelling scholarship, which he wanted to hear in detail.

'How remarkable!' he exclaimed, 'What is there nowadays for a musician to profit his art in Italy? *Tempi passati*! – there is quite enough for us to study and learn at home. How very much we need some sort of Foundation to permit this – the Festival perhaps ought to do that, or make it possible.' (This idea, as is well known, became the foundation of the Richard-Wagner-Stiftung). The Master was deep in silence. Then he asked me of my other plans. I told him I was on the point of going to Sicily.

'That will be good for you – see everything worth seeing and do not forget Palermo, there you shall be in good hands. I may go there myself. When you return, come here again and see me – perhaps you may learn something new up here.'

The conversation was interrupted by the entrance of the Master's wife who, with her eldest daughters, was home from a visit to the Museum. I was introduced and then, in a friendly way, dismissed with 'Goodbye, until May!'

May came. Back from Trinacria's shores I found waiting for me an invitation to the Villa Angri. I received a welcome like an old acquaintance. There I got to know the Master's family; the blossoming daughters – Lulu, Boni, Eva and Loldi – and jolly little Fidi, as well as two of Wagner's associates, the painter Paul Joukowsky (who did the décor for *Parsifal*) and Josef Rubinstein, an admirable musician and celebrated pianist. To these were added Martin Plüddermann, the gifted composer and ballad singer who died at an early age, and a colleague from the Munich 'Order of the Grail' – the young sculptor, Fritz Hartmann.

All were avidly engaged in preparations to celebrate the Master's birthday – the not inconsiderable plan of the little group was a performance – the first – of the Communion Scene from *Parsifal*. Rubinstein and Plüddermann had taken upon themselves the task of rehearsing a children's choir in the far from easy Grail Scene which, at that moment, had just been written out. Day after day they worked at it, until it came off. Then came 22 May – Wagner's birthday. The fiery rays of the sun were gleaming over Vesuvius, the spreading beams bathing the mountains and the coast with an intoxicating beauty as the first bars of the Transformation Music began to sound.

To the right of the piano, at which sat Rubinstein, were the gaily-jewelled girls, arranged like a row of pearls, their youthful faces radiant with anticipation and excitement. Opposite them I stood with Plüddermann, each of us with a Knights' score in our hand, while, in the background, Frau Cosima Wagner and her son Siegfried were listening, Joukowsky and Hartmann by their side. In the middle of the circle sat Wagner, behind a desk on which was the outline sketch of *Parsifal*, from which he sang as well as directed – he was soloist, conductor and producer, all in one. With his not large, but tuneful and well-produced voice, capable of all registers, he took all the parts in a most expressive manner – admonitions from Gurnemanz, Amfortas's cry to the deserted sanctuary and the woeful, sepulchral tones of Titurel. In between, the singers from above sounded like angels – their voices ringing the changes on the rugged tones of the Knights and Esquires. And, if a soprano came to grief, or a tenor was conspicuous by his absence, then the Master helped out and brought the piece to a successful conclusion.

Dusk was already about us as the final sounds hung in the air – 'Selig in Glauben' – everyone was left in silent rapture, in another world, until the spell spontaneously dissolved – but nevertheless, the rapture remained. 'Now my children, may I not be well satisfied with myself?' laughed the Master. 'I was not dropped on my head when I wrote that. Now – outside – we all need some fresh air!'

So we streamed out into the garden where there were refreshments already laid out. The balmy perfumed air of the warm night was laden with the distant strains of song and lute coming up from the sea shore. It was late when I took my leave. The Master deliberated about me for a while before he said, 'My young friend, have you it in mind to come to Bayreuth? There would be plenty for you to do, and it might amuse you.'

Who could have been happier than I? My heart's desire fulfilled as quickly as the words were spoken. With joy I told him. Then the work to be done was discussed – Rubinstein was to make a piano edition of the *Parsifal* score and I a copy for general, everyday use and, in addition to this, I was to help in the preparations for the stage performances of the work.

'Yes, my dear boy,' added the Master, 'all the Old Masters had to learn how to grind colours before they were allowed to begin their work.'

'Fine,' I replied, 'I will come as a colour-grinder,' and so took my leave of Wagner and his family.

Plüddermann, Rubinstein and I went down in the mild moonlit night. As we arrived at the gate we heard a familiar voice singing above us, 'Drei Knablein, jung, schön, hold und weise, begleiten euch auf eurer Reise.' It was the Master sending us a farewell greeting from the balcony of the villa.

'Auf Wiedersehen,' we returned our Mozart, 'Auf Wiedersehen.'

Winter 1881 saw me in Bayreuth. At Angermann's Inn, in the secluded pub district, long since disappeared, I found a large set of rooms, big enough to accommodate a large family and its entourage. I contented myself with a couple of the most pleasant of the rooms – part of the remainder later became the so-called 'Parsifal Chancellery'.

Soon after my arrival I got down to work. I received from the Master's hand the first sheets of his manuscript, beautiful thirty-stave Paris paper covered with bluish-coloured notation. Anyone who has seen a Wagner original manuscript score will know how neat and accurate and how decorative are the strokes of the pen – just like an engraved page. No sort of abbreviation or short cuts such as others use are to be seen – every instrument, every key signature and all the performing directions are written out in full. There was not the slightest error in any of the details – a very time-consuming way of writing, it must be remembered. In spite of this, hardly a daỹ went by without some sheets of paper, 'ganz frisch noch die Schrift und die Tinte noch nass', shuttling in a briefcase between Angermann's and Wahnfried. I was taking great pains to keep the script of my copy neat and even, but in spite of Wagner devoting only a few hours each day to the score, I was never completely able to keep up with him.

I soon discovered the reason for this – it was the sketch book I had glimpsed from time to time. This, a sort of miniature score, contained *in nuce* the whole outline of the composition, laid out in two or three lines, in a special system legible only to Wagner himself. It gave not only details of the orchestration but everything else in the score and, from it, the final full score was worked out in its pages and bar lines. This sketch book had been written out by Wagner only after he had worked out the complete composition in his head.

Wagner, no friend of excessive thriftiness, who gave away money with open hands (when he had it), this same Wagner, who surrounded himself with costly velvets and silks, was stingy when it came to manuscript paper – to him it was as if it was pure gold. Every scrap of paper was examined twice, and if possible three times, to see if there was any blank area going to waste. What was the reason for this peculiar stinginess? Was it because his complex scores necessitated excessive working out in rough? We saw it rather as his self-discipline, his way of imposing order on his materials, his craftsmanship – such as had led to the creation of the wonderful edifice of the Grail. From this economy of material came the noble architecture and line – not one note too many, not one note too few – and from this the clarity and transparency of the parts at which we marvelled so greatly.

I soon found that 'colour-grinder' was no bad occupation for me, and I realised that I had learned more and gained more experience in these few months at Bayreuth than in as many years at the Conservatory.

Nor was there any lack of stimulation outside the work. Evenings were frequently spent at Wahnfried where the Master, surrounded by his family, took recreation after his daily labour among the epic heroes. For preference, he liked to read the works of Calderon, Lope de Vega, Shakespeare and Goethe, but from time to time he would give a section of his great autobiography. Other evenings were musical – his favourite pieces were the Preludes and Fugues of Bach and Beethoven's quartets, and these were played on the piano by Rubinstein. Occasionally, he himself sat at the piano and performed a Loewe ballad but most interesting were those times when, with delightful freshness of characterisation, he gave scenes from the operas of Mozart, such as *Seraglio*. He also went over classical symphonies with me at the piano (I was to direct these at the Bayreuth

Musical Society), explaining their form and content and instructing me as to how they should be performed.

In the late autumn Wagner and his family settled in their winter residence at Palermo – as he had prophesied to me. It was there, in January, that *Parsifal* was finished. In the meanwhile, without his knowing it, I had started to prepare for the performance of *Parsifal* – and thereby hoped to surprise the Master on his return. I got together a choir of boys from the Bayreuth Municipal School and rehearsed them in their parts for *Parsifal*. The little Bayreuthers, most of them by now respected family men, were eager and intent on making the best possible impression with their fresh, unspoiled voices. But nothing came of our plan to welcome back the Master so, as Frau Cosima wished, we prepared for the imminent birthday celebrations. On 22 May the troop gathered in the Hofgarten early in the morning and were let into Wahnfried by a back door, and, felt soles on their shoes, they were led up a back stairway to the Gallery, where they stationed themselves without a sound. At the moment when the Master appeared to receive the congratulations of his family they broke out in full voice, 'der Glaube lebt, die Taube schwebt, des Heilands holder Bote'. All present listened attentively to this splendid chorus, the Master, quite overcome with astonishment, declared himself quite satisfied with what he heard – and gave 'Humpy' permission to bring his young troupe to the Festspielhaus for rehearsal and to take part in the actual performances.

Now began the endless preparation with soloists and chorus, who were turning up in ever-greater numbers. The faithful Heinrich Porges looked after the chorus of Flower Maidens and was dubbed 'Blumenvater' by Wagner. The orchestra was to be directed by Hermann Levi from Munich. It had not been easy for him to overcome the original opposition of the Master who had set his heart on a conductor of Aryan extraction for his *Parsifal* but by his ceaseless devotion and reliability in the service of the Grail he soon won over the Master and became his most intimate friend.

I will never forget those days when Wagner first took the stage chorus through the details of the production. Anyone who has attended a performance of *Parsifal* will realise how much work is involved in bringing together and keeping going the manifold apparatus of the action. And in this, unforeseen problems can occur, as this example will demonstrate:

One day, a rehearsal was taking place, with soloists, chorus, the special bells for the Grail, the stage music *e tutti quanti*, so that their effect could be ascertained upon the open stage. Everyone was playing and singing away, right up to the highest point above the stage, where the temperature was like an oven (gas lights were used in those days). It all sounded splendid, the Master was fully satisfied with it and wished for nothing better. But, unfortunately, the joy was not of long duration, for, as soon as the stage action began, everything went to pieces, nothing would work properly and even the acoustic balance was upset. We were in despair – it would all now have to be worked out anew, then tried out and rehearsed from scratch. But, with true malevolence, worse was to come – this time involving the moving scenery of the Transformation Scene.

This was painted on canvas and mounted on rollers which stood at each side of the stage – it was reeled off, from one side to the other, to give the effect of 'moving time and space'. This device, common in the Parisian theatres of the 1840s, may have arisen from Wagner's seeing it during his Paris years.

When the music ran out and came to an end the scenery went on – it was too long! The usually equable Brandt stood, watch in hand, noting just how much more music was needed as the scenery went rattling on. Wagner let out a cry, 'What, have I now to write music by the metre?' There was nothing to be done about it – the machine could not run faster, the scenery could not be replaced, it had cost a ransom, and besides there was not time. Wagner was beside himself, swore he would have nothing more to do with rehearsals and performances and hurried off in great agitation.

Wagner had, at first, been amused, commenting that for years he had been told his operas were too long and ought to be shortened – it was only upon realising how serious the situation was that he took this attitude of despair.

We gazed after him perplexed. What could we do? Because of a stupid mis-calculation the total effort of the performers was at stake. Levi was of the opinion that things were not so bad as to involve cancellation, and he thought it could be put right. I considered the matter myself: that the overburdened Master should be expected to undertake such extra work at the last moment – that would not do at all. I ran home, made out a rough copy of some transitional bars of music, set them out in full score and joined them up to the rest. Then, full of apprehension, I took the manuscript to the Master. He scrutinised the sheets, gave me a friendly nod, and said, 'Well, why not? So be it! Now off to the Chancellery and write out the voice parts, and come back when it is finished.' And so it was done. Now the music was co-ordinated with the scenery and nobody at any of the public per-formances suspected that anywhere a bit of honest cobbling had been done on it. Naturally, in the following years the scenery was put right . . . and the original music restored.

The final dress rehearsal took place – with the work the enthusiasm had grown, and everyone exerted his full power to give the drama the best possible presentation. Already there were visitors arriving, all wanting to gain admission to the Temple. Most were permitted – among them Dr Strecker, head of the firm of Schott, who had come to discuss publication with the Master.

'Children, pull yourselves together,' Wagner called out merrily to the orchestra, 'out there sits a publisher who is listening carefully to what we do – if you do the thing well, he may want to do it too!'

The 25th of July arrived. The whole of Bayreuth swarmed with visitors, passing through the gaily-decorated streets in dense flocks. At four in the after-noon the fanfares signalled the start of the first public performance of *Parsifal*. With profound emotion the assembled throng heard revealed the noble music of the Master's last testament. As the curtains were opened once again on the closing scene there broke out a storm of enthusiasm such as is rarely heard. All were calling for the creator of the wonderful work, to see him face to face. He did not appear.

A splendid victory for art had been won, a promising new era of the Bayreuth Festival was under way.

The wider fortunes of the Festival of 1882, to which the visit of the German Kaiser added a brilliant episode, are well known to all. Once more the Master had taken a part in the performance of one of his works – he had, unseen by the audience, taken the baton in the final performance and with his own hand brought the last Act to a triumphant close.

The first *Parsifal* performances were now at an end and everyone involved dispersed to the four winds. My work too was finished. . . . I went to Wahnfried to take my leave. There I met the Master, surrounded by his artists, who had gathered for the same purpose as I. Each of them received a souvenir – a photograph, inscribed and autographed. When Wagner saw me he stopped short and exclaimed, 'You here too! You will get no picture – for we shall see you again, soon.'

Humperdinck saw Wagner for the last time when he was summoned to Venice, where the Wagner family was spending the winter of 1882–3. There he was to have conducted a concert of music by Liszt and Wagner, but this had to be cancelled when the authorities prevented any form of assembly following civil disturbances. Instead, Wagner himself conducted his own early Symphony in C (dating from 1832, it had recently been resurrected in Dresden) on 24 December, in honour of his wife's birthday on Christmas Day.

Humperdinck ends his recollections with a moving account of how he took his leave of Wagner; shortly afterwards, when he had returned to Mannheim, he heard of Wagner's death in Venice.

Angelo Neumann

Angelo Neumann, returning to Bayreuth, recorded his impressions of the first performance of Parsifal. He also noted Wagner's wishes concerning applause after this work, wishes rarely taken account of even today.

The first performance of *Parsifal* took place on 29 July and was an epoch-making occasion to all those present. The audience itself naturally on such an evening was tremendously interesting. Interest and expectation were at their greatest height.

Forster and I had seats in the third row of the stalls and, as chance would have it, Albert Niemann, the great Wagner singer, and his wife sat directly behind us.

Words fail me to express the deep impression this work made upon us all. A lofty ecstasy came over me and I felt I had taken part in a sacred service.

As to the interpretation – Materna and Winkelmann were marvellous; as was the orchestra too under Hermann Levi. But above all Scaria's Gurnemanz was a masterpiece, and without exaggeration I may say it was the perfection of art.

This singer, who had triumphed so as Wotan in Berlin and then failed so lamentably in London, had risen under Wagner's guidance to such an interpretation as to enrapture the audience and even delight the Master himself.

After the performance we drove back in pouring rain to our supper at the 'Fantasie' – it was laid out for us on a long, communal table. We were joined by the Klingsor of that evening, Siehr from Munich, with his wife and daughter. It was remarkable that this famous bass, who went on to sing Gurnemanz, was one of the most violent public adversaries of Wagner's school, and remained so until the close of his days.

Eduard Hanslick sat next to me at supper. That redoubtable critic was evidently still under the spell of *Parsifal* and was noticeably silent and thoughtful. Naturally the sole topic of our conversation was the wonderful experience of the day. Hanslick joined enthusiastically in our conversation, making no adverse or caustic comments, and we felt he had been now quite converted.

During our talk, each giving his impressions of the day, Forster made a statement that struck us all with horror: 'You shall see – Wagner is not long for this world!' Our animation faded at these words and we sat there unspeakably shocked, till I managed to stammer, 'What makes you say a thing like that?' Forster answered, with quiet conviction, 'A man who is capable of producing a work of that order can *not* be long for this world, his work is finished!' Earnestly he spoke, almost with tears in his eyes – and his words impressed us with such a weight of foreboding that it was long before we recovered from their effect. But our earlier light gay mood was gone for that whole evening.

That season I heard seven performances of *Parsifal*. It was at the close of the first – when Wagner, amid the thunders of the audience, appeared on the stage surrounded by his artists – that he begged the public not to applaud again as they had during the course of the performance. So the second performance passed with a calm and reverent silence. This called forth another speech from the Master. He must explain, he said, that it was only *during* the performance itself that he objected to applause; but the appreciation due to the singers at the fall of the curtain was quite a different matter. So, at the next performances, the people expressed their enthusiasm at the close of each of the Acts.

At the third of the *Parsifal* performances, some hitch having occurred in the moving scenery, Fritz Brandt, at the risk of his own life, climbed up the swaying side wall, and clinging to a post at a dizzy height, took out his knife and cut the obstruction. It seemed hours before they could get at him with a ladder and help him down from his precarious perch.

Eduard Hanslick

Eduard Hanslick, whose contemplative mood after the performance of Parsifal *was noted by Angelo Neumann in the preceding extract, went on to describe the re-opening of the Bayreuth Festival in July 1882 in the following dispatches to his paper, the* Neue Freie Presse.

And so we found ourselves once again in the friendly little Bavarian town of Bayreuth, once famous for courtly splendour and twice hallowed by the power of the spirit. Half a century ago the devotees of Jean-Paul made the pilgrimage one by one; six years ago it was made in whole caravans by the admirers of Richard Wagner.

Yes – six years have passed since the Festival Theatre was first opened to cast the spell of Wagner's four-day wonder, *Der Ring des Nibelungen.* Since then, the odd theatre in the mountains has been closed and the hot, dusty road leading up to it deserted. It had been differently planned. Wagner had hoped for annual productions. He had even expressed the intention of having his theatre, in ever-expanding scope, undertake 'every type of dramatic work which, because of the originality of its conception and its truly German character, could lay claim to a particularly correct production'.

Nobody of course believed that he would ever produce any but his own works at Bayreuth. And quite properly so, for in order to hear a good *Fidelio* or *Don Giovanni* nobody had to travel to Bayreuth, still less to construct a special theatre. More credible and reliable seemed the other promise: an annual repetition of the *Ring* cycle in Bayreuth. This was in keeping with Wagner's definite public pronouncement that he would not permit the production of the *Nibelungenring* on any other stage. As sincere as this edict may have been originally, I doubted its durability from the start and predicted, back in 1876, that once Europe had travelled to Bayreuth, Bayreuth would have to come to Europe.

And so it has been – to the real advantage of the work and its creator. The *Nibelungenring* has, in the past six years, travelled to every court and municipal theatre worth mentioning. And the Wagner temple in Bayreuth has remained shut. Only now have its doors been re-opened, and for a new work, *Parsifal,* to which Wagner has given special significance by the term 'Bühnen-weih-festspiel' (Consecrational Stage Festival).

Hanslick completed this first section of his review with a detailed account of the text of Parsifal *running to some eight pages of print. He recommended a study of the text, which on its own gave some idea of the work's effectiveness on the stage, and commented on the language: in comparison with the* Ring *he found it simple and natural – so far as Wagner was capable of saying anything simply and naturally. Hanslick went on to review the first performance, which he (or his editor) dated incorrectly; it took place on 26 July 1882.*

The first performance of *Parsifal* took place on 25th July. It was an unqualified success. It proclaimed in its grand outline, as well as in the smallest detail, the individuality of its creator. Like the Babylonian ruler who had his monogram burned into every single brick of new public buildings, so also has the author of *Parsifal* impressed an invisible R.W. upon every bar. Future researchers will be able to recognise every torn-out page of the score.

Certain parts seemed strong and elevating, others indifferent and oppressive. Always, however, there is the spell of a forceful personality. The energy of a strong will, undisturbed by doubt, has an impressive effect in art as well as in life. It commands respect, if not always sympathy. Compared with the *Nibelungen*, *Parsifal* proves the advantage of compact form and, consequently, of unified impression. The mere circumstance that Wagner had discarded the dramatically false, unhappy form of the trilogy or tetralogy – which made the artistic pleasure of 1876 a tortuous exertion – assures a cleaner effect for *Parsifal* which will one day certainly be appropriated by the theatres of the world.

The method of musical composition is essentially the same. It is in the style of the 'endless orchestral melody' which Wagner first carried out strictly in *Tristan und Isolde*. In *Die Meistersinger* he enlivened it with flowering oases of melodic and multiple-voiced song and in the *Ring* he imposed upon it a rigid conformity. This method, which purports to elevate opera to true drama, involves the exclusion of the old organic forms, assigning the leading role to the ceaselessly moving orchestra and leaving the voices to declaim rather than sing.

The materials from which the orchestra spins its ever-changing, infinite web are the so-called leitmotives. In *Parsifal* too, each character has his own special musical leitmotive, or rather several of them, according to the various dramatic references. Wolzogen's *Leitfaden* lists twenty-six such motives; another, by Heintz, sixty-six; and a third, by Eichberg (there is already a small library of such Bayreuth booklets) only twenty-three. These twenty-three, however, as the author points out, are especially suitable for memorisation.

This explicit direction is characteristic. If the listener is to understand and enjoy *Parsifal* he must have first committed the leitmotives to memory. In the surging waves of a restless orchestra, he is faced with the endless test of detecting the 'Grail' motive, the 'Love Feast' motive, the 'Promise' motive, etc. These are all connected with the Grail. There are, in addition, a number of Kundry motives (Kundry's wild Ride, Kundry's Love and Kundry's Laugh, etc.) as well as those for Parsifal, Klingsor and others. These leitmotives, in ever-new combinations, variations and instrumentations, provide a continuous symphonic web. He who has not heard it from Wagner's intimate friends should be able on his own to detect that Wagner, as a rule, writes the orchestral accompaniment first and then sketches in the vocal parts; the integrated and integrating whole is the self-sufficient orchestra; what is sung to it are fragments whose sense is in the words, not in the tones. Thus, with the exception of a few conspicuous examples of melodious, intelligible song, *Parsifal* also offers the spectacle of a busy orchestra, rich in allusions and significance, in which float the flakes of an agitated song-speech.

A second essential characteristic of Wagner's later style is boundless freedom of modulation. In *Parsifal* there is no longer any real modulation but rather an incessant undulation, in which the listener loses all sense of a definitive tonality. We feel as though we were on the high seas, with nothing firm under our feet. Wagner has got himself into a chromatic-enharmonic way of thinking quite his own, continuously twisting in and out of the most remote keys. *Parsifal* does have individual moments of tonal equilibrium. They are welcome exceptions, some of them even charming; but exceptions they are, and usually fleeting.

The tyrannical domination of the leitmotives in the orchestra and the licence of the modulations strike me as serious shortcomings in operatic music; Wagner and his disciples prize them as the ultimate in progress. These are basic differences of opinion about which it is no longer possible to quarrel.

A simple, sustained, lengthy prelude, whose solemn dullness can have no other purpose than to set the mood, introduces the first Act and, at the same time, the three principal Grail motives. In the various leitmotives in *Parsifal* I find neither charm nor any particular characterisation. The model for a leitmotive and its application has been provided by Wagner in *Lohengrin*: 'Nie sollst du mich befragen.' Proclaimed by Lohengrin like a dogma, the theme stands forth at the outset in all its full significance. It does not have to be looked for or guessed at; it cuts through the score like a bright sword. The leitmotives in the *Ring* and *Parsifal* have nothing like the same sharply-etched physiognomy, nor the same striking effect, if only because there are too many of them. Where every little sequence of notes is supposed to lead somewhere and signify something there can be no guidance and no significance.

The Grail motives from the Prelude continue, as orchestral accompaniment, to colour the restrained first scene, notable for a manner of expression conspicuously more natural than the *Ring* dialogues and much the better for it. Gurnemanz, the bass, for all his ceremoniousness, is an amiable old man compared to Wotan. By way of declamation, on which, of course, the main burden of the Wagner roles rest, he does some odd jumping around; one notes that he knows *Meistersinger* – he repeatedly declaims words such as 'Linderung', 'lindern', 'schaden' and 'hamisch' with an intentionally false emphasis on the last syllable, with upward leaps, now of a sixth, now of an octave.

The episodes preceding Parsifal's entry offer nothing outstanding with the exception of isolated imaginative phrases and sound effects in the orchestral accompaniment; there is no want of these, indeed, in any page of the score. After these monotonous, attenuated episodes – and not a moment too soon – comes the wounded swan on the wing, a splendid bit of stage mechanics. The Knights and pages, dashing up in great excitement with the miscreant Parsifal, fill the stage with lively animation. It is a dramatic, masterfully composed picture, in which we greet a reference to the Swan motive from *Lohengrin* as a pleasant reminiscence. Parsifal's entrance has a sympathetic effect. The stupidity of the inexperienced boy is represented simply, without false pathos. It is a phenomenon, psychologically well founded, that we tend to admire in others those virtues which we ourselves do not possess. Wagner, the reflective, sharp-witted artist, loves to glorify naïve simplicity, but in this case even naïvety sounds much too calculated. One need only think back to the song of the sailors in *Tristan und Isolde*, the song of the cobbler in the *Meistersinger* and the forging song in *Siegfried* – these most unnatural of all the singing children of nature. It is otherwise with Parsifal in the first scene; he is just what he should be. Kundry is something else again! She is, to be sure, just what the poet would have her – but that is exactly the unnatural, the contradictory. A psychological and physiological hybrid, she sings, or rather cries and stammers, brokenly and in the most hair-raising intervals, at the same time being required to accomplish unheard of tasks in the art of pantomime.

Now comes the wonderfully effective Transformation Scene. This masterpiece of scenic art receives only step-motherly musical support. Until their arrival in the Temple of the Grail, Parsifal and Gurnemanz march to heavy, tiresomely monotonous chords. From here on the composition gets under way and rises to significant realisation, supported by the magnificent and original impressions of the setting. Admirable in their effect are the solemn unison song of the knights, the chorus of the young men and, finally, floating down from above, the promise, 'Durch Mitleid wissend – der reine Tor.' In this surprising blend of pure high voices the promise motive makes exactly the desired impression; in itself the rather empty ascending theme in fifths would hardly appear original or interesting.

The Holy Communion of the Knights of the Grail in the vaulted hall, with the three singing groups of knights, youths and boys (above in the cupola), with the heavy ringing of the bells, the strange painting-like walls, the solemn unveiling of the Grail – all this combines to make a wonderful picture. The finale belongs unquestionably among those dazzling musico-scenic achievements in which Wagner has no rival. It may be my fault, or the fault of too great expectations, but the fact remains that I found the effect less powerful and brilliant than I had imagined it in reading the text and the score. I expected, particularly, an extraordinarily dazzling brilliance from the orchestra and an almost overpowering impression from the chorus, a relentlessly cumulative crescendo of sound right to the finish. As a rule, he who reads the Wagnerian scores finds his expectations far surpassed in the actual performance; this time, for me at least, hopes were not fulfilled. The conspicuously slow tempi in this very long first Act may have contributed to this disappointment, as well as the familiar structural peculiarities of the sunken and hidden orchestra at Bayreuth, which does not permit of a supremely brilliant sound effect. In any event, after a first Act vocally declaimed and orchestrally swallowed, the second part is a musical treat, bringing with it rhythmically ordered and melodically self-sufficient song, and multiple-voiced song at that. Only one thing disturbs this pleasure: each scene is so endlessly drawn out. This inability to stop is as damaging to *Parsifal* as it is to the *Ring*. Everything is endless, everything too long, from the largest to the smallest, from the Holy Communion to Kundry's impossible kiss.

The evil sorcerer, Klingsor, opens the second Act with his conjuring up of Kundry. The demoniacal is represented by not uncommon yet nevertheless gripping means. The vocal line is again precipitate, jerky and recitative, the orchestra a witches' cauldron of bubbling leitmotives; and Kundry a musical-dramatic convulsion. Did Wagner intentionally offer here every kind of sulphuric vapour just to render us doubly receptive to the fragrance of the flowers in the following scene? If so, then he achieved his purpose to the utmost. The poesy of these lovely Flower Maidens sinks in places to questionable doggerel. But then, who pays any attention to the words when they flow, charmingly sung, from the lips of thirty pretty girls? Even their pell-mell entrance amidst the swarming triplets in the violins is full of dramatic life; and so is the second half of this scene, the appearance of the Maidens as flowers. Their A flat episode – 'Komm, Komm, holder Knabe' rather in the tempo of a slow waltz, melodically charming, piquantly and yet simply harmonised, belongs to Wagner's happiest inspirations. With what fine calculations are the thirty voices grouped, alternated, joined together, now and then making way for little solo passages! Of all the scenes in *Parsifal* I would rate this the highest, for it achieves the purest and most certain effects through the simplest means – charming expressive melody. Among all of Wagner's tone poems this chorus of the Maidens, difficult as it is to perform, stands out, almost unique, as the only large-scale scene in a light gracious genre, and at the same time a masterpiece of that genre.

The Flower Maidens finally disappear, laughing; Kundry, now young and seductively beautiful, calls Parsifal by name. There follows the great scene in which she first tells him of his mother, and then, with ever-increasing ardour and desire, presses herself upon him. Her narrative begins simply and singably, one of those promising melodic buds which, with Wagner, frequently peep out, only to be broken off before becoming blooms. From there on, the composition builds up ever higher in forced emotionalism. The composer seems perpetually on the point of running out of breath. He who does not know his leitmotives by heart is helpless in the face of the raging orchestral ferment, and he who does is hardly better off. It is too much to ask of the listener that he keep up with all the un-motivated, frightful changes of mood in which Parsifal and Kundry are tossed about throughout the whole long scene: from tedious narrative to sensual ardour, from ardour to religious ecstasy, and always in flight from everything musically beautiful and moderate. In Wagner's music certain stereotyped phrases have evolved for just such scenes of ultimately passionate expression, and by now they have hardened into what is almost a mannerism. I am aware that the sworn Wagnerians accept these standard phrases as natural sounds of deepest feeling, and that they prize this scene between Kundry and Parsifal as the finest the Master has written. It depends on the point of view. To me, the whole scene appears fundamentally untrue, the music outwardly ardent but inwardly cold, like baked ice. Then, just as we are beginning to grow tired and distracted amidst this tumult of fruitless passion, Parsifal's hand grasps the Holy Spear and we are saved. The magic castle collapses under the weight of truly shattering music, and the curtain closes on Klingsor's realm.

The third Act begins with a kind of religious idyll, composed with much affection, but also with the utmost breadth. It is a poetic, peaceful picture – Parsifal, in snowy white ecclesiastical robes, sitting by the Holy Well enjoying the beauty of the verdant scene, while Kundry washes his feet, and old Gurnemanz anoints his head. The scene belongs among those, quite characteristic of Wagner, which fascinate us as an atmospheric picture. But one can contemplate a painted picture longer than the most beautiful static tableau in a drama, where the situation soon presses for movement and development. In this case the author has seemed incapable of satiety in the plastic quiet of the scene; the music goes its bucolic way with impressive monotony. A fragrant surprise is Parsifal's lyric excursion on the beauty of the flowering meadow, but this, too, is soon lost in the quicksand of instrumental infinity.

Parsifal, Gurnemanz and Kundry finally make their way to the Mount of the Grail. Here, according to the directions of the text and the score, another transformation scene, like that of the first Act, should perform its pleasant office and charm the three stationary pilgrims through all kinds of landscape to their destination. Technical considerations, resulting from the experiences of rehearsal, persuaded Wagner that it would be better to pass it up, and thus, in the performance, we had only a simple curtain closing over the three pilgrims as they set forth. This is certainly more appropriate. The repetition of one and the same device of scenic magic, reminiscent of fairy tales and children's theatre, appeared questionable from the very beginning, a testimony to the poverty of the author's fantasy. This third Act brought a second and equally praiseworthy departure from the directions of the libretto: the dead Titurel, who is supposed to arise from the coffin to give his blessing, does not arise but remains at rest, as a corpse should. The introductory funeral music is too extended.

How badly the plot, after lengthy lyric contemplation, needs a moment of dramatic energy is apparent in the great effect of Amfortas's passionate upward leap against the Knights of the Grail crowding about him. From the words 'mein Vater', his song (over an expressive accompaniment, first in the cellos and then in the violins) is gripping. The final scene is executed with the same extraordinary brilliant material – the same, to be sure, which served the Grail scene of the first Act. The solemn sounds of the harp, the song of the boys sounding from the cupola, the bright radiance of the Grail, the appearance of the dove – all contribute again to a dazzling spectacle, similar to the first finale.

The third Act may be counted the most unified and the most atmospheric: it is not the richest musically.

And Wagner's creative powers? For a man of his age and of his method they are astounding. He who can create music as charming as the 'gambols of the flowers' and as vivid as the final scene possesses powers which our youngest composers may envy. *Parsifal* on the other hand does not consist solely of such lucid intervals. It would be pure foolishness to declare that Wagner's fantasy, and particularly his specifically musical invention, has retained the freshness and facility of yore. One cannot help but discern sterility and prosaism, together with increasing long-windedness. Are not the irresistible Kundry's attempts at seduction rather stiff and cool in comparison with the similar scene in *Tannhäuser*? And is the prelude to *Parsifal* not of the same origin and intent as the prelude to *Lohengrin*? It is the same tree, but in one case in full bloom and in the other in autumn – leafless and chilly. Or compare the song of Gurnemanz in the 'Good Friday Music' to the melodically related description of the Feast of St John in *Meistersinger*. Pogner's poetic song seems to have recurred to Wagner in the composition of the 'Good Friday Music', but where is the inner strength, the singing soul of the model? Even the most powerful episodes from the *Ring*, considered individually and apart, have no equal parts in *Parsifal*, always excepting the chorus of the Flower Maidens, which stands quite alone. When one considers that those great moments in the *Ring* are distributed throughout four full evenings, the comparison may, to be sure, show a favourable balance. And *Parsifal* has the advantage of a more effective libretto. Although utterly inadequate as a 'dramatic poem', it is a better opera text. It is, in a word, more musical. If we regard it as a festive, magic opera, if we ignore, as we often must in any case, its logical and psychological impossibilities and its false religious-philosphical pretensions, we can find in it moments of artistic stimulation and brilliant effectiveness.

The question of whether *Parisifal* should really be withheld from all theatres and limited to an occasional (and in the long run, very doubtful) revival in Bayreuth was naturally on all tongues. Wagner himself, in an open letter from Palermo dated 1 April 1882, emphasises the 'thoroughly distinctive character of the work' and assumes that he has made any performance of it outside Bayreuth impossible in that he has, 'with this poem, entered upon a sphere rightfully and eternally foreign to our opera houses.' I fail to see the 'impossibility' of it. I have already pointed out the odd, and even improper aspects of the church scenes. But since when has impropriety been an obstacle to the performance of Wagner operas? I find the ardent love scene between Siegmund and his sister Sieglinde in *Die Walküre* a thousand times more offensive than the religious scenes in *Parsifal*. The latter may be irritating to confirmed Christians, but they are no way so shocking to human sensibilities as the scene cited above, once characterised by Schopenhauer as infamous! I must state here that the church scenes in *Parsifal* did not make the offensive impression on me that others and I had been led to expect from reading the libretto. These are religious situations – but, for all their earnest dignity, they are not in the style of the church but completely in the style of the opera. *Parsifal* is an opera, call it a 'stage festival' or a 'consecrational stage festival' if you will. It cannot even be called a 'spiritual opera' as the term was used by Anton Rubinstein for in such an opera the voluptuous second Act of *Parsifal* would be impossible. The way in which the Wagner of the Venusberg, that splendid old theatrical devil, jumps out of the habit of the pious monk in this second Act is simply too stimulating.

Why should *Parsifal* not be given in a theatre? Is the Bayreuth Festspielhaus, for which it was written, not a theatre? Is it a church or a concert hall? No! It is a theatre, and one in which *Parsifal*, like any other opera, is played by professional singers in costume, with the most brilliant operatic apparatus conceivable, and for a continuously changing, paying public. Why should a performance of *Parsifal* offend religious sensibilities everywhere but in Bayreuth? We do not doubt Wagner's earnest resolve to prohibit it in Europe – he may have ulterior motives in reserving it for Bayreuth. But so far as inner motives, derived from the work itself, are concerned, I am unable to grasp the impossibility of performing it on other stages. And I should sincerely regret the latter prohibition. Just as it would have been a pity for all the cost and effort of the *Ring*, which was also supposed to have been expended solely for Bayreuth, so it would be a pity – and even more of a pity – for *Parsifal*. It is easier to produce than the Tetralogy, more compact, and more effective. Its music (with the single exception of the Kundry scene) has more repose and nobility. Assuming expedient cuts to be indispenable, it may prove more valuable and successful for the stages of the world. For the past quarter-century we in Central Europe have been badly off for new operas capable of survival, and we seem to be growing poorer in this respect from year to year. One need not be a Wagnerite to complain in all sincerity of this threatened withholding of *Parsifal*. I know very well that Wagner is the greatest living opera composer and the only one in Germany worth talking about in the historical sense. He is the only German composer since Weber and Meyerbeer whom one cannot disregard in the history of dramatic music. Even Mendelssohn and Schumann – not to speak of Anton Rubinstein and the newer ones – can be ignored without leaving a gap in the history of opera. But between this admission and the repulsive idolatry which has grown up in connection with Wagner and which he has encouraged, there is an infinite chasm.

According to all that has been said and intimated here, an annual repetition of *Parsifal* at Bayreuth appears to be no less than a certainty. And then what? And if, for the lifetime of Wagner it should be really withheld from other theatres – what then? Without Wagner's personality, the magnetic eye, and the strong hand which draws all, artists and audience to Bayreuth and holds them there, nobody after him would be able to accomplish the same feat. The Bayreuth Festivals will probably die with Wagner, but certainly not his *Parsifal*. The great theatres will give this interesting devout opera without much religious scruple, and audiences in Vienna, Munich and Berlin will hear and see it, just as do the audiences here, without imagining for an instant that they are in church. People will enjoy the *Ring* and *Parsifal* until, one fine day, they will get tired of being pitched around on a sea of endless melody and led around by stereotyped leitmotives. At that time let us have for the opera a new 'reiner Tor', a naïve composer of natural genius, possibly a kind of Mozart who will master the 'Master' and restore the natural balance between music and drama in the opera.

Felix Weingartner

Felix Weingartner (1863–1942), the Austrian conductor who took over the directorship of the Vienna Opera from Mahler in 1908, obtained a free student ticket for the Festival of 1882. He described his visit in his autobiography, Buffets and Rewards *in 1937:*

My first sight of the Festival Theatre gave me a shock, as I had not imagined it would loom so large. In majestic harmony it crowns the hill over the town, framed by the range of hills in the distance. No better site could have been found for a festival building.

In the streets of the town we soon came across a number of friends. . . . Our first walk took us to Wagner's house in the hope of catching a glimpse of him, but nothing stirred. The house of the master lay wrapped in its mid-day slumbers. We lunched at what had then already become the historic Restaurant Angermann and at half-past two ascended the Festival Hill.

As the Festival Theatre grew larger and larger, until I actually stood before it, I was a prey to the tensest anticipation, curiosity and impatience. As we approached it we dared hardly utter a word aloud.

At last we heard the first flourish of trumpets. Their tones resounded through the summer air and must have been audible far up in the woods. We produced our tickets, walked up a few steps and the interior of the building opened up before us. It was beautiful with the beauty of symmetry and simplicity, there were no conspicuous colours, no superfluous decorations. I entered between two pillars and found my seat easily. A soft light illuminated the auditorium. Below, in front of the stage where, as a rule, one's view is disturbed by lights, dazzlingly white sheets of music and restless musicians, nothing was to be seen but a simple rounded screen. True, there was a subdued humming as of soft tones far down in the depths, but this did nothing to disturb the mystic silence which broods over this hall and which compels all-comers to lower their voices.

My seat was at the back, not far from the line of boxes reserved for Wagner and his family and for royal visitors. In the year 1876 the old Emperor Wilhelm had sat there for two evenings; it was there that Ludwig II was vainly expected, there that Wagner listened to his own work. Would he come today? Would he be visible? The whole row of boxes was enveloped in impenetrable darkness.

Once more the flourish of trumpets. The performance was about to begin. Only about half the seats were occupied. In later years, when the standard of performance had fallen far below the early ones, the auditorium was packed. In the year 1882, Bayreuth was a place of pilgrimage, not a fashionable resort.

Darkness descended on the audience. Like another voice from another world the grandly conceived opening theme of the overture resounded. Incomparable!

In later years I attended performances of *Parsifal* in Bayreuth which disappointed me painfully, but the devotional effect of the opening remained. Inspiration, orchestration, acoustics and in a negative sense the optical effects were here combined in a unique manner which would be possible nowhere else.

The curtain rises comparatively slowly. The stage becomes visible, unveiling a solemn, beautiful picture; Gurnemanz awakens, aroused by the distant trombones. Emil Scaria's imposing figure is before us, his glorious voice awakens the henchmen. The cast was that of the original performance and was a triumph not only for Bayreuth, but also for Vienna, as nearly all the principal parts were taken by artists from the Vienna Court Opera House. . . . Hermann Levi, at first rejected by Wagner because he was a Jew, conducted. If Wagner had not withdrawn his objection, King Ludwig would have failed to allow the Munich orchestra to co-operate. It was not till Hermann Levi had ceased to conduct the Bayreuth performances that the excellence of his work – by comparison with that of his successors – became clear to all but blind partisans.

When Gurnemanz prepared to accompany Parsifal to the Castle of the Grail, I was seized by a slight giddiness. What was happening? It seemed to me as if the whole house with the audience was moving. The transformation accomplished with the help of shifting scenery had begun and the illusion was complete. It seemed as if one were being borne aloft. At each side of the stage there were two or three pillars on which the appropriate dissolving views appeared successively until the last wall of rock disappeared and the nobly-proportioned interior of the Castle of the Grail opened up before our eyes. As the C major chord resounded light flooded the majestic picture. The simplest of means had brought about an overwhelming effect. When much later *Parsifal* was free to be performed on other stages, plastic pillars, massive domes and, in some cases, still more pretentious devices were utilised without producing the same effect, while the shifting scenic arrangement was dropped with the convenient argument that it was 'out of date'.

During the first scene of the second Act there was loud talk in a box behind us, so loud that attention was distracted from the music and Hill's great performance. It sounded as if someone were giving orders in excited tones. Could it be Wagner himself who had so little consideration for his own work? At last one of my neighbours turned his head and gave vent to an energetic hiss in the direction of the box. For an instant a powerful-looking spectacled face appeared over the parapet and glanced in the direction from which the reproachful hiss had come. My excited imagination led me to think I had recognised Wagner. In any case the disturbing conversation ceased.

A most surprising effect was produced by the sudden transformation of Klingsor's tower into the magic garden. Some years later, when I had been present behind the scenes at several rehearsals and performances of *Parsifal* I had an opportunity of studying and admiring the simplicity of this transformation scene mechanism. When the performance was given in our own theatres the curtain fell at this point. How helpless we have become in many ways despite our much-vaunted progress! Our scenic apparatus is heavy and overladen, and anything but plastic, and where it strives for simplicity it is devoid of imagination.

The Flower Maidens' costumes showed extraordinary lack of taste, but the singing was incomparable. Heinrich Porges, the 'Blumen-Vater' as he was generally called, had trained them and therewith made a better name for himself than he achieved by his activities as a critic in Munich. During the lovely diminuendo, 'Wir welken und sterben dahinnen', a hearty 'Bravo!' was heard from one of the boxes. That was really Wagner's voice. I had already been told that at this point of the performance he was accustomed thus to signify his approval.

The great scene between Kundry and Parsifal made the greatest impression of all. The finale of that Act too, with its collapse of Klingsor's magic castle and the withering of the flower-garden, was a masterpiece of scenic art. Wagner's opponents had declared that *Parsifal* was a plagiarism of his own earlier works and this scene one of his usual protracted love duets. No reproach could be more foolish. Wagner never repeated himself, either here or anywhere else. Only small men work to a prescribed pattern.

I thought the climax had been reached but the third Act rose higher still. Scaria's performance as Gurnemanz was inspired. In appearance he was a fighting giant, and yet he was as tender and highly-strung as a child. I can still hear the little break in his voice over the words which tell of the death of Titurel. Wagner had excelled himself – that act placed him among the immortals.

When the curtain had been rung down on the final scene and we were walking down the hill, I seemed to hear the words of Goethe, '– and you can say you were present.' (He had said them in connection with an important historical event.) The *Parsifal* performances of the year 1882 were artistic events of the supreme interest and it is my pride and joy that I participated in them.

I had not yet seen Wagner. He never showed himself in the street or a restaurant and he used to drive to the Festival Theatre in a closed carriage, entering and leaving the theatre by a different door each time, so as not to be subjected to any annoyance.

Weingartner went to Parsifal *again two days later. There was a different cast for this performance, an expedient Wagner adopted so that sixteen performances of the new work might be given in thirty days; it further lessened the risk of cancellation should a principal singer fall ill. The Kundry of Marianne Brandt made a great impression on Weingartner, though Wagner himself expressed doubts about her. Weingartner kept up his pursuit of the elusive Master:*

One of my friends had discovered by which door Wagner would emerge from the house that day. Breathless with haste we rushed there when the performance was over. The carriage which was at other times to be seen in front of Wahnfried was there waiting. One of us went up to the coachman and asked him if Wagner were still in the theatre. 'Don't know' was the answer – given with an unmoved countenance. There was a drizzle of rain and the gas lantern in front of the entrance was flickering in the night air. We cowered under umbrellas a short distance away, expecting that any minute somebody from the theatre would come and ask us our business. No one came, however. Suddenly we heard the sounds of an animated conversation from inside the house, we went as close as we dared and now heard a voice speaking in a decidedly Saxon accent. That must be he! We already knew that Wagner had never dropped the peculiarities of his native dialect. A tall slim lady left the theatre and entered the carriage – presumably Frau Cosima. A gentleman accompanied her who we recognised as Josef Rubinstein, the man who had arranged *Parsifal* for the piano, an intimate friend of the Master's. He exchanged a few words with the lady in the carriage. Then there were quick footsteps and a strikingly short man came out, went up to Rubinstein saying, 'Well, goodbye, my dear Rubinstein, hope we meet again soon, remember me to your father.' That was the gist of the rapidly uttered words. For a few seconds I was able to see the man's face illuminated by the flickering light of the lantern. It was Richard Wagner. Those sharply defined features were unmistakable. Spectacles reposed on the bridge of his prominent nose, on his head he wore a top hat. He was wearing the light yellow overcoat to which, it was rumoured, he was so attached that his wife's urgent pleading could not induce him to change it for a new one. Hardly had I realised the fulfilment of my long-standing wish to see the Master's face than the carriage with its precious burden had driven away and was lost to sight in the darkness. I gazed after it almost bereft of my senses. What a tremendous life, what gigantic power was being carried away in that insignificant vehicle. How negligible and almost unreal the physical presence seemed in comparison with the magnitude of the spirit it encased.

For the third and last performance I applied to Emil Heckel for help. His wisdom and energy had contributed much to the foundation of the Bayreuth theatre. Rugged in appearance, forceful in character, by profession a music dealer, he was a true admirer of and a helpful friend to Wagner. He procured me the ticket I asked for. Not till the next day did I know that Wagner himself had conducted the last scene of the performance.

Bi-weekly receptions took place at Wahnfried to which, it was said, everyone was invited who left cards there bearing an address. Accordingly, I summoned up sufficient courage to approach the door of the villa and give the manservant who opened the door our cards, on which we had written our addresses. I am seized with reminiscent sadness when I look at the unassuming note addressed to me on which are the words:

Mr and Mrs Richard Wagner at home
every Thursday and Monday evening at 8.30
from July 27th to August 28th

On the evening on which we went to Wahnfried there was a heterogeneous collection of people present. The venerable figure of Franz Liszt caught the eye at once; he had been away from Bayreuth for a short time and had returned that same day. I recognised Hans Richter, Hermann Levi and many of the artists who had taken part in the performances. Frau Cosima wore an elegant dress with a train, her ash-coloured hair was beautifully dressed and she held court as if she were a princess. Girls in white frocks, Wagner's and Bülow's daughters, moved gracefully among the crowd. Siegfried, still a boy, spoke English to the foreign visitors and I envied him this accomplishment.

Would Wagner appear? He often stayed away from these parties. Heinrich Porges, the 'Blumen-Vater', had promised to introduce me if he should come. So I mastered my impatience and gazed at the numerous books and Schopenhauer's remarkable head which, painted by Lenbach, hung over a writing-desk.

I saw Liszt go into a neighbouring room which was separated from the reception room by a half-drawn curtain. Instinctively, I followed him and could see everything that passed there without entering the room itself. A door opened – Wagner hurried to meet Liszt, threw his arms about his neck and poured out a spate of excited affectionate words. This touching scene, which I witnessed by a mere chance, was only a prelude. Immediately afterwards Wagner entered the reception room and greeted his guests. He seemed to be in a particularly good temper, as he had donned evening dress – a thing which he seldom did. In his hand he carried a collapsible opera hat which from time to time he would balance on his head – in its collapsed state! What astonished me most, however, was a large star of some exotic Order which he wore round his neck, he who despised all decorations. The riddle was soon solved; he was only wearing it in order to present it to Fräulein Horson of Weimar, his First Flower Maiden, with a few pleasant words. It was rumoured that he had only that day received the Star from some Oriental potentate and had already perpetrated a good deal of nonsense with it, such as hanging it round the neck of his favourite dog.

Wagner's antics with the decoration, which was from the Bey of Tunis, were doubtless at the expense of Liszt, who revered such honours. Liszt had returned to Bayreuth for his granddaughter's wedding.

Wagner had very brisk and nervous movements; no one watching him would have imagined that he was nearing his seventieth birthday, still less that he would not live to see that day. He was somewhat stout, his beautifully formed by by no means abnormally large head was no more disproportionate to his small stature than were his small hands and feet. He looked ever so much younger than Liszt, who had the appearance of a very old man, though he was only two years older. Wagner's hair was only partially grey. His eyes shone brightly out of his pale face and seemed to be now dark, now light in colour. Restlessly, he moved hither and thither, engaging now one person, now another in conversation. From a feeling of respect I avoided coming too close to him, so that I missed a good deal of what he said. Once, however, I stood quite close to him as he was discussing the tempo of the *Tannhäuser* march – he could not understand why it was so often wrongly played. Pacing slowly up and down he hummed the melody as he wished it to be. If I had dreamt at the time that this was the only occasion on which I should be near him, I should have behaved less discreetly and should have been able to treasure more of his utterances.

For a short time he withdrew into the next room where some food was served to him. A glance at the dish set before him showed that he did not put into practice the vegetarian principles which he advocated.

People were leaving as I went up to Porges and reminded him of his promise. Both my friends were with me; Porges introduced us. Wagner shook hands with us all amicably and asked us whether we had seen any of the performances. He seemed to notice that I was agitated, for he suddenly laid his hand on my chest and called out, 'Your heart is palpitating!' When I was silent in surprise and confusion, he said in an unadulterated Saxon dialect: 'Well, well, for a young man such as you are, the Flower Maidens are the principal attraction in *Parsifal*, but they mustn't make you lose your heart.' Then he shook hands with us again. We were already at the door when his voice rang out again: 'But don't lose your heart.' I turned round. There stood Wagner, alone in the middle of the room. Smilingly he waved his hand to me.

On 25 August, Cosima's daughter Blandine was married to Count Gravina. As the groom was a Catholic, a religious ceremony was held the following day, and Weingartner went to the church in the hope of getting yet another glimpse of the Master.

At Blandine von Bülow's wedding, Frau Cosima, the bride's mother, sat between Wagner and Liszt, the latter listening with a pious expression on his face to the address of the Catholic priest, Wagner obviously fidgety because the address was so long. When the ceremony was over, Wagner, his arm in that of his wife, stood for a fairly long time in the church porch, waiting for his carriage to come up. Thus I had one more opportunity of seeing him; it was the very last.

Weingartner went to Bayreuth again in 1886. This year saw the first production there of Tristan und Isolde, *the fulfilment of one of Cosima's greatest ambitions. Weingartner recorded:*

At the first performance of *Tristan*, which was a sensational success, I sat next to [Liszt] in a box on the so-called Princes' Gallery. 'How is your cough, Master?' I ventured to ask once, when a long pause between his otherwise frequent gasps and coughs made me feel anxious. 'It is civilised,' he answered, with a faint smile; 'it leaves me alone during the music and will surely start again in the interval.'

Weingartner was with Liszt a few days before he died on 31 July 1886; his dying words are said to have been 'Tristan, Tristan'.

PART IV

Bayreuth in the 1880s
and early 1890s

Sir Henry Wood

Bayreuth in the 1880s attracted something like a wider public, but one still largely occupied with the arts. Sir Henry Wood (1869–1944), the conductor and founder of the Promenade Concerts, was a regular visitor to the Bayreuth Festivals, which he recalled in his autobiography, published in 1938. His enthusiasm for the old days of the 1880s and 1890s was perhaps justified by what prevailed at Bayreuth in succeeding decades.

I first visited Bayreuth for the Festival the year Liszt died [1886] since when I have made it the scene of many pilgrimages. The London agent for these Festivals was Schulz-Curtius who became my constant companion during these visits, introducing me to the great German artists and conductors. . . .

One of the conductors I met at Bayreuth was Mottl. Conversation was something of an effort as neither of us was fluent in the other's language. Mottl liked me, and he took great interest in my conducting of Wagner and demonstrated his own interpretations at the piano, explaining many traditional points. These have been invaluable to me, not alone when conducting concert excerpts, but when teaching Wagner roles. My full scores of the *Ring* contain many of his remarks; most valuable of all are his orchestral finishes for concert use in his own handwriting. I am proud to possess them.

In 1899 Wood took his first wife with him; she was a Russian soprano, the Princess Olga Urussov, whom he married in 1898 (she died in 1909).

Except for the last two, I had not missed Bayreuth for many years. So well did I know it that I felt I was showing Olga something of my own. The Bayreuth atmosphere remains as ever it was – and what a lovely theatre it is! I am a great believer in the picture-frame type of proscenium, and Bayreuth has it *par excellence*, but there is a very good one at Munich, though the auditorium there is too large.

At each succeeding visit to Bayreuth I have noticed improvements: in the presentation of *Lohengrin* (in which Siegfried Wagner helped so much) the device of the interstices of the trees hung right across the proscenium borders on strong netting was most effective. And again – in *Tannhäuser* – the new Paris version of the scene with the wonderful little flight of cherubs with their marvellous arrows which they shot on exactly the right chord.

Olga's musicianship rendered her deeply sensitive to Bayreuth. We both revelled in the simplicity of the daily life there; in the courtesy displayed at every turn; in our pleasant meals with the good wines; the meetings after the performances when we discussed all we had seen and heard. Everything simple, untouched by petty jealousies and wire-pulling. . . .

In the old days Bayreuth was the Mecca of all true Wagnerians. To go there was regarded almost as a pilgrimage, for Wagner's tradition held good through the influence of Cosima and Siegfried Wagner. All that is now [1938] gradually disappearing. Everything is commercialised. There must always be a 'star' conductor – Toscanini or Furtwängler – and this famous soprano or that famous tenor. In the old days we never knew who was singing and we certainly never knew who was conducting. The names were not advertised and we had to find out as best we could. We went there for Wagner and Wagner alone; but tradition broke down when the copyright of *Parsifal* ran out. It never ought to have been performed outside Bayreuth. One no longer thinks of Bayreuth as a pilgrimage: one just 'goes to the opera'.

Sir George Grove

Sir George Grove (1820–1900), civil engineer, biblical scholar and writer on music, is most remembered for the compilation of the Dictionary of Music and Musicians *which bears his name. He visited Bayreuth with August Manns in 1889, on his way to Vienna (he also stopped at Frankfurt to see Clara Schumann, but she was away). Grove had met Wagner in London in 1877 and was greatly impressed by him, but he was puzzled by the music dramas and remained out of sympathy with them. He was in Bayreuth on 10 August and on the 28th he wrote to a Mrs Wodehouse, from Interlaken:*

I should probably agree with Manns about *Meistersinger*, but as to *Tristan*, never! To it I have a distinct and strong moral objection which with me will always strongly affect my judgment about art. Art exercised on an immoral subject may be the finest art, but I want it not: the world must not be corrupted, however fine the music or the painting or the writing in which the corruption is conveyed, and therefore I never can or will admit such creators as Wagner or Gustave Flaubert, or many of the great French painters to the first rank. I am sure I am right. If art must be immoral then let it perish; but it need not be so. See Dict. vol. i 196b for my sentiments. Also I do think the tendency to make music so long and ultra-earnest is wrong. If everything is to take the same road what amusements will the world have in the end? Music is turned from a relaxation into a study, but no other relaxation is put in its place. Surely this is wrong. It is one of the main arguments for me against what they call 'women's rights'– who is to amuse and soothe us and help us along the dull road if women are themselves pulling the cart as hard as we are. . . .

In another letter, to Dr Charles Wood on 15 September, Grove wrote:

I had a very good time abroad – the first point was Bayreuth, where Manns and I heard *Parsifal*.

Well, of course one hearing of such a work is nothing – and of this *less* than nothing.

The circumstances of the dark theatre, the hidden orchestra, the very prominent and brilliant stage, and the *extraordinary* stage effects and machinery – are all so new that of themselves they throw you off balance, and then the piece is so unusual in its form, and the necessity of knowing it beforehand so essential, that all goes against a first hearing, especially in one so slow of taking things up as I am.

I confess I was disappointed and very wearied . . . but this I have not said to anyone but you, and I don't wish it repeated, because I should have probably have said much the same after hearing the Ninth Symphony. . . .

Bernard Shaw (1889 and 1891)

Bernard Shaw (1856–1950), the critic, dramatist and political writer, wrote music criticism in the late 1880s and early 1890s for a number of London periodicals. His first visit to Bayreuth was in 1889 and he wrote the following account for the magazine The Hawk. *It appeared on 13 August 1889. Shaw signed the piece 'By Reuter' – it was nothing of the sort, and his editor felt it necessary to point out that 'the joke lies in the pronunciation of it.' Shaw's distinctive style of spelling and punctuation has been retained in the extracts which follow.*

Oh, Bayreuth, Bayreuth, valley of humiliation for the smart ones of the world! To think that this Wagner, once the very safest man in Europe to ridicule, should turn out the prime success of the century! To be reduced to a piteous plea that you always admitted that there were some lovely bits in Lohengrin! To know beyond all shifts of self-deception that, when you got your one great chance of discovering the great man of your age, you went the fools among, and made an utter, unmitigated, irretrievable, unspeakable ass of yourself! To humbly and anxiously ask whether there are any tickets left – to pay a pound apiece for them – to crawl, seasick and weary, hundreds of costly miles to that Theatre which you so neatly proved to be the crazy whim of a conceited, cacophonous charlatan, there to listen to Tristan and the Meistersinger with the hideous guilt upon you of having once thought Lucia and Favorita worth a dozen of such. This is the sort of thing that takes the starch out of the most bumptious critic.

Yes, the cranks were right after all. And now – now that it is not merely a question of whether he or Offenbach is the more melodious, but of whether he is to be accepted as the Luther of a new Reformation, the Plato of a new philosophy, the Messiah who is really to redeem the fall and lead us back to the garden of Eden, now that the temple is up and the worshippers assembled, now that we are face to face with pretensions for the 'Master' in comparison with which the old simple claim to rank as artist and man of genius was a mere joke, dare we pick up our weapons and resume the fight? No, thank you, the fellow is too dangerous. Better call him a man of extraordinary ability as if we had thought so all along and then lie low and see whether he will really pull off his philosophical and religious venture as he undoubtedly pulled off his musical one, confound him!

You would not catch me talking in this strain if my own withers were wrung. No, I am not confessing my own mistakes; I am only rubbing in the mistakes of others. The first time I ever heard a note of Wagner's music was in my small boy days, when I stumbled upon a military band playing the Tannhäuser march. I will not pretend that I quite rose to the occasion; in fact, I said just what Hector Berlioz said – that it was a plagiarism from the famous theme in Der Freischütz. But a little after this bad beginning I picked up a score of Lohengrin; and before I had taken in ten bars of the prelude I was a confirmed Wagnerite in the sense the term then bore, which committed me to nothing further than greatly relishing Wagner's music. What it commits a man to now, Omniscience only knows. Vegetarianism, the higher Buddhism, Christianity divested of its allegorical trappings (I suspect this is a heterodox variety), belief in a Fall of Man brought about by some cataclysm which starved him into eating flesh, negation of the Will-to-Live and consequent Redemption through compassion excited by suffering (this is the Wagner-Schopenhauer article of faith); all these are but samples of what Wagnerism means nowadays. The average enthusiast accepts them all unhesitatingly – bar vegetarianism. Buddhism he can stand; he is not particular as to what variety of Christianity he owns to; Schopenhauer is his favourite philosopher; but get through Parsifal without a beefsteak between the second and third acts he will not. Now, as it happens, I am a vegetarian; and I can presume enormously upon that habit of mine, even among the elect. But for an unlucky sense of humor which is continually exposing me to charges of ribaldry, I should have been elected a vice-president of the Wagner Society long ago.

However, these be matters into which this is not the place for a deep dip. The question of the moment is, what is Bayreuth like? Well, it is a genteel little Franconian country town among the hills and fine woods of Bavaria, within two or three hours' rail from Nuremberg. It is not old enough to be venerable, nor new enough to be quite prosaic; and the inhabitants either live in villas on independent incomes or else by taking in one another's washing and selling confectionery, scrap books and photographs. There are plenty of street fountains, a nonsensically old-fashioned monument to a person generally described by vulgar English visitors as 'old stick-in-the-mud', a factory chimney, a barrack, a lunatic asylum, a very quaint eighteenth-century opera house, the Wagner Theatre halfway up the hill, and the inevitable *Sieges Turm*, or tower commemorative of 1870–1, quite at the summit, among the pines. Half the main street is the Maximilianstrasse, and the other the Richard Wagnerstrasse. The Master's house is a substantial villa, undistinguishable from other villas except by the famous inscription – Hier wo mein Wähnen Frieden fand Wahnfried sei dieses Haus von mir benannt – and by a *sgraffito* cartoon much in the manner and taste of Mr Armitage, representing Wotan as the Wanderer. Behind the Master's house is the Master's grave; for Wagner, as I heard an indignant Englishman exclaim, is 'buried in the back garden sir, like a Newfoundland dog.' I shall never be a true Wagnerite after all for I laughed at this expression of bourgeois prejudice, whereas any decently susceptible disciple would have recoiled horror-stricken. At certain hours the gate between the Wahnfried domain and the Hofgarten is left open and the faithful go in to deposit wreaths on the colossal granite slab which covers the Master's last bed, and to steal ivy leaves as souvenirs. The only other sentimental journey available at Bayreuth is to the cemetery at the country end of the Erlangenstrasse, near the old town, where you see a boulder of unhewn stone on Jean Paul Richter's grave and an inartistic and useless outhouse which is the mausoleum of Liszt.

The imagination rather declines to face the notion of life at Bayreuth without Wagner. Walks on the hills through the scented pine woods are always available, but dwellers in the next county to Surrey do not spend twenty pounds to walk in Bavaria when a few shillings would land them in Guildford or Dorking. There are a couple of show places – the Fantasie to the south-west, and the Eremitage to the east, which give some sort of aim for a couple of excursions, each capable of slaying two or three hours. They are something between a Wicklow glen and an Isle of Wight chine; and the Eremitage has a chateau with a Temple of the Sun, a pseudo-Roman bath, dolphins, tritons and general rococo. On the whole, Bayreuth has to be put up with for Wagner's sake rather than enjoyed for its own. Business begins at the Wagner Theatre at four; but after two the stream of people up the hill is pretty constant, their immediate destination being the restaurant to the right of the theatre, and their immediate object – grub. At a quarter to four a group of men whom you at once recognize as members of the orchestra, as much by a certain air of Brixton or Kentish Town about them as by the trombones and cornets they carry, troop out of the centre door. These, by fearsome blasts, right and left, proclaim that the entertainment is about to begin. In spite of the vile noise they make, they are audible only for a very short distance partly because they stand under the portico instead of on top of it, partly because brass instruments should be blown quietly and musically if the sound is to travel (always excepting the nothing-if-not-violent bugle). In ten minutes or so it will be time to go into the famous theatre.

You have already bought your playbill in the street for a penny; and you will have to find your own seat among the fifteen hundred in the auditorium. However, this is easy enough, as your ticket directs you to, say, Door No 2 Left Side. That door delivers you close to the end of the row in which your seat is, and as each corner seat is marked with the highest and lowest number contained in the row, you can, by a little resolute brainwork, find your place for yourself. Once in it, you have a stare round at the theatre. It is republican to begin with;

the 1,500 seats are separated by no barrier, no difference in price, no advantages except those of greater or less proximity to the stage. The few state cabins at the back, for kings and millionaires, are the worst places in the house. All this is pleasant; for if you are an aristocrat, you say 'Good – a man can be no more than a gentleman' and if a democrat, you simply snort and say 'Aha!' The wonder is that though this theatre has been built and known to the public for thirteen years, yet we have during that time run up a little host of playhouses, and never once dreamt of departing from the old cock-pit-and-scaffold model. What a capital architectural feature is that series of wings, each with its pillar and its branch of globes, causing the stage to grow out of the auditorium in the most natural manner! Sh-sh-sh! The lights are lowered. Sit down everybody. Why do the ladies not take off their hats as requested by a placard? Ah, why indeed? Now the lights are almost out; there is dead silence; and the first strain of the prelude comes mystically from the invisible orchestra. And so on. When the act is over, there is a pause of an hour for late afternoon tea. After the second act comes another pause for supper. Thus do these ascetics emulate the Buddha.

It is too late in the day to describe the three lyric plays being repeated at Bayreuth. Tristan – would you believe it? – is thirty years old. Die Meistersinger will be twenty-two next October. Certainly, Parsifal is quite a novelty – only ten years and a half; but Parsifal is not an affair to be sketched in a few lines. All that I shall say here, then, is that though the accounts of the tremendous effect they produce in the Wagner Theatre are not exaggerated, yet the process of getting tremendously affected is by no means a blissful one. I am a seasoned Wagnerian; and there is no veil of strangeness between me and the ocean of melody, with all its cross-currents of beautiful and expressive themes, in Die Meistersinger. But at Bayreuth, after the third act, I had just enough energy to go home to my bed, instead of lying down on the hillside and having twelve hours' sleep *al fresco* there and then. That third act, though conducted by Hans Richter, who is no sluggard, lasts two hours, and the strain on the attention, concentrated as it is by the peculiarities of the theatre, is enormous. Consider, too, that the singers are not like De Reszke or Lasalle, refreshing to listen to. They are all veterans – hale and respectable veterans, irreproachably competent, with thick voices and intelligent declamation; but they are terribly dry. You are driven for a reviving draught of beauty of sound to the orchestra. Having heard that before, you are thrown back on the inner interest of the poem, and so forced to renew your grip with a closer and closer application on the very thing you sought a moment's relief from. When it is over you are glad you went through with it, and are even willing to face it again; but you recognise that you have achieved edification by a great feat of endurance, and that your holiday, your enjoyment, your relaxation will come when the work of witnessing the performances is finished, and you are returning home down the Rhine.

Parsifal, in spite of its prolonged and solemn ritual, is less fatiguing than the Meistersinger, although to the Philistine it is a greater bore; for the Meistersinger, long as it is, is bustling, whilst the shorter Parsifal is slow and serious. Not that the boredom saves any Philistine from the spell of the work; the merest scoffer is impressed, and would not unsee it, even if he could get his pound back at the same time. Tristan neither fatigues nor bores, except for a while at the end of the second act, if King Mark is dull, and during the first half of the third if the tenor is uninteresting. The rest is one transport; deafness and impotence combined could alone resist it; you come away hopelessly spoiled for Roméo et Juliette after it.

As to the merits of the Bayreuth mode of performance, they are simply the direct results of scrupulous reverence for Wagner, thorough study, and reasonable care. What has been said lately about the inferiority of the staging to that at the Lyceum is quite true. Admirable as the orchestra is, we can beat it in London as certainly as we can build the theatre the moment we are wise enough to see that it is well worth our while. And the sooner the better, say I, for the sake of our English millions to whom Bayreuth is as inaccessible as the North Pole.

Shaw also contributed an article to The English Illustrated Magazine *in October 1889 about this visit. Unlike the above review, which is here given in full, the following one has been somewhat shortened – a number of references to long-forgotten theatrical personages and events have been left out, as have points which Shaw had already made in the foregoing article.*

There are many reasons for going to Bayreuth to see the Wagner Festival plays. Curiosity, for instance or love of music, or hero-worship of Wagner, or adept Wagnerism – a much more complicated business – or a desire to see and be seen in a vortex of culture. But a few of us go to Bayreuth because it is a capital stick to beat a dog with. He who has once been there can crush all admirers of Die Meistersinger at Covent Garden with – 'Ah, you should see it at Bayreuth' or, if the occasion be the Parsifal prelude at a Richter concert – 'Have you heard Levi conduct it at Bayreuth?' And when the answer comes sorrowfully in the negative, the delinquent is made to feel that in that case he does not know what Parsifal is, and that the Bayreuth tourist does. These little triumphs are indulged in without the slightest remorse on the score of Richter's great superiority to Herr Levi as a Wagnerian conductor and of the fact that a performance of the Parsifal prelude by a London orchestra under his direction is often much better worth a trip from Bayreuth to London than a performance by a German orchestra under Levi is ever worth a trip from London to Bayreuth. It is not in human nature to be honest in these matters – at least, not yet.

Those who have never been in Germany, and cannot afford to go thither, will not be sorry when the inevitable revolt of English Wagnerism against Bayreuth breaks out; and the sooner they are gratified, the better. Ever since the death of Beethoven, the champions of Music have been desperately fighting to obtain a full hearing for her in spite of professorship, pedantry, superstition, literary men's acquiescent reports of concerts, and butcherly stage management – all trading on public ignorance and indifference. Wagner, the greatest of these champions, did not fight for his own hand alone, but for Mozart, Beethoven and Weber as well. All authority was opposed to him until he made his own paramount. . . .

Wagner did not succeed in putting dulness out of countenance until he became a classic himself. And now that he is a classic, who is to do for him what he did for his predecessors? For is he not going to escape their fate. The 'poor and pretentious pietism' which he complained of as 'shutting out every breath of fresh air from the musical atmosphere' is closing round his own music. At Bayreuth, where the Master's widow, it is said, sits in the wing as the jealous guardian of the traditions of his own personal direction, there is already a perceptible numbness – the symptom of paralysis. . . .

The law of traditional performances is, 'Do what was done last time' – the law of all living and fruitful performance is, 'Obey the innermost impulse which the music gives, and obey it to the most exhaustive satisfaction.' And as that impulse is never, in a fertile artistic nature, the impulse to do what was done last time, the two laws are incompatible, being laws respectively of death and life in art. Bayreuth has chosen the law of death. Its boast is that it alone knows what was done last time, therefore it alone has the pure and complete tradition, or, as I prefer to put it, that it alone is in a position to strangle Wagner's lyric dramas note by note, bar by bar, *nuance* by *nuance*. It is in vain for Bayreuth to contend that by faithfully doing what was done last time it arrives at an exact copy of what was done the first time when Wagner was alive, present and approving. The difference consists just in this, that Wagner is dead, absent and indifferent. The powerful, magnetic personality, with all the tension it maintained, is gone; and no manipulation of the dead hand on the keys can ever reproduce the living touch. Even if such reproduction were possible, who, outside Bayreuth, would be imposed on by the shallow assumption that the Bayreuth performances fulfilled Wagner's whole desire? We can well believe that in justice to those who so loyally helped him, he professed himself satisfied when the most that could be had been done – nay, that after the desperate makeshifts with which he had had to put up in his long theatrical experience, he was genuinely delighted to find that so much was possible. . . .

It is extremely likely that when A Midsummer's Night's Dream was first produced, Shakespear complimented the stage manager, tipped the carpenters, patted Puck on the head, shook hands with Oberon, and wondered that the make-believe was no worse; but even if this were an established historical fact, no sane manager would therefore attempt to reproduce the Elizabethan *mise en scène* on the ground that it had fulfilled Shakespear's design. Yet if we had had a Shakespear theatre on foot since the seventeenth century, conducted on the Bayreuth plan, that is the very absurdity in which tradition by this time would have landed us. . . .

In a footnote to the last comment Shaw points out that this is, in fact, the very state of affairs prevailing at the Comédie Française – the stage arrangements are as close as possible to those of the time of Molière. Shaw attributes to this the inferiority of the French as actors compared with the English. He continues to develop his theme:

If Bayreuth repudiates tradition, there is no mortal reason why we should go so far to hear Wagner's lyric dramas. If it clings to it then that is the strongest possible reason for avoiding it. Every fresh representation of Parsifal (for example) should be an original artistic creation, and not an imitation of the last one. The proper document to place in the hands of the artists is the complete work. Let the scene-painter paint the scene he sees in the poem. Let the conductor express with his orchestra what the score expresses to him. Let the tenor do after the nature of that part of himself which he recognizes in Parsifal; and let the *prima donna* similarly realize herself as Kundry. The true Wagner Theatre is that in which this shall be done, though it stand on Primrose Hill or in California. And wherever the traditional method is substituted, there Wagner is not. The conclusion that the Bayreuth theatre cannot remain the true Wagner Theatre is obvious. The whole place reeks of tradition – boasts of it – bases its claim to fitness upon it. Frau Cosima Wagner, who has no function to perform except the illegitimate one of chief remembrancer, sits on guard there. When the veterans of 1876 retire, Wagner will be in the condition of Titurel in the third act of Parsifal.

It would be too much to claim that the true Wagner Theatre will arise in England; but it is certain that the true English Wagner Theatre will arise there. The sooner we devote our money and energy to making Wagner's music live in England instead of expensively embalming its corpse in Bavaria, the better for English art in all its branches. Bayreuth is supported at present partly because there is about the journey thither a certain romance of pilgrimage which may be summarily dismissed as the effect of the bad middle-class habit of cheap self-culture by novel reading; partly by a conviction that we could never do the lyric dramas at home as well as they are done at Bayreuth. This, if it were well founded, would be a conclusive reason for continuing to support Bayreuth. But Parsifal can be done not merely as well in London as in Bayreuth, but better. A picked London orchestra could, after half-a-dozen rehearsals under a competent conductor, put Herr Levi and the Bayreuth band in the second place. Our superiority in the art of stage management is not disputed. . . . There remain the questions of the theatre and the singers.

Shaw continues with a description of the Bayreuth Theatre and its fine acoustic – he comments on the ventilation and the freedom from stuffiness and compares the building and the behaviour of the audiences gathered in it with the more conventional theatres. He remarks that if such a theatre were to be put up in London it would not be wasting for much of the year, as at Bayreuth, but would be used for works by Mozart, Beethoven, Weber and Verdi – as well as plays by Shakespeare, Schiller, Goethe and Ibsen.

The doubt as to the possibility of finding singers for an English Wagner Theatre might be disregarded on the ground that London is accustomed to pick and choose from the world's stock. But this plan has not hitherto answered well enough to justify us in relying upon it in the future. Fortunately, Bayreuth has shewn us how to do without singers of internationally valuable genius. The singers there have not 'created' the lyric drama; it is the lyric drama that has created them. Powerful as they are, they do not sing Wagner because they are robust: they are robust because they sing Wagner. His music is like Handel's in bringing into play the full compass of the singer, and in offering the alternative of either using the voice properly or else speedily losing it. Such proper use of the voice is a magnificent physical exercise. The outcry against Wagner of the singers who were trained to scream and shout within the five highest notes of their compass until nothing was left of their voices – and not much of that – has now died away. . . . Plenty of English singers would set to work at the Niblung Ring tomorrow if they could see their way to sufficient opportunities of singing it to repay them for the very arduous task of committing one of the parts to memory. Singers of genius, great Tristans and Parsifals, Kundrys and Isoldes, will not be easily obtained here any more than in Germany; and when they are found, all Europe and America will compete for them. But Bayreuth does without singers of genius. . . .

Next comes a commentary by Shaw on several of the singers he heard at Bayreuth – and their lack of 'genius'.

Can we hope to replace the three great conductors? The chief part of the answer is that there is only one great conductor, and him we have bound to us already. Whoever has heard the Tristan prelude conducted by Richter . . . or the Parsifal prelude . . . knows more than Bayreuth can tell him about these works. Herr Levi shews what invaluable results can be produced by unwearying care and exhaustive study. Herr Felix Mottl's strictness, refinement, and severe taste make the orchestra go with the precision and elegance of a chronometer. Discipline, rehearsal, scrupulous insistence on every *nuance* in a score which is crammed with minute indications of the gradations of tone to be produced by each player: these, and entire devotion to the composer's cause, could do no more. But they are qualities which exist everywhere, if not in everyone. If Wagner's work can call them into action in Germany it can call them into action here. With Richter the case is different. He, as we know, is a conductor of genius. To make an orchestra play the prelude to Parsifal as Herr Levi makes them play it, is a question of taking as much pains and thought as he. To make them play the introduction to the third act of Die Meistersinger as they play it for Richter is a question of the gift of poetic creation in musical execution. The perfection attained by Herr Mottl is the perfection of photography. Richter's triumphs and imperfections are those of the artist's hand.

Before Wagner, the qualities which distinguish the Bayreuth performances were rarer in Germany than they are now in England. His work inspired them there: what is to prevent it doing so here? No more of Bayreuth then: Wagnerism, like charity, begins at home.

Shaw returned to London on 4 August 1889, having spent ten days in Germany visiting Nuremberg, Frankfurt, Mainz, Koblenz and Cologne as well as Bayreuth. He did not go to Bayreuth for another five years, though he advised the readers of The World *on 25 February 1891 that advance booking was essential:*

It is by no means too soon to secure seats now. The Festspielhaus is so admirably constructed that people are apt to think that it does not matter where their seats are, so perfect is the view from all parts of the auditorium. But the distance of the back seats from the stage makes a considerable difference to all but very long-sighted persons. If you want to see the facial play of the artists, take my advice and secure tickets in the front half of the house.

Shaw failed to take heed of his own advice, and tried to make last minute arrangements in the summer of 1891, when he was about to leave for Venice on behalf of the Workers' Art Guild. He wrote to Percy Bunting, Editor of the Contemporary Review:

29 Fitzroy Square
30th July 1891

Dear Mr Bunting,

Does the Contemporary ever meddle with music? My reason for asking you is that ever since I found that all the Bayreuth tickets were gone, I have felt that I must go there at all hazards. Parsifal Van Dyck* engages to find seats for me. I now want an excuse in the shape of a magazine article for spending the money, which I cannot afford, as I stand committed to a trip to Venice as well. However, I would rather stay at home than repeat the usual Bayreuth article, with illustrations, portraits, etc. What I want to do is deal at large with the lesson of Bayreuth for England, to compare Covent Garden etc. If I find that I have anything of this sort to say when I come back, would you care to have an article?

I need not start until the 13th August; but as Van Dyck is waiting for my reply to his offer I should be glad to know as soon as possible.

yours faithfully
G. Bernard Shaw

Shaw failed to secure this commission, and described what happened in The World *on 16 September 1891:*

As a matter of fact I have not been to Bayreuth. Those who remember how earnestly I warned my readers to secure tickets in good time will not be surprised to hear that I spoke as a man taught by his own incorrigible remissness in the past. When at the eleventh hour, being wholly unprovided, I found that there was not a ticket to be had in Europe – that there were two hundred and fifty names down for returned tickets for every performance, and that the average of returns was not above twenty-five, I became quite mad to go. But in a day or so, resigning myself to the inevitable, I came to the conclusion that Bayreuth was an

* Ernest Van Dyck, the Belgian tenor, who was singing Parsifal.

overrated place, and made arrangements for an excursion of a different sort. No sooner had I done this than the difficulty about tickets vanished: Carl Ambruster offered to manage it for me: Van Dyck offered to manage it for me: Messrs Chappell actually did manage it for me: Europe, in short, had realized the gravity of the situation, and Bayreuth was at my feet. But it was too late: the other arrangements stood inexorably in the way; and I now had to refuse. Nobody will be surprised to learn that the proffered seats were no sooner sorrowfully disposed of to mere ordinary Wagnerians, than circumstances again modified my arrangements so as to remove all obstacles to my going. I braced myself up once more to face that forty hours' rush from Holborn to Bavaria, with its eight hours' *malaise* between Queenborough and Flushing, less deadly in its after effects than a railway journey from Calais or even Ostend to Brussels; its inevitable inspection of the latest improvements in the Cologne cathedral, in which every inch of new steeple adds an ell of insignificance and vulgarity to the whole structure; its endless joggle along the Left Rhine Railway, with the engine depositing a ring of soot between one's neck and collar, and the impermanent way disintegrating into whirlwinds of dust; its two or three hours' wait after midnight at Würzburg for the Bamberg train, or else push on to Nuremberg, there to pay a mark for every penn'orth of sleep you have time for; and the final entry into Bayreuth within four hours of the trumpet call to the theatre, hoping desperately that the novelty of the place and the stimulus of Wagnerian enthusiasm will enable you to keep awake during the first performance. I had run it so close that no easier stages were practicable. But I was spared after all: the tickets were gone this time in earnest. At least the Committee thought so, and telegraphed 'Impossible,' though it afterwards turned out that they were wrong, as they usually are about everything except lodgings. Howbeit, I took their word for it; and now the Bayreuthites may boast as outrageously as they please about the Tannhäuser: I shall never be able to contradict them.

There follows Shaw's remedy for all this bother and inconvenience – the 'lesson of Bayreuth for England' was the construction of the English Wagner Theatre on Richmond Hill. This became a regular theme of Shaw's and is substantially repeated and augmented in a postscript to The Perfect Wagnerite.

Mark Twain

Mark Twain (Samuel Langhorne Clemens, 1835–1910), the American writer, was no stranger to Wagner's work and was very fond of the early operas – Tannhäuser in particular. So, although he was an enthusiastic traveller, he was not at Bayreuth in 1891 as a mere sightseeing tourist – his favourite work was being performed there for the first time.

AT THE SHRINE OF ST WAGNER

Bayreuth, Aug. 2nd, 1891

It was at Nuremberg that we struck the inundation of music-mad strangers that was rolling down upon Bayreuth. It had been long since we had seen such multitudes of excited and struggling people. It took a good half-hour to pack them and pair them into the train – and it was the longest train we have yet seen in Europe. Nuremberg had been witnessing this sort of experience for about two weeks. It gives one an impressive sense of the magnitude of this biennial pilgrimage. For a pilgrimage is what it is. The devotees come from the very ends of the earth to worship their prophet in his own Ka'aba in his own Mecca.

If you are living in New York or San Francisco or Chicago or anywhere else in America, and you conclude, by the middle of May, that you would like to attend the Bayreuth opera two months and a half later, you must use the cable and get about it immediately or you will get no seats, and you must cable for lodgings, too. Then if you are lucky you will get seats in the last row and lodgings in the fringe of the town. If you stop to write you will get nothing. There were plenty of people in Nuremberg when we passed through who had come on pilgrimage without first securing seats and lodgings. They had found neither in Bayreuth; they had walked Bayreuth streets a while in sorrow, then had gone to Nuremberg and found neither beds nor standing room, and had walked the quaint streets all night, waiting for the hotels to open and empty their guests into the trains, and so make room for these, their defeated brethren and sisters in the faith. They had endured from thirty to forty hours' railroading on the continent of Europe – with all which that implies of worry, fatigue, and financial impoverishment – and all they had got and all they were to get for it was handiness and accuracy in kicking themselves, acquired by practice in the back streets of the two towns when other people were in bed; for back they must go over that unspeakable journey with their pious mission unfulfilled. These humiliated outcasts had the frowsy and unbrushed and apologetic look of wet cats, and their eyes were glazed with drowsiness, their bodies were adroop from crown to sole, and all kind-hearted people refrained from asking them if they had been to Bayreuth and failed to connect, as knowing they would lie.

We reached here (Bayreuth) about mid-afternoon of a rainy Saturday. We were of the wise, and had secured lodgings and opera seats in advance.

I am not a musical critic, and did not come here to write essays about the operas and deliver judgment upon their merits. The little children of Bayreuth could do that with a finer sympathy and a broader intelligence than I. I only care to bring four or five pilgrims to the operas, pilgrims able to appreciate them and enjoy them. What I write about the performance to put in my odd time would be offered to the public as merely a cat's view of a king, and not of didactic value.

Next day, which was Sunday, we left for the opera house – that is to say, the Wagner temple – a little after the middle of the afternoon. The great building stands all by itself, grand and lonely, on a high ground outside the town. We were warned that if we arrived after four o'clock we should be obliged to pay two dollars and a half apiece extra by way of fine. We saved that; and it may be remarked here that this is the only opportunity that Europe offers of saving money. There was a big crowd in the grounds about the building, and the ladies' dresses took the sun with fine effect. I do not mean to intimate that the ladies were in full dress, for that was not so. The dresses were pretty, but neither sex was in evening dress.

The interior of the building is simple – severely so; but there is no occasion for colour and decoration, since the people sit in the dark. The auditorium has the shape of a keystone, with the stage at the narrow end. There is an aisle on each side, but no aisle in the body of the house. Each row of seats extends in an unbroken curve from one side of the house to the other. There are seven entrance doors on each side of the theatre and four at the butt, eighteen doors to admit and emit 1,650 persons. The number of the particular door by which you are to enter the house or leave it is printed on your ticket, and you can use no door but that one. Thus, crowding and confusion are impossible. Not so many as a hundred people use any one door. This is better than having the usual (and useless) elaborate fire-proof arrangements. It is the model theatre of the world. It can be emptied while the second hand of a watch makes its circuit. It would be entirely safe, even if it were built of lucifer matches.

If your seat is near the centre of a row and you enter late you must work your way along a rank of about twenty-five ladies and gentlemen to get to it. Yet this causes no trouble, for everybody stands up until all the seats are full, and the filling is accomplished in a very few minutes. Then all sit down, and you have a solid mass of fifteen hundred heads, making a steep cellar-door slant from the rear of the house down to the stage.

All the lights were turned low, so low that the congregation sat in a deep and solemn gloom. The funereal rustling of dresses and the low buzz of conversation began to swiftly die down, and presently not the ghost of a sound was left. This profound and increasingly impressive stillness endured for some time – the best preparation for music, spectacle or speech conceivable. I should think our show people should have invented or imported that simple and impressive device for securing and solidifying the attention of an audience long ago; instead of which they continue to this day to open a performance against a deadly competition in the form of noise, confusion and a scattered interest.

Finally, out of darkness and distance and mystery soft rich notes rose upon the stillness, and from his grave the dead magician began to weave his spells about his disciples and steep their souls in his enchantments. There was something strangely impressive in the fancy which kept intruding itself that the composer was conscious in his grave of what was going on here, and that these divine sounds were the clothing of thoughts which were at this moment passing through his brain, and not recognized and familiar ones which had issued from it at some former time.

The entire overture, long as it was, was played to a dark house with the curtain down. It was exquisite; it was delicious. But straightway thereafter, of course, came the singing, and it does seem to me that nothing can make a Wagner opera absolutely perfect and satisfactory to the untutored but to leave out the vocal parts. I wish I could see a Wagner opera done in pantomime once. Then one would have the lovely orchestration unvexed to listen to and bathe his spirit in, and the bewildering beautiful scenery to intoxicate his eyes with, and the dumb acting could not mar these pleasures, because there is not often anything in the Wagner opera that one would call by such a violent name as acting; as a rule all you would see would be a couple of silent people, one of them standing still, the other catching flies. Of course I do not really mean that he would be catching flies; I only mean that the usual operatic gestures which consist in reaching first one hand out into the air and then the other might suggest the sport I speak of if the operator attended strictly to business and uttered no sound.

This present opera was *Parsifal*. Madame Wagner does not permit its representation anywhere but in Bayreuth. The first act of the three occupied two hours, and I enjoyed that in spite of the singing.

I trust that I know as well as anybody that singing is one of the most entrancing and bewitching and moving and eloquent of all vehicles invented by man for the conveying of feeling; but it seems to me that the chief virtue in song is melody, air, tune, rhythm, or what you please to call it, and that when this feature is absent what remains is a picture with the colour left out. I was not able to detect in the vocal parts of *Parsifal* anything that might with confidence be called rhythm or tune or melody; one person performed at a time – and a long time, too – often in a noble, and always in a high-toned, voice; but he only pulled out long notes, then some short ones, then another long one, then a sharp, quick, peremptory bark or two – and so on and so on; and when he was done you saw that the information which he had conveyed had not compensated for the disturbance. Not always, but pretty often. If two of them would but put in a duet occasionally and blend the voices; but no, they do not do that. The great master, who knew so well how to make a hundred instruments rejoice in unison and pour out their souls in mingled and melodious tides of delicious sound, deals only in barren solos when he puts in the vocal parts. It may be that he was deep, and only added the singing to his operas for the sake of the contrast it would make with the music. Singing! It does seem the wrong name to apply to it. Strictly described, it is a practising of difficult and unpleasant intervals, mainly. An ignorant person gets tired of listening to gymnastic intervals in the long run, no matter how pleasant they may be. In *Parsifal* there is a hermit named Gurnemanz who stands on the stage in one spot and practises by the hour, while first one and then another character of the cast endures what he can of it and then retires to die.

During the evening there was an intermission of three-quarters of an hour after the first act and one an hour long after the second. In both instances the theatre was totally emptied. People who had previously engaged tables in the one sole eating-house were able to put in their time very satisfactorily; the other thousand went hungry. The opera was concluded at ten in the evening or a little later. When we reached home we had been gone more than seven hours. Seven hours at five dollars a ticket is almost too much for the money.

While browsing about the front yard among the crowd between the acts I encountered twelve or fifteen friends from different parts of America, and those of them who were most familiar with Wagner said that *Parsifal* seldom pleased at first, but that after one had heard it several times it was almost sure to become a favourite. It seemed impossible, but it was true, for the statement came from people whose word was not to be doubted.

And I gathered some further information. On the ground I found part of a German musical magazine, and in it a letter by Uhlig, written thirty-three years ago, in which he scorned and abused people like me, who found fault with the comprehensive absence of what our kind regards as singing. Uhlig says Wagner despised 'Jene plaperude Musik' and therefore 'runs, trills and *schnorkel* are discarded by him'. I do not know what a *schnorkel* is, but now that I know it has been left out of these operas I have never missed it so much in my life. And Uhlig further says that Wagner's song is true: that it is 'simply emphasized intoned speech'. That certainly describes it – in *Parsifal* and some of the other operas; and if I understand Uhlig's elaborate German he apologizes for the beautiful airs in *Tannhäuser*. Very well; now that Wagner and I understand each other, perhaps we shall get along better, and I shall stop calling him Waggner, on the American plan, and thereafter call him Wagner as per German custom, for I feel entirely friendly now. The minute we get reconciled to a person, how willing we are to throw aside little needless punctilios and pronounce his name right!

Of course I came home wondering why people should come from all corners of America to hear these operas, when we have lately had a season or two of them in New York with these same singers in the several parts, and possibly this same orchestra. I resolved to think that out at all hazards.

Tuesday. Yesterday they played the only operatic favourite I have ever had – an opera which has always driven me mad with ignorant delight whenever I have heard it – *Tannhäuser*. I heard it first when I was a youth; I heard it last in the last German season in New York. I was busy yesterday and I did not intend to go, knowing I should have another *Tannhäuser* opportunity in a few days; but after five o'clock I found myself free and walked out to the opera house and arrived about the beginning of the second act. My opera ticket admitted me to the grounds in front, past the policeman and the chain, and I thought I would take a rest on a bench for an hour or two and wait for the third act.

While seated on the bench outside the Festspielhaus Mark Twain dwells, in republican fashion, and at some length, on the European phenomenon of Princes (thoughts occasioned by his observing one such entering the theatre casually and at the very last minute) and the deference paid to them in their native lands.

In a moment or so the first bugles blew, and the multitude began to crumble apart and melt into the theatre. I will explain that this bugle-call is one of the pretty features here. You see, the theatre is empty, and hundreds of the audience are a good way off in the feeding-house; the first bugle-call is blown about a quarter of an hour before time for the curtain to rise. This company of buglers, in uniform, march out with military step and send out over the landscape a few bars of the theme of the approaching act, piercing the distances with the gracious notes; then they march to the other entrance and repeat. Presently they do this over again. . . .

I saw the last act of *Tannhäuser*. I sat in the gloom and the deep stillness, waiting – one minute, two minutes, I do not know exactly how long – then the soft music of the hidden orchestra began to breathe its rich, long sighs out from under the distant stage, and by and by the drop-curtain parted in the middle and was drawn softly aside, disclosing the twilighted wood and a wayside shrine, with a white-robed girl praying and a man standing near. Presently that noble chorus of men's voices was heard approaching, and from that moment until the closing of the curtain it was music, just music – music to make one drunk with pleasure, music to make one take scrip and staff and beg his way round the globe to hear it.

To such as are intending to come here in the Wagner season next year I wish to say, bring your dinner-pail with you. If you do, you will never cease to be thankful. If you do not, you will find it a hard fight to save yourself from famishing in Bayreuth. Bayreuth is merely a large village, and has no very large hotels or eating-houses. The principal inns are the Golden Anchor and the Sun. At either of these places you can get an excellent meal – no, I mean you can go there and see other people get it. There is no charge for this. The town is littered with restaurants, but they are small and bad, and they are overdriven with custom. You must secure a table beforehand, and often when you arrive you will find somebody occupying it. We have had this experience. We have had a daily scramble for life; and when I say we, I include shoals of people. I have the impression that the only people who do not have to scramble are the veterans – the disciples who have been here before and know the ropes. I think they arrive about a week before the first opera, and engage all the tables for the season. My tribe have tried all kinds of places – some outside of the town, a mile or two – and have captured only nibblings and odds and ends, never in any instance a complete and satisfying meal. Digestible? No, the reverse. These odds and ends are going to serve as souvenirs of Bayreuth, and in that regard their value is not to be overestimated. Photographs fade, bric-à-brac gets lost, busts of Wagner get broken, but once you absorb a Bayreuth restaurant meal it is in your possession and your property until the time comes to embalm the rest of you. Some of these pilgrims here become, in effect, cabinets; cabinets of souvenirs of Bayreuth. It is believed among scientists that you could examine the crop of a dead Bayreuth pilgrim anywhere on the earth and tell where he came from. But I like this ballast. I think a 'Hermitage' scrape-up at eight in the evening, when all the famine-breeders have been there and laid in their mementoes and gone, is the quietest thing you can lay on your keelson except gravel.

Thursday. They keep two teams of singers in stock for the chief roles, and one of these is composed of the most renowned artists in the world, with Materna and Alvary in the lead. I suppose a double team is necessary; doubtless a single team would die of exhaustion in a week, for all the plays last from four in the afternoon till ten at night. Nearly all the labour falls upon the half-dozen head singers, and apparently they are required to furnish all the noise they can for the money. If they feel a soft, whispery, mysterious feeling they are required to open out and let the public know it. Operas are given only on Sundays, Mondays, Wednesdays and Thursdays, with three days of ostensible rest per week, and two teams do the four operas; but the ostensible rest is devoted largely to rehearsing. It is said that the off days are devoted to rehearsing from some time in the morning till ten at night. Are there two orchestras also? It is quite likely, since there are one hundred and ten names in the orchestra list.

Yesterday the opera was *Tristan und Isolde*. I have seen all sorts of audiences – at theatres, operas, concerts, lectures, sermons, funerals – but none which was twin to the Wagner audience of Bayreuth for fixed and reverential attention. Absolute attention and petrified retention to the end of an act of the attitude assumed at the beginning of it. You detect no movement in the solid mass of heads and shoulders. You seem to sit with the dead in the gloom of a tomb. You know that they are being stirred to their profoundest depths; that there are times when they want to rise and wave their handkerchiefs and shout their approbation, and times when tears are running down their faces, and it would be a relief to free their pent emotions in sobs or screams; yet you hear not one utterance till the curtain swings together and the closing strains have slowly faded out and died; then the dead rise with one impulse and shake the building with their applause. Every seat is full in the first act; there is not one vacant one in the last. If a man would be conspicuous, let him come here and retire from the house in the midst of an act. It would make him celebrated.

This audience reminds me of nothing I have ever seen and nothing I have read about except the city in the Arabian tale where all the inhabitants have been turned to brass and the traveller finds them after centuries mute, motionless, and still retaining the attitudes which they last knew in life. Here the Wagner audience dress as they please, and sit in the dark and worship in silence. At the Metropolitan in New York they sit in a glare, and wear their showiest harness; they hum airs, they squeak fans, they titter, and they gabble all the time. In some of the boxes the conversation and laughter are so loud as to divide the attention of the house with the stage. In large measure the Metropolitan is a show-case for rich fashionables who are not trained in Wagnerian music and have no reverence for it, but who like to promote art and show their clothes.

Can that be an agreeable atmosphere to persons in whom this music produces a sort of divine ecstasy and to whom its creator is a very deity, his stage a temple, the works of his brain and hands consecrated things, and the partaking of them with eye and ear a sacred solemnity? Manifestly, no. Then, perhaps the temporary expatriation, the tedious traversing of seas and continents, the pilgrimage to Bayreuth stands explained. These devotees would worship in an atmosphere of devotion. It is only here that they can find it without fleck or blemish or any worldly pollution. In this remote village there are no sights to see, there is no newspaper to intrude the worries of the distant world, there is nothing going on, it is always Sunday. The pilgrim wends to his temple out of town, sits out his moving service, returns to his bed with his heart and soul and his body exhausted by long hours of tremendous emotion, and he is in no fit condition to do anything but to lie torpid and slowly gather back life and strength for the next service. This opera of *Tristan und Isolde* last night broke the hearts of all witnesses who were of the faith, and I know of some who have heard of many who could not sleep after it, but cried the night away. I feel strongly out of place here. Sometimes I feel like the sane person in a community of the mad; sometimes I feel like the one blind man where all others see; the one groping savage in the college of the learned, and always, during service, I feel like a heretic in heaven.

But by no means do I ever overlook or minify the fact that this is one of the most extraordinary experiences of my life. I have never seen anything like this before. I have never seen anything so great and fine and real as this devotion.

Friday. Yesterday's opera was *Parsifal* again. The others went and they show marked advance in appreciation; but I went hunting for relics of the Margravine Wilhelmina, she of the imperishable *Memoirs*. I am properly grateful to her for her (unconscious) satire upon monarchy and nobility, and therefore nothing which her hand touched or her eye looked upon is indifferent to me. I am her pilgrim; the rest of this multitude here are Wagner's.

Tuesday. I have seen my last two operas; my season is ended, and we cross over into Bohemia this afternoon. I was supposing that my musical regeneration was accomplished and perfected, because I enjoyed both of these operas, singing and all, and, moreover, one of them was *Parsifal*, but the experts have disenchanted me. They say: 'Singing! That was not singing; that was the wailing, screeching of third-rate obscurities, palmed off on us in the interest of economy.'

Well, I ought to have recognised the sign – the old, sure sign that has never failed me in matters of art. Whenever I enjoy anything in art it means that it is mighty poor. The private knowledge of this fact has saved me from going to pieces with enthusiasm in front of many and many a chromo. However, my base instinct does bring me profit sometimes; I was the only man out of thirty-two hundred who got his money back on those two operas.

Richard Strauss

The first production of Tannhäuser *at Bayreuth was assessed on a very different level by Richard Strauss. He was a musical assistant at the Bayreuth Festival in 1889 and 1891, and was one of the five conductors of* Tannhäuser *in 1894. He wrote the following article, giving his views on the best methods of fulfilling the composer's intentions, for the* Bayreuther Blätter *in 1892.*

ON THE PRODUCTION OF 'TANNHÄUSER' AT
BAYREUTH

Amongst the flood of nonsense I had to hear or read last summer concerning the festival in general and the incomparable performance of *Tannhäuser* in particular originating from people who always knew better but invariably failed to do better or at least to make really concrete suggestions as to how one could do better, I noticed particularly that the professional critics, having duly shown that *Tannhäuser* was no drama and should therefore be performed in accordance with the 'laws' of opera, almost unanimously admitted that the playing of the festival orchestra had been of a very high order. It is of course extremely nice of these gentlemen to find something complimentary to say about the Bayreuth *Tannhäuser*, but even this compliment loses in importance if we remember that these same critics are in the habit of concluding their reports on performances at their local theatres of operas such as *Asrael* in Dresden, *Manon* in Vienna, *Cavalleria* in Berlin, *Rose von Strassburg* in Munich, etc., with the words: 'Chorus and orchestra under the practised and careful guidance of our (at times inspired) Mr X were excellent.' But excellent, after all, means excellent and nothing else, and I have been unable so far to find in any German dictionary an indication that there are degrees of 'excellence'. This is rather unfortunate.

In defence of the critics I can only assume that this indifferent use of the word 'excellent' constitutes nothing more than looseness of style, since I do not imagine for a moment that these critics would wish to compare the performances of their local orchestras with those in Bayreuth. If we assume that the performance of the orchestras in the above-mentioned theatres was characterised by the epithet 'excellent' because their playing did in fact excel the performance on the stage, we should in this particular case have to examine in what respect the instrumental presentation of the *Tannhäuser* score in the festival theatre excelled the orchestral performances mentioned above, i.e. the stylistically perfect realisation of the Master's intentions. . . .

In the seventh volume of his collected works, Wagner calls an opera in which the dramatic tendency is at no point allowed to become clearly defined 'a chaos of the most confusing kind', precisely because so many artistic media are used. 'A purely musical effect,' he says, 'is made impossible if the dramatic action is left obscure.' What unprejudiced spectator has not himself heard the musical effect of the Bacchanale of the Paris version when played in one of our larger opera houses, as an extremely unpleasant, and violent noise. All that was to be seen was an orchestra struggling in vain with figuring designed for a far more moderate tempo, and in its midst 'one of the sergeant-majors of the baton' (*Taktprofessen*, as Liszt once called us) radiating fortissimo glory, whilst the puppets up there on the stage performed their ancient, outmoded, indifferent ballet steps without rhyme or reason, a performance not inclined to attract the attention of the most naïve of patrons nowadays. In short, this scene did not achieve the slightest effect.

This had to be explained by the critic. It did not occur to anybody to point to the real cause of the trouble, namely that the stage presentation was not in agreement with the author's intention, or rather, that not a single one of the author's intentions had been carried out; but the composer of *Lohengrin, Tristan, Meistersinger,* could not very well be accused of having made a complete mess of the *musical* revision of the first scene of *Tannhäuser.* What was to be done? A gentleman who had been particularly good at looking up dictionaries ever since his days at the Berlin Conservatoire at last discovered – in a Hebrew dictionary I imagine – a wonderful slogan, 'Stylistic difference'. In other words: the music of the new Venusberg scene, being 'Tristanesque', differed stylistically from that of the old *Tannhäuser.* Note that this applied only to the music! Not even the worthiest people have so far had the audacity to claim that the poetic and dramatic content of the Bacchanalia and of the following scene between Venus and Tannhäuser is out of keeping with the text of the old *Tannhäuser.* But since it may be presumed that nobody will argue that in what is still only the first scene of *Tannhäuser,* poet and musician (forgive the tautology) are for once out of step, or that the means of expression used by the 'musician' are inadequate to express the poetic idea, and considering that the revision of the text of the first scene is in complete stylistic agreement with the old *Tannhäuser* text, we are forced to conclude that the music of the first scene would agree in the same way with the music of the rest of *Tannhäuser* if only the performance were right, i.e. stylistically accurate, and if the dramatic intentions of the author were clearly realised on the stage, so that the conductor of the orchestra were suddenly to find himself in a position to achieve agreement with these dramatic intentions.

How incomparably beautiful was the effect of the Bacchanalia in Bayreuth!

In that performance there was complete agreement between the living gesture, embodied in a dance of formal Greek beauty, and its moving expression in the language of the modern orchestra, an agreement which constituted a stylistic achievement of the first order. The spectator was justified in saying of this first scene of *Tannhäuser* in the Bayreuth performance: this is *the* Venusberg and I have seen a true picture of Hellenic *joie de vivre.* In this scene, as at the end of the first act and during the second act, where he found himself in the chivalrous atmosphere of the medieval cult of the Virgin, and again at the beginning of the third act when he was deeply moved by the noblest expression we have of the mystic expectancy of Christianity, eye, ear and heart alike were fascinated by the glorious impression of a wonderful dramatic poem, fully brought to life by a performance in which all the means of expression used by the author – sculpture, painting, poetry and music – were equally matched. All 'stylistic differences' were suddenly dispelled like 'eitler Staub der Sonne'; let who will dare to assert after this that the Venusberg is out of place in Wagner's *Tannhäuser.*

The measured beauty of the ancient dance as manifested in Bayreuth naturally induced the orchestra to adopt a slower pace than usual, so that the rhythms of the dance ... played by the orchestra were imbued with the full significance required by the events on the stage. ... The Master says: 'The choice and designation of the right tempo, which allows us to determine immediately whether the conductor has understood the piece, enables good musicians, once they are familiar with the music, to find automatically the right way of playing it because the former involves the conductor's recognition of the latter'. This means that the right tempo is the decisive factor in a good performance which corresponds to the composer's intentions. Now, leaving aside for the moment the quality and quantity of orchestra and cast, the training of the orchestra, the individuality of the conductor, his lively or quiet manner, his sense of rhythm, etc., the following factors in the drama have a considerable effect on the tempo (and the performance) of the orchestra:

1. The singer's delivery; his temperament, his vocal talent, his feeling for significant declamation, his . . . ability to accentuate sharply.

Thus the moderate tempo of the chivalrous song to Venus, which I heard delivered correctly for the first time by the singer who played Tannhäuser in Bayreuth, is of such decisive importance for the tempo of the overture that the whole of the B major central scene of the allegro passage of the overture, if played at this speed, appears to be badly orchestrated, because the figuring in the viola and cello parts can no longer be carried out so that, as I have often found in other performances of the *Tannhäuser* overture, the melody and bass only and not the middle parts can be heard. Furthermore, the right tempo and delivery in Elisabeth's prayer, 'Ich fleh' für ihn', are of the utmost importance for the prelude to Act III, and those of her aria in Act II for the prelude to Act II.

2. The singer's ability to act, to express realistically on the stage the gestures described by the orchestra – and even *Tannhäuser* contains far more of these than one could have imagined before the Bayreuth performance. In connection with this point I should like to draw attention to the dramatic and musical delivery of the orchestral prelude; to the three songs of Tannhäuser to Venus, to Tannhäuser's 'Den Gott der Liebe sollst Du preisen' in the duet of the second act; I would remind you of the wonderful co-ordination of gesture and its musical expression before the words of Venus, 'Wie hätt ich das erworben'; before Elisabeth's, 'So stehet auf' and 'Verzeiht wenn ich nicht weiss was ich beginne', before the Landgraf's words 'Dich treff ich hier in dieser Halle', and 'So sie's! Was der Gesang so wunderbares'.

All these moments and many others, such as the Landgraf's action before the words 'Ein furchtbares Verbrechen ward begangen,' made an indescribable impression in Bayreuth because of the exactitude of dramatic execution and the co-ordination between orchestra and stage.

I do not suppose that any of the spectators, who followed the dramatic development attentively, noticed while watching the incredibly gentle movement amongst the troubadours in the first act just before Wolfram's song, 'Als du in kühnem Sange uns bestrittest,' how much the conductor had slackened the pace of the short orchestral ritornello, or how the great breadth of orchestral playing during Elisabeth's miming in Act III seemed natural because the singer who played the part of Elisabeth was able to carry out her movements in an atmosphere of dignified calm in agreement with the orchestra.

3. The size of the stage: in the pilgrims' chorus, for example (the pilgrims, by the way, should remain in motion and should *not*, as is usual in 'cleverly' directed theatres, go down on their knees before the statue of the Virgin which detracts attention from the main action) and in Elisabeth's exit in the third act.

4. Dramatic and musical training of the chorus, and size of the chorus: in connection with this I would remind you of the wonderful diction and rhythmic perfection of the welcoming chorus of Act II, which enabled the conductor to attain the right tempo and playing of the march without the chorus which precedes it; further, of the excellently enunciated pilgrims' chorus in the third act which (according to Wagner) is so important for the phrasing of the first few bars of the overture; finally of the 'enthusiastic rising' of the whole assembly of knights (end of Act II) at 'Mit ihnen sollst Du wallen,' after the Landgraf's words to Tannhäuser pointing the way to salvation. The dramatic realisation of this incident as achieved in Bayreuth fully justifies Mottl's considerable increase in pace at this point.

I should like to mention, as an interesting exception, the considerably slower tempo of the prelude to Act III (crotchet = 50) as compared with the tempo of Tannhäuser's narration (crotchet = 60). The explanation of this is to be found in the epic character of the latter, in contrast to the actual event which the prelude, marked by the master himself 'Tannhäuser's pilgrimage', is meant to describe.

The examples mentioned above show how difficult it is to play the purely instrumental symphonic parts of the *Tannhäuser* score. In the *Tannhäuser* overture, and the preludes to the second and third acts, the conductor is faced as in none of the later works with the task of uniting a number of elements often diametrically opposed by the composer into a symphonic whole. As I have already indicated above, the events on the stage pre-determine in the overture the tempo and delivery of the pilgrims' chorus, of the Bacchanalia, of the song to Venus and the latter's song to Tannhäuser, 'Geliebter, komm'. As for the prelude to the second act, the fundamental tempo of which is determined by the aria of Elisabeth, the deciding factors are, apart from the subjects of this aria, the radiant motif from the finale of Act I announcing Tannhäuser's arrival and the curse of Venus, 'Suche Dein Heil und finde es nie,' immediately following on the pert violin passage which I imagine expresses the jubilant spirit of the hunt ('Die Erde hat ihn wieder'); similarly, for the prelude to Act III, it is the motifs of the pilgrims' choruses, of Elisabeth imploring and dying a sacrificial death in part immediately contrasted with the Pope theme, the Pope's curse and the motifs of the repentant Tannhäuser which are all-important.

Only a conductor of genius like Felix Mottl could succeed in bringing out these sharp contrasts with the clarity postulated by the action on the stage and in welding them into complete unity by the artistry of his transitions and the restrained modifications of his tempo. He was assisted by the festival orchestra: a body of artists who combine with complete mastery of all technical difficulties that intuition which alone enables the conductor to support the singers and the dramatic action, and to give full expression to the feelings aroused by complete impregnation with the demands of the drama.

The prominence of the solo element is a peculiarity of the *Tannhäuser* score which, partly still imbued with Weber's spirit, so frequently poses to individual players the most difficult of problems concerning sensitive delivery and delicate phrasing. Only a conductor steeped in the poetic content of the drama like Felix Mottl could, assisted by the members of the orchestra, almost conjure up before the eye of the listener in his rendering of the clarinet melody in the overture or the oboe solo passages in the preludes to Acts II and III the very characters whose fate, as portrayed on the stage, was to compel the sympathy of the listener and to move and elate him profoundly. Only an artist with Mottl's intensity of feeling could have had the audacity to take the tempo of the 6/4 bar in the prelude to Act III as slowly as he did, because he sensed that his own fervour would inspire even the brass with the strength to play the 'Pope Scene' even at this length: *fff sustained*, as prescribed by the Master. . . .

It is very difficult to define in words impressions made by a work of art. . . . But very few people were privileged last year as I was to attend the festival rehearsals, thus being able to listen to the performances themselves well-prepared for and receptive to all the subtleties and beautiful passages which demand, for their full appreciation, that our eyes and ears, spoiled as they are by a hundred years of indifferent performances, must first be carefully attuned. It often grieved me to see that many who were unable to attend more than one performance, without having seen the preceding rehearsal, were almost dazed at the idea of missing so much of what they were accustomed to (no matter how inept that had been), whilst they were not yet ready on the other hand to appreciate fully the wonderful phenomenon which was being enacted before their eyes in all its purity of style: the rebirth of the genuine *Tannhäuser*. The opera *Tannhäuser* had been resurrected as a drama and, blinded by its glory, the 'laws' of the opera, the common tempi and the traditional canonic age of Elisabeth and many other spectres slunk back into the obscurity of their respective Hof- and Stadt-Theatres.

Perhaps this little pamphlet will at least succeed in drawing the attention of men 'of good will' who will make their pilgrimage to Bayreuth this summer to those things which matter most in a performance of *Tannhäuser*: not to individual virtuoso achievements (which are usually lacking in genuine virtuosity), not to 'great voices', but to purity and perfection of style as indicated above. Nor shall I ever desist from the hope that men will eventually discover why we go to Bayreuth and why festivals are organised there. We must just have a little patience, because in Germany everything takes a little longer than elsewhere.

The Elisabeth at Bayreuth in 1891 and 1894 was Pauline de Ahna, whom Strauss married at Weimar on 10 September 1894. Pauline was a demanding person and did not get on with Cosima. She gave up the stage after her marriage. Strauss returned to Bayreuth to conduct Parsifal *in 1933, to fill the gap when Toscanini dropped out.*

Strauss wrote the next passage in 1912 for the Hamburger Fremdenblatt *– the copyright of* Parsifal *was due to expire in 1913 and Bayreuth wished to have it extended (in fact, it was put on in New York in 1903 in spite of Cosima's legal action against Conried, Director of the Metropolitan Opera).*

For me there is only one consideration in the *Parsifal* question – respect for the will of a genius.

Unfortunately, it is not those who are concerned with the preservation and refinement of our culture who have the power to decide the *Parsifal* performing-rights question, but mere lawyers and politicians whose horizon does not reach to the understanding of the unlimited rights of spiritual ownership.

I was present myself at the eight-day deliberation of the German Parliament where the representatives of the German people, with few exceptions, debated the material concerning the copyright privileges and their duration, with enviable ignorance. I myself heard a Mr Eugen Richter, through shameless lies, drive the rights of two hundred poor German composers into the ground in favour of two hundred thousand German inn-keepers.

Things will not change as long as the stupid general right to vote remains and as long as votes are counted and not weighed, as long as, for example, the vote of one Richard Wagner does not count as a hundred thousand and those of one hundred thousand servants as one.

Then I would perhaps no longer hear remarks (even in the Goethe-league) about the rights of the German nation which is supposedly authorised to plunder, thirty years after his death, the Genius which it ridiculed and banished during his lifetime and to prostitute his work on the smallest of the provincial stages.

A few of us will protest in vain and in two years time the German philistine will be able to hear *Parsifal* for fifty pfennigs on a Sunday afternoon between lunch and dinner instead of going to the cinema or the music-hall.

Is it any wonder that the French and Italians still consider us barbarians in all questions of culture?

Richard Strauss's polemic on the question of the copyright of Parsifal *is understandable – he was a creative artist himself and doubtless wished to protect his rights concerning his own compositions; his assiduous business deals over their performance are legendary. Indeed, in 1898, he had set about forming the Guild of German Composers to protect their rights by law.*

The other side of the case, at least as far as performing Parsifal *outside of Bayreuth is concerned, was put by Shaw, writing in* The World *on 25 March 1891:*

For the life of me I cannot see why the recent suggestion that the score of Parsifal may find a place on [the conductor's] desk at Covent Garden should be scouted as 'profane'. I leave out the question the old-fashioned objection, founded on the theory that all play-houses and singing-halls are abodes of sin. But when a gentleman writes to the papers to declare that 'a performance of Parsifal, apart from the really religious surroundings of the Bayreuth Threatre, would almost amount to profanity' and, again, that 'in the artificial glare of an English opera-house it would be a blasphemous mockery' I must take the liberty of describing to him the 'really religious surroundings' since he admits that he has never seen them for himself. In front of the Bayreuth Theatre, then, on the right, there is a restaurant. On the left there is a still larger restaurant and a sweetstuff stall. At the back, a little way up the hill, there is a cafe. Between the cafe and the theatre is a shed in which 'artificial glare' is manufactured for the inside of the theatre; and the sound of that great steam-engine throbs all over the Fichtelgebirge on still nights.

Between the acts the three restaurants are always full, not of devout Wagnerites (The Meister advocated vegetarianism), but of Spiers & Pondites, who do just what they will do at the Star and Garter when my Festspielhaus on Richmond Hill is finished. The little promenade in front of the theatre is crowded with globe-trotters, chiefly American and vagabond English, quite able to hold their own in point of vulgarity, frivolity, idle curiosity, and other perfectly harmless characteristics, with the crowd in the foyer at Covent Garden or the Paris Opera. When they have seen every celebrity present pass and repass some twenty times, they become heavily bored, and are quite excited at seeing a small contingent from the orchestra, with the familiar German-band equipment of seedy overcoat and brass instrument, assemble under the portico and blare out a fragment of some motive from whatever music-drama is 'on' that evening. This is the signal for entering the theatre, but nobody moves, as everyone knows that it is only the third blast that means business, when you do not happen to be at a distance – in which case, however, you hear nothing, unless you are dead to windward, with a strong gale blowing. Inside, the 'honorable ladies' are requested by placard to remove their towering head-gear; and not one of them is sufficiently impressed with the really religious surroundings to do so. Then the famous 'Bayreuth hush' is secured by a volley of angry sh-sh-sh-es, started by the turning down of the lights; and the act begins. What sanctity there is in all this that is not equally attainable at Boulogne or Bayswater remains to be explained.

Mr Charles Dowdeswell's position on the subject is safer than that of his fellow-correspondent. He claims special sanctity, not for Bayreuth, but for Parsifal, and says (what is perfectly true) that the Bayreuth Festspielhaus is the only existing theatre in which justice can be done to the work. But as to his practical conclusion – that for the immense majority here who cannot afford to go to Bayreuth it is better that they should never see any performance of Parsifal at all than see one even as good as the Covent Garden Meistersinger – no practical Wagnerite critic can endorse it. Let us build a Wagner Theatre, by all means, as soon as possible.

Richard Strauss's mature views on the stage production of Wagner's operas are found in a book entitled Betrachtungen und Errinerungen, *published in 1949; the following essay was written about ten years earlier, when the composer was in his mid-seventies.*

REMARKS ON RICHARD WAGNER'S WORK IN GENERAL
AND ON THE FESTSPIELHAUS AT BAYREUTH

As Richard Wagner began his great reforming work on the re-birth and fulfilment of the German and Christian Mythos and, as he explained in his learned writings, he found opera in such a state that with a few exceptions (Gluck's *Orfeo*

and *Iphigenia, Fidelio, Figaro, Freischütz*) the music of these classics far surpassed the paltry novels which were set to music. It was natural that, because of
his own great dramatic talent, he was drawn to the forming of the actual drama
itself and to the ancient classical dramas in which the chorus commented on and
interpreted the action and his inspiration was to replace this with the orchestra of
the symphonists. This is only partly the case. It no longer requires proof that the
range of expression of the modern orchestra (especially since the days of Weber
and Berlioz) is completely at variance with that of the commenting and explaining chorus in a tragedy by Aeschylus or Sophocles.

Not only does the modern orchestra paint in the background, not only does it
serve to explain and remind, but it provides the content itself, reveals the ideal
and embodies an inmost truth. It seems understandable that, in view of the
advanced stage of development music had reached by the time of Beethoven, the
talented musician should almost take for granted the role of the orchestra in
opera – but that he should have felt that everything on the stage had to be
recreated if the complete work of art which he envisaged (already foreshadowed
in the writings of Goethe and Schiller) was to equal the masterpieces of these
heroes of the past, or even excel them – with the assistance of music. Therefore
the Master was more concerned with the drama itself – and its realisation – than
with the orchestra, of whose miraculous powers its creator was much less aware
than we are.

Hence the concept of a covered, invisible orchestra which I consider to be
justified and beautifully effective only in *Parsifal* and, after my own experiences
at Bayreuth from 1889 to 1894, in *Tristan* and the *Ring*. Admittedly voice and
word are used to better effect in the Festspielhaus than in a theatre with a visible
and frequently raised orchestra. But many of the inexhaustible riches of the score
are lost at Bayreuth – I need only remind you of *Meistersinger*. And in which,
after all, is a civilised audience more interested – in the opera and singers? Or the
orchestra? I think the latter. Nor do I believe that I am speaking solely as a
listener and spectator – when I have seen *Tristan* three times I know the
dramatic action and poem and from then on the things which interest me on the
stage are a good new production or new singers. The orchestra in *Tristan* or
Meistersinger on the other hand, no matter how carefully and frequently I study
the score at home, reveals something new every time. I suppose I have heard
Parsifal and the *Ring* some fifty times each (usually when I have been conducting them) yet I cannot have enough of the orchestral part and I discover in it new
beauties and I am grateful for new revelations every time. The directors who
consider a brightly-lit orchestra pit and a brilliantly-illuminated rostrum detract
from cleverly-lit stage-settings are therefore against me. It does not disturb me to
see before me an orchestra playing well and a conductor who really leads and
inspires it (he must not be too demonstrative) if it means that not a single wonderful detail in the magical score of *Meistersinger* is lost, and that I am in a position
to enjoy complete harmony between orchestra and stage such as I have been fortunate enough to experience at various houses under Kraus, Blech and Böhm. I
know there are many musical people who share this opinion.

So let us continue to make pilgrimages to Bayreuth to hear *Tristan* and *Parsifal* in tribute to the great Master and to see and hear the works in the form he expressly wished. But on the whole I am for the old Italian-style theatres! With of course an orchestra of eighty to a hundred players – sixteen first and sixteen second violins, twelve violas and cellos and eight double basses.

Bernard Shaw (1894)

The Festival of 1894 saw Bernard Shaw at Bayreuth once more. There are two letters about the Festival from Shaw to his friend and fellow-journalist, W. T. Stead (1849–1912). Stead, child of the manse and social reformer, had had himself prosecuted for procuring a child prostitute to prove to complacent authorities that such a thing was possible. Stead had a deep distrust and dislike of the theatre, although, it appears, he had never been in one. He went down with the Titanic.

29 Fitzroy Square W
4th July 1894

Dear Mr Stead

What a man you are – to talk of making a round of the theatres, as if they were brothels! Why, how many years do you suppose it takes to learn to see and hear in a theatre? However, if you begin, you had better begin with the most serious attempt yet made to treat the theatre as a temple – I mean, of course, Bayreuth. I have just had an offer of tickets for the first four performances this year at par (£1 apiece) – July 19th Parsifal, 20th Lohengrin, 22nd Tannhäuser & 23 Parsifal again (it is the regular thing to do Parsifal twice). Will you take these tickets if I can secure them for you? Remember, in Parsifal the Holy Ghost descends and the hero's feet are washed with a woman's tears and dried with her hair. Ober Ammergau was a miserable, genteelified, Sir Noel Patonesque Sunday School piece of illustrated Bibleism: Bayreuth is very different.

What do you say?

yrs sincerely
G. Bernard Shaw

29 Fitzroy Square W
8th July 1894

My dear Stead

This is most noble of you; I believe you wont regret it. I enclose the four tickets which were purchased on the 9th March last, and were the best then left available. The theatre holds about 1000 people; and only one of your seats (652) is far enough back to be more than half way from the stage to the royal boxes, which bring up the rear. All the seats are equally good as far as being in full view of the stage is concerned; and the acoustic conditions are perfect; but the very high numbers are the least desirable because of the distance from the stage.

Your being 'an utter barbarian' is a great advantage, Wagner stands or falls by the success of his appeal to 'the folks' – that is to the unsophisticatedly receptive natural man. If you want to read up on the subject, read Wagner's 'Communication to My Friends' – the part concerning Lohengrin and Tannhäuser – translated in W. Ashton Ellis's Wagner's Prose Works in English, Vol I, Kegan Paul, Trubner &c. If you have any difficulty getting it from the London Library or wherever you borrow books, let me know & I will see whether I cannot hunt you up a copy. Parsifal you had better deliver yourself up to without further preparation than reading the text. You can get the books of all the operas in the Bayreuth shops for about a shilling – English translations.

To secure lodgings, write to the Wohnungs Committee, Bayreuth, describing what you want & what days you will arrive and quit. The office is in the railway station. When you get out of the train you give your name at this office; and they hand you a card with full particulars of where you are to go. For a clean room in the main street, high up over a shop, I have paid eighteen shillings for a week, including breakfast. As you can get the same accommodation in Berlin for a month for about the same money, you will be highly welcome on these terms. Of course, there are hotels, if you prefer them.

You wont want to arrive in Bayreuth until the morning of the 19th nor stay there after the fall of the curtain on the 23rd unless you go Wagner mad, and make frantic bids for all the subsequent performances. I write all this in case I should be unable to hit you off by a visit.

The season is pretty heavy on my time just now. I am going to drop out of The World now that Yates is gone.

Next winter the greatest music critic in Europe will be silent on the subject unless he gets an extremely handsome inducement to go on.

yours sincerely

G. Bernard Shaw

P.S. Let me know if I can give or get you any further information.

Shaw left for Bayreuth on 16 July and took in Darmstadt, Würzburg and Nuremberg on his way there. He returned by way of Ostend and Dover and arrived back on 26 July. His reviews appeared in The World *on Wednesday 1 and Wednesday 8 August 1894. A number of irrelevant passages are omitted.*

When I ran across to Bayreuth the other day I was fully aware that the cost of my trip would have been better spent in bringing a German critic to England. And I greatly regret that this article is not written in German, and for a German paper, since it is now evident that, as far as any musical awakening and impulse can come from one country to another, it must come for the present from England to Bayreuth and not from Bayreuth to England.

First, as to the wonderful Bayreuth orchestra, to the glories of which we have been taught to look with envious despair. I beg to observe here, in the most uncompromising manner, that the Bayreuth orchestra, judged by London standards, is not a first-rate orchestra, but a very carefully worked-up second-rate one. The results of the careful working-up are admirable: the smoothness, the perfect sostenuto, the unbroken flow of tone testify to an almost perfect orchestral execution in passages which lend themselves to such treatment. But there are two factors in the effect produced by an orchestra: the quality of execution, and the quality of the instruments on which the execution is done. How much this may vary may be judged by the wide range of prices for musical instruments, even leaving out the scarcity values reached by certain exceptionally desirable old fiddles and bassoons. Take, for example, the cheapest and most popular wind instrument in the orchestra – the cornet. Heaven knows how low the prices of the vilest specimens of cornet may run! but between cheapest orchestrally presentable cornet and a first-rate one by a good English maker the variation in price, without accounting for electro-plating or decoration of any sort, is from about thirty-five shillings to eight or ten pounds. Fiddles range from a few shillings to the large sums any orchestral player can afford to give for them: and the scale of prices for wood wind-instruments varies from one to three figures.

Now, if there were such a thing as an international musical parliament, I should certainly agitate for a return of the prices of the instruments used in the Bayreuth and Crystal Palace orchestras respectively: and I should be surprised if the German total came to as much as half the English one.

In the brass especially, the peculiar dull rattle of inferior thin metal at once strikes an ear accustomed to the smooth, firm tone of the more expensive instruments used in England. There is a difference of brightness too; but I leave that out of the question, as possibly due to the difference between Continental and English pitch, a difference which is all to the bad for us. In judging the wood wind I am on less certain ground, since the tone is so greatly affected by the way in which the reed is cut. The strings, as compared with ours, are deficient in power and richness: and even in the case of the horns, which we somehow or other cannot play, whilst the Germans can, the tone is much rougher and more nearly allied to that of the Alpine cowhorn than what may be called the standard tone here. The inferiority of the German orchestra to the English is not an inferiority in natural capacity, but an inferiority in the current national standard of musical beauty . . . that this inferiority is no new thing, and was well weighed by Wagner himself is clear from the stress which he laid upon the superiority of the instruments used by our Philharmonic band.

All the other points he so strenuously urged on conductors have been mastered at Bayreuth . . . but the material of it all – the brute physical sounds of the instruments which are so ably handled – still remains comparatively cheap and ugly: and the worst of it is that no German seems to care. As far as I can make out, the payment of an extra five pounds to an instrument maker for the sake of a finer tone would strike both conductor and player as an unreasonable waste of money.

And yet this German indifference to the final degrees of excellence in instrumental tone is conscientiousness itself compared to their atrocious insensibility to the beauty of the human voice and the graces of a fine vocal touch. The opening performance of Parsifal this season was, from the purely musical point of view, as far as the principal singers were concerned, simply an abomination. The bass howled, the tenor bawled, the baritone sang flat, and the soprano, when she condescended to sing at all, and did not merely shout her words, screamed. except in the one unscreamable song of Herzeleide's death, in which she subsided into commonplaceness. The bass, who was rather flustered, perhaps from nervousness, was especially brutal in his treatment of the music of Gurnemanz; and it struck me that if he had been a trombone-player in the band instead of a singer, Levi of Munich, the conductor, would have remonstrated. Accordingly, having the opportunity of exchanging a few words with Levi afterwards, I expressed my opinion about the bass in question. Levi appeared surprised, and, declaring that the singer had the best bass voice in Germany, challenged me to find him anyone who could sing the part better, to which I could only respond with sufficient emphasis by offering to sing it better myself, upon which he gave me up as a lunatic. It had to be explained to him that I was accustomed to the 'smooth' singing popular in England. That settled the question for the Bayreuth conductor. Good singing there is merely 'glatt', obviously an effeminate, silly, superficial quality, unsuited to the utterances of primeval heroes. The notion that this sort of smoothness is one of the consequences of aiming at beauty of tone and singing in tune is apparently as strange in Germany as the notion that it is more truly virile to sing like a man than a bullock.

It is true that the German singers at Bayreuth do not know how to sing: they shout; and you can see them make a vigorous stoop and lift with their shoulders, like coalheavers, when they have a difficult note to tackle, a pianissimo on any note above the stave being impossible to them. . . .

Sitting, as I am today, in a Surrey farmhouse with the sky overcast, and a big fire burning to keep me from shivering, it seems to me that it must be at least four or five months since I was breathing balmy airs in the scented pine woods above Bayreuth. If only I could see the sun for five minutes I could better recall what I have to write about. As it is, I seem to have left it all behind with the other vanities of the season. I no longer feel any impulse to describe Lohengrin or Tannhäuser . . . or to draw morals for Frau Wagner. . . .

What I feel bound to record concerning the Bayreuth Lohengrin – remember that this is the first time the work has been done there, and probably the first time it has been done thoroughly at all, if we except the earliest attempt under Liszt at Weimar – is that its stage framework is immensely more entertaining, convincing and natural than it has ever seemed before. This is mainly because the stage-management is so good, especially with regard to the chorus. In Lohengrin there are only two comparatively short scenes in which the chorus is not present and in constant action.

The opera therefore suffers fearfully on ordinary occasions from the surprising power of the average chorister to destroy all stage illusion the moment he shambles on the scene with his blue jaws, his reach-me-down costume, his foolish single gesture, his embarrassed eye on the prompter, and his general air of being in an opera chorus because he is fit for nothing better. At Covent Garden he is, in addition, generally an old acquaintance: it is not only that he is destroying the illusion of the opera you are looking at, but that he has destroyed the illusion of nearly all the operas you have ever seen. . . .

As to the ladies of our opera chorus, they have to be led by competent, sensible women: and as women at present can only acquire these qualities by a long experience as mothers of large families, our front row hardly helps the romance of the thing more than the men do. . . . A physically and artistically superior class of singers who regard it as an honour to sing at Bayreuth, even in the chorus, certainly help the illusion as far as the Saxon and Brabantine warriors in Lohengrin are concerned: but this difference in raw material is as nothing compared with the difference made by the intelligent activity of the stage manager. One example will suffice. Those who know the score of Lohengrin are aware that in the finale to the first act there is a section, usually omitted in performance, in which the whole movement is somewhat unexpectedly repeated in a strongly contrasted key, the modulation being unaccountable from the point of view of the absolute musician, as it is not at all needed as a relief to the principal key. At Bayreuth its purpose is made clear. After the combat with Telramund and the solo for Elsa which serves musically as the exposition of the theme of the finale, the men, greatly excited and enthusiastic over the victory of the strange knight, range themselves in a sort of wheel formation, of which Lohengrin is the centre, and march round him as they take up the finale from Elsa in the principal key. When the modulation comes, the women, in white robes, break into this triumphal circle, displace the men, and march round Elsa in the same way, the striking change of key being thus accompanied by a correspondingly striking change on the stage, one of the incidents of which is a particularly remarkable kaleidoscoping of the scheme of colour produced by the dresses. Here you have a piece of stage management of the true Wagnerian kind, combining into one stroke a dramatic effect the value of which was proved by the roar of excitement which burst forth as the curtains closed in. . . .

Walter Crane

Walter Crane (1845–1918) was an artist associated with William Morris and the Socialist League. He became Principal of the Royal College of Art and, although he painted many water-colours, he is chiefly remembered for his illustrations in children's books. His reminiscences include two vignettes, 'A German Official' and 'Pilgrims to Baiyreuth', as well as the following description of his visit to the Festival:

For our summer holiday the following year (1894) we had planned a trip to Baireuth [*sic*], at the suggestion of our friend Rowley, and a tour was arranged to include visits to many other places by the way. We went by the Hook of Holland route to Rotterdam, and thence to Cologne, and up the Rhine by steamer, and from Mainz and Aschaffenburg across Germany, making a rapid journey to Rothenburg, where, leaving the main line at Steinach, we made a stop of a night or two, enjoying that delightful old town, a unique example of a medieval city, and apparently untouched since the sixteenth century. It had been a happy hunting-ground with German artists for some time, I believe, and was becoming known to those of other nationalities. The stream of English pilgrims to the Wagner festivals at Baireuth had lately discovered it, and our hostelry, the 'Goldener Hirsch', was full of tourists. The quiet charm of the place, complete within its old walls and embattled gates, was very great. Rothenburg reminded one of the fortified towns so often seen in the backgrounds of Albert Dürer's designs, and carried one back to the Middle Ages, the timber-built covered warder's walk inside the walls being complete. The streets were lit at night by lanterns at intervals slung over the middle of the roadway, and a woman lamplighter attended to them. The inhabitants seemed unspoilt and guileless. The little children would come up and trustfully put their hands in ours, smiling.

We were sorry to leave so pleasant and interesting a place, but we were booked to hear Wagner at Baireuth, and time would not allow a longer stay.

We touched at Nuremberg, my second visit, paying our duty at its shrines, but it looked comparatively modern after Rothenburg, save the great towers, but even these had been darkened in the factory smoke.

Baireuth was reached at last, where an *appartement* had been secured beforehand, and we duly made our way with a crowd of visitors of different nationalities to the temple on the hill – the Wagnerian opera-house, with its surrounding restaurants; for music, in spite of its charms, is exhausting, and between the acts the audience were glad to dine.

It was an ideal way to enjoy the opera. One strolled or drove up in the afternoon, and leisurely took one's seat in the vast theatre – the seats rising tier on tier from the stage. By degrees the audience poured in and filled them up. Only a faint glimmer of light came from where the orchestra was concealed in front of the stage. Silence fell on the vast audience, only broken by the occasional snapping of fastenings of opera-glass cases. This year only the three operas were given – *Lohengrin* was the first, and I recall the wonderful effect of the first bars of the overture on the violins – the far-off swan-music – a delicate vibration in the air, at first, rather than a sound – stealing on the silence in the darkness in a way that reminded one of a creeping mist over the lowlands, or the silver windings of a river flowing ever nearer, until it reached one's feet in full flood.

Truly it was a wonderful orchestra, which had the unity of a single instrument.

I was not struck by any artistic superiority in the treatment of the scenery or the dresses in this opera and Lohengrin did not look sufficiently romantic.

Tannhäuser was better mounted, and there were some rather rich and impressive scenes in Venusburg, the chorus acting with much more spirit and realism than usual, and the pilgrim scene was good.

Parsifal, then only performed at Baireuth, was also very impressive in parts, such as in the cathedral scene, with slow march of the knights and the illumination of the Holy Grail, but others were stagey and unconvincing, and the hero was unfortunately insignificant-looking, someone even suggesting that in his curious brown armour in one of the scenes he resembled a water-rat. The music was wonderful, of course.

Between the acts there was a long break, and the audience all streamed out – to be recalled when the performance re-commenced by a fanfare of trumpets sounded from the main entrance. One was at liberty to stroll off into the woods near by, or to fortify oneself for the next act at the restaurant.

During the progress of the opera, an American lady was overheard to remark to her companion, 'Em'ly, this excitement is breaking me up fast!'

- PILGRIMS - TO - BAIYREUTH -

National Viewpoints

IT SHOULD SURPRISE very few people that such an ardent Wagnerian as Anton Bruckner was to be found on the Bayreuth scene as early as 1873, three whole years before the Festivals got under way. He worshipped Wagner it is true – but mere worship of the Master was no passport to Wahnfried while Wagner was alive. In fact, Bruckner had already made the acquaintance of Wagner during the time of the *Tristan* productions at Munich in 1865, and eight years later, in 1873, he felt able to write to him from Karlsbad, where he was taking the cure, asking if the Master would look over and pass judgment on some of his compositions. Bruckner valued Wagner's opinion more than anything and, failing to get a reply to his letter, he went in person to Bayreuth in September and presented himself at the Wagner residence with the scores of two symphonies – the second and the yet unfinished third. Wagner took in the scores for consideration and asked Bruckner to come back and see him in a few days' time.

Bruckner returned as arranged; he was well received by Wagner, drank several glasses of deceptively strong Weihenstephaner beer (the day being warm and Wagner being hospitable) and was so overcome, both by the effects of the drink and Wagner's interest in his work, that when he left he had completely forgotten to which of his symphonies Wagner had accepted the dedication. There was no other way out than to ask Wagner himself; Gustav Kietz, who had been present making a bust of the Master, could offer little help to Bruckner, but thought it might perhaps have been the piece with the trumpet tune. So Bruckner sent a note, 'The D minor Symphony, with the opening trumpet tune?' to which came the reply 'Yes, yes, warmest greetings!' This opening of the Symphony greatly appealed to Wagner and, whenever he met the composer in later years, he would greet him, 'Ha! Bruckner, the trumpet tune!' A more formal acceptance came via Cosima soon afterwards, in which Wagner thanked the forty-nine-year-old Austrian for 'the beautiful gift and the honourable and moving dedication'. Cosima's diary makes little of this, merely recording the visit of the 'poor organist Bruckner' from Vienna.

Ten years after this meeting, not long before he died, Wagner gave his opinion. 'I know only one who approaches Beethoven and that is Bruckner.' In spite of his high opinion of Bruckner's work, his friendliness towards the man and his often-repeated assurances that his music would survive and be performed, Wagner gave him little practical help to this end. However, Bruckner for his part considered that he owed everything to Wagner, remembering perhaps the time when he first heard *Tannhäuser* in Linz and decided to devote his life thenceforth to composition.

Bruckner returned to Bayreuth for the Festival in 1876 and in 1882, and on both occasions he was honoured by Wagner's special attention and favour. After the Master's death Bruckner continued to visit the Festivals regularly until 1892. He became a familiar figure about Bayreuth and there are many anecdotes about his quaint behaviour there. Friedrich Klose, the Swiss composer who eventually became his pupil, recalled how he came to meet Bruckner, forty years his senior, in Angermann's Inn after the first performance of *Parsifal* in 1882. Bruckner offered to show the young man the sights of Bayreuth the next day. It was a day, Klose relates, he would not be likely to forget. First there was a tour of the Festspielhaus, and here Bruckner blundered into a rehearsal; pausing only to invite the assembly of Flower Maidens to visit him in Vienna, to their general astonishment, he began to show off the stage and all its marvels. Expecting tips they did not get, the stage-hands regarded this behaviour with aggrieved hostility. Outside the Festspielhaus, Bruckner began counting, compulsively, all the architectural features of the building – the windows, the panels in between them and so on – one after the other, even going back later to make sure for himself that both sides of the house were the same. Young Klose was quite dismayed, especially when Bruckner repeated the process at every other building they visited. After taking in the Margrave's Opera House in the centre of the town, the pair ended up in a church; by this time Klose confesses he was thinking more of his midday meal than religion. However, the sacrifice was well worth it, for Bruckner seated himself at the organ and delivered one of his celebrated mighty improvisations. After this a belated meal was considered but only when they had been on a circuit of the Hofgarten and inspected all the statues and Bruckner had had each one named for him, pausing for an unlikely encounter with a young lady with whom the composer claimed an imaginary acquaintance, only then did they find their way to an accommodating household for the lunch it was far too late for any restaurant to serve. Klose, faint with hunger and anticipating a solid Bavarian meal to revive him, was quite astounded when just as he was about to fall on his food at last, Bruckner let out a cry and hauled him up from the table and out of the house. Somebody, it seemed, had made a disparaging remark about Wagner in Bruckner's hearing and that was enough – he would never eat under a roof where such blasphemy prevailed!

Bruckner's compulsive counting (a habit that also affected Dr Johnson at one stage) is said by those conversant with these matters to indicate an anxious disposition. Maybe poor Bruckner had good cause to be so – on one occasion he was made the butt of a cruel practical joke by a female harpist and had to make a premature departure from the Festival town. The residents of Bayreuth, who had not yet developed an indifference to every degree of odd behaviour among their guests, would shake their heads in wonderment as Bruckner took himself off to Wahnfried, where he would station himself for hours on end, gazing up at the windows from the garden. For his visits to the Bayreuth Festival Bruckner would dress in trousers of incredible bagginess, a wide floppy hat and a well-worn jacket – but, in case he should happen upon Wagner in the street, he carried a new tailcoat over his arm. If the encounter came about Bruckner would slip into a doorway and change into the more festive garb to greet the Master.

Bruckner wrote to Hans von Wolzogen telling of his last meeting with Wagner and that he regarded memories of him as his most precious bequest. He ends the letter 'till up there!' This sentiment was taken up by Otto Bohler in a little silhouette, showing Bruckner being welcomed into heaven by Wagner, surrounded by other German masters, while Bach plays the organ in the background.

The true depth of Bruckner's feelings for Wagner may be measured by the end of the Adagio of his Seventh Symphony; here is eloquence that words cannot match.

Bruckner returned to Bayreuth in 1884 for the Festival and also to pay a visit to Liszt. Two years later, when *Tristan* was first performed at Bayreuth, Bruckner arrived just in time to accompany that master to the Festspielhaus for the last time. A few days afterwards Bruckner delivered his funeral oration for Liszt in the form of one of his colossal improvisations on the organ, using themes taken from *Parsifal*.

With his subsequent visits to the Festival in 1888, 1891 and 1892 Bruckner saw all of Wagner's works that had so far been given at Bayreuth – the exceptions were *Der fliegende Holländer* and *Lohengrin* which were first performed there in 1901 and 1894 respectively.

Of all great musicians Bruckner, with the possible single exception of Liszt, had the closest connections with the Master of Bayreuth, and yet the music of Bruckner and Wagner is as disparate as the men themselves. It was Tovey who first suggested that, in place of 'bleeding chunks' of Wagner, orchestras in concert halls should play the symphonies of Bruckner. Is this a fair substitution? Are Bruckner's symphonies merely Wagnerian music-drama with the voices left out as this suggestion would seem to imply? The form in its entirety and most of the content differ greatly except to the most casual listener; stage dramas (even with some symphonic development of the musical matter) contrast strongly with the classical form of the symphony (no matter how 'romantic' the nature of the content); Wagner's scores call for an array of special instruments and battery of percussion – Bruckner used the developed 'classical' orchestra augmented only by a quartet of Wagner tubas on three occasions and two cymbal strokes (one of doubtful authenticity) on others. These quite obvious differences, a few amongst many, outweigh any superficial similarities. In addition, Bruckner appears to have been uninterested in much of the stage action in Wagner's dramas – he was shocked by the behaviour of the principal protagonists in the middle acts of both *Tristan* and *Parsifal* and did not bother to unravel for himself the convoluted story of the *Ring* – it was the music alone, not the drama, that held his interest. He could be seen at performances sitting with closed eyes, or in a seat which offered no view of the stage. He is reported as having once asked, 'Why do they burn Brünnhilde at the end of *Walküre*?'

Unlike many other composers who fell under the spell of Wagner at Bayreuth, Bruckner possessed sufficient musical individuality to withstand the potent influences at play there. If Bruckner is to be classed as an artistic legatee of Wagner, his is a spiritual inheritance rather than a musical one.

*   *   *

The music of Hugo Wolf, by contrast, shows considerable influence of Wagner –
yet, unlike Bruckner, he knew the Master hardly at all, and his meetings with
Wagner were too brief to show little except the temperament of the impetuous
young student. During Wagner's visit to Vienna in the winter of 1875–6 to raise
money for Bayreuth and look out for new singers, the Director of the Opera,
Franz Janner, persuaded him to participate in the preparation of productions of
Tannhäuser and *Lohengrin*, even though he flatly refused to conduct them
himself. For the first *Tannhäuser* Hugo Wolf, then fifteen years old, queued for
four hours for a standing place in the gallery. He later recalled that he applauded
the performance until his hands hurt and called out 'Bravo! Wagner, bravissimo,
Wagner!' so loudly that people turned to look at him instead of the famous composer. A few days later he approached Wagner ('very respectfully', he wrote to
his father) as he was leaving the Hotel Imperial to attend a rehearsal of
Lohengrin. He got nothing but a stare from Wagner so he ran to the Opera
House and arrived there just before the Master. Here Wolf tried to open the cab
door for his idol but the driver, no doubt pursuing a tip, beat him to it.
Afterwards, by devious means, Wolf wormed his way into Wagner's rooms in
the hotel and the maid took him to see Wagner, who had just returned from a
Philharmonic concert. In response to Wolf's anxious request for an opinion on
his own compositions, Wagner replied that he had no time to look at them and it
was quite impossible anyway to judge from immature works whether the
composer would come to anything later on, illustrating this point with the words,
'Look at my *Rienzi*, there are poor things in that!'

In 1876 Bayreuth was beyond Wolf's reach, but he went in 1882. Wolf's
friends in Vienna had contributed to the cost of his journey to Bayreuth and his
accommodation there – they even bought him a new suit of clothes but with
Wolf's diminutive stature this proved to be a tailoring disaster.

His free student's ticket failed to reach him in time so he had to pay out quite a
large sum of money to see *Parsifal* on 13 August 1882 and again two days later.
He was overwhelmed by the experience: 'colossal – Wagner's most inspired,
sublimest creation'. He attempted to meet Wagner, but the Master's entourage
would not allow him to be approached and even Wolf's friendship with Amalie
Materna proved to be of little value – Wagner was immune to the blandishments
of his Kundry. Nevertheless, Wolf found everything else in the Festival town to
his liking; he made a journey to the Hermitage and paid a visit to the grave of
Bayreuth's other famous artistic figure, Jean Paul, bringing away leaves of ivy
and lilac. He left Bayreuth on 16 August.

1883 saw the young composer at Bayreuth once again. He wrote home to his
father, 'I only wish you had been able to be here – Wagner's greatness would
have revealed itself to you through his mighty work – yes, these are quite unforgettable days, true milestones, and must be considered the happiest of one's
life. Bayreuth will indeed be always foremost amongst my memories.' To his
friend Henriette Lank Wolf wrote a postcard:

Parsifal is without doubt by far the most beautiful and sublime work in the whole field of Art. My whole being reels in the perfect world of this wonderful work, as if in some blissful ecstasy, becoming ever more enraptured and blessed – I could die even now, a thought that has not occurred to me for a long time. I can do no better than to exhort you under all circumstances to get to Bayreuth – think less about it and act the more!

In 1884 Wolf took a post as critić with the fashionable Viennese paper the *Salonblatt* but left soon afterwards. On 21 August 1884 Wolf and his friends Eckstein and Zweybruck left for Bayreuth on the Vienna Wagnerverein train. They heard *Meistersinger* and *Parsifal* and Wolf was once more deeply affected by the latter work. Zweybruck, who was hearing *Parsifal* for the first time, left the Festspielhaus at the end of the first act and, not feeling like chatting through the interval, went off into the grounds. He heard someone sobbing behind a bush and came upon Wolf on a bench, head in hands, shaking with emotion; Zweybruck left him alone.

His other companion, Friedrich Eckstein, had met Wolf in a vegetarian restaurant in Vienna in 1882. A qualified chemist and Classical scholar, Eckstein did much to widen Wolf's cultural horizon. He had an excellent musical knowledge; he studied composition with Bruckner and acted for a time as his unpaid secretary. Eckstein, at various times, made the acquaintance of Mark Twain, Edison and Freud. He took his first pilgrimage to Bayreuth so seriously that he journeyed all the way from Vienna on foot – not, as legend has it, with penitent's sandals on his feet but, as he was always ready to point out, a pair of stout hiking boots.*

In 1889 Wolf returned to Bayreuth for *Parsifal, Meistersinger* and *Tristan* and accompanied the Belgian bass Emil Blauwert, who was singing the part of Gurnemanz, in a recital of his songs. This recital led to Wolf's meeting Mrs Elizabeth Fairchild from Boston, who was so taken with the songs she paid for the publication of his Goethe and Eichendorff settings and handed out some two hundred copies of each volume to her acquaintances in America.

1891 was the year of Wolf's final visit to Bayreuth and it was not an entirely happy one, for the syphilis which was eventually to bring about his miserable death in 1903 was already affecting his nervous system. Humperdinck had found him lodgings for the Festival, but the rooms were very uncomfortable and noisy and Wolf could not get a night's sleep; to his distress he fell asleep during the first and third acts of *Parsifal*. Two days later he moved to other accommodation but his nervous condition did not improve and, in a state of agitation, he took his final leave of Bayreuth at four o'clock one morning.

Hugo Wolf was a Wagnerian in the best sense, appreciating Wagner as a musician and dramatist in the first instance and as a musical theorist only second – if at all. He wrote, 'Without *Meistersinger* I could never have written *Der Corregidor* – oh, yes, the old magician takes us with his spells and shows us the path to take!'

*Walter Legge, who met Eckstein in Vienna in 1937, recounted these anecdotes in the Introduction to the second edition of Ernest Newman's *Hugo Wolf* (1966).

Amongst his friends and acquaintances Wolf could count such Bayreuth stalwarts as Humperdinck, Mottl, Richter and Weingartner as well as, for a time, Mahler.

Whilst Wagner was in Vienna in 1875–6 various groups of musicians sympathetic to his cause gathered to honour him. At one of these gatherings Gustav Mahler, then just fifteen years old, found himself in a cloakroom with the great man; he was to regret all his life that he was too overcome with awe to address the Master or even extend the courtesy of helping him with his coat.

Wolf and Mahler, both students at the Vienna Conservatory, were close friends at this time but a few years later, in 1880, they fell out over a libretto that each of them believed the other was secretly setting to music. (This was a pre-Humperdinck fairy-tale opera called *Rübezahl* – or would have been, for neither of them did in fact set it.) When the two met again, in 1883, it was on the road up to the Festspielhaus at Bayreuth and, according to Alma Mahler, not even their great common passion for Wagner could unite them in his own citadel, and they cut each other dead.

Mahler had not been able to go to Bayreuth with the contingent of Viennese vegetarians for the *Parsifal* première in 1882, and the death of Wagner in 1883 made him regret all the more the diffidence he had shown seven years previously on the only occasion he had found himself in the Master's presence. However, during a season of Italian Opera at the Carl-Theater in the Wiener-Vorstadt the young Mahler earned enough money to make the journey to Bayreuth in 1883. When he returned to Ighan he wrote to his friend Fritz Lohr: 'I can hardly describe my present state to you. When I came out of the Festspielhaus, completely spellbound, I understood that the greatest and most painful revelation had just been made to me, and that I would carry it unspoiled all my life.'

In 1887 Cosima Wagner, then in sole charge of the Bayreuth Festival, went to Leipzig and there heard Mahler conduct *Tannhäuser*. Whatever impression she formed of the young conductor she did not invite him to direct any performances at Bayreuth, so Mahler's next visit to the Festival was as a visitor once more. In 1891 he heard *Tannhäuser* and *Parsifal* – the latter twice, as was the custom in those days. He again made the journey through the Fichtelgebirge to Wunsiedel to pay homage to Bayreuth's earlier celebrated man of the arts.

In 1894 there came an invitation from Cosima to Mahler to attend the Festival – but as a mere spectator, not as participant. He was working at this time on the last movement of his second symphony (composition for Mahler was a holiday pastime) but he was quite prepared to suspend his composing for a week or two. He declared his visit 'successful from every point of view' and he visited Wahnfried every day and watched the performances from the Wagners' box in the Festspielhaus, seeing *Parsifal* and *Lohengrin* (which was being given for the first time at Bayreuth) as well as *Tannhäuser* conducted by, amongst others, Richard Strauss. The music critic Karpath later recalled approaching Mahler during an interval at one of these performances; he offered the composer a cigarette, but Mahler passed him by without a word, lost in a world of his own.

Mahler returned to Bayreuth for the new production of the *Ring* in 1896 (a year that saw the first visit to Bayreuth of the twenty-seven-year-old Hans Pfitzner). He saw the third cycle, conducted by Felix Mottl. Mahler was this time coolly received by the Wagners, and he suspected the singer Ernestine Schumann-Heink of intrigue against him. Henri-Louis de la Grange, Mahler's recent biographer, suggests that this change of attitude was due to Cosima's wishing to have Mottl (who, unlike Mahler, was not a Jew) appointed to the post of Director at the Vienna Opera in Mahler's place. Cosima never invited Mahler, the greatest conductor of his day and an unsurpassed Wagnerian, to direct any Bayreuth performance – but then the choice of conductors for the Festivals has rarely favoured musical distinction at any time. Cosima did, however, from time to time request and follow Mahler's advice concerning singers, and in 1905 she prevailed upon the Director she had tried to depose to get one of her son's operas performed in Vienna.

Max Reger, who produced a vast amount of music, may be one of those composers such as Hans Pfitzner and Franz Schmidt who, like Bruckner some years ago, may be said to be waiting in the wings for public recognition; there has been music worse than Reger's, at first dismissed by the critics, that has subsequently found favour with the larger musical public. As in many other cases, his initial visit to Bayreuth in 1888 made Reger decide to take up composition. During his final year of study with Adalbert Lindner, who later became his biographer, Reger got to know Wagner's music well, though he had earlier discovered it in a series of piano arrangements belonging to his father, himself a keen Wagnerian. When Reger had acquitted himself successfully in his examinations, his father gave him the money to go to Bayreuth. (In 1902 Anton Webern received a similar reward, and when he returned home he wrote a piece called 'Young Siegfried'.) Reger was only fifteen when he saw *Meistersinger* and *Parsifal* and, like many of his age, he was overwhelmed by the experience. He later wrote to Karl Wenderling, 'One does not easily speak about things such as love for one's mother – when I first heard *Parsifal* at Bayreuth I was fifteen, I cried for two weeks and then became a musician.' Reger also observed, 'I give the world five hundred years before such a work as *Meistersinger* is heard again', and even Wagner's detractors would be inclined to agree with him on that.

In 1903 Reger wrote to a friend in Leipzig, 'Yesterday at Bayreuth I became acquainted with Siegfried Wagner.' Two years later Reger renewed his friendship with Siegfried and the following year he went to Bayreuth as the Wagners' guest and shared their box in the Festspielhaus. This was his last visit. The Festivals were brought to an end by the outbreak of war in 1914 and did not resume for another ten years. Reger died in 1916 at the early age of forty-three.

The composer Alban Berg, one of the so-called Second Viennese School (with Schoenberg, Webern and others), went to Bayreuth in 1909 for *Parsifal* which was still the only place where it was performed. His brother Hermann bought him the ticket. Berg's impressions of his brief visit were recorded in his letters to Helene

Nahowski whom he married two years later. He was twenty-four years old and had already experienced many fine performances of Wagner at the Vienna Opera where Mahler had just completed a legendary ten years as Director.

By Viennese standards Bayreuth was found wanting. Berg compared the standard of performance to the pre-Mahler period in Vienna; the staging was cheap and the orchestra and chorus not of the top standard. The soloists were outstanding, however, even if Siegfried Wagner's direction of the work was not.

Writing immediately after his return from the Festspielhaus, Berg described *Parsifal* as 'magnificent, overwhelming' and a couple of days later he was still enraptured by the work. Of the Festival he wrote:

. . . Nobody decent here at all – 'except for yours truly'! Altogether, Bayreuth is an empty delusion. I'd never want to set foot in it again, but for the unforgettable *Parsifal*. If Wagner had not long ago turned in his grave, I am sure, he would rise and take flight in disgust at what goes on in and around Wahnfried. . . .

. . . Picture the scene. Left and right of the Festspielhaus a Festspiel beerhouse and a Festspiel restaurant. I arrived at the theatre in devout mood to find the entire audience (mostly Bavarians and Americans) disporting themselves in those places – led by Siegfried Wagner and his friends. After the first act the same business started again, and I could have run off into the fields nearby and wept. People strolled around laughing and chattering, feeling they simply must have a drink. . . . And again Siegfried Wagner set the tone – wearing a fresh stand-up collar he had put on after the heat and exertion of conducting. He circulated wherever somebody might ask him for an autograph. . . .

The people sitting near Berg were from Munich 'like caricatures out of *Simplicissimus*' and when Cosima entered to take her seat everybody turned to peer at her, 'Bayreuth's talented Business Manageress'. The second interval was worse than the first as the audience clamoured for its food and drink:

. . . The Bavarians drank beer, the Americans champagne. Siegfried Wagner had changed from his immaculate white tennis kit into a dark suit, and with all the autograph hunters hardly had time to enjoy his 'Parsifal steak' with rice and stewed fruit, before it was time to go back for Act Three. . . . The whole place is a horrible exploitation of the Wagner idea. Extremely distressing, to see what the 'German nation' had done to the greatest of all Germans.

Berg's essentially romantic temperament was much in sympathy with Wagner, especially the later works; his own compositions, which progress from extended tonality to free atonality and serialism, seem always to keep in touch with tonality in the accepted sense. Berg takes over not far from where Wagner, in *Parsifal*, left off. His first opera, *Wozzeck* (a transitional work) shows the influence; the psychological drama is contained in the orchestra while the vocal parts, developing out of the Wagnerian declamation, more closely resemble speech. The fragments that constitute the fabric of the work can be picked out just as the 'leitmotives' can be picked out of the Wagner operas. Also there are passages in *Wozzeck*, albeit brief ones, that show secondary influence of Wagner – flashes of late Strauss, Mahler and even Debussy.

Of all the members of the Second Viennese School Berg's music is perhaps the most approachable (or the 'least difficult' to understand) although there is a lot of truth in Schoenberg's repeated insistence that what *his* works needed were good performances and all such 'difficulties' would be resolved. Wagner, in his time, had said much the same.

* * *

During the years of the Third Republic, the French – that is to say, a handful of susceptible Parisians – found themselves infected by a surprisingly welcome new malady, the curiously debilitating disease of Wagnermania. However, even before 1876, that significant year in the Wagner annals, the society known as 'Petit Bayreuth' had been founded by a Paris magistrate, Antoine Lascoux, and, when the theatre at Bayreuth opened its doors to the public for the first time, there was a small band of French pilgrims on hand for the event – Camille Saint-Saëns (whose account is to be found in Part II of this book), Ernest Guiraud (professor at the Conservatoire, where Debussy was one of his pupils) and the writer Catulle Mendès, amongst others. Again, in 1882, for *Parsifal*, the faithful assembled – this time Ernest Chausson, Vincent d'Indy, Jules de Brayer (notable for introducing Auguste Renoir to Richard Wagner) and Mendès with his wife Judith Gautier the writer, daughter of Théophile Gautier. More unexpectedly this French contingent included Léo Delibes. His visit provided an anecdote which scandalised the more devout: asked for his opinion of *Parsifal*, Delibes, according to d'Indy, replied that he adored the second act 'parce qu'il y avait des petites femmes, et que, les petites femmes c'est toujours amusant'.

When the Bayreuth Festival lay dormant and the theatre was closed from 1876 to 1882, Munich provided first-hand experience of the Wagnerian music drama, the idea of which had so gripped the French imagination. But of course only for those who were willing or able to visit Munich. Their number was small, and the conclusion must therefore be drawn that French Wagnérisme was based on inadequate local performances of fragments taken from the dramas, on the accounts of returning pilgrims (exaggerated, like all travellers' tales) and on the reading of Wagner's writings. This may perhaps be the reason for (or the cause of) the large proportion of non-musical devotees to be found in Parisian Wagner circles – but then Wagner's works have always been in the unhappy position of being music adopted by the non-musical, something for which Wagner himself is not free from blame with his attempt at a synthesis of all the arts and, of course, his theorising.

Such enthusiasm for Wagner as prevailed in Paris at this time did not, however, extend to the actual performance of his works; in fact it was not until 1914 that *Tristan*, and 1921 the complete *Ring* cycle were given anything resembling truly representative productions. Even as late as 1884–5 Lamoureux gave untold joy to Chabrier when he allowed him to take part in rehearsals for the first performance in Paris of *Tristan*. Not that the work was being given on the stage where it belongs – it was to have mere concert performances, and heavily cut, too. Emmanuel Chabrier, who is usually considered 'the embodiment of the grace and wit and charm so characteristic of French music', is said by James Harding, in his book on Saint-Saëns, to have 'tortured his southern genius into the composition of a flatulent opera' by the name of *Gwendoline* under the influence of Wagner. Mr Harding (only one of a series of writers to make the same mistake) gives Bayreuth as the scene of Chabrier's conversion, but it was in reality Munich, in 1879. Chabrier was there in the company of Henri Duparc and Vincent d'Indy, who gave the celebrated account of Chabrier's sobbing 'I've waited ten years of my life to hear that A on the cellos' during the opening bars of the *Tristan* prelude. He was then thirty-eight years old, and forthwith he abandoned his post in the civil service to devote his life to musical composition.

Ernest Chausson underwent a similar conversion at Munich that same year. He had qualified in Law in 1877, but the Wagnerian experience convinced him that he too must be a composer and on his return to Paris he enrolled in the classes of Franck and Massenet. *Tristan* brought him back to Munich in 1880 and, as already mentioned, he was at Bayreuth for *Parsifal* in 1882. In spite of these enthusiasms, however, Chausson's Wagnerism is less intemperate than that of others in his group; his music avoids the extremes of intense passion and intense despair and, it may be said, anything like greatness.

Chabrier's opera *Gwendoline*, to a libretto by Catulle Mendès, was produced at Brussels in 1886. Ernest Reyer, another Wagnerian, dismissed it as worthless but, as his own opera *Sigurd* had been performed there just two years previously, the opinion may be not uncoloured by his own mild lack of success. When Chabrier's next opera *Le roi malgré lui* was staged in Paris in 1887 Fauré declared that he would rather have written that than the entire *Ring*. Clearly, Chabrier was rid of his flatulence.

It was Shaw's friend, the tenor Van Dyck, who introduced Chabrier to the conductor Felix Mottl who, in spite of his devotion to Cosima's Bayreuth, displayed a catholicity of taste that (unlike Richter's) admitted the existence of French music and indeed went so far as an enthusiasm for Berlioz. The outcome of the meeting was a production of *Gwendoline* by Mottl at Karlsruhe in 1889.

Chabrier had planned to visit the Bayreuth Festival in 1888 (where Van Dyck was to sing Parsifal) to meet Cosima but the serious illness of a member of his family prevented him from leaving home. Even when he got there the following year, in the company of Chausson, d'Indy and Lamoureux, he felt obliged to leave before his visit was complete due to the illness of his childhood nursemaid – but not before he had seen his first performance of *Parsifal*:

Yesterday, Sunday 21st July 1889, I heard *Parsifal* for the first time. I have never in all my life had an artistic experience at all comparable to this; it is overwhelming; one comes out after each act (I do, at least) absolutely overcome with admiration, bewildered, distraught with tears running down one's cheeks. It is worse than *Tristan* at Munich. What can I say? It is sublime from beginning to end.

During his 1889 visit to Bayreuth Chabrier also heard *Tristan* and *Meistersinger* and paid a visit to Wahnfried, where he played the piano for Cosima, choosing the prelude to *Gwendoline* and his most famous piece, *España*. He took home as a souvenir a sprig of ivy from Wagner's grave (a common enough practice before it was fenced off) which was duly displayed at the Chabrier Centenary Exhibition in Paris in 1941.

Chabrier's appreciation of all things Wagnerian stopped short of the sunken orchestra pit in the Festspielhaus – he felt it resulted in loss of tone during quiet passages, '[it] sounds as if the music is coming from the room next door'. Others, seated in the wrong part of the theatre, have thought the same.

Along with Lekeu and Duparc, Chabrier was perhaps the most prominent of this generation of French Wagnerians. Lekeu, on a visit to Bayreuth (also in 1889) had to be hauled out of the Festspielhaus unconscious during a performance of *Tristan* – an event not unknown to the visitor today, the new cramped seating, introduced in 1968, making such proceedings difficult and noisy. Duparc, a curious figure of a composer, with only a tiny output to show for a long life of eighty-five years, was not as consumed by Wagner's music as his fellows, perhaps due to his lack of active composing, but found himself more involved with the Bayreuth Master's ideas and theories. Duparc and d'Indy were veterans of the Wagnerian music drama, having been to Munich for the first performances of *Rheingold* and *Walküre* under Wüllner in 1869 and 1870. Wagner himself, disapproving of these performances, had stayed away, though curiously Brahms, of all people, was there.

Vincent d'Indy, born of an aristocratic military family, wrote music which shows considerable influence of Wagner, and his teacher Albert Lavignac, himself considered an advanced theorist in his day, did much to encourage this. D'Indy was a regular visitor to Bayreuth, and Munich too – his enthusiasm for Wagner the artist made him, like many another Wagnerite, an equally enthusiastic Teutonophile and this, together with his dislike of Jews (an attitude common enough amongst his class) earned him the hatred of Saint-Saëns as well as others.

But it was doubtless Wagner himself who had made it difficult for almost any true Frenchman to be devoted to his cause (unless they took up the position of d'Indy) with his anti-French farce *Eine Kapitulation*, written in heat in November 1870 when Paris was under siege, and subsequently published, in cold blood, in 1873. This work, mocking the hardships of the beleaguered French, was Wagner's personal revenge for the misery he had suffered in Paris during the corrupt years of Napoleon III, when Meyerbeer sat on his throne at the Opéra and Wagner's energies were, of life's necessity, diverted from music drama to the making of popular piano arrangements of selections from the operas of Auber, Donizetti, Halévy and suchlike. The scandal and failure of *Tannhäuser* in 1861 added injury to the previous insults. *Eine Kapitulation* did more than simply harm Wagner's cause – it cost him valuable friendships, such as that of Mendès and Judith Gautier. He was also reproached by Saint-Saëns, who confronted him at Wahnfried in 1876 while paying a call on Liszt. Mendès, however, may well have been glad to have an excuse to break with Wagner the man, though he continued to be devoted to the works. It had always been a strained relationship. Mendès, together with Judith Gautier, his mistress before their marriage in 1867, had visited Wagner many years previously when he was living at Tribschen and, stimulated by his advanced concepts of art and drama, they had introduced them into their Parisian circles – thus infecting the susceptible with the Wagner germ. Nevertheless, Wagner had been far too attentive to the desirable young Judith for Mendès's liking and, using Wagner's Francophobe play as his excuse, he published in 1881 a novel entitled *Le roi vierge* parodying the composer and his relationship with King Ludwig. Saint-Saëns, for his part, asking Wagner how he could have penned such a piece as *Eine Kapitulation* was told 'it was a harmless joke'.

Against this background, French Wagnermania none the less continued to flourish, reaching a peak around the year 1885. On 8 February 1885 the first issue of the *Revue Wagnérienne* appeared; it was founded by Edouard Dujardin, a young novelist who originated the 'stream of consciousness' style and who is the subject of Toulouse-Lautrec's *Le divan japonais*. The *Revue* lasted some three years, was supported by Houston Stewart Chamberlain, and counted amongst its contributors Liszt, Saint-Saëns, d'Indy, Fauré, Reynaldo Hahn and Florent Schmitt as well as the literary figures, Mallarmé, Huysmans, Verlaine and, inevitably, Catulle Mendès.

French Wagnerphilia, extending to the founding of journals but not to the staging of the music dramas, continued to depend on Bayreuth pilgrimages for cultural nourishment when the Festival was under way, and on that particularly Gallic institution, the Parisian soirée, when it was not. Performers were hired for these occasions to play the works of the Master on the piano, a totally inadequate representation to be sure, but they no doubt counted it better than nothing – for those who frequented these soirées were, for the most part, literary or pseudo-literary figures. Claude Debussy found himself one such hired pianist and was by this means introduced to the music of Wagner – a not insignificant event, as it turned out. With financial help from Etienne Dupin, Debussy made two journeys to Bayreuth, the first in 1888, the second the following year. As with many other musicians it was *Parsifal* that impressed Debussy most – its influence remained with him and persisted even though he did not see the work again until 1914. Certainly the influence is apparent in *La Damoiselle élue*, which was completed in 1888, and it can be seen in later works too, notably *Pelléas et Mélisande*, perhaps the most successful of that series of post-Wagnerian music dramas from the French composers, and *Le Martyre de Saint Sébastien*. Debussy's tirades against 'old Klingsor' are well known and show that he recognised the extent to which Wagner's influence could stifle a composer's individuality. However, he was also prepared to accept the benefits of such an influence – the mature

Debussy, in 1914, told André Caplet that the orchestration of *Jeux* should produce 'a colour like illumination from behind such as the wonderful effects in *Parsifal*'.

Edward Lockspeiser, in his fine work on Debussy, quotes a passage from a book by a French lawyer, Emile de Saint-Auban, called *Un pèlerinage à Bayreuth*; this came out in 1892 and tells of a devotee's experiences in a less than earnest fashion:

> The sight of the station, on arriving at Bayreuth, was most odd. Such a mass of people were waiting, excitedly walking about or rushing forward, waving handkerchiefs, it was like the crowd at a harbour greeting the arrival of the steamer. I stepped down on to the platform.
>
> 'Komm, mein Herr!'
>
> Who is this soprano piping these words into my ear? I turn round, and a delicate little hand catches hold of my arm. Is this charming damsel a Customs official? I am not aware of having done anything wrong, to be set upon in this way.
>
> 'Komm! – es ist billig!'
>
> Well, it cannot be the Customs. But surely I have read of something of this sort in *Parsifal* with the difference that the Fool is there assured that his experiences will cost him nothing at all! Can it be, by any chance, that the Flowermaidens' scene is to be enacted on the station platform? My Flowermaiden, however, with her skinny figure and her hair plaited around her temples, is hardly a rose.
>
> 'Komm – es ist billig!'
>
> What? another!
>
> 'Komm!'
>
> A third?
>
> 'Komm, mein Herr,' suddenly growls a deep bass. Upon my word this must be Klingsor! At last it all becomes clear. We are being offered rooms. It is not a competition of Flowermaidens, it is a competition of hotel-keepers, which is much more to the point. Since, then, we are to be put up and not seduced let us make a choice. Klingsor is a pleasant enough fellow. I decide for him and I stay in the Rue Richard Wagner.

M. de Saint-Auban, no doubt convinced of the possibility by the closed pit, tells of the Bayreuth orchestra sitting down to play with large jars of beer to hand – there have been cartoons, too, of brass players quaffing beer during the performances, in between cues – but this picturesque scene is purely one of imagination – shirt-sleeves, yes – but beer, never! Anyone who has been in the pit when the orchestra is installed there and playing will know there is barely room to play an instrument let alone lift the elbow.

To consider a brief roll of this generation of Bayreuth pilgrims from the ranks of French composers – Duparc, Chausson, Augusta Holmès (a colourful figure who composed in the grand manner and who appealed to even the homosexual Saint-Saëns), Lekeu, Paul Dukas (a pilgrim in 1886) and Chabrier, is to muster the pupils of the venerable César Franck. But Franck himself would have no truck with the Bayreuth master or his corrupting Festival – needless to say he never went there, but he was familiar with Wagner's works and even if he did write the word 'Poison' on his score of *Tristan* he felt it worth keeping by him. His disciples d'Indy, Duparc and Chausson, with their unequalled idolatry of Wagner, were also the most devoted to Franck himself. Did they perhaps perceive a common element in the two masters? A link may be found in the person of Liszt – he certainly influenced Franck in his early years to a greater or lesser degree. Some questions remain unanswered: did Franck actually know Wagner's works in their entirety so well as to be secure in his anti-Wagner stance? And how did so many of his pupils find their way so readily into the opposing camp?

Towards the end of the 1880s French Wagnermania began to show signs of abating – at least as far as the Parisian salons were concerned; the Bayreuth excursions continued, with Massenet, Messager, Dukas, Raymond Bonheur and Paul Bourget in 1886, and Pierre Louÿs and Ida Rubinstein in 1891, while the new production of the *Ring* in 1896 brought Fauré, Romain Rolland* and Colette.

Colette was a regular visitor to Bayreuth up to the turn of the century – she set her novel *Claudine and Annie* there, calling it the 'Holy City', and used it to demonstrate her attitude to Wagner. This seems to have been one of admiration for and acknowledgment of his achievements, coupled with a merciless deflation of his grandiloquence. This was done by means of the caustic quips to which she was so addicted and which did so much for her reputation. *Tristan* was held in high esteem and so was the 'Forest Murmurs' passage from *Siegfried* (this latter was something of a cult piece for her circle). Colette claimed Siegfried Wagner as an acquaintance and made bitchy remarks about him ('his bottle-shaped figure') and the Festspielhaus at Bayreuth was, for her, the 'Gasometer Theatre'.

Nevertheless, the attack on Wagner in 1888 by his fallen disciple Nietzsche was made even more pointed, to the French at least, by his choice of *Carmen* as the work best fulfilling his ideals. After this the feverish attitude of the French to Wagner could rarely break out again. Fauré and Messager collaborated on a set of popular quadrilles for piano duet and published them under the title *Souvenirs de Bayreuth*. The mighty motives of the *Ring* (even those in triple time) were distorted into an uncompromising four-in-a-bar – if the intention of these pieces was parody was it meant to be the *Ring* cycle or, less likely perhaps, the popular dance sets that inevitably came out when any operatic success caught the public imagination? (An especially shaming case had been that of the publisher Diabelli who, not enthusiastic about taking the songs of Schubert in his lifetime, brought out *Erlkönig- und Wanderer-Galoppe* only six weeks after Schubert died and in that composer's name, although most likely they were put together by Diabelli

* For Rolland's comments see page 218.

himself.) Whatever their reason the two French composers were doing nothing more than Gottfried Sonntag, the bandmaster of the Bayreuth garrison, had done with his *Nibelungenmarsch* – and that had been given Wagner's enthusiastic approval.

If the *Souvenirs* were bad, worse was to follow, for in 1906 Debussy published his *Children's Corner* Suite and this contains, of all possible horrors, a parody on the death of Tristan!

French music had gradually shed the influence of Wagner (other German music of the time had made little impression, Brahms was virtually unknown and what was known was not liked) and it was soon to yield to the influence of the Russians, just as before Wagner the influence had for the most part been from Italy, none of these succeeding influences having had, it would seem, a less than beneficial effect.

Not one of the French musicians so far discussed could be said to have had any practical involvement with the Bayreuth Festival – they were visitors only and thus quite apart from the routine work of musical and stage preparation. This, however, was not the case of Alfred Cortot who actually worked at the Bayreuth Festival. Cortot won first prize at the Paris Conservatoire when he was nineteen years old, and the head of the firm of Pleyel offered him a trip to Bayreuth as reward. That was in 1896 but Cortot, like Debussy before him, was already a veteran of the Wagner soirées; his work at the piano having made him quite familiar with the reduced score of the *Ring*, he was ready for this opportunity to see and hear the mighty work as its creator had intended. As in the case of so many of his predecessors, Cortot's Bayreuth pilgrimage proved to be a most significant event in his young life – and as had happened so frequently before it caused him to choose the path his future career would take. After his brilliant success at the Conservatoire he had been uncertain whether to take up teaching, composition or concert work. Now, he decided, he must be a conductor – to direct the works of Wagner!

During his first visit to Bayreuth the young Cortot was invited to a Wahnfried reception where he received the distinction of being asked to play the music of Liszt on the Master's own piano. Cosima, with her shrewd perception, was impressed by his personality as well as his musicianship, and so requested Cortot to return to Bayreuth to take the place of the pianist Edouard Risler, who was then establishing his career as a touring virtuoso.

Cortot worked at Bayreuth for several seasons as a musical assistant and in the years 1901 and 1902 was involved in rehearsals for the *Ring, Parsifal* and the first Bayreuth production of *Der fliegende Holländer*, all of which were directed by Richter and Mottl. Stage rehearsals were taken by Cosima in person and Cortot was often called from the *répétiteur's* position at the piano to help her to demonstrate some point – he would be placed at her side as Siegfried or Parsifal, while she, as was her custom, acted out the part of Brünnhilde or Kundry for the benefit of the singer. Cortot emphasised the strangeness of this experience, in the light of Cosima's striking resemblance, at this period of her life, to her father Franz Liszt.

Profiting from his Bayreuth experiences Cortot, on 7 May 1902, conducted the first performance in Paris of *Götterdämmerung* and followed this in June of the same year with a successful performance of *Tristan*. Whether these were fully staged or concert performances is not clear from Cortot's account – they took place in a theatre (not the Opéra) but that fact does not itself make the issue clear.

In 1905 Cortot founded the celebrated trio with Jaques Thibaud and Pau Casals, and from then on his career took a direction other than that of Wagner conductor. Casals himself visited Bayreuth in 1907, but found the singers not very good. In spite of this he did recognise the power of *Tristan*.

Alfred Cortot retained his devotion to Wagner and Bayreuth, and as late as 1957 gave an interview in which he spoke of both in the warmest and most affectionate terms.

And so the French made their contribution to Bayreuth, largely in the form of onlookers at the spectacle – but as Curt von Westernhagen, writing in 1976, points out, their mere attendance helped to secure the existence of the Festival in its early critical years. In 1886, for instance, when *Tristan* was first presented at Bayreuth, there were at times only three hundred in the audience – and that with a 'star' singer, Rosa Sucher, in the part of Isolde. Under these circumstances, Cosima was forced to consider closing the Festspielhaus for good until, according to Hans von Wolzogen, the French began to take notice of Bayreuth and flock there in considerable numbers to occupy the places that the largely indifferent Germans were prepared to leave empty. Bayreuth and its Festival were now on the French tourist map and, Lavignac in hand and handbag, the visitors made their artistic journey up the green hill. They continue to do so. Wagner performances in Paris are even now not remarkable for their frequency or success, but nevertheless, it may be said that the French have truly helped to make the Bayreuth Festival what it is today.

*   *   *

In the two foregoing sections it was possible to group together the French Bayreuth visitors in one case and the German-speaking, if not actually German-national, visitors in the other. This section is less well ordered. There are the English to begin with, then a Finn, an Italian and one or two others, having very little in common except that they were all musicians and visited the Bayreuth Festival.

In the last quarter of the nineteenth century the influences at play on English music were predominantly German; but the Germans were Mendelssohn, Schumann and Brahms rather than Wagner. When he visited London in 1855 Wagner had found no great interest in his work and what interest he did find was, for the most part, ill-informed. The music critics, as ever arbiters of public taste, were hostile, and the musicians taking part in his concerts bewildered. Some years afterwards, Wagner declared that the only stimulating moments of his entire stay were when he chatted with the Queen and Prince Albert during the interval of one of these concerts. Perhaps their understanding of his language helped, for Wagner spoke little English.

With this background, as might be expected, only a few of the leading English musical figures went to Bayreuth for the opening of Wagner's Festival in 1876, and those who did were largely indifferent to what they saw and heard and, as a man, against Wagner as a person.

One exception was Hubert Parry. When he was twenty-eight years old he joined that select band that made the journey to the first Bayreuth Festival, travelling there via Cologne and the Rhine Valley to Bamberg, where he spent a day. He found it 'a superb place with a wonderful cathedral.' The description still holds good today; Bamberg is one of the pleasanter excursions from Bayreuth *en fête*. Parry saw the second cycle of the *Ring* and recorded in his diary:

I gave up attempts to describe my feelings. I was never so perfectly satisfied in my life. *Rheingold*, first of all, was perfect to my mind. Then *Die Walküre* came up to my expectations which were of the highest. *Siegfried* I found certainly hard to understand, and did not enjoy it so much as the others at the time, but on looking back upon it I got to enjoy it more and more and the impression afterwards was very strong. As for *Götterdämmerung* it utterly surpassed my expectations. I was in a whirl of excitement over it and quite drunk with delight. The first Act satisfied me most with its three great climaxes piled one on the other like Andes on Himalayas. Before the performance I met Otto Goldschmidt in the street, and he was rather pooh-poohy about it. After *Götterdämmerung* he came into the restaurant with a very solemn face and said, 'I suppose it must be the finest thing since *Fidelio*.'

A year after the Festival, Parry's diary reports on 2 May, 'In the evening I went to Dannreuther's to meet Wagner.' The Master of Bayreuth was in London once again, giving a series of concerts in the vain hope of raising enough money to pay off the Festival debts. Parry went to all the concerts and, at Edward Dannreuther's, heard Wagner read part of the *Parsifal* poem, at that time not yet set to music. Parry does not tell how Wagner struck him as a person but his biographer, Charles Graves, assures the reader that Parry was interested in Wagner only as a musician; an instance of the fashion that disapproved wholeheartedly of Wagner as a person, a fashion persisting in some quarters even today.

In 1882 Parry, by now an enthusiastic Wagnerian, went to Bayreuth for *Parsifal*. He left London on 21 July and, in the company of Edward Dannreuther, travelled via Bonn and the Rhine to Würzburg. He records his disapproval of the cathedral interiors they inspected *en route*; Bayreuth itself he described as 'a barbarous city which is distinguished for its unsurpassable stinks and the stupidity and backwardness of its inhabitants'. Parry saw *Parsifal* three times and enjoyed it 'beyond measure', even though he returned home afterwards 'tired and good for nothing'. Of the work's very first performance on 26 July his diary entry runs:

All the singers did better than I ever heard them do before. Scaria was superb as Gurnemanz; Materna even better as Kundry; Winkelmann excellent as Parsifal and Hill's Klingsor as good as possible. Scenic management and tableaux supremely effective and all the difficult points I had dreaded – the swan, the Flower Maidens, the washing of the feet and the dove – were all just perfect. As a work of art it is at the very highest point of mastery. The religious element makes it seem to me a little hollow, and I was not satisfied with the climaxes of the first and last Acts being chiefly scenic and not humanly emotional. But the impression was very great.

After the second performance Parry wrote, 'the work took possession of me very powerfully and I enjoyed it beyond measure.' However, for this performance the second cast took the stage and Parry found them less good than the first; for the third performance the original singers returned and he reckoned that their efforts on this occasion surpassed the first.

Foul weather prevailed during that week in Bayreuth – what the local people call, with justification, 'Festival-weather' – and Parry was prevented from making the excursions into the totally unspoiled countryside that have provided the Bayreuth visitor, down to the present day, with added recreation, pleasure and satisfaction. He did, nevertheless, go to a reception at Wahnfried. The house made a great impression on him and he noticed, on display, a fragment of Beethoven's manuscript of the B flat piano sonata. Of the inhabitants he wrote:

It was crowded with all the notabilities and nullities and Mme Wagner did the royal person. Wagner only appeared for a little while and looked like a lively irrepressible boy. Liszt seemed to be caressing everyone sweetly, and looked a veritable old bogey.

Before he left Bayreuth Parry made a tour of the novel theatre and was taken by the sheer size, the backstage appointments and, most particularly, the huge metal canisters, so large they had to be mounted on wheels, that served as the bells of the Grail Temple before being replaced, in recent years, by a tone-producing electronic device.

Wagner occupied something like a central place in the few external musical interests of Frederick Delius, in the company of Bach, Chopin and Grieg – an eclectic group, to be sure. A visit to Covent Garden as a youth, when he saw a performance of *Lohengrin*, aroused Delius's interest in Wagner and, in later years, when he was working with no great enthusiasm as a commercial traveller for his family's textile firm in Bradford, he had the opportunity to see many other operas during his trips to Germany, most notably *Die Meistersinger*. Following a spell in America and returning to his old haunts in Europe, Delius heard on one occasion in Leipzig a truly unforgettable performance of *Tristan und Isolde*, directed by the celebrated Nikisch.

His enthusiasm for Wagner took Delius to Bayreuth in 1894. He was thirty-two years old – and still going by the name of Fritz. At this time he was living in Paris, and was a member of a circle that gathered around William Molard, a mere clerk in the Ministry of Agriculture but one endowed with deeply Bohemian tastes that encompassed the playing of entire Wagner operas on the piano for his own edification, if not that of his listeners. Other members of the circle were Edvard Munch, Strindberg and Sinding, as well as other, lesser-known Scandinavians. One of these was Jutta Bell-Ranske; she had been a neighbour of Delius's in Florida and had come to Paris to study speech and singing. While there she helped him with the text of his second opera, *The Magic Fountain*. Delius wrote to her at the end of May 1894:

> I want to tread in Wagner's footsteps and even give something more in the right direction. For me the dramatic art is almost taking the place of religion. People are sick of being preached to. But by being played to they may be worked upon.

A worthy enough *Credo*. It is interesting to ponder whether Delius would have considered that he, and his music after him, had fulfilled this early testament. Or is his Brave New Musical World one of those several false dawns that have since beset western music? Perhaps it is best regarded merely as a casual remark, made *en passant*, and not as a standard by which his achievement should be measured. At any rate Delius went on to compose no less than six operas in the succeeding eleven years.

While he was at the Bayreuth Festival in August 1894 Delius wrote to Jutta Bell-Ranske, who was staying at his flat in Paris, telling her of his impressions of *Tannhäuser* and *Parsifal*. As was the custom then he went to *Parsifal* twice and described it as 'magnificent – the finest work of Wagner.' Such a reaction to the work was common to almost all visitors to Bayreuth in those days, when the Festival held the exclusive rights of performance. It was not possible to see it elsewhere until 1913, although it was staged in New York in 1903 against the Wagner family's wishes. So *Parsifal* involved a pilgrimage to Bayreuth and, with the superficially religious nature of the piece, it became imbued with an aura of dedication; those who had seen it regarded themselves as apart from those who had not. Shaw, in 1891, had regarded all this as so much humbug and said so; it was, he wrote, an opera like any other and, as such, should be put on in every opera house that wanted it, and the public freed from the air of false sanctity that Cosima Wagner had created at Bayreuth. Shaw, of course, was right.*

His Bayreuth visit did not satisfy Delius's appetite for Wagner and he went from the Festival to Munich where he saw the complete *Ring* cycle, *Tristan* and *Meistersinger* no less than three times each. In Munich he dined with the

* See page 161 above.

Bjørnsen family but failed to meet Richard Strauss even though a friend tried to bring this about – perhaps Delius could not be persuaded to take an evening off from the Hoftheater.

The two great pillars of English music, Elgar and Vaughan Williams, both paid visits to the Bayreuth Festival. Edward Elgar was there in 1892 and saw *Parsifal* (twice) as well as *Tristan, Meistersinger* and *Tannhäuser*, and again in 1902 when *Parsifal, Holländer* and the *Ring* were given. He was also a regular visitor to the summer festivals at Munich, which in those days were largely devoted to Wagner. It is a pity that no observations of these events are recorded in Elgar's correspondence or the diary kept by his wife. It is known, however, that although a great admirer of *Meistersinger*, the only opera he ever cared for was *Parsifal*; and that, of course, meant a journey to Bayreuth.

Ralph Vaughan Williams may be a surprising figure to find amongst the pilgrims to the Bayreuth shrine – what was this embodiment of English pastoralism doing in such company? He did study for a time in Germany, with Max Bruch in Berlin, and that could have influenced him – but the effect was no more lasting than that of his period of study with Ravel (three years his junior). He was twenty-four years old when he went to Bayreuth in 1897. *Parsifal* and the *Ring* were performed that year but, as with Elgar, there is no record of Vaughan Williams's impressions, or any evaluation of what he saw.

It is tempting to see in the work of these two composers the influence of that seminal music drama *Parsifal*; in Elgar's *Dream of Gerontius* and in Vaughan Williams's opera *Pilgrim's Progress*, for example. The influence in the latter case is more evident in the form – it is essentially a static work, too static for its own good (which has lost some fine music to the public). Vaughan Williams was perhaps misled, when he came to write the piece, by the apparently static nature of *Parsifal*. Elgar, adopting the form of the oratorio, was on more secure ground. Both of these works, however, are essentially religious in their concept and content, something that *Parsifal* in essence is not.

Elgar, it may be noted, brought home a tradition of a more practical nature, one that did not then survive for long but which was only recently revived: a series of fanfares, derived from Bach, to summon the audiences to performances at the Three Choirs Festival.

The now virtually-forgotten composer Granville Bantock went to the Bayreuth Festival in 1889 when he was twenty-one years old. He saw *Tristan* and *Parsifal* and developed his enthusiasm for their composer.

Ethel Smyth went to Bayreuth in 1892, when her career as a composer was causing her much doubt and misgiving, as the guest of a friend – 'a moneyed maiden', as she put it. Dame Ethel recalled her trip in a volume of autobiography, *As Time Went on . . .*, published in 1936 when she was an established figure in English musical life; these recollections she based on letters, diaries and a rather fallible memory. She remembered 'the old days when many were alive who had

The fanfare players, 1904

Cosima, 1904

Cosima, 1904

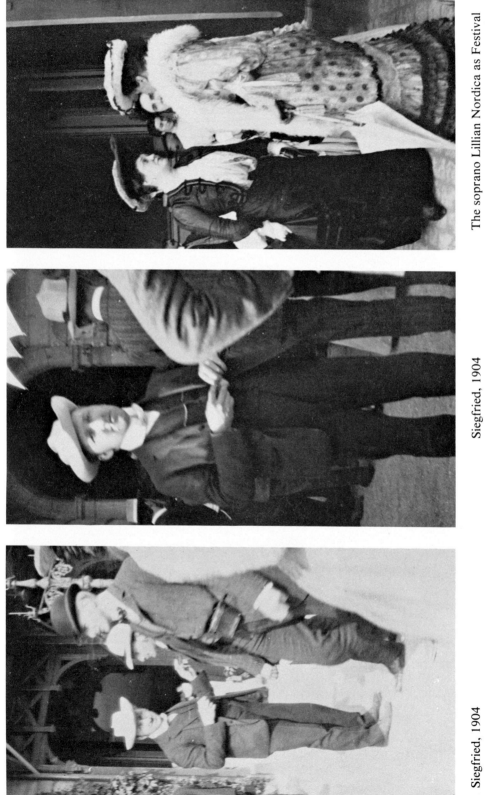

The soprano Lillian Nordica as Festival visitor, 1904

Siegfried, 1904

Siegfried, 1904

Hans Richter stung by a wasp, 1904

Hans Richter and his wife at breakfast, 1904

Hans Richter on his way to conduct the *Ring*, 1904

c

b

Cosima, 1906

Siegfried and Eva, 1906

Engelbert Humperdinck
and his wife, 1908

Engelbert Humperdinck
as Festival visitor, 1908

'Have you got me lighted properly', Bernard Shaw, 1908

Bernard Shaw and his wife with
Hans Richter, 1908

The tenor Ernst Van Dyck as
Festival visitor, 1911

The Valkyries with their répétiteur Carl Kittl, 1914

Hans Richter walking down the hill from the Festspielhaus in 1914. By now retired he was attending his last Bayreuth performances as an onlooker

known Wagner and before the Festival had become a commercialised summer excursion', and states that although she had never been a Wagnerian herself, in 1892 she found Bayreuth at a state of perfection, with Cosima keeping everything up to the Master's ideal. The spirit of the audience was impressive 'not owing to any concentrated effort of earnestness but to the fact that the hurry and bustle of life is inaudible at Bayreuth'. Life in the festival town she found all so marvellously simple – 'the life in all sorts of queer little burgher dwellings, the meals out of doors (and very, very bad they are)'.

Concerning the performances she saw Ethel Smyth makes no comment, but she does assure one correspondent that 'there is nothing at Bayreuth to make you laugh. The days of the far-seeing ridiculous old Wagnerians are past, for all the world is Wagnerian now, and Bayreuth is a world's fair.' Curiously, she was unable to remember whether she visited the Wagners at Wahnfried 'in the flesh or only in the illustrated papers'. Years later she met Cosima in Berlin and Frau Wagner said, 'Oh, I remember you perfectly at Wahnfried.' Dame Ethel darkly hints that Cosima probably had other reasons for this recognition, not unrelated to the company they were in at the time. Her final comment on the episode is 'to enter, as a non-worshipper, places where divine worship is going on, is neither decent nor pleasant'.

Jean Sibelius visited the Bayreuth Festival in 1894 – it was his only visit, or visits, for he was there on two occasions, going to Munich in between. He went with his brother-in-law, the composer Armas Järnefelt, and saw *Parsifal*, *Lohengrin* and *Tannhäuser* (conducted by Richard Strauss). It is illuminating to study his observations on these works, written as he saw them, in the light of his later attitude to Wagner and Bayreuth: 'I have bought the vocal scores of *Tannhäuser* and *Lohengrin* and I am studying *Lohengrin* as best I can.' Sibelius took his visit to Bayreuth seriously enough to prepare himself for it. His friend, companion and teacher, Martin Wegelius, believed every true Wagnerian should make the journey down the Rhine; as far as possible they did this, travelling from Hamburg to Mainz. The day he arrived in Bayreuth Sibelius went to a performance:

Heard *Parsifal*. Nothing in the world has ever made so overwhelming an impression on me. All my innermost heart-strings throbbed. I was beginning to think of myself as a dry old stick but it is not the case. . . . I cannot begin to tell you how *Parsifal* has transported me. Everything I do seems so cold and feeble by its side. *That* is really something.

The following day Sibelius saw *Lohengrin* and reported:

It did not have the impact on me that I had expected. I cannot help feeling it old-fashioned and full of theatrical effects. In my opinion *Parsifal* stands head and shoulders above everything else. You can judge the effect *Lohengrin* had on me when I say that when the performance was over I thought of my own opera (*The Building of the Boat*) and went around humming bits of it.

Sibelius deplored the social aspects of the Bayreuth Festival and the adulations of the ardent Wagnerites: 'Every hansom cab that Wagner has been in is labelled "historisch"; everything in this town is like that', and there were those 'who behaved as if they had taken Holy Communion', although others munched salami during the performances. The Kaiser's sister he described as 'looking like a kitchen-maid'. Nevertheless, he discovered an awareness of a deep cultural tradition at Bayreuth.

Sibelius and his companions went on to Munich for more Wagner. He was taken by only parts of the *Ring* cycle and appears not to have seen *Rheingold* at all. *Meistersinger* he enjoyed tremendously: 'It surpassed all my expectations and completely bowled me over.' He was persuaded by his friends to go back to Bayreuth for another *Parsifal* and this impressed him more than before.

Sibelius's attitude to Wagner was one of love and hate. For a time he certainly loved the music, but detested the effect it could have on a creative artists such as he aspired to be; he was, however, never completely indifferent. In later years, when he was famous and celebrated as a national hero, he deliberately set out to mislead his biographers on this subject. He told them he was never really interested in Bayreuth, even when he was there, and that he saw only *Tannhäuser* and *Lohengrin*, concealing the fact he had been to *Parsifal* twice as well as *Tristan, Meistersinger* and the greater part of the *Ring* at Munich. Nor did he allow that he got his head down into at least two of these works. He dismissed Wagner in later years as 'gross, brutal, vulgar and totally lacking in finer feelings'. But there is evidence that Sibelius did find some attraction in Wagner's deep sense of mystery and in his use of the orchestra, and himself employed many of Wagner's effects of colour, notably in the *Legends* for orchestra.

The Italian composer of *verismo* operas, Giacomo Puccini, the most prominent of a large family of ecclesiastical musicians rivalled in extent only by the Bachs, showed a notable catholicity of taste in music: Beethoven he held to be the supreme master and, in his own field of opera, he worshipped the diverse idols, Verdi and Wagner.

Verdi, of course, reigned supreme in Italy. Of Wagner's works the first to be performed in that country was *Lohengrin*, given at Bologna in 1871. Before that, however, one Giovannina Lucca, wife of the Milanese music publisher (whose firm was taken over by Ricordi), had already made the journey to Lucerne in July 1868 to see Wagner about presenting *Rienzi* to the Italian public; her choice of work was appropriate but nothing came of it. Later, in 1880, this enterprising lady once again approached Wagner, this time to see if he would be prepared to condense the entire *Ring* cycle into a single evening. He replied that he was not prepared to do it, but suggested that Signora Lucca do it herself, if she felt up to it. There is no evidence that she did, or was.

Puccini paid a visit to the Bayreuth Festival in 1889, the year his opera *Edgar* was produced at La Scala. He went at the instigation of the music publisher and business man Ricordi who himself had no time for Wagner or his works, but was nevertheless prepared to make a bit of money by them. Puccini's commission was to report on *Die Meistersinger*; in particular to see if it could be cut, and by how much, for the Milanese audiences – even *Bohème* and *Tosca*, not long operas by any means, were subsequently given in shortened versions at La Scala. *Meistersinger* was eventually put on at that house on 26 December 1889: it is not known by how much it was cut, if at all. Puccini thought it well done, but the audience on the first night was a poor one (an influenza epidemic was raging at the time) and such as turned up for the performance seemed to be bored by the work.

Puccini was especially fond of *Meistersinger*, *Tristan* and *Parsifal*. During work on *Turandot* he opened the score of *Tristan* and observed: 'Enough of this Music! We are mandolinists, amateurs; woe to him who gets caught by it! This tremendous music destroys one and renders one incapable of composing any more.'

Puccini reserved his greatest admiration, however, for *Parsifal* and once, in Vienna in 1923, he booked seats for three successive performances, intending to take in only one act from each and to concentrate on that. The spell was too great; he ended up sitting through all three performances in their entirety. Like Debussy before him, Puccini was attracted most by the orchestration of *Parsifal*, for the theme of the drama, with its overtly religious content, would not be of irresistible appeal to anyone with the aetheistic inclinations admitted by Puccini.

Ferrucio Busoni went to the Bayreuth Festival in 1888 as a guest of the piano manufacturer Steinway. Busoni had never regarded Wagner's music very highly and, like other composers, Debussy amongst them, dreaded the influence it could have on a creative artist striving to establish an individual style.

Sergei Rachmaninov visited Bayreuth in 1902 and saw the *Ring*, *Holländer* and *Parsifal*. He was on his honeymoon and the tickets for the performances were a wedding present from his fellow-pianist, Alexander Siloti. While there he met his fellow-countryman, Nikolai Rimsky-Korsakov.

By the turn of the century these clearly defined national attitudes to Wagner and Bayreuth were beginning to disintegrate. The Festival was becoming a feature on the tourist map and many of the visitors (like tourists in any age) were aggrieved rather than pleased to encounter their fellow-countrymen abroad. Mingling with habitués were many who had surely never set foot in their native opera houses but felt it necessary to be able to say back home that they had taken in the spectacle of Bayreuth after the fashion of say, Oberammergau.

With the musical developments of the succeeding decade Wagner took on an old-fashioned aspect and, for the young progressive musician, to be seen at Bayreuth was to risk being labelled an incorrigible reactionary. The changes in the Festival audience that were to be so marked after the 1914–24 hiatus were already starting to manifest themselves.

PART V

The Festival Established,
1896–1914

Albert Lavignac

Albert Lavignac, (1846–1916) was a French musicologist and teacher at the Paris Conservatoire (where he counted Debussy among his pupils). His book Le voyage artistique à Bayreuth *contained, in addition to the following description of life at the Festival in the 1890s, a catalogue of leitmotives after the manner of Wolzogen, and a detailed account of the stories of the dramas. Published in 1896 it is still in use by the French, and the American edition, called the* Operas of Richard Wagner, *is still in print.*

Bayreuth, as is witnessed by the beauty of many of its monuments and the width of its streets, had its period of splendour when it was the residence of the Margraves during the seventeenth and the first half of the eighteenth century. It has now again become a fine provincial town, quiet and easy-going; life should be comfortable and peaceful there, to judge from several imposing private hotels which are almost palatial, the smart houses which line the aristocratic quarters, and the fine theatre, whose interior, a veritable marvel of the rococo style, attests past grandeur. This theatre, which keeps a respectful silence when its celebrated and overpowering neighbour begins to speak, offers all the sweetness of Italian music, of opera comique, and even of operettas to the inhabitants of Bayreuth, who seem to welcome with interest such offerings as *Lucia.*

But it is on the approach of the performances in the Festival Theatre that the town is to be seen departing from its accustomed calm and adorning itself to welcome its guests, who become more numerous each season.

A full month in advance the performers, coming from all parts of Germany, and even from abroad, to co-operate in the great work, begin to animate the usually silent streets with their presence, gathering in the inns, and from morning to night dotting the road leading to the Theatre to which they are called by the numerous rehearsals.

The hotels make their toilette; private houses, destined also to entertain strangers, are put in their best order – nothing is too good, according to the idea of these kind and hospitable people, for the expected lodgers. The householder, who has cleaned her house from top to bottom with scrupulous care, in honour of her visitors deprives herself of all her ornaments to decorate their rooms lavishly, adding garlands and bunches of artificial flowers. She selects the finest embroidered sheets from her chests, and provokingly puts covers, which are always too narrow, on them by means of a complicated system of buttons. The first night or two we are a little out of our bearings, but we quickly grow accustomed to this strange fashion and soon come to sleep peacefully under the benevolent eyes of the host's family portraits, among which a bust of Wagner and a lithograph of Franz Liszt are always found.

During this period of preparation and work, it is especially in the neighbourhood of the Festival Theatre that activity is concentrated. The artists have not always the time, after the morning rehearsals, to go back to the town at the lunch hour, and often take their meal in the spacious restaurant, which is nearby, and which is also smartened up and festooned with the Bavarian colours to receive in a few days the numerous guests to whom it will serve the most varied menus of a good French cuisine. In the meanwhile, it supplies the personnel of the Theatre with a very comfortable dinner (in Germany they dine at one o'clock), for the modest sum of one mark. There is nothing more amusing than these groups in which Siegfried is seen fraternising with Mime, and Parsifal in no wise terrified by the presence of the Flower Maidens. At a table set in the open air, and always surrounded by a family group, dines Hans Richter, who with his sandy beard, large-brimmed hat, and short velvet coat, would be recognised among a thousand.

But the hour strikes; it is time to get back to work – the large carriage drawn by two white horses, well-known to the inhabitants of Bayreuth, arrives, and after describing a skilful curve, sets down before the porch of the Theatre the inspirer and oracle of all this little world, Frau Wagner, the valiant custodian of the traditions and wishes of the Master, whose activity never forsakes her and who is present at all the rehearsals, watching over the smallest details. Here also is Herr von Gross, who seconds Frau Wagner's efforts with his wide knowledge of affairs and enlightened devotion.

We next direct our steps to the hall, where the door is shut, conscientiously guarded by an old servant of Wahnfried. The silence lasts until nightfall and is only broken by an occasional pedestrian – inhabitants of the town who sometimes stroll as far as this to enjoy the view and the splendid sunsets which are to be seen from the terraced gardens adjoining the Theatre.

The ordinary rehearsals are strictly private; but to the general rehearsals of each work, which take place just before the opening of the season, Frau Wagner invites her friends in Bayreuth (who have no seats in the series, which are all reserved for strangers), and also the families of her faithful auxiliaries, the artists.

It would be impossible, moreover, to judge the desired sonorous effects if these rehearsals took place in an empty hall; the presence of the spectators very sensibly improves the sound.

The date fixed months before for the first performance at last arrives: everyone is at his post, armed and ready; the town is adorned with flags, and, let it be said in passing, there is no fear of missing the French colours from among the flags of all nationalities, which will at once reassure those people who are doubtful – if any remain – of their kind reception by the Bavarians.

In a few hours Bayreuth is full of the animation of its great days. People very limited with regard to time often arrive at the last moment; but that is a bad plan, and we cannot advise too strongly those who can do it to reserve at least half a day for rest, during which they may familiarise themselves with the very special moral atmosphere of this little district, before they climb the leafy road which leads to the Theatre. People do not go there as they go to the Opéra in Paris, or in any other city, taking with them their cares of yesterday and their worldly indifference. Or at least they should not go thus, for it would be voluntarily depriving themselves of one of the world's most intense artistic emotions it is possible to experience, if they entered the hall of the Festival Theatre at Bayreuth without being sympathetically attuned to what they have come to hear. Unfortunately that is what often happens now that the Wagnerian pilgrimage has become as fashionable as it is to go to Spa or to Monte Carlo. I know perfectly well that it is impossible to make all the spectators pass an examination before permitting them to enter the hall, or to make sure that, either by their musical education or by the intelligent interest which they take in matters of art, they are worthy to enter the sanctuary; but it must be confessed that it is painful to hear the remarks which, by their absurd nature, show how unworthy is a certain portion of the public that now frequents Bayreuth. I have heard one woman ask who was the author of the piece to be given the next day; and another rejoiced that they were going to perform 'Sifurd' [*sic*] which she liked so much. Her companion, an enlightened musician, to whom she made this astonishing remark, set himself respectfully, though greatly distressed, to correct her grave error, and began to sketch for her the subject of the Tetralogy, which indeed interested her very much, for she had not the least notion of it; when darkness enveloped the hall and the grumblings of the prelude to the first Act of *Die Walküre* were heard, it was then necessary to interrupt this education, alas so tardily begun.

More than an hour before the time fixed for the opera a long line of carriages forms to bring the public to the Theatre. These carriages, too few for the numbers of rich enthusiasts, are taken by assault; it is well to engage them in advance if you do not wish to go on foot, which you can do in a delightful walk of about twenty minutes along the shady lanes parallel with the principal avenue. The landaus and victorias, somewhat out of date and made to be drawn by two horses, have never more than one – harnessed to the right of the shaft, as horses are scarce here, which produces the most comical effect.

If you are among the first to arrive, you have ample leisure to examine the newcomers and notice that the toilettes have singularly gained in elegance during the past few years. Formerly everyone was contented with a simple travelling costume; then, little by little, the standard rose and if tourist costume is to be seen now it is in the minority. I speak here principally of the ladies, who display bright and fresh toilettes. The sole annoying point about them is the hat, which they will not consent to leave with the attendants during the performance, when it is strictly forbidden to keep it on the head. They resign themselves to holding it on their laps, which is scarcely comfortable.

This moment of waiting in the open air and daylight, for the performance begins at four o'clock, is perfectly charming. The situation of the Theatre, admirably chosen by Wagner, commanding a smiling country with the town in the foreground and the woods and meadows of green Franconia for the horizon, is absolutely enchanting. However it must not rain, for the novel building, so well arranged for everything else, offers under its external arcades, which are open to every wind, only very poor shelter – here at such times the public huddles under umbrellas streaming with rain. But doubtless God protects the spectators of Bayreuth, for it is generally fine and it is possible to stay outside till the last moment.

Now let us go into the auditorium and make its acquaintance while it is still brightly illuminated.

You enter it in the simplest way: no black-coated gentlemen seated behind a desk. One employee only is found at each of the numerous entrances to see that you have not mistaken your door and to tear off the coupon for the performance of that day. You can come back again after each interval without anyone bothering about you.

The hall . . . before the curtain rises gives one the impression of an aviary in full activity; everyone is moving about, more or less excited, and talking with his neighbour, exchanging his impressions, or else relating his previous visits to this musical spot; then you search the distant rows for friends or simply for the familiar faces of those you know to be attending the same series as you.

During this time the gallery reserved for the crowned heads fills up. Frau Wagner's seats are filling in their turn. Her aristocratic profile is to be seen – she seats herself in the front row with her delightful daughters and Siegfried Wagner, the living image of his father, joins them when his duties do not call him to the orchestra or to the stage. However, the last call of the trumpets sounds outside and the rare late arrivals enter. Suddenly darkness envelopes the hall and there is perfect silence. I should like it better if people were silent from the very first. It seems to me that all this agitation is a bad preparation for what is to come but it cannot be prevented.

The eye can distinguish nothing at first, then it gradually becomes accustomed to the feeble light produced by some lamps near the ceiling. From this moment one might hear a pin drop – everyone concentrates his thoughts and every heart beats with emotion. Then amidst the luminous and golden tone which arises from the depths of the 'mystic abyss' there mount warm, vibrant and velvety, the incomparable harmonies unknown elsewhere and which, taking possession of your whole being, transport you to a world of dreams. The curtain parts in the middle and moves to each side of the stage, exposing to view scenery which, as a rule, is very beautiful. Criticism, which never gives up its rights, disapproves of many things, though almost always wrongly in our opinion; but let us set that question aside to recall our impressions at the end of the act when we start from our ecstasy to go out, the last chord having sounded, and breathe the pure fresh air outside.

Let us state in passing that the atmosphere of the hall, due probably to an ingenious system of ventilation, has never seemed mephitic to us, like the majority of theatres we know; on returning we do not experience that asphyxiating sensation that is usually so disagreeable.

Nothing could be more delicious or more restful than these intervals passed in the open air, nor could anything be more gay; we find many people there, we hear French spoken on all sides and we have the feeling of being at home, as if coming out of the Conservatoire, or the Lamoureux or Colonne concerts – but homesickness never enters our heads.

Usually at the end of the performance people go to supper in one of the large restaurants immediately adjoining the Theatre. There is a third a little higher up and a little more isolated, where those who like to prolong their impressions will find a calm, quiet and comfortable retreat.

It is prudent to engage a table in advance at the large restaurant, for without doing so we risk a very late supper. The cuisine there is excellent. We can either select a very fine meal for which we will have to pay accordingly, or we can be quite well satisfied at a more reasonable price. The artists often meet here, and when after a performance one who has greatly delighted the public enters, it is not rare to see everybody rise spontaneously to give him a warm and vociferous ovation. And this is much the more willingly because they never appear on the stage to receive the plaudits of their admirers. This is a custom which Wagner established from the first. At first it was even strictly prohibited to applaud at the end of the work, and the first performances of the *Ring* which during the first year comprised the programme of the Festival, ended in a respectful and affecting silence, which certainly agreed better with the poignant impression left by the marvellous final scene than noisy demonstrations; however, several regrettable infractions of the rule took place, the enthusiasm manifesting itself in the usual way, which was against Wagner's wish and which he had much trouble in repressing. It has always remained the tradition not to applaud *Parsifal* but for the other works the public has had its way: it is not possible to prevent the bravos breaking out at the end of the performance. The public even took it into its head, in 1896, at the end of the first cycle, to call for Richter, who had conducted the Tetralogy in a masterly manner. For more than a quarter of an hour frantic applause and shouts, enough to bring the house down, were heard on every side; but the noble and modest artist, faithful to the established rule, did not yield to the general wish and remained obstinately out of sight; he even avoided showing himself at supper where he doubtless feared a renewal of the demonstrations. A similar scene recurred over Mottl eight days later. He had literally electrified the audience by his admirable conducting of the orchestra, but being just as retiring as his rival, he kept out of sight with the same modesty. And when Siegfried Wagner's turn came to conduct his father's work, he also respectfully conformed to the tradition notwithstanding the sympathetic recalls of the entire audience.

The mornings pass quickly in Bayreuth; while waiting for the Theatre to open we visit the town and the monuments, which to tell the truth have only a secondary interest – but it is pleasant to lounge about there. The local guide books will tell the reader that he must see the old castle where there is a tower, to the top of which you can drive in a carriage and from which a beautiful view is to be had of the surrounding country – pleasant, smiling and fertile. The new castle too, which contains a collection of indifferent pictures; also indicated are the statues of kings, writers and pedagogues which adorn the squares, the churches which ought to be visited (enumerating the while, the tombs of the Margraves contained therein). The conscientious tourist will certainly not neglect to make this round in detail. Others, on the contrary, maintaining that they have come solely on a musical pilgrimage, do not wish to know anything else than the road leading to the Festival Theatre.

Many people employ their mornings in reading over a score of the work they will hear in the evening – and they are not the worst employed. You can produce a passable piano at a large price, but you need to be a millionaire to hire a good grand piano! In every street are harmonious noises to be heard and from numerous open windows float the well-known leitmotives.

The indolent, to rest their minds, content themselves with quiet walks through the streets and with visits to the bookshops, where are to be seen the classic collections of portraits of the Master, photographs of the principal artists, and lithographs representing an evening at Wahnfried. Formerly there were also shops full of souvenirs of Bayreuth which offered all possible extravagances and were highly amusing. But they have now become more quiet and this year you would have great difficulty in finding foulards with the Festival Theatre printed in two colours or shirts with their fronts embroidered with leitmotives.

The lunch hour comes quickly – then, according to our purse or our tastes, we go either to one of the fine and famous restaurants which are found in the principal streets and in all the large hotels (there we can meet the stars and main personalities from the Theatre) or to the more picturesque and characteristic inns, such as Vogl's garden, where the artists and the old inhabitants of Bayreuth often meet after performances. Here in the open air we can try the excellent beer of the country, served in a mug of extraordinary height and capacity, surmounted by a pewter lid, which is as embarrassing to novices as the long-necked vase was to the fox in the fable. For one of these mugs you pay the astonishing price of fifteen pfennigs. With this Bavarian beer it is not unfitting to take an omelette aux confitures, or those delicious *pfannkuchen* of which only the German cuisine has the secret, or a dish of sausages and sauerkraut. Let not delicate palates exclaim at this: what seems gross at home often becomes quite delicious when served in its proper surroundings. The buffet at the railway station also offers those who would lunch a source which is often overlooked – but there you are well treated and served much more speedily than elsewhere.

Let it be said here that, contrary to the accepted opinion, the trip to Bayreuth does not necessarily mean 'an excessive expenditure' and it is within reach of even modest purses.

Lavignac then gives a carefully calculated list of expenses which would be incurred variously by a young man of the student type, by someone of less stringent means and by a person who required to indulge himself with every available comfort. The amounts are now of as little interest as such values ever are – except that there is a ratio of only two to one between the highest and lowest figures.

During the days of rest which separate the performances, or in the mornings, it is pleasant to make some of the excursions which the environs offer.

You can go to Bad Berneck – the trip is about two hours in a carriage; it shows you the picturesque corner of a smiling valley and the little town is beautifully situated on a rock in a wild and rugged countryside – it makes for delightful walks. There is also the Eremitage whose beautiful park and celebrated elm grove merit more attention than the hideous structure of the castle, encrusted from top to bottom in shell-work and cut coloured pebbles. Let us mention, however, a quite graceful colonnade in a semi-circle and the ornamental ponds in which different jets of water can be made to play in your honour – like the far distant ones of Versailles.

The Fantasie, the park of which is open to the public, is a private estate and is almost always rented during the season to some distinguished visitor. From the terrace of this castle there is a lovely and melancholy view, which reminds you of certain works of Gustav Doré.

All of these places are naturally provided with restaurants where you can lunch; here are to be found our neighbours of yesterday and tomorrow, as well as the artists, who come with their families to rest after their interesting but severe labour. Sympathetic relations are quickly established and you cannot resist the pleasure of seizing their hand, even if you do not know them, and congratulating them on their intelligent interpretation. You can express yourself in French if you do not speak German – such things are understood in all languages. In my opinion one of the charms of life at Bayreuth is this frequent meeting with the artists whose lives are so often full of interesting particulars.

You also have the chance of seeing them at Wahnfried, if good fortune gives you the right of introduction there.

Frau Wagner, triumphing over all the fatigues caused by her arduous occupation, every week during the season gives entertainments, to which she invites her personal friends and a small number of the fortunate elect. As precious as any other memories are those passed in the house of the Master, which is so full of him, and amongst those who have known him and been with him.

How can we describe the exceptional charm of the mistress of the house and the exquisite affability with which she receives the most modest as well as the most authoritative of the admirers of Wagner? We, for our part, are profoundly touched by it, as well as by her gracious and very particular courtesy to the French visitors. Frau Wagner is admirably seconded in her role by her son and her very charming daughters, who rival each other in the amiable reception of their guests.

At these receptions the interpreters from the Theatre are often heard (as are artists from outside) marvellously accompanied by Herr Mottl who, not contenting himself with being a great orchestral conductor, is also a pianist of the highest order.

The large central salon of the villa, where they have the music, is ornamented with a very handsome bust of Wagner, and statues of his principal heroes – the Flying Dutchman, Lohengrin, Tannhäuser, Walter von Stolzing and Hans Sachs. A frieze also represents the principal scenes of the *Ring*. The superb library adjoining this salon proves by the number and choice of its volumes the rare erudition as well as the eclecticism of the man who formed it. Here also, among a

profusion of objects of art and valuable souvenirs, we admire interesting portraits of the Master and his wife.

The villa is situated in a fine park at the end of the Richard-Wagnerstrasse,
originally called the Rennweg, one of the principal arteries of the town. It is built
in the style of a Roman villa and in the front, above the door, is an allegorical
fresco representing Wotan and his two ravens with the muses of tragedy and
music on either side, and by them the young Siegfried. Beneath it is an inscription
telling how Wagner found peace here.

It is in the grounds of this estate, in a spot selected by himself, that the Master
sleeps his last sleep, near those who loved him so much and who only live to
venerate and glorify his memory. On Sunday morning, making a pious
pilgrimage, you can pass through this gate which is left open then, to the austere,
bare tomb overlooking the town recreation area, a beautiful park laid out with
ancient trees.

The auditorium of the model Theatre contains 1,344 seats, arranged as a fan-
shaped amphitheatre within a rectangular building. Each seat consists of a large
folding cane-seat without arm rests. Because of the fan-shaped layout the
number of seats is not the same in each row; the first contains only thirty-two
while the thirtieth row has fifty-two – the seats are placed alternately in each of
the rows so that everyone is obstructed as little as possible by those in front and a
good view may be had from every point. However, it is certain that the best seats
for seeing as well as hearing are in the middle of the fourth to eighth rows.

Behind this amphitheatre, and consequently at the very back of the hall, is a
row of nine boxes reserved for important guests and the Wagner family and their
invited guests. Although I believe that the public may sometimes get seats here at
a price, officially they are not at the public disposal, which is not a matter for
regret, for they are so far away from the stage that you are better off elsewhere.

Finally, above these boxes, there is another large gallery containing two
hundred seats, for which the personnel of the Festival have first call. There you
can hear marvellously well but you have a bad view and it gets very warm. So, including these places, the auditorium altogether contains about 1,500 spectators.
There is no ticket office – the entrances and exits are ten side doors, five on each
side, opening directly from the outside and each giving access to a certain
number of rows.

The lighting consists of a double row of incandescent electric lamps; the lower
row, midway up the columns which surround the hall, is entirely extinguished
one minute before the beginning of each act; the other, quite close to the roof, is
simply turned down – there is then almost total darkness.

The ventilation is perfect; it is never too warm and yet no draught is ever felt.

The orchestra, which is hidden out of sight by means of a double screen which
partly covers it, is arranged upon steps, which are a continuation of those on
which the seats of the spectators are placed, and descend a long way under the
stage as if into a kind of cave which has been called a 'mystic abyss'. There the instruments are grouped by families exactly as at any large symphony concert,

except that things are reversed – the conductor and violins being above and the heavy instruments below at the back; moreover, the first violins are to the right and the second to the left, as if the normal orchestra were reversed.

The backstage accommodation is a little larger in overall space than the auditorium – the curtain therefore divides the building into two as far as its length is concerned. The stage is very deep, perhaps unnecessarily so, for the whole of it is never used and the back merely serves as a kind of store room for the properties. There is nothing unique about the arrangements – it is almost the same as you would expect to find in any well-equipped theatre, the height of the roof and the depth under the stage are adequate to allow of an entire scene being raised or lowered. It also may be taken into the wings on either side. The artists' dressing-rooms are spacious but extremely simple. A little room serves as a foyer for the instrumentalists to tune up in, as this is not allowed in the orchestra where silence is maintained before the performance.

There is no foyer for the public – the surrounding countryside takes its place when it is fine, as it generally is in July and August; in case of bad weather people take refuge in one of the café-restaurants which have been established in the vicinity since the Theatre was opened in 1876. On the same floor as the various boxes is a little annexe (built in 1882) with three fine rooms, one of which is a dining room with a buffet, serving as ante-rooms for the principal privileged guests. These rooms are also used for rehearsals but are never opened to the public. Finally, above, on the gallery level, is a long room in the form of a lobby where the innumerable wreaths sent from all over the world on the occasion of Wagner's funeral are piously preserved on the walls; there too may be seen, under a protective glass, the slate on which he was accustomed to write the hours for the next rehearsal, and which still bears his last commands. In the adjoining room the already voluminous archive is kept.

The exterior of the edifice is not at all remarkable. It is a large building of red brick, with projecting beams and a base of free-stone, with very little of the artistic in its appearance. Its best feature is the little court in the form of a loggia, added afterwards, with the balcony and reception rooms. It is all without any architectural pretension – it was planned solely with a view to practical use and this end has been well attained.

I once experimented with myself in a way which I do not now regret but which I would not repeat for anything in the world because it was most distressing. The series of performances I was to attend consisted of *Parsifal, Meistersinger, Tristan* and *Parsifal* again. I had devoted several weeks to a profound study of *Parsifal* so that there would be no surprises in it for me, I already knew the *Meistersinger* pretty well, but – and *this* is the important part of my experience – I had not read a note of *Tristan*, a few fragments of which was all that I knew and those from poor performances.

Now this is what happened: the two days of *Parsifal* were for me two days of the most pure and never-to-be-forgotten happiness, I was actually living amongst the Knights of the Grail, and I seemed to be in a dream as I strolled about outside between the acts smoking my cigarette; the scenic illusion was as complete as possible and the happy impression it left upon me will never be effaced from my memory. I was more highly amused by the buffooneries (although somewhat coarse) of the *Meistersinger* than I had ever been at the Palais Royal; at the same time I was profoundly moved by the tender kindliness of Sachs and his very touching spirit of self-sacrifice. But as for *Tristan* I understood nothing at all, nothing, nothing, absolutely nothing – is that fully understood?

It does take a certain amount of courage to admit these things, especially when one has subsequently succeeded in penetrating the innumerable beauties of *Tristan und Isolde* – but I wish my sad example to be of service to others and therefore it is necessary to relate it.

We must not go to Bayreuth then without having first made a serious preparatory study of the works which we are going to hear, and this study is just as necessary for the words as for the music. The more the study is prolonged and the more it is intelligently conducted, the more the pleasure and satisfaction we may promise ourselves from it.

The characteristic of every Wagnerian artist-interpreter, as we find him at Bayreuth (and there only), is complete disinterestedness, the abnegation of his own personality, as well as his own interests – according to the example set by the Master, he goes there with no other motive than the pure desire of producing Art for the sake of Art. Therefore no one, neither the singers nor the members of the chorus, the players in the orchestra nor the scene-shifters, the trainers nor the musical assistants, receive anything in the nature of money or reward; all they receive is a simple indemnity which scarcely covers their living expenses – sometimes they refuse even that. Their travelling expenses are paid, and they are lodged in a local house at the charge of the administration; when the performances come to an end they depart without having realised any pecuniary profit – for they have not come for that. The happiness of co-operating in the great work, of participating in a magnificent manifestation of beauty, is quite sufficient for them, they are the priests of Art and artists in the purest and highest sense of the word – and, with rare exceptions, they are religious artists, convinced of the greatness of their mission.

For the singer who is heard in Paris, Munich, Berlin or elsewhere, the greatest composer will always be the one who has afforded him the greatest number of successes; the best work that in which the best role is allotted to him; he thinks more of the business side than of the artistic, seeking above all to please the public, to have himself entrusted with an important and effective role (so as to be able afterwards to look forward to more advantageous engagements) and finally, to get rich. But on the day he comes to Bayreuth all such ideas of money are dismissed – it is a pilgrimage that he is performing, and from the first moment his whole will and intelligence are directed solely to a respectful interpretation of the work, putting aside the sordid considerations and petty jealousies of the green-room. His sole aim henceforth is to render as faithfully as possible the part which is assigned to him without attempting to introduce into it any other effects than those which are written in it, conforming to the exact letter and to the tradition which is now still alive in the minds and memories of the surviving collaborators of the revered Master.

We can well understand, their individual worth apart, what cohesion and veracity the execution and interpretation will gain when the performer is inspired with such feelings, when he sees his function as part of a proud ritual, when he sees around him colleagues impregnated with a like respect for the dignity of Art.

It is not, therefore, the perfection of personal virtuosity of this singer or that to which the exceptionally striking and captivating character of the Bayreuth performances must be attributed, but to that intimate solidarity, to that boundless devotion to the common cause which allows an artist, who is everywhere else accustomed to play leading parts, to accept here, without loss of dignity, the most insignificant role, in which he will acquit himself with as much zeal and conscientiousness as if he were the hero. The same singers may well be seen elsewhere on other stages but they will never be as they are here, because they have not the same inspiration.

The performer who intends to tackle the Wagner repertory must be endowed with rare and manifold qualities. Above all he must have a natural artistry, be an excellent musician and one who is not baffled by any demands of intonation, for Wagner, by the very essence of his style, treats the voice as a chromatic instrument, or rather as a keyboard with a high and a low compass and various registers. The Wagner interpreter must also have the true qualities of a dramatic actor for there is as much action and byplay as singing and the slightest fault, the least degree of awkwardness on the stage, in this theatre becomes the equivalent of a wrong note – it jars like a discord.

Every role has been minutely mapped out by Wagner down to the smallest detail, effects are not to be sought after and those that are intended are there to be observed. The best interpreter is therefore the one who is most faithful to the score. Above all let it not be thought that this docile and respectful manner of interpretation lessens in the smallest degree the singer's prestige – on the contrary it shows that he is possessed of the purest and most exquisite artistic sensibilities.

Bayreuth then should not be visited for the sake of hearing or seeing the performer but for hearing and seeing the work – but considering ourselves fortunate if we happen to chance upon an interpretation of the highest order which sometimes happens, but it is in no way necessary for the understanding of the work.

The orchestra at Bayreuth, although large, is never noisy. If any fault is to be found with it, it is rather that of being sometimes too subdued; it never drowns the voices of the singers and every syllable is distinctly audible. This may arise from the articulation of the performers, which is exceedingly clear in general, and from the numerous consonants of the German language, but it is certain that the underground situation of the orchestra, like an inverted amphitheatre and covered with a screen, also has a lot to do with it. The blending of brass and string tone from these depths sometimes produces an organ-like tone which is only to be heard at Bayreuth.

In addition, there is nothing more curious than the sight of the orchestra during a performance but unfortunately no one, without a single exception, is allowed to go into the pit – it is heavily guarded. The carefully shaded incandescent lights illumine the music stands in front of each player (the majority of these in their shirt sleeves for it is warm in July) who is giving his whole heart to his work. People are fond of telling how large tankards of beer are set beside the players from which they drink when they have a few bars' rest – but this is quite untrue. In fact, when their part does give them a rest, the neglected ones of the orchestra, the trombones and tubas who dwell in the depths of the cave, creep surreptitiously among the music stands to try to get a momentary glimpse of a corner of the stage, a delight which is reserved solely for the violins who are placed up at the top edge of the orchestra.

The conductor is above too (like the others he takes off his jacket and cravat) and has his face lighted by two lamps whose powerful reflections ensure that no one in the orchestra or on the stage may lose any of his gestures or facial expressions; it is not his score that is illuminated – he knows that by heart and rarely glances at it – it is himself, the absolute master, the sole one on whom the final responsibility of the performance falls.

Wagner attached great importance to the scenery, which he planned himself and which was executed under his direction by the scene-painters. The smallest detail was not allowed to escape his notice. It is easy to understand that in a completely darkened auditorium, where the eyes of the spectator are neither dazzled by the footlights nor distracted by any trifling or passing incidents, the expressive force of the scenery is singularly enhanced. Even the curtain is expressive – it does not rise as in every other theatre but parts in the middle and gracefully rises towards the top corners with rapidity or with a deliberate majesty according to what is appropriate, regulated like everything else by the scrupulously careful Master, who left nothing to chance. For instance, after the tremendous closing scene of the *Ring*, the curtain closes somewhat regretfully; on more joyous scenes it falls as if a blow.

If the Wagnerian decor is not always of extraordinary richness, it is more sober than that of the Opéra in Paris and therefore more harmonious – by this I mean it is more appropriate to the work and more fitting to produce the desired effects.

Among the parts which seem to me to be less effective I will particularly mention the Flower Maidens' scene with its loud and brutal hues and monstrous and improbable blooms which remind one of provincial hotels rather than the domain of magic and sorcery; the rainbow in the last scene of *Rheingold* which seems to be made of wood; the tableau of the Venusberg, which has never been a success on any stage and may well be impossible to realise; Loge too must be reproached for extreme parsimony in the matter of flames around the sleeping Valkyrie; the *Ride* is childish too. But these are small details to which we attach little importance when we are captivated by the whole concept.

Despite all that has been said about it the stage machinery is not at all extra-ordinary – it is that of any well-equipped theatre. Sometimes it is very ingenious, but with simple means; thus the scenery in *Parsifal* which passes from one side to the other, giving the onlooker the impression it is he who is moving. To avoid having to close the curtain at the change of some scenes there is a clever system of jets of steam which rise from the ground and mingle with the clouds painted on gauze, concealing from the audience what is happening on the stage. The Rhine-maidens, who seem to be actually swimming in the waters, moving with sur-prising ease, and covering the whole height of the stage, darting up to the top as if to breathe the air at the surface of the water, are simply lying in a kind of metal cradle, raised by hidden ropes (this device dates from 1896 – the means used in 1876 were more complicated and less effective). At the first rehearsal one of these sprites fainted, but she was in no danger for each has a group of six stagehands controlled by one of the musical assistants who are there to make sure the gyrations coincide with the music and the impotent flounderings of Alberich. The dragon is little more than an ordinary fairy-stage contrivance; a man makes him open his jaws and roll his eyes while the singer of the part of Fafner, standing behind the back of the scenery, bellows and roars into an enormous speaking-trumpet.

The stage business is quite different from ours. The singers play much less to the audience than to each other, they look at each other when they sing, they are not afraid of turning their backs on the audience when the dramatic action so demands – for example, Parsifal stands in this position in the foreground without moving during the latter half of the first act – they behave on the stage as they would in real life, without being conscious of the audience in front of them. This is so natural to them that it does not seem at all remarkable to us, but if one of them does it differently and acts in the conventional manner, addressing his gestures and words to the audience, we are immediately taken aback and alarmed. When there is a chorus the members do not arrange themselves in two symmetrical rows, like soldiers drawn up on parade, or in a semi-circle exactly facing the audience, all raising their arms together like automata at the loudest note. Each one has his individual part which he plays sings and acts, the result being a feeling of dramatic truth and faithfulness to life that is infinitely satisfying.

The costumes of the men are generally very beautiful; those of the women do not lend themselves to splendour so readily as does the brilliant armour of the knights. With the exception of the martial equipment of the eight Valkyries, a few rich female toilettes in *Lohengrin* and the betrothal outfits of Eva and Isolde, Queen of Cornwall, the heroines by the very nature of their characters are not intended to make a display of elegance. But let us take note, in passing, of the adornment of Freia in *Rheingold* which was copied from a figure in Botticelli's *Spring*.

At Bayreuth there are no bells to announce the end of the intervals, when the time has arrived a small band of trumpets and trombones provided by the regiment in the garrison of Bayreuth, but dressed in civilian costume, comes out of the Theatre and sounds a loud fanfare to the four cardinal points in succession. These are made up of motives from the work that is being played and, written out by Wagner himself, contain a phrase from the act about to begin. The number of these players varies in accordance with the importance of the motive serving as the call, and in accordance with the degree to which it is set out in harmony – the last calls of *Lohengrin* and of the *Ring* may employ as many as twenty-four.

The three traditional blows are not struck – when all have seated themselves in obedience to the commands of the fanfares, darkness follows in the auditorium, bringing with it profound silence. A whole minute or so passes in deep reflection and then the first sounds are heard issuing from the orchestra.

The effect is solemn, dignified and full of respect. There is nothing anywhere to offer comparison with the fascination of Bayreuth – the only way to experience it, as no description, however true and however enthusiastic, can do it justice, is to make the journey.

'He who would understand the poet must visit the country of the poet.'

Lilli Lehmann

Lilli Lehmann, who sang Woglinde in 1876, returned to Bayreuth to sing Brünnhilde in four of the five Ring cycles in 1896. In the years between she had become established as one of the leading Wagner singers outside Bayreuth. Personal reasons had prevented her from leading the Flower Maidens for Wagner in the 1882 Parsifal and when, in 1886, Cosima offered her a part in Tristan she turned it down when she discovered it was not Isolde but Brangäne. In these passages from her memoirs she contrasts the Bayreuth of 1896 with that she had known previously, in the days of Richard Wagner.

If there was ever anything to excite my delight and enthusiasm it was the revival of the *Nibelungen Ring* at Bayreuth. For me it was the celebration of the end of a period of internal conflict and heavy personal losses – I wanted to let my Brünnhilde express my feelings about all this – I longed to carry everybody away to the lofty heights, to make them rejoice or make them weep, just as I had experienced throughout the last twenty years. I yearned to do it in this very place – I wanted to sing in remembrance of those who were here no longer – I desired to be submerged in my task and so to seek release from all material cares.

Memories immediately overcame me as I entered the Villa Gerber, for it was here that Niemann and Betz (Siegmund and Wotan of 1876) had lodged. From upstairs one had a view of the little town and the Fichtelgebirge beyond. Soon I hastened to the Festspielhaus, which was not far off, where Frau Cosima, swathed in black, sat on the stage and directed the placing of the scenery for the third act of *Walküre*. Siegfried dashed back and forth, as his father used to do – the image of him in all his actions!

When I went back to the Festspielhaus at about four o'clock the first act was being rehearsed with the singers – my heart turned to stone. With the exception of Frau Sucher (Sieglinde), who acted beautifully, I saw and heard only wooden puppets and I thought, with sorrow, of 1876 when Niemann, with but one glance, set the seal on the whole first act.

I did not speak to Cosima and the children until the evening, when they greeted me quite cordially. Cosima was more happy and cheerful than she had ever been – she was full of energy and vitality and occupied at the theatre from nine in the morning to nine at night. Dinner and supper she took at the theatre, with artists invited to her table – which they called the 'High Table' but which was very lively and uninhibited. Cosima, apart from being clever and well-informed, assumed an authority of judgment so that what she proclaimed was, like some aristocrat, accepted as infallible. The result was some wonderful judgments! For example, one day we were discussing the closing scene of *Götterdämmerung* and I mentioned Frau Vogl's dramatic ride to death as Brünnhilde. She was an accomplished horsewoman, usually taking her own Grane with her to guest appearances. In the finale she would unbridle her horse, swing herself up on to his back, and together they would leap into the flaming funeral pyre. Cosima called this a circus stunt, not fit to be seen on the stage. I remarked that it was what Wagner had instructed and when there was a Brünnhilde who could do it the effect produced was very fine. But she did not agree with that and the matter was not raised again. Myself, I had promised to represent a 'warrior maid' and not an expert rider as my contribution to the Festival work.

I soon realised, hearing such pronouncements, that there remained little affection for the artists of 1875–6 and that their best was now considered 'quite unacceptable'. So I tempered the edge of my tongue until I had fully discovered the extent of the present Bayreuth judgments and no longer had any doubt that these were in opposition to the 1875–6 tradition – and thus to Wagner's own ideas.

Mottl had already informed me that Cosima had changed the whole of *Parsifal* in 1883, so it was not surprising that she had no respect for 1876 and now relied on her own taste and desires exclusively. During the first few days, I was present at a quite ridiculous acting rehearsal when the bass, Grengg, who had a divine voice and was the most good-natured Viennese rogue, was being initiated in the part of Hagen by Cosima. She explained Hagen's antecedents fully and systematically – but what interest was this to Grengg? In the end he took his instruction in bad part and, telling me, 'Well I am lacking in the demonic', he took himself off. He was begged to return and, in spite of telegraphing a reply, 'I will not', he sang after all.

Cosima's manner had never been easy: her close friend, Countess von Schleinitz, commented after the 1876 Festival, 'Bayreuth is the graveyard of friendships', and even her fawning biographer, the Graf du Moulin Eckart, has to record that she was known as the 'Margravine von Bayreuth' on account of her imperious ways.

The Rhine-maidens' swimming apparatus, now a splendid flying machine, worked beautifully – it was therefore more regrettable that the three voices failed to blend. The second Rhine-maiden was chiefly to blame for this. She was terribly unmusical and ruined all the trios. *Rheingold* was beautifully staged and while it was more animated than in 1876 this animation was too restless and frequently distracted from the pleasure of the spectator. During the music which follows Loge's narration the gods all made obeisance to Wotan – the effect was really quite comical to see. This passage should express the echoing lamentations of the Rhine-maidens for the return of the gold. How could Frau Cosima make such a blunder? And how remote from Wagner's own direction! Fafner felled his brother with a single blow – while the orchestra hammered out four of them. Wagner would surely have wanted this followed more closely!

The everlasting standing in profile was carried to the point of madness. The spectator saw no acting – the singers stood with their backs always towards one side or other of the auditorium.

There was not a lot to attract me – my devotion to Wagner's own staging, to the artistic unity I had known, the deep impression these made, would not allow it. I suffered to see how the form of the *Ring*, which we had all so lovingly absorbed and taken away with us, together with our thoughts of its creator, was now being dislocated in the very place that was its home.

There were changes not only in *Rheingold* but also in the *Walküre* – in the love duet Siegmund and Sieglinde sat in reversed position; in contrast to 1876, Sieglinde was placed in a corner by the wings and Siegmund, gazing upon her, had to sing into the wings. The second act, in its staging and action, departed completely from 1876. In that year the fight took place on a broad path that ran across the whole stage, above the rocks – in 1896 it was acted out on the left side because the rocks were divided now by a path in the middle. In the first scene Brünnhilde stood on a rock at the right and went off to the right whereas in 1876 she had stood on the left side and, taking the path above the rocks, went off to the right. After the Annunciation of Death scene she now goes into a cave under the rocks, to the right, and reappears at the fight, for no clear reason from the left – and in a small wheeled apparatus, where she is confined like a dummy, unable to move shield or spear to protect Siegmund, let alone take part in any other action.

Splendid though the scenery was in itself it must be considered in the light of a need to provide a brilliant picture in order to contrast with the gloomy first and third acts – 'auf wolkigen Höh'n wohnen die Götter' sings Wotan, but black rocks such as these are not to be found on the cloudy heights – nor do they present an attractive setting. The impression ought to be brilliant, sunny and clear – it was so under Wagner and it was beautiful that way.

In 1896, in the second scene, the stage was covered with uneven lumps and the singer had not a foot's width of secure standing room – a very uncomfortable innovation. Equally removed from 1876 was the flat setting of the third act; it failed to offer the slightest elevation on which a number of figures might be grouped. Previously, several small protruding rocks enabled us Valkyries to rush on and take up lofty positions – but that was no longer possible with the 1896 sets, and the Valkyries had to stand in a row like soldiers.

From all sides came complaints of endless alterations to the staging and the posing of the singers – what one day would be stated as permanent would the next be rejected as wrong. With all this uncertainty for even the principal artists in 1896, Bayreuth contrasted with the administration and model of the true Master which all of us took away in 1876. These 1876 artists must surely have the correct perspective. I may be understood better if I say that Cosima, during the preliminary rehearsals for the *Ring*, was putting quite important decisions to her son, saying, 'You remember, Siegfried, do you not, that it was done this way in 1876?' Whereupon Siegfried always answered, 'I believe you are right, Mamma.' Siegfried was about six years old in 1876 and was rarely at rehearsals. I was often compelled to observe that it had not been as Cosima said and that she was incorrect in her opinion – but as soon as she was told that this or that had been different in 1876 the same answer always came – 'Quite so, but it was subsequently changed in this way.' Now, it is certain that some explanation of 'subsequently' would have been produced, so it became worthless to pursue the matter any further. Those who had been participants themselves could be forgiven if much had slipped from their memories in twenty busy years but to assume that a boy who was only six years old and who had taken no part should still remember anything – this was extremely audacious!

Shortly before the beginning of the dress rehearsals Hans Richter asked me whether, in 1876, Wotan had raised the sword from the hoard at the words 'so grüss ich die Burg' at the end of the *Rheingold*. I recalled the many deliberations but not the outcome, as we Rhine-maidens were occupied behind the scene at this point and could not see the stage. So I consulted Betz who told me it was not done at the commencement in 1876 but taken up later.

Artistic considerations caused me to call out frequently to the Rhine-maidens, 'Do it this way, sing it like this, move your body to give expression.' But I was never consulted and there was no demand for my experience and knowledge. No one had any time for us artists of 1876 and so much passed me by, passages I knew to be of great beauty, without moving me or rousing my interest. Love, heart and soul were wanting – as was the technique of revealing the inner beauties for the listener. The Rhine-maidens' final appeal to Wotan was given without expression – there were cries but no true lamentations. No one in present Bayreuth recalled 1876, when the tones of the Rhine-maidens were wrenched from their throats in mourning – but carrying too something of the brilliance of the gold with them.

Apart from Vogl, Mottl and Richter, my sister (who found herself singing the third Norn without knowing just how that came to happen) and myself, there were none present of those engaged in the 1876 *Ring* cycles. Hans Richter, the personification of selflessness, did for the young son of his old master what nobody else could, indeed would, have done. Already he had taken forty-six orchestral rehearsals with Siegfried diligently listening to see how it should be done. Richter took the first dress rehearsal, Siegfried the second and Mottl the final one. Of the actual public performances, Richter did the first and fifth, Mottl the third, and Siegfried the second and fourth cycles.

Richter was indeed a devoted servant of Bayreuth – he was associated with the Festivals until 1912 and took nothing for his work, not even expenses, declaring that the Master taught him all he knew and he did not expect to be paid for it. Richter lived in Bayreuth until his death in 1916.

The Lehmann memoirs continue with her account of an illness (an infection behind her ear) which almost caused her to cancel her appearances. But it responded to treatment, of a necessarily primitive nature, and she resumed her preparations.

Cosima, fearing that those she had ordered might be too late, asked me to bring my own costumes with me. She was right, for it was midday on the day of the *Walküre* performance when a suit of armour was sent to me – I took it as a mistake and informed the theatre that I would be wearing my own coat of chain mail in the *Ring*. However, it was no mistake. Poor Burgstaller, who was to sing Siegfried, approached me with the words, 'Look, dear lady, look at the Joan-of-Arc suit of armour they have dressed me up in.' Only after he had almost expired inside this armour was it retired in favour of the old type of loose chain mail.

There is detailed consideration of Brünnhilde's costume and the rightness and wrongness of cloak and gown and their respective colours in relation to the action and mood of the drama. Lehmann records her preference for a white gown and a red-blond wig. Much of this appears to have been of the fashion to which Shaw so much objected.

Nowadays, when dramatic art is reduced to nothing, when the use of space and scenic design is carried to extremes by producers, it is not possible to completely do without some form of gesticulation to convey expression – as Cosima feels herself compelled to assume. Stage heroes and heroines (and nearly everybody on the stage has to become one at some time or another) should not be allowed to look and behave like ordinary mortals and they should not be divested of their characteristic setting.

I write this free from any wish to reproach the great, strong and indomitable will of Frau Cosima with having thought too literally and with too little regard for practical stagecraft. I write it only to state an artistic standpoint which coincides with that of Richard Wagner himself and which only the experienced practitioner – distinct from the 'producer' or 'director' – can understand. For such reasons it was particularly startling when Waltraute came on in *Götterdämmerung* dressed in a costume so different from what was usual that I hardly recognised her. I was told at Wahnfried that this costume (like that of Fricka) with its long sleeves of six puffs falling over the hands was inspired by Botticelli's paintings of the Madonna. In vain I asked myself what Botticelli's Madonnas had to do with pagan goddesses. In 1876 the Valkyries wore long flowing robes but in 1896, by way of contrast, they were clad in short ones. In addition, in 1896, one of the sisters, Waltraute, underwent a disfiguring change into her *Götterdämmerung* costume – but I do not think Cosima was fully to blame for this.

In spite of all that went against the spirit of 1876 my memory of Cosima and my stay at Bayreuth does in no way lessen my esteem, artistic considerations apart, for such a remarkable and strong-willed woman. Her life was certainly not free from conflict and she had borne a great deal that the eyes of the world had not seen. On the contrary I believe that, in fact, in many ways we drew closer to one another and our relationship could well be expressed as the attraction of opposites. Cosima was the complete woman of the world and I was the complete artist. We understood each other very well while retaining our opposing outlook – and we did each other full justice, as one strong nature is able to sympathise with another. This was our point of contact. A fine lady and an artist can get on well at most times – until they both lay claim to perfection. Natural talent and personality lead each individual in a different way. Cosima is not an artist and I am not a woman of the world – this was fundamental to the contradictions of our ways.

All roads may lead to Rome but to the Bayreuth of today there is but one – the road of slavish subjection. There is no true conception of how valuable individual artistry can be. Without it nothing great can be created and the audience, no matter where it is, will not be moved nor transported. It wants to be carried away and so it must be. I do myself when I go to the opera house (I consider myself a very appreciative listener). In 1876 Richard Wagner left the individuality that made those performances so memorable to each artist – he interfered only to correct dilettantism or lack of understanding. Harmony prevailed between him and the artists and between each artist and his work – that is an uncontestable fact; but the ideals of individuality have now given way to a tyranny that demands submission as a prime requisite. Even if the tyrant's rod is wielded with much amiability it still remains just that – a tyrant's rod.

To be sure, only the best was desired and much that was beautiful has been achieved – but the heart has gone out of it and nothing is so sorely missed at Bayreuth as that! If only they would follow memory more closely!

Many persons visit Wahnfried, the elect and the non-elect, and amongst them are many who have no idea of art or of an artist's sensibility. There they listen to all kinds of things and go away to write about the work and the artist just as it has been suggested to them. They yield their souls to Wahnfried, thinking that by so doing they are being true to the Master! But no!

If Lilli Lehmann's attitude to Cosima was hostile this was doubtless due to the slight of the Isolde-Brangäne episode. She had demanded a substantial fee for her appearances as Brünnhilde and this brought a rebuke from Cosima – who, it must be said, was otherwise full of admiration and praise for her art. But

Lehmann, in reply, adding 10,000 marks of her own, used her fee to endow a bed for sick musicians, something that she says was Wagner's own wish.

In spite of (or perhaps, because of) a brilliant career in all the major female Wagner roles Lilli Lehmann did not sing at Bayreuth after 1896 although she did return as a Festival visitor.

Romain Rolland

Romain Rolland (1866–1944) French author, biographer, music historian and critic; his chief work is the ten volume novel Jean-Christophe, *which is about the life of a musician. Rolland's journal of his 'Four Days at Bayreuth' dates from 1896, when the* Ring *was given for the first time since the première of 1876.*

The Bavarian Railway and its usual easy-going tardiness. At the Bayreuth station – not a carriage to be seen. On foot we cross the deserted, chill, dark little town from one side to the other. About midnight we arrive at Professor Egerich's – 17 Rathausstrasse. Two rooms on the ground floor. Frightful colour prints of Luther, Melanchthon, Mozart and Beethoven on the walls. Artificial flowers. Silver wedding souvenirs. Out-of-tune piano!

On Saturday morning (August 8th) we paid a visit to Wahnfried which was not far away. Wagner's house and Wagner's grave – the two most modest and tasteful things he ever did. The cool, shady approach, bordered by grass verges. The massive, ivy-covered slab of marble under the dome of the dappled, leafy trees.

Eva and Daniela (Thode) receive us in their modest salon and invite us to a soirée. Daniela really captivating with her comical French. Eva's sharp and obstinate profile – just like Wagner's but without his spirituality. For the rest, they are both quite amiable. But one may speak only about Bayreuth. Everything else has to compete with that. They are living off their father's glory. Humperdinck and Chamberlain are the limits of their horizon. The Germanic details . . . the dress. . . .

The seventeenth-century Park, always deserted, always shady, which I have dreamed of for five years. This morning I found once more the same atmosphere among the leafy trees. Here, involuntarily, speech is hushed, as though in the presence of the dead.

The Wagner shops. Nibelung pins with Fricka's rams, Grane. Table crockery with Wagner's stubborn features. Busts – bare or black-draped. Wagner cravats – a black cravat with a photograph stuck in the middle. A picture of a Wagner soirée decorating a visiting-card case. A dozen plates with scenes from the dramas. Wagner at the hair-dressers' . . . Wagner at the cobblers' . . . .

The evening reception at Wahnfried – Frau Wagner with a black veil covering her hair and forehead and extending as far as her feet. She has grown old, but nevertheless has something attractive about her eyes and mouth. Unfortunately, she is not natural – very outspoken, superficial, brilliant. She occupies herself constantly with matters of serious import – and she meditates a lot. When she is at the piano she plays on her features what she plays in the music. But she is amiable to all and she speaks excellent French. Her four daughters made a favourable impression on me five years ago. Isolde, ever indifferent to what is happening about her, is large and vigorous, she has not too bad a figure – but she has a fearfully Semitic profile, and that not of the aristocratic sort (it is remarkable how this is found in the Wagner blood). Countess Gravina (Blandine) appears ever more handsome, a little sickly and tense, but she has an agreeable high colour (more so than the other Bülow-Wagner daughters). Eva, nevertheless, with her slim figure, is an elegant sight. Thode, a pale, bald-headed and pock-marked figure, is incessantly making faces – and thus has a look that is not a little macabre.

Siegfried, who is to conduct tomorrow, is not down in the salon. I introduce myself to Houston Stewart Chamberlain. Very big, fair and lean, he is still young and looks about thirty-five, he has a blond beard and a square, rather bushy moustache. I recall to him the *Revue Wagnérienne* – he knows my name but not my book. Our conversation is interrupted by Frau Wagner.

Among the French is the small, pale Fauré – of somewhat equivocal appearance, less like an artist than a man of the world of business – I do not know why, but in spite of his fine features, he always reminds me of a Levantine. . . .

Gabriel Monod and Germaine, she in a buttoned-up woollen dress, looking like a girl with her decided opinions and her awkward innocence.

The Bayreuth singer, Burgstaller – the Siegfried, a local woodsman, very big, very ugly, with a silly, unattractive pock-marked face, nevertheless he is sympathic due to his naïvety and his awkward behaviour.

The gigantic fleshy Gods of Valhalla. Refreshments and music – as only Wahnfried could provide. Henri took the champagne for lemonade – 'it has a fine refreshing sour taste!' The piano is crushed under blows of the fist and there is over-loud singing. Risler and a Pole play, like fury, a mediocre march by Schubert. A singer gives Susanna's aria from *Figaro* – in a tragic manner! Another pianist plays Brahms's *Lied der Parzen*. Frau Schumann-Heink sings a pious Schubert song in her extraordinarily powerful and dramatic voice; but it is effortful and ugly and when she opens her mouth one can well conceive that her voice is less part of her than an instrument she is playing on with clumsy fingers. Eventually, Risler mauls the *Meistersinger* overture on the piano. He is now quite the German with his red face . . . Clothilde attempted to have a chat with him. He seemed to be exceedingly stupid; however, he does understand how to create a position for himself here. It can be foreseen he will be put in second place when Siegfried takes over the conducting.

All of this company at the soirée is mediocre. It would be a better thing too if the Wagners brought more artistic interest or else more kindheartedness into the conversation.

I do like these reception rooms, especially the hall, about which so much unfavourable has been said – the arrangement is very beautiful with some noteworthy works of art – Lenbach's Schopenhauer is most interesting and the Liszt is fascinating.

Rolland now moves on to the performances. His time for the duration of Rheingold *is excessive by any standards – according to the Bayreuth Festival records it took the twenty-seven-year-old Siegfried Wagner 2 hours 21 minutes to conduct this particular performance.*

Sunday 9th August, 3 o'clock to 7.30 – *Rheingold* (no interval)

That appears not too long. Hardly so – in the middle something does harass the nerves – a little weariness due to the prolonged strain. I am sensible of no deep excitement whatsoever – but merely pleased, charmed and curious. For that the piece itself is a little to blame, this stuff is mediocre, and the music is less rich than in the other parts of the tetralogy – except in the opening and closing scenes.

The orchestra too is to blame, it is too quiet, too subdued and too discreet (the flood of sound is reduced to a trickle). I was not receiving the quantity of sound needed . . . to move me deeply. The voices prevail greatly over the instruments, and that is a misfortune which Wagner had doubtless not foreseen.

The first scene is an enchantment for the eye and the ear – the lullaby of the murmuring waters as they rise up out of the depths – the pleasing sight of the Rhine-maidens at play. They slip about in the grey-green waters, up and down, taking in the whole height of the stage in the space of one breath. They are held suspended in a corset arrangement (previously this corset was attached to a pole which was moved about) and it would have been perfect had they been less wrapped up in clothing. Splendid effects of sunlight through water were given out from the river-bed.

There follow some comments, not very favourable, on the singers, before Rolland proceeds to describe the characters' appearance:

Above all, the costumes are in totally inharmonious colours and glaring shades. Wotan has the curly head and curly beard of an Indian Bacchus . . . Froh is dressed in a gown of improbable green and he is equipped with a crook like an eighteenth-century shepherd. Freia has a floral gown with wide sleeves like the heroine of a pre-Raphaelite pastoral play; Fricka is a classical Juno, and Donner, a flint hammer over his shoulder, has the rough-hewn appearance of a primitive early German figurine.

There was much to reproach too in the frightful Valhalla décor – I do not know why but someone had the idea of making it like an Arabian temple, an accumulation of domed mosques grouped around an enormous observatory dome. In the foreground, a clumsy array of trees and flowers.

However, the various scene changes were well managed, with a multiplicity of clouds and steam. The underground cavern, the Nibelungs' forge – these were done with an epic sublimity.

Several ladies had to leave the auditorium during the performance. There was nearly a fist fight beside us between a squint-eyed Italian tenor and his uncouth American neighbour – the cause being a rudely delivered, and badly taken 'Shut up!'

Upon leaving the theatre after the performance, as always, there was a crowd of Bayreuthers and people from the country round about – come to mix with the procession of visitors and to mock them and make jokes at their expense.

Monod remarked, indicating a singularly hideously-dressed person, 'Wagner would have shown her to the door and told her, "You are much too fine for me"' – to which Clothilde replied, 'Then he would have shut out his own daughters, too.' They are about in their luminous silks – Eva in red, Daniela in green and Blandine in white. . . .

Monday 10th August – *Die Walküre*

Brünnhilde, a young Norwegian (Gulbranson), is excellent; in the Wagners' salon she seemed to be too corpulent but in the perspective of the theatre she is beautiful, gripping and natural and, above all, she is young – the prime requisite and the rarest at Bayreuth. The others are mediocre. Wotan is vocally inadequate. Old Vogl is miscast as Siegmund. Sucher made me despair with her stupid acting, her heavy-handed emphasising and her shrill, half-baked screaming. Her vast padded bulk – from bust to backside, she is as wide as a city wall. . . . I found the orchestra more imposing than yesterday – it is richer in its perfect precision of detail and in its greater delicacy of expression.

Rolland expends two whole pages being impressed by the storm at the beginning, and the removal of the sword towards the end of Act 1, as well as by the close of the Wotan-Brünnhilde scene in Act II – but he expected more from the 'Ride'.

Brünnhilde apart, they all act in conventional, self-conscious 'tableaux vivants' which quite appalled me and spoiled Bayreuth for me. Monod, to whom I expressed this feeling, was also struck by this – he replied that in '76 the acting was quite different: Wagner was an uncompromising realist and wanted his characters to live on the stage and not stand about like statues. Then, Niemann as Siegmund had run to Sieglinde and held her tightly as he sang out his Spring song. Today, they sat quietly side by side. In general, one can well believe they would be afraid to embrace one another here at Bayreuth – Wotan had almost to stop and consider whether to put his pursed lips to Brünnhilde's brow as he was laying her to rest. Damn it – it is not worth coming to Bayreuth if one is not to be allowed to witness – in these epic dramas – an uninhibited outburst of passion! I suspect that the inspiration behind all these frozen countenances and fanciful, pseudo-Greek salon-pictures is Frau Wagner and her son-in-law Thode.

A miserable public – phonies, Jews, snobs, hypocrites, Yankees, slow-witted English and repulsive Germans, stinking as high as the Alps. . . .

A violent storm on the way up to the theatre. Lightning flashing quite close by down in the valley.

Tuesday 11th August – *Siegfried*

At last my intellect is silenced – I am moved! This performance is not to be compared with the foregoing. The first Act is something wonderful and would alone be sufficient to justify the Bayreuth 'school' and make it indispensable – the pupils were Hans Breuer (Mime) and Burgstaller (Siegfried). Never have I seen acting and music united in such animation. Mime was an amazing sight, no higher than Siegfried's elbow, dirty, shuffling, shaggy-haired like an ancient ape, red-eyed and grimacing of face . . . but with a voice, the tones of which are produced with consummate accuracy. . . .

The bulky and rather repellent Burgstaller was, at distance, a young, outgoing, charming Siegfried with a lissom, naturally graceful way of moving, a heroic lack of affectation and a pleasant voice. . . . The music of this Act, especially the close, is magnificent. The Hymn to the Sword sounds like an air by Bach or Handel.

The last part of Act III is, in the end, a little over-emphatic and declamatory, and it was rather less well played and sung. Siegfried was tired and Brünnhilde not as good as yesterday: she now looked fat and dumpy, she was puffed-up with drowsiness and had her powerful bosom and neck openly exposed. There were the conventional gestures too – fear at being disarmed; meanwhile the sweat was pouring off Burgstaller's grease paint. None of this, however, can make me forget the perfect beauty and power of the first Act. That remains, for this year, the greatest impression of Bayreuth.

This was not merely a passing enthusiasm on the part of Rolland. Later, in 1908, in Musicians of Today, *he devoted most of the section on Wagner to* Siegfried, *which seems to have been his favourite. He recalls this same performance of Act I and made the same extraordinary comparison with the two Baroque masters.*

Between Acts II and III Clothilde and I took the path out from the left side of the theatre into the open air, amongst the well-tilled, rain-soaked fields of rye. The earth gave off a powerful odour. Crickets chirped. The red sun set behind the pine forest. Here was peace bestowed by contented Nature, in which the valiant Old Man, after his conflicts, was reconciled with the world once more – and died in serenity.

It appears Rolland did not stay for the final part of the Ring. *He writes (in* Musicians of Today) *that he finds it depressing – to those (presumably like himself) with sensitive feelings; and comments, 'One would like to end with* Siegfried *and escape the gloomy* Götterdämmerung.'

Gabriel Fauré

Gabriel Fauré (1845–1924), the French composer who reminded Rolland variously of a businessman and a Levantine, had been to the first Ring cycle of 1896. He wrote his impressions in a letter to his wife:

6 August 1896

I thought I was going to find the people round me all dazzlingly intelligent . . . but it is just the contrary . . . we are all finding one another duller than usual. We are incapable of talking about anything other than the performances. . . . The Tetralogy is packed with philosophy and symbolism that merely serve to demonstrate our poverty, our emptiness. When it comes to an end it leaves one convinced of universal misery, eternal suffering and that is all! It is penitence in the noblest meaning of the word, it is almost contrition.

Two days later another letter shows his developing enthusiasm, but it is surprising that he should be so taken aback with his personal reactions – he was not unfamiliar with the Ring and had attended a complete cycle at Munich in 1879.

8 August 1896

. . . I am full of this Tetralogy. . . . It soaks into you like water into sand.

Bernard Shaw (1896)

Bernard Shaw returned to Bayreuth for the Ring in 1896 and wrote reviews for the magazine The Star, a paper he had joined on its foundation but which he left soon afterwards as it was not, for him, sufficiently Socialist in its outlook. However, he continued to contribute to it, writing music criticism under the name of 'Corno di Bassetto'. Shaw, as before, is critical of certain aspects of Bayreuth – 'the effect on pious Wagnerians was as though I had brawled in Church', he wrote in 1905. A similar attitude at the International Socialist Congress of 1896, where he went straight after Bayreuth, almost convinced the delegates (as unused as Wagnerians to criticism) that Shaw had deserted them for the enemy.

19th July

There are moments when Providence takes a joke seriously by way of restraining our sense of humor. We all know (or ought to know) the moment near the close of Das Rheingold, when, the ring being disposed of to the giants, and Freia and her apples of eternal youth restored to the gods, Donner, mounting the rock, calls the clouds to him, and, when their black legions, crowding about him, have hidden him in their mists, swings his hammer, splits them with a thousand blinding ribbons of lightning, and reveals the skiey towers of Valhall, with Froh's rainbow-bridge spanning the valley to the gate of the wonderful castle – the home of the gods. The effect of this on the stage of the Wagner Theatre is magnificent, but the management, not content to wait for this, took advantage of the Bayreuth custom of summoning the audience by sound of trumpet, to blare out Donner's call to the real heavens before the performance began. What was the result? No sooner was the call sent echoing from hill to hill than the cloudless sky darkened, and the trombones were answered by a distant roll of thunder. I was up in the pine woods at the time, discussing high themes with the brilliant editor of a paper which I will disguise as the D***y Chr*****e. He had persisted in whistling I dreamt that I dwelt in marble halls all the way from Victoria to Nuremberg (the turbulent part of the Channel excepted), and I was trying to get him off that subject when I heard the brazen voices sending forth their *He da! He da! Duftig Gedunst Donner ruft euch zu Heer!*

The thunder – the real thunder – answered, and we sprang up from our carpet of scented pine needles and made for the theatre precipitately. Just as we reached it the rain came down in torrents. Consequently the entry of the audience to the first performance, usually a gay, busy, eager, hopeful function, was this time a damp scuttle. Nearly every seat in the house was filled a quarter of an hour before the performance began.

Das Rheingold, being only the prologue to the colossal music-drama of the Niblung's Ring, which takes three nights to perform, is not divided into acts, and therefore compels the audience to sit for about two hours and a half without a rest. I sat it out without turning a hair; and my companion did not whistle a single bar during the hundred and fifty minutes; but some of the audience found their powers of endurance somewhat strained. One lady fainted and her removal, with the curious flash of bright sunlight into the dark theatre and across the lurid picture of Nibelheim as the door was opened to let her out, made an unwelcome distraction.

The performance was, on the whole, an excellent one. Its weakest point was Perron's Wotan, a futile impersonation. The orchestra, although it was too good, as orchestras go, to be complained of, was very far from being up to the superlative standard of perfect preparedness, smoothness, and accuracy of execution expected at Bayreuth. We in London have taught Richter to depend too much on his reputation, and on his power of pulling a performance through on the inspiration of the moment. The result of our instruction is now apparent. The effect of the Das Rheingold score was not the Bayreuth effect, but the London effect: that is, it sounded like a clever reading of the band parts at sight by very smart players, instead of an utterance by a corps of devotees, saturated with the spirit of the work, and in complete possession of its details. The strings were poor; the effects were not always well calculated – for instance, the theme of the magic helmet was hardly heard at first; and in the prelude, the great booming pedal note – the mighty ground tone of the Rhine – was surreptitiously helped out, certainly with excellent effect, by the organ.

The stage management is – I can no longer conceal it – radically bad at all the points where ordinary amateur intelligence, devotedly exercised, is not sufficient to find out the right way. The plain truth is that Madame Wagner does not know what acting can and cannot do, or how much the imagination of the audience will do when the situation goes beyond the resources of acting. Over and over again, when overwhelming crises of emotion are reached – crises which occur in the minds of the spectators as they follow the drama, and which, though they are supported with the most powerful sympathy by the orchestra, are not provoked by any particular action of the figures on the stage, and are utterly beyond expression by any such means – we find the Bayreuth artists making the most violent demonstration, striking the most overcharged attitudes, and trying to look ineffable things at the very moment, in short, when the slightest betrayal of any share on their part in the excitement of the audience must mar the whole effect – the moment, consequently, when a skilled actor allows the play itself, helped by the imagination of the spectators, to do all the work. This is the whole secret of the amateurishness of Bayreuth. Madame Wagner is beyond question a very clever lady, and a most able woman of business; but she knows so little how dramatic effects are produced technically that at the very points where her husband's genius and the emotions to which it appeals are producing their most searching effects she assumes that no effect will be produced at all if the prima donna does not exhibit the most demonstrative consciousness of it. I call this amateurish, but from the Bayreuth point of view it is even worse than amateurish: it is heretical, being the most foolish characteristic of Italian operatic acting. I do not say that Wagner himself was free from it. Though his tendency always seemed to me to be to err in the direction of taking too much of the work for the music – that is, for himself – and leaving too little to the actor, who is often instructed to stand motionless for long periods whilst the orchestra conveys, often with the most extraordinary vividness, not only how he feels, but what he is thinking about, yet it may be that the vehemence of Wagner's imagination, and the success with which he had himself enlarged the limits of forcible expression by mechanical means in the orchestra, may have led him occasionally to demand superhuman demonstrations from his actors. But I rather doubt this in view of the care with which his scores, with all their wealth of instrumentation, are contrived so as not to overwhelm the singer. He was perhaps the most practical of all the great composers, and the last man in the world, apparently, to demand impossibilities. At all events, whether the fault lies with the Wagner tradition or Madame Wagner's present supervision, there can be no doubt of the fact that a stage-manager who understands acting – if the world can produce so unusual a phenomenon – is badly wanted at Bayreuth.

There is a good deal to be done too, in the way of getting rid of mere old-fashionedness. . . . I do not for one moment dare to suggest the Rhinemaidens should take a hint from our 'living pictures' and dress like Rhinemaidens. The world is not decent enough for that yet. But is it necessary for the three ladies to go to the other extreme and swim about in muslin *fichus* and tea-gowns? They gave me a strong impression that they had forgotten their gloves and hats; and even a parasol to save their complexions when the sunlight came shimmering down through the water on the Rhinegold would hardly have been out of keeping with their costumes. Happily, their movements were fairly mermaidenly. The old fire escape machinery of 1876 has been discarded, and the three are now suspended from above . . . with plausible and graceful results.

Another antiquated stage trick which Bayreuth clings to is that of attitudinizing on the stage with a corner of your mantle held between the fingers, in the manner of the antique Niobe. But whereas Niobe held up her mantle to screen herself and her children from the arrows of Apollo, the Bayreuth prima donna does it solely to display her drapery in the German historico-classical manner, with unspeakably ridiculous effect.

One more disparagement. In 1876 the use of jets and clouds of steam for stage effects was a novelty . . . but it cannot be denied that from the very first it carried with it a prosaic flavor of washing day, totally irreconcilable with the magical strangeness of the wishing cap or *tarnhelm*. It is effective only for one purpose – that of producing an illusion of a cloud of fire when a powerful light is turned upon it; and to that use, I suggest, it cannot be too strictly limited.

For the rest, I have nothing but praise, although there certainly was a Rhine-daughter whose top note was distressingly flat. The singing, on the whole, was much better than I expected it to be. The Germans are evidently becoming conscious that there are in the world De Reszkes and other people who have demonstrated that Wagner's music can be sung beautifully, and that even a basso should not deliver himself as if the Bayreuth audience were a Hyde-park demonstration. I admit, of course, that Friedrichs as Alberich occasionally howled and shouted in the old Wagnerian style; but he also sang at times – even at most times – and sang not badly either. The veteran Vogl who played Loge at Bayreuth twenty years ago, played it again last Sunday with a vocal charm which surpassed the most sanguine expectations. Both he and Freidrichs acted with great spirit and intelligence. Burgstaller, who is to play Siegfried presently, took the small part of Froh, and made his mark in it by a certain radiant sensitiveness and enthusiasm which became him very well. Frau Heink Schumann . . . was magnificent as Erda. Calvé herself could not have surpassed her in dramatic power and beauty, and her voice was at its best. Marie Brema, the only English member of the cast, was Fricka, never a very popular goddess, her modern name being Mrs Grundy. Miss Brema sang very well and shewed no diminution of her old energy; but she devotedly does (and occasionally overdoes) what she is told to do by Madame Wagner, besides wearing what she is told to wear. No human prima donna could make a perfect success under these conditions, and I urge Miss Brema, whose ability is of a high order, to take her fate into her own hands for the future. Acting is her own business: it is not Madame Wagner's; and the sooner that is realized, the better for Bayreuth. The rest of the cast was adequate – Breuer as Mime perhaps a trifle more than that.

You shall hear further from me presently. My friend the editor has now got I dreamt that I dwelt mixed up with the Rhine-daughters' trio. The combination of Balfe and Wagner is novel, and somewhat trying at first, but it grows on one with use.

C. di B.

P.S. – The first act of Die Walküre has just been rescued from a *succès de sommeil* by the perennial and passionate Sucher, who suddenly broke into one of her triumphs as Sieglinde. Gerhäuser, as Siegmund, made up as a stout middle-aged gentleman in sheepskins and a red beard, has been as null and wooden as anybody could desire. With the assistance of Wachter as Hunding, he all but put us to sleep in the first half of the scene. In pulling the sword from the tree he was much less exciting than an English vestryman taking his hat from a peg. But Sucher carried everything before her. She could not transfigure Gerhäuser, but she made us forget him and remember only the Siegmund of Wagner's poem – that poor devil of a hero to whose moment of happiness our hearts all go out. Bravo Rosa!

20th July

Die Walküre is endured by the average man because it contains four scenes for which he would sit out a Scotch sermon, or even a House of Commons debate. These are the love duet in the first act, Brynhild's announcement to Siegmund of his approaching death in the second, the ride of the Valkyries and the fire charm in the third. For them the ordinary playgoer endures hours of Wotan, with Christopher Sly's prayer in his heart, 'Would twere over!' Now I am one of those elect souls who are deeply moved by Wotan. I grant you that as a long-winded, one-eyed gentleman backing a certain champion in a fight, and letting himself be henpecked out of his fancy because his wife objects to the moral character of the champion, he is a dreary person indeed, and most ungodlike. But to those who have seen on the greater stage of the world how Religion has fortified itself by an alliance with Law and Order and Morals and Propriety; how it has gained temporal power at the cost of that eye which is not the eye to the main chance; how it has become so entangled in these alliances and bargains that when new and higher forces are born of its holiest wisdom it is driven first to use its authority over them to make war against Truth as dangerous, and Love as an unnatural vice, and then when they defy its authority, in spite of that filial love, to silence them in sleep (since they cannot be killed), and surround their couch with juggling fires to scare away all mankind from waking them – to those who have seen all that, there is nothing trivial, nothing tedious in Die Walküre.

Wotan's one eye is not ridiculous; his spear, the symbol of his temporal power, with the runes and bargains engraved on its shaft, is no mere stage property; his wife Fricka, shuddering with horror and wrath at her broken moral laws, and forcing him to abandon his love-child to the 'justice' of her worshipper, is no mere henpecking Mrs Caudle; and when Brynhild, the child of his wisdom, rebels against the command which Fricka has forced from him, and is put to sleep on the mountain peak, surrounded by the fires of Loge, there is more in it than the somewhat fifth-of-Novembery pyrotechnics – mostly squibs and steam – of the Bayreuth stage machinist. You, Mr Star Editor, familiar as you are with the tragedy of Religion married (for money) to the State; with a people frightened away from truth and knowledge by a display of brimstone that can scorch no hand that is fearlessly thrust into it; and with other matters which are no doubt mentioned in your political columns – you would understand Die Walküre well enough. And in a dim-way, many of the people who have no general ideas, and who yawn and fidget when Wotan is at the seven hundred and seventy-seventh bar of one of his disquisitions, with no sign of any intention of stopping, do perceive that something of public importance is going on and must be put up with. They may not see exactly why or how the god finds that all the power he has built up has only enslaved himself, still less do they understand the apparent contradiction of his secret hope and longing for his own downfall and destruction even whilst he is working with all his might to defend himself and make Valhall impregnable and eternal; but they see his trouble, and, after all, it is trouble that moves us to sympathy, and not the explanation of the trouble.

At the same time let me confess that Die Walküre at full length, beginning at four and ending at half-past nine, and involving three hours and a half of concentrated attention, is hard work for a critic, and a considerable test of the endurance of an amateur, except when the performers are sufficiently gifted to make you forget everything but the drama. The Bayreuth artists cannot do all this; in fact, some of them excel in the art of making five minutes seem like twenty. In Die Walküre the all-important performer is Wotan; and as I hinted in my last communication, Perron is not the ideal Wotan. He is tall but an awkward and straddling person, and is perhaps as clever in private life as many other people who appear stupid on the stage. His acting consists of striking a graceless attitude and holding on to it until the fear of cramp obliges him to let go. Why then, you will ask, was he selected for such a part on such an occasion? Well, simply because he has an excellent voice, of which he takes commendable care. From its low G to its top F it comes without effort, is clear, resonant, powerful without noisiness or roughness, and agreeable in quality. At the end of Die Walküre he shewed no sign of fatigue. And that is why he takes the place which so many keener artists, without this physical endowment of his, must deeply envy him. Gerhäuser's voice has matured since he sang the part of Lohengrin here a couple of years ago; but as Siegmund the Unlucky he was quite overparted – conscientious but slow, dull, and resourceless almost beyond bearing. Wagner has provided such formidable lengths of dumb show in the work that, unless an actor is inventive, highly accomplished in pantomime, and able to make himself personally fascinating, he must inevitably be left again and again helplessly staring at the conductor and waiting for his cue. And that is just what Siegmund and Hunding were doing most of the time. Of Sucher's great success as Sieglinde I told you in the hurried postscript which I dispatched after the first act. The second act began with a very fine performance of Fricka's scene by Miss Marie Brema, whose performance entitles us to say in England we have produced one of the very best living Wagnerian artists. It was a first-rate piece of work, having the vocal qualities that the Germans neglect as well as the dramatic quality they value, with, to boot, the excellent quality of Miss Brema's own individuality, which happily got completely the better of the Bayreuth tradition this time. Miss Lilli Lehmann, now Frau Lehmann-Kalisch, played her old part of Brynhild: but she was ill, and had to be helped by both prompter and conductor in passages which she has had at her fingers' ends for many years.

Die Walküre has the advantage over Das Rheingold of being much more frequently performed. Probably everybody concerned, from the stage carpenters to the prima donna, knew it better. The difference was very noticeable in the orchestra. Richter was in his best form, interpreting the score convincingly, and getting some fine work from the band. In the scene of the apparition of the Valkyrie in the second act, the effect of the wind instruments was quite magically beautiful. The deep impression made, in spite of the fact that none of the men could cope with the parts, and that Brynhild, though capably played, was not altogether suitably impersonated, was due largely to the force with which Richter, through his handling of the orchestra, imposed Wagner's conception on the audience.

The weather here is excellent; and we all wish that the old plan of giving the audience one day's holiday were in force. Parsifal also is badly missed. But Der Ring is Der Ring, and there is an end. Among the visitors the Germans seem to be in a large majority this year, but no doubt the American and English tourists will turn up and assert themselves later on.

C. di B.

P.S. 6.15pm. The first act of Siegfried has been the worst disappointment so far. Grüning, as Siegfried, is hardly to be described without malice. Imagine an eighteenth-century bank clerk living in a cave, with fashionable sandals and cross garters, an elegant modern classic tunic, a Regent-street bearskin, and a deportment only to be learnt in quadrilles. Or, rather, do not imagine it; but pray that I, who have seen the reality, may not be haunted by it in my dreams. He only needed a tinder-box instead of a furnace, and a patent knife-cleaning machine instead of an anvil, to make him complete. I really cannot conscientiously advise Englishmen to come to Bayreuth until Grüning comes to England. Fortunately there was some relief. Breuer was excellent as Mime; and Perron, in the Wanderer scene, where voice alone can do almost anything, and the costume makes awkwardness impossible, was at his best. And the orchestra is keeping up to its Walküre standard.

22nd July

With all possible goodwill towards the Bayreuth management, I cannot bring myself to congratulate it on Siegfried. If the performance had been given at an ordinary German theatre, with ordinary German prices, I should have been delighted with the orchestra and the mounting; but I should have roundly denounced the choice of the principal artist. And since Siegfried is a drama which depends as much on the actor who plays the title-part as Hamlet does, my condemnation of Herr Grüning practically gives away the whole performance. I must add that Madame Wagner – who is understood to be responsible for the casting of Der Ring – is not in this case the victim of an unexpected collapse. Herr Grüning is no novice. I have never yet succeeded in visiting Bayreuth without hearing him sing. He has played Parsifal and Tannhäuser, and Madame Wagner knows to a hair's breadth, as well as I do, what he can do and what he cannot do. Consequently the people who have made tedious and costly pilgrimages from the ends of the earth to Bayreuth, as the one place in the world where Wagner's music-dramas can be witnessed in their utmost attainable excellence and fidelity of representation, have every right to remonstrate indignantly at being put off with a third-rate Siegfried. As far as I can judge, there can have been no attempt to make even the best of him by careful rehearsal. We have seen how Alvary can manage the business of the Wagnerian stage with the precision of a French pantomimist, at a scratch performance in London, with everything behind the scenes at sixes and sevens and only enough interval between the acts to clear away one scene and tumble another on. Why cannot the same result be obtained here, where the intervals are an hour long, and the simple-minded pilgrims are fed all day long with stories of the months of rehearsal, the scrupulous observance of the Master's wishes, and the inexorable conscientiousness of Madame Wagner? The truth is that all these devout professions are borne out by the carpenters, machinists and gasmen and by them alone. The changes of scene, the wonderful atmospheric effects, the jets of steam, and so on are worked with a smoothness and punctuality that are beyond praise. Once only, in the change of scene from the depths of the Rhine to Valhall, did I hear something tumble with a thud behind the gauzes, accompanied by a strenuous whispering of instructions. That was no doubt an accident – a very trifling one to me, who have so often sat in Covent Garden during the change from the second to the third scene of Boito's Mefistofele, listening to the mysterious strains of the orchestra, whilst dim figures of stage carpenters stumbled and rushed wildly about the stage twilight, stimulating and exhorting one another in language which owed its frantic force to profanity rather than to grammar. At Bayreuth the clouds move, night follows day, and calm follows storm apparently without human agency. But it is one thing to drill a staff of workmen, and quite another to drill a tenor. If any of the men at work in the flies had botched his work last night as Grüning several times botched his, he would be an unemployed man this morning.

Yet, on the whole, the tenor was more conscientious than the prima donna. Frau Lilli Lehmann-Kalisch is famous for her Brynhild – famous in America. She has a bright soprano voice, brilliant at the top, but not particularly interesting in the middle – just the wrong sort of voice for Wagner. When dressed as the warmaiden, she is plump, pretty, very feminine . . . therefore just the wrong sort of person for Brynhild. She is clearly conscious that her golden hair is hanging down her back, and since she refuses, as she lies asleep on the mountain top, to allow her face to be covered by the vizor of her helmet, she is, in that attitude, so unmistakeably and indeed aggressively a conventionally pretty woman, emphasizing a well-developed bust with a toy cuirass, that Siegfried's assumption that she is a man, and the emotional shock with which he subsequently discovers that the supposed sleeping warrior is a young woman, are made incredible and ridiculous. And this, if you please, is Bayreuthian fidelity to 'The Meister'.

However, I quite admit that Frau Lehmann-Kalisch is an artist of considerable qualifications; and I should like to see her as Marguerite in Gounod's Faust. Her singing is open to exception in the manner of phrasing: in fact, she absolutely destroys one of the most characteristic turns in that section of the great duet (excuse the word; but it *is* a duet, and actually has a concerted cadenza in it) with which the familiar Siegfried Idyll begins. But her offences in this respect were as nothing beside Grüning's. Even in the sword-forging scene, when he was comparatively cool, the swinging triplets which occur in the bellows music were too much for his powers of execution; and at the end, when he was wracked with emotion over which he had not an artist's mastery, the manner in which he gasped his way from note to note, producing effects which had exactly the same relation to Wagner's shapely phrases as a heap of broken glass has to a crystal goblet, is not to be described.

In justice to Herr Grüning, let me add that he has some agreeable points. He is handsome and, in a pleasant, robust, very German way, elegant in the manner of the last century. In a periwig, as a sympathetic young man of sensibility, with a not too exacting vocal part, he would pass as a tenor who ought to be doing better things. Apparently he loves Wagner, and is anxious to do him justice; and when he fails, he fails honestly. But I must not insult him by an open attempt to spare his feelings on this occasion; and I have no desire to spare the feelings of the managers. He was overparted as Siegfried; and I repeat that they knew beforehand that it would be so. The guarantee of a first-rate performance – that guarantee which is the basis of the authority and prosperity of the Wagner Theatre – has been broken, and broken deliberately, not for the first time.

Let me now forget Marguerite-Brynhild and her young man, and recall the moments when neither were on the stage. Then, I grant you, the representation was splendid. Perron, with his straddling legs, knock knees, and unhappy expression hidden by the gown, the beard, and the wide hat of the Wanderer, and with his fine voice in full play, did nothing to contradict the majesty of the Wotan music. He missed the humor of the passages with the dwarf and with Siegfried at the foot of the mountain; but that was only a small deduction from the satisfaction of the general effect. Breuer, as Mime, repeated himself a good deal; but his play was so clever that it was worth repeating. Frau Heink-Schumann as Erda, and Friedrichs as Alberich, sustained the impression they made in Das Rheingold; and the orchestra was again very fine, especially in Mime's nightmare after Wotan's visit, and the tragic thunderclouds of music in the first scene of the third act. Die Götterdämmerung tonight will probably redeem all that was lost last night, since it depends so much less on Siegfried. At all events, we are full of hope.

C. di B.

P.S. There is joy over Die Götterdämmerung: Grüning has vanished, and Burgstaller, the alternative Siegfried, reigns in his stead. So far, the improvement is due more to the faults of Grüning than to the qualities of Burgstaller, but he promises well. We are all somewhat exhausted after a first act lasting two hours, yet most of us are ready to go through it again. The scene between Brynhild and Waltraute has effected us beyond all my adjectives: not even Frau Heink-Schumann's combination of black-blue Valkyrie armor and shield with a summer gown and fashionable sleeves could spoil its sublimity. I shall start for London after the performance (unless it kills me). The interval is too short to write more.

23rd July

The completion of the first cycle of the Nibelungen tetralogy at Bayreuth has been celebrated by applause lasting for seven minutes, the object being to bring Richter and principal artists before the curtain. But at Bayreuth nobody takes a curtain call, except the – well, the dove in Parsifal. Nevertheless the audience hammered and bravoed very lustily, the English taking a lead in the noisier part of the demonstration. . . . The enthusiasm was certainly justified by the performance. The new Siegfried, Burgstaller, a product of Bayreuth and its Wagner school, won the audience over completely in the second and third acts. In the first act he was a little handicapped by a certain novelty (after the Germanically handsome Grüning) in his aspect, and by a helmet which had to be rescued from falling off whenever he ventured on an impulsive advance on his Brynhild.

He is a young man of the build and features which we associate rather with Syria and Maida-vale than with the primeval Rhineland, and in his make-up he aimed only partly at Siegfried, and chiefly at – say, Parsifal. But he has none of the pretentiousness and lack of simplicity which sometimes distinguish the clever Oriental from the stupid Saxon. On the contrary, his chief personal charm lies in a certain combination of courageous shyness and a touch of the unformedness of youth in his movements, with impulsive enthusiasm and an artistic judgement very remarkable at his age. In the third act, when he comes to tell that story of the ring and the helmet, the sword and the dragon, which everybody in the tetralogy tells at full length whenever the smallest opening for it is perceptible, he quite charmed us by his bright delivery. In narrating the incident of the wood-bird, he was far more interesting than the wood-bird itself had been; and this result was largely due to clever and skilful singing. Not only did he give us some very pretty contrasts of tone, but he made the rhythm dance in a way that was quite delightful after the trudging and tramping of those who had been over the same ground before him. He has, too, qualities of joyousness and humour in his temperament that are invaluable in relieving the heavy earnestness which occasionally oppresses Bayreuth. In the first act he accidentally slipped into his head register on a high note, the effect being by no means unhappy; and immediately the foolish people whose ears are just sharp enough to distinguish the note of a piccolo from that of a trombone began to wonder whether his voice would stand the strain of the performance. They might have spared their anxiety; his voice was never in the slightest danger. His success was complete and legitimate. . . .

Nobody who is acquainted with Der Ring will need to be told by me that The Dusk of the Gods brought the sensation of the tetralogy to a climax. The truth is – I may dare to say so now that I am clear of Bayreuth in full flight for London – Das Rheingold, Die Walküre and the first two acts of Siegfried are music-drama in the fullest possible integrity of that genre; but Die Götterdämmerung, like the end of Siegfried, is opera. In it we have choruses and finales; we have a great scena for the prime donna with the chorus looking on very much as they used to do when Semiramide was singing *Bel raggio*; above all, we have the tenor stabbed to death and then coming to life to sing pretty things about his love before he finally expires, just like Edgardo in Lucia de Lammermoor. The resemblance is not shirked at Bayreuth. When two stalwart members of the chorus picked up the slain Siegfried, and pretended to support him while he stood up and had a few more bars about Brynhild, it was impossible not to see that we had come round again to Valentine in Gounod's Faust. It is true that we had come round like the Hegelian spiral, on a higher plane – a prodigiously higher plane; but the fact remains that Wagner, instead of abandoning opera for ever after Lohengrin, only abandoned it for a time to invent and create the music-drama, since his great world-poem could not find its musical expression otherwise. But the powers which he acquired in creating Das Rheingold, Die Walküre and most of Siegfried – powers so gigantic in comparison with those which Meyerbeer, Gounod and others acquired by practice in mere opera-composing on the old scale that it is hardly possible now to conceive Meyerbeer and Wagner as beings of the same order and species – completely changed the situation for him. It gave him a technical command over the dramatic music which made him as complete a master of the opera as Beethoven was of the symphony, Bach of the fugue or Mozart of the decorative forms into which he poured his apparently spontaneous and unconditioned dramatic music. Die Götterdämmerung, Die Meistersinger and Tristan are just as much operas as anything else: the fact that they are dramatic poems, and that Il Barbiere and Fra Diavolo are not, is no more an objection to the inclusion of the four under the same general heading of opera than the fact that Beethoven's Ninth Symphony is a dramatic poem is an objection to its being called by the same technical name as Haydn's Surprise Symphony. On the other hand, I should hesitate to call Das Rheingold an opera, since it deliberately excludes all operatic features, whereas Die Götterdämmerung excludes nothing, the composer like a true past-master of his art availing himself of all forms and methods with entire freedom, even when they led him, as they sometimes did, to all the outward and visible signs of Italian opera.

No doubt this is the explanation of the popularity of those works of Wagner which followed his relapse, as music-drama doctrinaires should call it, into opera in the last scene of Siegfried. Certainly the effect of Die Götterdämmerung was very rich and splendid on Wednesday. The music is from beginning to end the very luxury of sound woven into a gorgeous tissue by a consummately skilful master. I shall make no attempt to describe it: those who know the music will understand when I say that the conductor and the band knew their work, and that Waltraute's description of Wotan waiting in Valhall for his doom surpassed expectation in its beauty of sound, and majesty of movement, and psychological luck in producing the golden moment of the first act. And to those poor barbarians who do not know the work, why should I address myself at all, since they would not understand me?

In point of technical execution, perhaps, the worst feature of the performance was the Hagen of Grengg. His voice, once described to me by Levi as 'the best bass voice in Germany' is coarsened and shaken by abuse. He breaks his phrases in the worst pseudo-Wagnerian style, pumping out almost every note with a separate effort, and seldom conveying more than the roughest broken outline of the phrase. His acting is heavy and undistinguished. They are possibly proud of him at Bayreuth. . . . The English singer, Miss Marie Brema, had been announced as one of the Norns, but she did not appear, to my great disappointment, as her Fricka in Die Walküre proved her to be, by temperament, one of the most powerful and accomplished Wagnerian heroines Madame Wagner has yet discovered. Her place was filled by the somewhat provincial expedient of doubling the part of the first Norn with that of Waltraute. Madame Heink-Schumann has thus played three parts in the tetralogy, the third being Erda, and in all of them she has made a deep impression by her fine contralto voice and the passion and power of her delivery. The contrast, vocally, was a little hard on the other Norns, one of whom was no less an artist than Sucher. In the river scene, the Rhinemaidens, no longer suspended by ropes, but still clinging to their *fichus*, rose out of the river with their hair elaborately dressed like three wax heads in a Bondstreet shop window, and would have been exceedingly ridiculous if the music and Siegfried and the drama had not swept away all such considerations. Frau Lehmann-Kalisch's high notes, bright and true, and her saturation with the feeling of a part so magnificent that no woman with a heart and brain could possibly play it without rising far out of her ordinary self, achieved a triumph which makes it ungracious to qualify a very warm commendation of her performance. I must not however, call her a great Brynhild. She acts intelligently, sings effectively and in tune, and she is attractive enough, attaining in all these respects a degree of excellence that makes it impossible to call her commonplace; but for all that she is conventional, and takes the fullest advantage of the fact that plenty of ideas suggested by Wagner will attach themselves to her if only she stands her ground impressively. Gunther and Gutrune did their work without distinguishing themselves remarkably one way or the other, and the chorus bellowed with a will, substituting real primeval roughness for an artistic representation of roughness, which is a very different and more difficult thing.

But these criticisms of executive details, though they are important inasmuch as it is only by the most vigilant and unsparing activity in making them that Bayreuth can be kept conscious of the fact that it must conquer fresh prestige from performance to performance, and never for a moment rest on its reputation and the Master's laurels, must yet seem trivial and impertinent to those who can feel nothing but the tremendous impression made on them by a representation, complete in every word, note and picture, of the mightiest art work our century has produced.

I exhort all those who have lazily made up their minds that Bayreuth is too far, or that they cannot spare the money for the trip, to reconsider their decision and insist on the ever-resourceful Mr Schulz-Curtius finding them tickets for one of the remaining cycles. If even I, to whom Bayreuth has no novelty, and who can detect faults at the rate of about three in each bar, can say that I have been more than overpaid for the trouble and expense of my trip, how much more will not a visit be worth to those who can add the enchantments of a fool's paradise to the genuine recreation – I use the word in its highest sense – to be gained from the prodigious sum of really successful artistic effort which each of the performances represents? Therefore hestiate no longer, but buy your tickets, pack up your traps, and away with you. Only, if you value a cordial welcome, perhaps you had better not mention that you have come on my recommendation.

C. di B.

In a letter to Beatrice Webb, dated 29 July 1896, Shaw says he has rushed 'from the thick of Bayreuth' to the 'thick of the International Socialistic Congress' held that year in London. These reviews of 1896 are the last formal notices of Bayreuth by Shaw, who gave up music criticism shortly afterwards.

Shaw's book The Perfect Wagnerite *was published on 1 December 1898 and went through three more editions (1901, 1913 and 1922), acquiring several prefaces and a number of postscripts in its course. Some of these appendages are about Bayreuth, and repeat the familiar Shaw theme of its lesson for England.*

When the Bayreuth Festival Playhouse was at last completed, and opened in 1876 with the first performance of the *Ring*, European society was compelled to admit that Wagner was a 'success'. Royal personages, detesting his music, sat out performances in a row of boxes set apart from the public for princes. They all complimented him on the astonishing 'push' with which, in the teeth of all obstacles, he had turned a fabulous and visionary project into a concrete and commercial reality, patronized by the public at a pound a head. It is well to know that these congratulations had no other effect on Wagner than to open his eyes to the fact that the Bayreuth experiment, as an attempt to evade the ordinary social and commercial conditions of theatrical enterprise, was a failure. His own account of it contrasts the reality with his intentions in a vein which would be bitter if it were not so humorous. The precautions taken to keep the seats out of the hands of the frivolous public and in the hands of the earnest disciples, banded together in little Wagner Societies throughout Europe, had ended in their forstalling by ticket speculators and their sale to just the sort of idle globe-trotting tourist against whom the temple was to have been strictly closed. The money, supposed to be contributed by the faithful, was begged by energetic subscription-hunting ladies from people who must have had the most grotesque misconceptions of the composer's aims: among others, the Khedive of Egypt and the Sultan of Turkey!

Since then, subscriptions are no longer needed; for the Festival Playhouse pays its own way now, and is commercially on the same footing as any other theatre. The only qualification required from the visitor is money. The Londoner spends twenty pounds on a visit: a native Bayreuther spends one pound. In either case the 'Folk' on whose behalf Wagner turned out in 1849, are effectively excluded: and the Festival Playhouse must therefore be classed as infinitely less Wagnerian in its character than Hampton Court Palace. Nobody knew this better than Wagner; and nothing can be further off the mark than to chatter about Bayreuth as if it had succeeded in escaping from the conditions of our modern civilization any more than the Grand Opera in Paris or London.

Within these conditions, however, it effected a new departure in that excellent German institution, the summer theatre. Unlike the old opera houses, which are constructed so that the audience may present a splendid pageant to the delighted manager, it was designed to secure an uninterrupted view of the stage, and an undisturbed hearing of the music, to the audience. The dramatic purpose of the performances was taken with entire and elaborate seriousness as the sole purpose of them; and the management was jealous for the reputation of Wagner. The sightseeing globe-trotter no longer crowds out the genuine disciple; the audiences are now as genuinely devoted as Wagner could have desired: the disconcerted, bewildered, bored followers of fashion have vanished with the sportsman on a holiday: the atmosphere is the right one for the work. There is, apparently, an effective demand for summer theatres of the highest class. There is no reason why the experiment should not be tried in England. If our enthusiasm for Handel can support Handel Festivals, laughably dull, stupid and anti-Handelian as these choral monstrosities are, as well as annual provincial festivals on the same model, there is no likelihood of a Wagner Festival failing. Suppose, for instance, a Wagner theatre were built at Hampton Court or on Richmond Hill, not to say Margate Pier, so that we could have a delightful summer evening holiday, Bayreuth fashion, passing the hours between the acts in the park or on the river below before sunset, is it seriously contended that there would be any lack of visitors? If a little of the money that is wasted on grand stands, Eiffel towers and dismal Halls by the Sea, all as much tied to brief annual seasons as Bayreuth, were applied in this way, the profit would be far more certain and the social utility prodigiously greater. Any English enthusiasm for Bayreuth that does not take the form of a clamor for a Festival Playhouse in England may be set aside as mere pilgrimage mania.

Besides, the early Bayreuth performances were far from delectable. The singing was sometimes tolerable, and sometimes abominable. Some of the singers were mere animated beer casks, too lazy and conceited to practise the self-control and physical training that is expected as a matter of course from an acrobat, a jockey or a pugilist. The women's dresses were prudish and absurd. It is true that after some years the Kundry no longer wore an early Victorian ball dress with 'ruchings', and that Freia was provided with a faintly modish copy of the flowered gown of Spring in Botticelli's famous picture: but the mailclad Brynhild still climbed the mountains with her legs carefully hidden in a long white skirt, and looked so exactly like Mrs Leo Hunter as Minerva that it was quite impossible to feel a ray of illusion whilst looking at her. The ideal of womanly beauty aimed at, reminded Englishmen of the barmaids of the seventies, when the craze for golden hair was at its worst. Further, whilst Wagner's stage directions were sometimes disregarded as unintelligently as at the old opera houses, Wagner's quaintly old-fashioned tradition of half rhetorical, half historico-pictorial attitude and gesture prevailed, the most striking moments of the drama were conceived as *tableaux vivants* with posed models, instead of as passages of action, motion and life.

I need hardly add that the supernatural powers of control attributed by credulous people to Wagner's widow, and later to his son, did not exist. Prima donnas and tenors were as unmanageable at Bayreuth as anywhere else. Casts were capriciously changed; stage business was insufficiently rehearsed; the audience was compelled to listen to a Brynhild or Siegfried of fifty when they had carefully arranged to see one of twenty-five, much as in any ordinary opera house. Even the conductors upset the arrangements occasionally. On the other hand, we could always feel assured that in thoroughness of preparation of the chief work of the season, in strenuous artistic pretentiousness, in pious conviction that the work was of such enormous importance as to be worth doing well at all costs, the Bayreuth performances deserve their reputation. Their example raised the quality of operatic performances throughout the world, even in apparently incorrigible centres of fashion and frivolity.

In 1898 I purposely dwelt on the shortcomings of Bayreuth to shew that there was no reason in the world why as good and better performances of the *Ring* should not be given in England, and that Wagner's widow nor his son could pretend to handle them with greater authority than any artist who feels the impulse to interpret them. Nobody will ever know what Wagner himself thought of the artists who established the Bayreuth tradition: he was obviously not in a position to criticize them. For instance, had Rubini survived to create Siegmund, Wagner could hardly have written so amusing and vivid a description as he did of his Ottavio in the old Paris days. Wagner was under great obligations to his heroes and heroines of 1876; and he naturally said nothing to disparage their triumphs; but there is no reason to believe that all or indeed any of them satisfied him as Schnorr von Carolsfeld satisfied him as Tristan or Schröder-Devrient as Fidelio. It was just as likely that the next Schnorr or Schröder would arise in England. Nowadays it seems odd that anyone should need to be told all this. British and American singers have long since replaced the Bayreuth veterans to considerable advantage.

When Shaw came to write a Preface for the fourth edition of The Perfect Wagnerite *in 1922 world events had moved greatly; and, as he points out, music and drama had not been untouched in the process. As the following paragraph, taken from this Preface, shows, Shaw's attitude to the Bayreuth he had known in the 1890s had changed too.*

One had to admit at Bayreuth that here was the utmost perfection of the pictorial stage, and that its machinery could go no further. Nevertheless, having seen it at its best, fresh from Wagner's own influence, I must also admit that my favorite way of enjoying a performance of the *Ring* is to sit at the back of a box, comfortable on two chairs, feet up, and listen without looking. The truth is, a man whose imagination cannot serve him better than the most costly devices of the imitative scenepainter, should not go to the theatre, and as a matter of fact does not. In planning his Bayreuth theatre, Wagner was elaborating what he had better have scrapped altogether.

So much for Wagner's own influence! And seeing it at its best! But, as should by now be apparent, Shaw was ever inconsistent – and provokingly so. Provocation is a feature of The Perfect Wagnerite *and it is a pity that what still remains a worthwhile commentary on the* Ring *should not be available now in print in England – especially as an English Wagner style had been triumphantly established in the 1970s, which, moreover, had put Bayreuth in the shade – as Shaw said it would!*

Sir Arthur Sullivan

Sir Arthur Sullivan (1842–1900), the English composer, left for Bayreuth shortly after being received by Queen Victoria during the Jubilee celebrations of 1897. The following extracts come from his diaries. It may seem surprising to find a writer of comic operas making his way to Bayreuth: less so, if it is remembered that Sullivan had ambitions to succeed with his more serious music, and also played a part in the re-discovery of Schubert.

August 11th – Put on light clothes and went to the performance of *Parsifal*. Although many points open to severe criticism, the work and performance impressed me immensely. Theatre, which holds over 1600, quite full. Saw many English friends, Prince and Princess of Wales, Lady de Grey, Balfour, etc.

The Prince of Wales had already seen the Ring *in London in 1882; it would be interesting to know what he made of Bayreuth and* Parsifal *– perhaps he took the line of Delibes's famous remark when confronted with the sacred drama, quoted on page 181 of this book.*

August 14th – Beginning of *Ring* performance, *Rheingold*, commenced at 5 and went on without break till 7.30. Then home to dinner. Much disappointed in the performance; all of them. Orchestra rough and ragged, conducted by Siegfried Wagner. Vocalists beneath contempt. Sometimes stage-management is good, but much is conventional and childish. It is difficult to know how Wagner could have got up any enthusiasm or interest in such a lying, thieving, blackguardly set of low creatures as all the characters in his opera prove themselves to be.

August 15th – Performance of *Walkurie* [*sic*] (House party – Lady de Grey, A. J. Balfour, Prince and Princess of Wales, etc.). Very pleasant party – good lunch. Back at 3.15. Unfortunately fell asleep and didn't wake till 5 and so missed the first act. Much that is beautiful in the opera – less dreary padding than the others.

August 16th – Performance of *Siegfried*. I think it intolerably dull and heavy, and so undramatic – nothing but 'conversations' and I am weary of Leit Motiven. Burgstaller (tenor) is young and good-looking and has a pretty voice, but he will kill it if he sings Siegfried and similar roles much more. He was dead beat at the end of the opera. What a curious mixture of sublimity and absolute puerile drivel are all these Wagner operas. Sometimes the story and action would disgrace even a Surrey pantomime.

The Surrey Theatre, in London, was at that time all the rage for the cheap melodramas it staged.

August 18th – Last *Ring* performance *Götterdämmerung*
    1st act – 4 to 6 – dull and dreary
    2nd act – 6.30 to 8 – just as dull and dreary
    3rd act – 8.45 to 10 – very fine and impressive – the Leit Motiven seemed all natural and not dragged in, and the whole act is more dramatic, and musically finer than any of the others.

Sullivan, it has been said, never openly criticised Wagner or any other musician – he knew what it was like to fail himself. Sullivan was drawn by the majesty and power of Wagner's music but felt there were in it passages of sham which Wagner unscrupulously passed off on his disciples as genuine.

Sir Charles Tennyson

Sir Charles Tennyson, lawyer, writer and relative of the poet, was born in November 1879. He gave this talk, 'Memories of Bayreuth', on BBC Radio 3 in April 1976 when he was in his ninety-seventh year. (He died in June 1977.)

The first time that I went to the Wagner Festival at Bayreuth was in 1899, when I was nineteen years old. I had gone out to Germany for a few months after leaving school at the end of 1898. First, I spent some time at Dresden, learning the language with a marvellous lady who devoted most of her time to teaching the language to candidates for our Foreign Office, Fräulein Gottschalk. She had developed a cast-iron method of teaching English people German. She had carefully analysed both languages and knew exactly what an Englishman would pick up naturally (and need not be taught at all), what, on the other hand, he would never suceed in learning, except by heart and as a matter of routine, and what he must acquire by a careful and intelligent study of the language – if at all. She proved so excellent a teacher that I was able to leave Dresden after about three months. While at Dresden I went to the Opera a good deal and heard a certain amount of Wagner. The Dresden Opera House was very strong at this time but I do not remember who the conductor was – two of the singers I remember very clearly; one was the principal baritone, Herr Scheidemantel (famous as Hans Sachs in *Meistersinger* to which I became devoted) and one was Fräulein Marten (who, I think, had been one of Wagner's favourite pupils). She was a massive lady and a very fine singer whom I think I saw in *Tannhäuser*, *Lohengrin*, *The Flying Dutchman* and also in *Rienzi* and *Die Feen*.

The 'Fräulein Marten' mentioned here was most likely to have been Amalie Materna – she was Wagner's Brünnhilde and Kundry. Materna would have been about fifty-five years old in 1899, but quite possibly still singing the principal roles. Alternatively, it could have been Therese Malten.

From Dresden I went, for a term, to the University of Jena to study Classics. Jena was not particularly famous for its Latin and Greek but it was famous at this time for *Pädagogie*, or the Theory of Education – in this it had a notable Professor (Rhein) who was drawing students from all over the world. There was quite a large English contingent which included F. T. Acland who was afterwards a member of Asquith's Government – his father was an eminent Liberal and a close friend of my stepfather, Augustine Birrell, also an eminent Liberal and a most delightful and entertaining man, but not at all interested in music – indeed I think he was the only man I have known who was completely tone-deaf. He used to say that the only reason why he recognised 'God save the King' was that people around him arose from their chairs.

I worked pretty hard at Jena and was joined there by a remarkable friend, Ralph Peter. Ralph was roaming about Europe preparing, I think, for the Foreign Office Examinations. One of his peculiarities was the suddenness of his decisions and his remarkable power of carrying them out, however great the difficulties. When term at Jena ended, Ralph decided that he and I should pay a visit to the Wagner Festival at Bayreuth. We neither of us had any money and we had no friends at Bayreuth to whom we could look for hospitality, but Ralph succeeded, in an incredibly short time, in obtaining invitations for us to stay with some musical Germans for a week – he even arranged for someone to pay for our seats!

Now as I made another visit to Bayreuth five or six years later, seventy years ago, I am apt to confuse details of the two visits – so postpone description until I am able to speak of my second visit. Two things, however, I indelibly remember in connection with my first visit. I remember that we used to go after the opera to drink and smoke in a café where an Austrian Countess sat at the head of a long table, entertaining the singers, while smoking cigars and drinking beer – I mean, the Countess was smoking cigars and drinking beer – not the singers! I remember also that we found Mrs Annie Besant staying in our house with two of her young male acolytes. She was a massive woman, about fifty years old and, by now, a fully-fledged Theosophist. Mrs Besant, swathed from head to foot in purple veiling, gave us and our hosts a most enthralling talk on *Parsifal*, which we had just seen and which I did not like, partly owing to the extreme plain-ness of the Kundry. I remember that the two acolytes claimed supernatural powers for Mrs Besant but, when pressed to give us demonstrations, excused themselves on the ground that she reserved such demonstrations for 'special occasions'.

My second visit to Bayreuth is about 1905. By then I had got called to the Bar and settled down to a bachelor life in London which included a certain amount of opera – not yet so expensive as it has now become.

I hovered, at this time, on the fringe of the Bloomsbury Group, my chief friend amongst whom, Thoby Stephen (my contemporary at Cambridge) died, unfortunately, in 1906. I remember meeting his sisters, Vanessa and Virginia Stephen, at Covent Garden when I was attending a performance of the *Ring* cycle. Virginia became afterwards the famous novelist Virginia Woolf and Vanessa became a famous painter.

At this time the attitude to Wagner's works was rather different from what it is today – we loved *Meistersinger*, felt that we ought to love the *Ring*, were rather snooty about *Tannhäuser*, *Lohengrin* and *The Flying Dutchman* – but inwardly enjoyed them! The Bloomsbury attitude was partly influenced by Shaw's musical criticism and partly by a reaction from Italian Grand Opera – I recall how an old friend of mine, Alfred Noyes, once rhymed the name of 'Verdi' with the word 'hurdy-gurdy' in a long-since-forgotten poem. I have certainly changed my mind about Verdi but I am unrepentant about Wagner and today, as in 1899, consider his *Meistersinger* the greatest dramatic masterpiece of the nineteenth century.

It was my privilege, at this time, to be very often entertained by some friends of my mother's who had daughters of my generation, and were devoted to music. One summer, these friends invited me to join a delightful party to Bayreuth, in which the mother and the two daughters supplied the female element and 'Blue-toothed' Baker (a Balliol contemporary and friend of the young Asquith), Conway Wertheimer (also of Balliol – son of Ashe Wertheimer, the art expert who had presented Sargent's portraits of his entire family to the Tate Gallery) and myself were to be the men. A party of this kind, seventy years ago, was a considerable undertaking – and so our voyage across Europe proved. We travelled, I think, by Harwich and the Hook and were to break our journey at some town at which our hostess had reserved accommodation. When we reached this hotel we discovered that by no means whatever could the party be fitted into the accommodation offered to it without serious violation of the proprieties. However, Conway Wertheimer found a solution – he asked to see the Manager and, assuming his most magisterial air (he afterwards became an eminent KC), said to the Manager, 'You, my dear Sir, are obviously unaware that I am a first cousin of Herr Karl Baedeker.' Fortunately, the Manager did not ask for the relationship to be established and suitable accommodation was immediately provided.

But our troubles were not over. On arriving at Bayreuth the same difficulty presented itself. This time it was not necessary to invoke Herr Baedeker – the lodging-house keeper, immediately recognising our dilemma, was able to recommend other accommodation, to which the ladies withdrew. Later, the ladies, in their new lodging, were somewhat disturbed by the Proprietor's habit of straying about the passages at night, in his dressing gown, and muttering to himself – especially when they learned that he had recently been tried for murder of a lodger and only acquitted on a technicality. However, they suffered no harm.

Both my visits to Bayreuth were during the regime of Frau Cosima Wagner and her son, Siegfried. Certainly, I have a very distinct memory of seeing a lean and leonine, white-haired Frau Cosima walking in the grounds of the Festspielhaus on the arm of Arthur Balfour – I think that was on my second visit, anyhow, it was a sight one was not likely to forget!

Cosima had been an extremely controversial figure in her time – the illegitimate daughter, by a Swiss Countess, of the famous composer and pianist, the Abbé Liszt. She had, before she ran away with Wagner, been the wife of von Bülow, the leading German musical-dramatic critic and chief defender of Wagner's new ideas as a composer. By now, however, Cosima was over sixty and Wagner had been dead for fifteen years. Bayreuth had become an international institution and Frau Cosima, although she did not die until 1930, was already a legend.

I do not think that Bayreuth under the direction of Cosima and Siegfried was very highly regarded in the musical world – their methods were thought to be too conservative – for example, their successors would not, I feel sure, have tolerated the Kundry of my *Parsifal*, nor do I think that the younger generation would have tolerated the massive Brünnhilde at the close of *Götterdämmerung*, smacking her equally massive grey horse on the rump and flopping into the stage bonfire while the complaisant beast trotted quietly off into the wings.

Of the musical direction I am not able to judge, but the performances at Covent Garden were considered, at this time, more satisfactory than those at Bayreuth, I believe.

Is this all that I can remember of my two visits to Bayreuth? I am afraid it is – but then the last of them was a long, long time ago and I am very, very old.

Sir Thomas Beecham

Sir Thomas Beecham (1879–1961), English conductor, impresario and founder of orchestras, made the journey to Bayreuth in 1899. His autobiography, from which this extract is taken, was, to universal regret, never completed. It appears that he enjoyed the countryside and the conversations he had with a group of young Germans more than the Bayreuth performances. Beecham was invited to Bayreuth in 1936 as a guest of Hitler, but he did not take up this offer.

It was during the summer of the same year [1899] that I paid my first visit to Bayreuth, and it may be imagined with what excitement I had been looking forward to this celebration, which inspired as much enthusiasm in the musically devout of the end of the nineteenth century as did a pilgrimage to some shrine such as that of Thomas à Becket at Canterbury in the Middle Ages. I journeyed by slow steps through Bruges, Brussels, Cologne, Frankfurt and Nuremberg, suitably preparing my mind for the great experience by a re-study of the music dramas I was to hear under ideal conditions, as well as an extensive dip into German history, folklore and lyric poetry, and after about ten days reached the little Franconian capital on an evening early in August. The town was hot, stuffy and packed, the only accommodation I could secure was inadequate and uncomfortable, and a large number of visitors seemed to be from my own country. This was an unwelcome surprise, for I had vaguely imagined that I should find myself in the pure atmosphere of an undiluted Teutonism, and the prevailing sound of my own tongue gave the place something of the tone of a holiday resort at home that dulled a little the edge of my expectations. With the splendid snobbery of youth I declined to believe that this accustomed crowd of knickerbockered sportsmen, gaitered bishops, and equine-visaged ladies could have any real affinity with the spirit of the mighty genius who had completed on the stage the task which Walter Scott a century earlier had begun in the novel, the reconstruction of the age of chivalry and romance. I coveted the happiness and applauded the prejudice of the royal Ludwig, and had I been a millionaire would have waited until the close of the Festival and engaged the company to play its programme all over again for the benefit of an audience of one, myself.

There were signs too that Bayreuth was ceasing to be the inviolate shrine of the Wagner cult and that the German public was beginning to lose some of an earlier faith in its artistic integrity. The air was filled with the din of controversy over the policy of Wahnfried as well as the quality of the performances at the Festspielhaus, and the redoubtable Felix Weingartner was to the front with a pamphlet in which he vigorously attacked both. The malcontents quite unambiguously proclaimed the decadence of the Festival, accused Cosima of having handed over the splendid musical machine of her husband as a toy for their son to play with, deplored the engagement of singers who had little knowledge of the true Wagnerian style, as well as conductors whose addiction to slow tempi weakened that force and liveliness which Richard had always demanded in the rendering of his music, and, worst of all, clamoured loudly for the removal from the chair of the youthful Siegfried, whose left-handed direction was denounced as feeble and uninspiring. Naturally the Wahnfried circle responded to its critics with the counter-accusations of intrigue and jealousy, and so far as I could judge, seemed for the moment to be having the better of the argument. The personal prestige of Cosima, a remarkable woman of considerable attraction and indomitable will, still ran high, and if she did not know what Richard's true wishes and intentions had been then no one did.

My own sympathies veered towards the opposition camp, as the representations I heard were distinctly disappointing. Although I had not seen the *Ring* before, and could not therefore judge in detail where I found them wanting, the singing, playing and stage production all fell below the level I had previsioned. The inevitable crowd of cranks and faddists swelled the ranks of worshippers and the bookshops overflowed with literary curiosities, some of them linking the music dramas with every recent 'ism' in philosophy, politics, science and even hygiene; one bright effort going so far as to allege that *Parsifal* was less of an art work than a piece of propaganda for the higher vegetarianism and not to be comprehended fully unless accepted as such. It was something of a relief to escape from this unidyllic environment into the country for a change of air during a pause in my cycle of performances, and as I had been told of a little spa, Alexanderbad, some twenty miles out where one went to drink the steel-water springs and take walks in the pine woods all around, I went, and remained there for the rest of my visit, going to Bayreuth only on the days of the performances.

Beecham, then, does not make any detailed assessment of the music he heard but he does end this section on Bayreuth with a comment in a typically provocative vein. It was at Bayreuth (of all places), he tells us, that he realised how much he appreciated the music of Brahms – 'generally at his best in smaller forms'.

Béla Bartók

Béla Bartók (1881–1945) the Hungarian composer, attended the Bayreuth Festival of 1904 when he was twenty-three years old. His impressions are briefly recorded in one quite continuous message spread over two picture postcards which he posted separately. The first one shows the Festspielhaus and the second (indicated by a stroke in the following text) the Neues Schloss.

Regensberg, 21 August 1904

Dear Kálmán

I am still under the spell of *Parsifal* as I write these lines. A very interesting work, though it did not make such a tremendous impression on me as *Tristan*. Anyone possessed of the slightest religious sentiment must be moved by / the plot. I feel disturbed by that continual praying on the stage. Contrary to my expectations, I found many innovations in the music. It is amazing that a man of seventy could write anything so fresh as the Flower Maidens' love song in the second act – and this without being repetitious. I shall be writing something more about Bayreuth, in any case. What I would like to know is whether you would come to see a few performances some time. I played my Scherzo to Richter who thinks it is a scherzo 'von und zu Ubermenschen'.

Yours ever
Béla

The recipient of these cards was Kálmán Harsányi (1876–1929), a Hungarian poet. Bartók wrote to him a few weeks later:

. . . When I was in Bayreuth, I learned that those Wagner Scholarships are not only for musicians but also for writers and poets. Perhaps you, too, could send in an application. Even if you do not obtain a full scholarship, you might still get tickets for six performances or so (not something to be scorned when tickets cost twenty marks). Applications have to be in by the end of Jan 1905 to a Count Festetich whose address I have forgotten. . . .

Bernard Shaw (1908)

Bernard Shaw, who by now had given up writing music criticism, visited Bayreuth in 1908. His wife, Charlotte Payne-Townshend, whom he had married in 1898 (the account of their wedding, in The Star *of 2 June, was written by Shaw himself and is a classic), had never been to Bayreuth; it was their intention to hire a car and drive there by way of Scandinavia. A letter to the impresario J. E. Vedrenne was accompanied by Bayreuth Festival programmes bearing Shaw's comments. The names of the singers have been inserted in parenthesis.*

25th July Das Rheingold conducted by Richter

The second scene was quite spoiled by the heavy dark brown foreground. One would think Turner had never painted, and Gaspar Poussin and the tradition of the yellow sun and brown tree had never been exploded. Great pity; for the castle was fine.

Wotan [Soomer] magnificent voice – man under 30.
Loge [Briesemeister] style of Barker.

The three Rhinedaughters [Hemel, Alten and Kraus-Osborne], not being able to sing like salmon, sang like pheasants instead, with amazing realism. First scene consequently very ugly beyond words – Alberich jolly well out of it.

27th July Siegfried

I forgot to get the bills of the Walküre and Götterdämmerung. The casts were not changed. Richter conducted the last three performances magnificently. He is too old to care much about the Walkürenritt & that sort of thing; but all the rest was masterly: not a stroke wrong and the broadest & grandest parts the best.

The Rheingold was not so good: the singers drowned the orchestra. I told Richter he would have to write additional accompaniments presently.

There were some very clever tricks of stage lighting in the second act of Siegfried, especially getting the sun behind the tree & casting a strong shadow *towards* the footlights with the bare sun glittering at you through the leaves.

Soomer ought to be captured for London (from a business point of view). His singing at the end of Die Walküre produced a wild demonstration from the audience. He talks to Brynhild on a low G as easily as a basso profundo, and gets pianos on a high D above middle C as easily as a tenor. Very rich voice and sings in tune. Too young for the 3rd act of Siegfried, but splendid in the first act with Mime & in the Walküre farewell. Talk to Schulz-Curtius or the opera people about it.

Siegfried [Burgstaller] very good – couldnt have believed it was the same man I saw at his debut on my last visit.

Mime [Breuer] excellent – really sings now.

Alberich [Dawison] a stick – also vibrato.

Brünnhilde [Gulbranson] sings in tune. Most matronly.

31st July Lohengrin

Wonderful stage pictures, very well composed. But I missed a certain manoeuvre by which, when Lohengrin was first produced in Bayreuth, the women (in the finale to the first act) suddenly swept forward & changed the whole color of the stage at the exact moment when the key changed.

Musically the performance was a little muzzy: the later Wagnerian style blots out something of the sharpness & brilliancy of the age of Spontini.

Heinrich der Vogler [Hinckley], deutscher Konig & Vibrato.

Elsa [Fleischer-Edel], in a flaxen wig, exactly like the doll in the second act of the Contes d'Hoffman.

Ortrud [Walker], looking very Irish in the 1st act.

1st August Parsifal

This was the most perfectly managed performance I ever saw (and I have seen 6 before at Bayreuth). The only sort of curtain call allowed by tradition there is a tableau curtain at the end of Parsifal; and this time the impression was so perfect that there was a shocked protest – quite a lot of hissing – when the curtain was taken up again.

Virginia Woolf

Virgina Woolf (Virginia Stephen) (1882–1941), English novelist, essayist and literary critic, went to the Bayreuth Festival in 1909 with her brother Adrian and Saxon Sydney-Turner (a friend of their elder brother Thoby who had died in 1906). Saxon, an intense Wagnerite, had arranged the trip; it was not a happy group and Virginia, who knew little about music, found her fellows dull company. She wrote to her sister Vanessa describing Bayreuth as 'like an English market town' and the people as 'gross' and 'hideous'. The German women were 'puddings of red dough' and the amount of self-indulgence by food and drink, to be seen wherever she went, disgusted her. Her first impression of Parsifal *was of 'vague, weak stuff' but a second performance a few days later almost brought tears. Virginia wrote (with some difficulty, she told her sister) the following article which appeared in* The Times *on 21 August 1909, under the heading 'Impressions at Bayreuth':*

The commonplace remark that music is in its infancy is best borne out by the ambiguous state of musical criticism. It has few traditions behind it, and the art itself is so much alive that it fairly suffocates those who try to deal with it. A critic of writing is hardly to be taken by surprise, for he can compare almost every literary form with some earlier form and can measure the achievement by some familiar standard. But who in music has tried to do what Strauss is doing, or Debussy? Before we have made up our minds as to the nature of the operatic form we have to value very different and very emphatic examples of it. This lack of tradition and of current standards is of course the freest and happiest state that a critic can wish for; it offers some one the chance of doing now for music what Aristotle did 2,000 years ago for poetry. The fact, however, that so little has yet been done to lay bare the principles of the art accounts for the indecision which marks our attempts to judge new music. As for the old, we take it for granted, or concentrate our minds upon the *prima donna*'s cold. It is criticism of a single hour, in a particular day, and tomorrow the mark has faded.

There is only one way open thus for a writer who is not disposed to go to the root of the matter and is yet dissatisfied with the old evasions – he may try to give his impressions as an amateur. The seats in the great bare house in Bayreuth are packed with them; they have a secret belief that they understand as well as other people, although they seldom venture an opinion; and, at any rate, there is no doubt that they love music. If they hesitate to criticise, it is perhaps that they have not sufficient technical knowledge to fasten upon details; a criticism of the whole resolves itself into vague formulas, comparisons and adjectives. Nevertheless, no one can doubt that the audience at Bayreuth, pilgrims many of them from distant lands, attend with all their power. As the lights sink, they rustle into their seats, and scarcely stir till the last wave of sound has ceased; when a stick falls, there is a nervous shudder, like a ripple in water, through the entire house. During the intervals between the acts, when they come out into the sun, they seem oppressed with a desire to disburden themselves somehow of the impression which they have received. *Parsifal*, in particular, lays such a weight upon the mind that it is not until one has heard it many times over that one can begin, as it were, to move it to and fro. The unfamiliarity of the ideas hinders one at the outset from bringing the different parts together. One feels vaguely for a crisis that never comes, for, accustomed as one is to find the explanation of a drama in the love of man and woman, or in battle, one is bewildered by a music that continues with the utmost calm and intensity independently of them. Further, the change from the Temple of the Grail to the magic garden, with its swarms of flower-maidens and its hot red blossoms, is too violent a break to be bridged conveniently.

Nevertheless, although they are great, these difficulties scarcely do more than disturb the surface of a very deep and perhaps indescribable impression. Puzzled we may be, but it is primarily because the music has reached a place not yet visited by sound. An anthem sung with perfect skill in some great church will suggest a part of the scene in the vast hall, with its green distances, and yet a part only. Ecclesiastical music is too rigidly serene and too final in its spirit to penetrate as the music of *Parsifal* penetrates. Somehow Wagner has conveyed the desire of the Knights of the Grail in such a way that the intense emotion of human beings is combined with the unearthly nature of the thing they seek. It tears us, as we hear it, as though its wings were sharply edged. Again, feelings of this kind that are equally diffused and felt for one object in common create an impression of largeness and, when the music is played as it was played on the night of the 11th, of an overwhelming unity. The Grail seems to burn through all superincumbrances; the music is intimate in a sense that none other is; one is fired with emotion and yet possessed with tranquillity at the same time, for the words are continued by the music so that we hardly notice the transition.

It may be that these exalted emotions, which belong to the essence of our being, and are rarely expressed, are those that are best translated by music; so that a satisfaction, or whatever one may call that sense of answer which the finest art supplies to its own question, is constantly conveyed here. Like Shakespeare, Wagner seems to have attained in the end to such a mastery of technique that he could float and soar in regions where in the beginning he could scarcely breathe; the stubborn matter of his art dissolves in his fingers, and he shapes it as he chooses. When the opera is over, it is surely the completeness of the vast work that remains with us. The earlier operas have always their awkward moments, when the illusion breaks; but *Parsifal* seems poured out in a smooth stream at white heat; its shape is solid and entire. How much of the singular atmosphere which surrounds the opera in one's mind springs from other sources than the music itself it would be hard to say. It is the only work which has no incongruous associations.

It has been possible, during these last performances, to step out of the opera-house and find oneself in the midst of a warm summer evening. From the hill above the theatre you look over a wide land, smooth and without hedges; it is not beautiful, but it is very large and tranquil. One may sit among rows of turnips and watch a gigantic old woman, with a blue cotton bonnet on her head and a figure like one of Dürer's, swinging her hoe. The sun draws out strong scents from the hay and the pine trees, and if one thinks at all, it is to combine the simple landscape with the landscape of the stage. When the music is silent the mind insensibly slackens and expands, among happy surroundings: heat and yellow light, and the intermittent but not unmusical noises of insects and leaves smooth out the folds. In the next interval, between seven and eight, there is another act out here also; it is now dusky and perceptibly fresher; the light is thinner, and the roads are no longer crossed by regular bars of shade. The figures in light dresses moving between the trees of the avenue, with depths of blue air behind them, have a curiously decorative effect. Finally, when the opera is over, it is quite late; and half way down the hill one looks back upon a dark torrent of carriages descending, their lamps wavering one above another, like irregular torches.

These strange intervals in the open air, as though a curtain were regularly drawn and shut again, have no disturbing effect, upon *Parsifal* at least. A bat from the woods circled Kundry's head in the meadow, and little white moths dance incessantly over the footlights. It was curious, although scarcely fair, to test *Lohengrin* two days after one had heard *Parsifal*. The difference which a chorus, alive in all its parts so that eyes and arms are moving when the voice is silent, can make to a work in which the chorus means so much is surprising certainly; and yet, recognising the admirable performance, other reflections were suggested by it. The same surroundings that were so congenial to *Parsifal* turn much of *Lohengrin* to tinsel and sham armour; one thinks of gorgeous skirts and the mantles of knights trailed along the dusty paths and pricked by the stubble. An opera-house which shelters such a troop should be hemmed in by streets with great shop windows; their splendour somehow dwindles away and falls flat in the empty country.

But although this was one of the impressions that *Lohengrin* gave rise to, can it be held to be any reflection upon the music? No one, perhaps, save a writer properly versed in the science, can decide which impressions are relevant and which impertinent, and it is here that the amateur is apt to incur the contempt of the professional. We know the critic who, in painting, prefers the art of Fra Angelico because that painter worked upon his knees; others choose books because they teach one to rise early; and one has only to read the descriptive notes in a concert programme to be led hopelessly astray. Apart from the difficulty of changing a musical impression into a literary one, and the tendency to appeal to the literary sense because of the associations of words, there is the further difficulty in the case of music that its scope is much less clearly defined than the scope of the other arts. The more beautiful a phrase of music is the richer its burden of suggestion, and if we understand the form but slightly, we are little restrained in our interpretation. We are led on to connect the beautiful sound with some experience of our own, or to make it symbolise some conception of a general nature. Perhaps music owes something of its astonishing power over us to this lack of definite articulation; its statements have all the majesty of a generalisation, and yet contain our private emotions. Something of the same effect is given by Shakespeare, when he makes an old nurse the type of all the old nurses in the world, while she keeps her identity as a particular old woman. The comparative weakness of *Lohengrin* urges one to such speculations, for there are many passages which fit loosely to the singer's mood, and yet carry one's mind out with a beauty of their own.

In the meantime, we are miserably aware how little words can do to render music. When the moment of suspense is over, and the bows actually move across the strings, our definitions are relinquished, and words disappear in our minds. Enormous is the relief, and yet, when the spell is over, how great is the joy with which we turn to our old tools again! These definitions indeed, which would limit the bounds of an art and regulate our emotions, are arbitrary enough; and here at Bayreuth, where the music fades into the open air, and we wander with *Parsifal* in our heads through empty streets at night, where the gardens of the Hermitage glow with flowers like those other magic blossoms, and sound melts into colour, and colour calls out for words, where, in short, we are lifted out of the ordinary world and allowed merely to breathe and see — it is here that we realise how thin are the walls between one emotion and another; and how fused our impressions are with elements which we may not attempt to separate.

The group had stayed in Bayreuth for two weeks (from 6 August) and afterwards went on to Dresden for more opera and the galleries. The pictures were a disappointment but they did see Strauss's Salome *which was four years old in 1909 and still considered unfit for the London stage; it was eventually given by Beecham in 1910. Virginia was greatly excited by the new discovery and wrote that Strauss 'gets great emotion into his music, without any beauty'. However, her companions still had their minds on Wagner and the petty bickerings that had plagued the trip from the outset broke out once more.*

Sir Adrian Boult

Sir Adrian Boult (1889–), conductor and champion of British music and composers, went to Bayreuth with his mother, an enthusiastic traveller, when he was an undergraduate at Oxford. They visited Munich first and were entranced by Bruno Walter's direction of Mozart's operas. It was later in 1912 that the twenty-three-year-old Boult went to Leipzig to study conducting with the celebrated Artur Nikisch.

The extract below comes from Boult's autobiography My Own Trumpet *which was published in 1973, when he was eighty-four. He does not say what he saw at Bayreuth but it sounds as if his disappointment was with* Parsifal, *the stage scenery of which dated from Wagner's original production of 1882 (it was, in fact, not replaced until the late 1930s, by which time it was literally falling to pieces).*

Bayreuth next day offered a sorry contrast: by 1912 the efforts to keep everything 'as the Master had left it' were wearing themselves out; the theatre was dusty (curtains included), props shoddy, mise-en-scène prehistoric. The chorus sang woefully out of tune, but the orchestra, and many soloists were magnificent.

Coming down from the theatre arm-in-arm with my mother, I suddenly realised that we were dashing along at a great pace, when we had a comfortable hour to spare before taking our train back to Nuremberg where we were sleeping. I suggested slowing down, but she pushed on, gasping as we dodged in and out of the crowd: 'I – hate – walking – behind – fat – people.' Each person or couple seemed fatter than the one we had just overtaken.

Igor Stravinsky

Igor Stravinsky (1882–1971) the Russian composer, went from his family estate in Russia to Bayreuth in 1912, interrupting work on his most celebrated composition to do so. He wrote about the Festival in 1936.

I was roused from that peaceful existence by an invitation from Diaghilev to join him at Bayreuth to hear *Parsifal* in its hallowed setting. I had never seen *Parsifal* on the stage, the proposal was tempting, and I accepted it with pleasure. On the way I stopped at Nuremberg for twenty-four hours and visited the Museum. Next day my dear portly friend met me at the Bayreuth station and told me we were in danger of having to sleep in the open, as all the hotels were filled to overflowing. We managed, however, with great difficulty, to find two servants' rooms. The performance which I saw there would not tempt me today even if I were offered a room gratis. The very atmosphere of the theatre, its design and its setting, seemed lugubrious. It was like a crematorium, and a very old-fashioned one at that, and one expected to see the gentleman in black who had been entrusted with the task of singing the praises of the departed. The order to devote oneself to contemplation was given by a blast of trumpets. I sat humble and motionless, but at the end of a quarter of an hour I could not bear any more. My limbs were numb and I had to change my position. Crack! Now I had done it! My chair had made a noise which drew on me the furious scowls of hundreds of pairs of eyes. Once more I withdrew into myself, but I could think of only one thing, and that was the end of the Act which would put an end to my martyrdom. At last the 'Pause' arrived, and I was rewarded by two sausages and a glass of beer. But hardly had I had time to light a cigarette when the trumpet-blast sounded again, demanding another period of contemplation. Another Act to be got through, when all my thoughts were concentrated on my cigarette, of which I had had barely a whiff. I managed to bear the second Act. Then there were more sausages, more beer, another trumpet-blast, another period of contemplation, another Act – Finis!

I do not want to discuss the music of *Parsifal* nor the music of Wagner in general. At this date it is too remote from me. What I find revolting in the whole affair is the underlying conception which dictated it – the principle of putting a work of art on the same level as the sacred and symbolic ritual which constitutes a religious service. And, indeed, is not all this comedy of Bayreuth, with its ridiculous formalities, simply an unconscious aping of a religious rite?

Perhaps someone may cite the Mysteries of the Middle Ages in contravention of this view. But those performances had religion as their basis and faith as their source. The spirit of the Mystery Plays did not venture beyond the bosom of the Church which patronised them. They were religious ceremonies bordering on the canonical rites, and such aesthetic qualities as they might contain were merely accessory and unintentional, and in no way affected their substance. Such ceremonies were due to the imperious desire of the faithful to see the objects of their faith incarnate and in palpable form – the same desire as that which created statues and ikons in the churches.

It is high time to put to an end, once for all, this unseemly and sacrilegious conception of art as religion and the theatre as a temple. The following argument will readily show the absurdity of such pitiful aesthetics:

One cannot imagine a believer adopting a critical attitude toward a religious service. That would be a contradiction in terms; the believer would cease to be a believer. The attitude of an audience is exactly the opposite. It is not dependent on faith nor on blind submission. At a performance one admires or one rejects. One accepts only after having passed judgment, however little one may be aware of it. The critical faculty plays an essential part. To confound these two distinct lines of thought is to give proof of a complete lack of discernment, and certainly of bad taste. But is it at all surprising that such confusion should arise at a time like the present, when the openly irreligious masses in their degradation of spiritual values and debasement of human thought necessarily lead us to utter brutalisation?

But to return to the *Sacre* . . .

'The Gradual Change'

On Saturday 31 January 1914, The Times *published an anonymous article about Bayreuth and the performance of* Parsifal *by 'one of the audience'. The occasion was the première of that work in London two days later (the copyright had run out on 31 December 1913), but the interest lies in the observations on Bayreuth in the light of the writer's regular visits to the Festival between 1882 and 1914.*

During the week of the two Patronatverein performances (1882) the aspect and 'feeling' of Bayreuth was altogether peculiar. In recalling that week my memory presents a picture of the place different in many respects from the Bayreuth of the next twenty years or so, during which I spent a week or a fortnight of every Festival month in the town or its near vicinity. The visitors were not then, as later, people mostly well off who had bought tickets for a renowned theatrical performance, but were members of a society, mostly poor, who had assembled to witness a performance of an interesting work of art to which their membership gave them free entrance. In later years the double string of carriages up and down the road from Bayreuth to the theatre was continuous for a good half-hour before the commencement; but on July 26th 1882, carriages were very scarce, and the two paths on either side of the road were thronged with pedestrians marching like pilgrims to a shrine.

A peculiar social atmosphere also pervaded the town. We felt that we were all, although unacquainted with each other, in sympathy and filled with the same enthusiasm. We had invaded, and, for the moment, intellectually annexed, Bayreuth.

It was, of course, impossible that the peculiar social atmosphere of that first week would ever again pervade Bayreuth in quite the same way; but such was the power of the master's spell that in subsequent years all who attended the Festival performances came to some extent under its power.

Now, in looking forward to the production of *Parsifal* on Monday, it is impossible not to feel curiosity as to the effect on those who have seen the work at Bayreuth of the new performance as compared with memories of the past. The preliminary spells by which the Bayreuth master entangled our spirits and prepared our minds for the reception of poetic impressions – the quaint old town, hidden away in romantic Bavaria, the people with but a single aim, the unique theatre – these are denied to the Covent Garden management and it is a serious demand to make on a member of the audience that he should walk straight out of Bow street into the 'Grals-Gebiet' and feel immediately at home there. Covent Garden also, unless it has made new arrangements, lacks the completely hidden orchestra which plays no small part in the general effect of the music. On the other hand, it has, or should have, an orchestra superior to the Bayreuth one; and, we have every right to expect scenery far better than all the Bayreuth scenery, except the Grail Hall. Klingsor's garden should be a delight instead of an eyesore; and our English scene-painters will certainly far surpass the Germans in all the landscape scenes. Even the most experienced Bayreuth visitor may, therefore, hope for entirely new impressions of the scenic elements of the drama.

With Parsifal *now available in every opera house that could stage it the unique claims of the Bayreuth Festival were lost; indeed, after the 1914 Festival there came the Great War and the Festspielhaus was shut for ten years, the longest break in its history. When it opened once more, in 1924, it was from a changed world that its visitors came.*

APPENDICES

APPENDIX I

Personalia
A guide to some of the figures mentioned in the text

BANTOCK, Granville, 1868–1946, English composer and champion of modern British music. His own output was considerable. Knighted 1930.

BARTÓK, Béla, 1881–1945, Hungarian composer who was influenced by the folk music of his country but did not imitate it. He spent his last years in exile in America.

BEECHAM, Thomas, 1879–1961, English conductor and impresario of exceptionally wide interests; renowned in Haydn and Mozart as well as Strauss and Delius. Knighted 1914.

BENEDICT, Julius, 1804–1885, English composer and conductor of German origin who studied with Weber. He met Beethoven in 1823. Moved to London 1835. Knighted 1871.

BENNETT, Joseph, 1831–1911, English critic and writer for many years with the *Daily Telegraph*. Wrote texts for oratorios by Barnett, Bottesini, Cowen, Mackenzie and Sullivan (*The Golden Legend*).

BERG, Alban, 1885–1935, Austrian composer. At first self-taught he became a pupil of Arnold Schoenberg in 1904 and embraced atonality and serialism in his later works. He wrote two operas, *Wozzeck* and the unfinished *Lulu* (this was completed by Friedrich Cerha only after Berg's widow died in 1977; it was first given complete at Paris in 1979).

BETZ, Franz, 1835–1900, German baritone who sang the first Hans Sachs at Munich in 1868 and Wotan (after Scaria dropped out) in the first Bayreuth *Ring* in 1876.

BJØRNSON, Bjørnstjerne, 1832–1910, Norwegian poet, novelist and dramatist. A friend of both Grieg and Delius he provided each of them with texts to set.

BOULT, Adrian Cedric, 1889–, English conductor who promoted modern British music. Studied with Nikisch and Reger. Knighted 1937.

BRAHMS, Johannes, 1833–1897, German composer who settled in Vienna in 1863. He had a reserved admiration for Wagner but in spite of this was taken as the figurehead of the anti-Wagner faction of his adopted city.

BREMA, Marie, 1856–1925 (real name Minny Fehrmann), English mezzo-soprano of German-American descent who sang in most opera houses and became a teacher at Manchester.

BRUCKNER, Anton, 1824–1896, Austrian composer and organist of humble origin. He became a friend of Wagner and espoused his cause without embracing his methods.

BÜLOW, Hans Guido von, 1830–1894, German pianist and conductor who was a lifelong champion of Wagner. He was the first husband of Cosima Wagner (divorced 1869) and the father of her daughters Blandine and Daniela.

BURGSTALLER, Alois, 1871–1945, German tenor who sang at the Bayreuth Festivals between 1896 and 1902. In 1903 he sang Parsifal in New York, which brought him into disfavour at Bayreuth.

BUSONI, Ferruccio Benvenuto, 1866–1924, Italian pianist and composer whose fame and fortune developed, as he himself lived, in the countries to the north of the Alps.

CAPLET, André, 1878–1925, French composer and conductor much influenced by his friend Debussy several of whose works he completed or orchestrated.

CASALS, Pau, 1876–1973, Catalan cellist and composer who, in 1905, joined the celebrated trio with Cortot and the violinist Thibaud. Much of his later life was spent in Puerto Rico.

CHABRIER, Emmanuel, 1841–1894, French composer who at first studied Law and composed as an amateur but, under the spell of Wagner, decided to devote his life to music.

CHAMBERLAIN, Houston Stewart, 1855–1927, English writer (on Wagner for the most part) who married Wagner's daughter Eva in 1908 and became a German subject. He was an avid propagandist for the Aryan theories that became current in the Bayreuth circle.

CHAUSSON, Ernest, 1855–1899, French composer who studied with Massenet and later with Franck.

CHORON, Alexandre, 1772–1834, French musical scholar and composer who compiled a musical encyclopaedia and books on composition.

CORTOT, Alfred, 1877–1962, French pianist who originally intended to be a conductor and in which role he gave the first performance in Paris of *Götterdämmerung*; he was on the music staff at Bayreuth as a young man.

CRANE, Walter, 1845–1915, English illustrator and designer chiefly known for his work on children's books. He was also an educator and influenced the spread of Art Nouveau.

CUI, César Antonovich, 1835–1918, Russian composer of French ancestry who joined the Balakirev group of nationalist composers before becoming a critic in 1864.

DANNREUTHER, Edward George, 1844–1905, English pianist, critic and teacher of German origin. Lived in London from 1861 and championed the cause of Wagner there against all odds.

DAVISON, James William, 1813–1885, English music critic who attended the Bayreuth Festival in 1876 for *The Times*.

DEBUSSY, Claude Achille, 1862–1918, French composer, pupil of Albert Lavignac. He fought, with some success, the bad influence of Wagner on French music of his generation.

DELIBES, Léo, 1836–1891, French composer who studied with Adam at the Paris Conservatoire, became chorus-master at the Opéra, and, in 1881, professor of composition at his old academy.

DELIUS, Frederick (originally Fritz), 1862–1934, English composer of German descent. He was a friend of Grieg, spent most of his life in France and had his first successes in Germany before Beecham championed his music in England.

DIAGHILEV, Sergei Pavlovich, 1872–1929, Russian impresario and founder of the Russian Ballet for which he had many famous works composed by Stravinsky, Ravel, Debussy and Prokoviev, as well as others.

DORÉ, Paul Gustav, 1833–1883, French painter and illustrator who was associated with Wagner in Paris at the time of the *Tannhäuser* production.

DUJARDIN, Edouard, 1861–1949, French novelist of the 'stream of consciousness' school who founded the journal known as the *Revue Wagnérienne* in 1885 in Paris.

DUKAS, Paul, 1865–1935, French composer who studied with Guiraud. He later became professor at the Conservatoire.

DUPARC, Henri, 1848–1933, French composer who began his musical career as a child prodigy of the piano. He took lessons with Franck. In 1885 he developed a nervous complaint and stopped composing. In spite of his long life his output is remarkably small.

VAN DYCK, Ernest, 1861–1923, Belgian tenor noted for his portrayals of Lohengrin and Parsifal (which he sang for the first time at Bayreuth in 1888). He was a friend of Shaw and of Chabrier.

ELGAR, Edward, 1857–1934, English composer, largely self-taught, who obtained first recognition in Germany. His first symphony was introduced by Richter at a Hallé concert in 1908, an event which established his success.

ELLIS, William Ashton, 1853–1919, English physician who was the pioneer translator of Wagner's *Prose Works*. Such was his devotion to this arduous task that he would have passed his final years in penury had not Shaw been instrumental in obtaining a Civil List pension for him.

FRANCK, César, 1822–1890, Belgian composer, originally a child prodigy pianist, he studied at the Paris Conservatoire, became a celebrated organist and teacher.

GAUTIER, Judith, 1850–1917, French poet and Orientalist, the daughter of the writer Théophile Gautier. She married Catulle Mendès in 1867, and left him in 1874. Her relationship with Wagner has not yet been fully clarified.

GRÉTRY, André Ernest Modeste, 1741–1813, Belgian composer of opera and writer on musical subjects.

GRIEG, Edvard Hagerup, 1843–1907, Norwegian composer of Scots descent who studied in Germany. An enthusiast for Norwegian national music, he worked largely in the smaller forms.

GROVE, George, 1820–1900, English civil engineer, biblical scholar and writer on music; editor of the Dictionary that bears his name. Knighted 1883.

GUIRAUD, Ernest, 1837–1892, French composer and academic who, whilst professor at the Conservatoire, counted Debussy amongst his pupils from 1876.

GULBRANSON, Ellen, 1863–1947, Swedish soprano who sang at Bayreuth from 1896 to 1914. She was much admired by Melba, who commanded private performances of her Wagner roles.

HALÉVY, Daniel Fromental Elias, 1799–1862, French composer who wrote numerous operas that made up the staple diet of the Paris Opéra. Wagner made piano arrangements of these, in the years 1839–42.

HANSLICK, Eduard, 1825–1904, Austrian music critic and lecturer on the history of music at Vienna University. Conservative by nature, he was unable to accept Wagner's innovations.

HELLER, Stephen, 1814–1888, Hungarian pianist and composer who took up residence in Germany, at Augsberg.

HOLMÈS, Augusta, 1847–1903, Irish-French pianist and composer who studied with Franck and was one of the most ardent of French Wagnerians (she took a German pseudonym, Hermann Zenta). One-time mistress of Catulle Mendès, she had a child by him. A woman of great personal beauty and charm she even roused the homosexual Saint-Saëns to ask for her hand. She wrote many songs and an opera which never succeeded.

HUMPERDINCK, Engelbert, 1854–1921, German composer who worked with Wagner at Bayreuth. Later he travelled in France, Italy and Spain and for a time taught in Barcelona. In the 1890s he was critic for the *Frankfurter Zeitung*.

D'INDY, Vincent, 1851–1931, French composer, pupil of Franck, he became a teacher of distinction with many famous pupils. A regular visitor to Bayreuth, where he frequently met Liszt whom he greatly admired.

JOACHIM, Joseph, 1831–1907, Hungarian-German violinist, composer and conductor who was a close associate of Brahms for many years.

KLINDWORTH, Karl, 1830–1916, German pianist and conductor, a pupil of Liszt, who made the piano arrangements of Wagner's works. His adopted daughter, Winifred Williams, married Siegfried Wagner in 1916.

LAMOUREUX, Charles, 1834–1899, French violinist and conductor who was at the Opéra from 1870 and who founded in 1881 the Concerts (and Orchestra) that bear his name. He introduced much of Wagner's music to Paris – but in concert form.

LAROCHE, Hermann Augustovich, 1845–1904, Russian music critic who was a fellow student of Tchaikovsky. He held academic posts in Moscow and St Petersburg.

LASALLE, Jean Louis, 1847–1909, French baritone who studied painting in Paris but eventually turned to singing.

LAVIGNAC, Alexandre Jean Albert, 1846–1916, French musicologist and teacher; author of numerous technical treatises, founder of the *Encyclopédie de la musique*.

LEHMANN, Lilli, 1848–1929, German soprano who sang at the early Bayreuth Festivals. Her career extended to the 1920s and encompassed 170 roles throughout the repertoire. As a teacher she had many famous pupils.

LEKEU, Guillaume, 1870–1894, Belgian composer who studied in Paris with Franck and d'Indy.

LEVI, Hermann, 1839–1900, German conductor, appointed director at the Munich Opera in 1872, he conducted the first performances of *Parsifal* at the Bayreuth Festival in 1882.

LISZT, Franz, 1811–1886, Hungarian pianist and composer who established the traditional life of the travelling virtuoso performer. He was a great champion of Wagner (who felt Liszt was wasting a great talent in performing). His daughter Cosima married Wagner in 1870.

LOUŸS, Pierre, 1870–1925, French novelist and poet, he was a friend of Debussy, who twice set some of his verses, the *Chansons de Bilitis*.

MAHLER, Gustav, 1860–1911, Austrian conductor and composer who, after many important posts, established a legendary regime at the Vienna Opera between 1897 and 1907. His compositions were part-time activities only.

MATERNA, Amalie, 1844–1918, Austrian soprano who sang mainly in Vienna. She was the first Brünnhilde at Bayreuth in 1876 and the first Kundry in 1882.

MENDÈS, Catulle, 1841–1909, French writer, poet and dramatist who wrote numerous libretti for Chabrier, Massenet, etc. He married Judith Gautier, his mistress for several years. His personal friendship with Wagner did not survive *Eine Kapitulation*, but his interest in the works remained.

MESSAGER, André, 1853–1929, French conductor and composer, he was director of Covent Garden from 1901 to 1906 (during which period Richter conducted the *Ring* there) and from 1901 to 1913 joint director of the Paris Opéra. The first performance of Debussy's *Pelléas et Mélisande* was given under his direction at the Opéra-Comique in 1902.

MONOD, Gabriel, 1844–1915, French historian and Teutonophile, a friend of Romain Rolland, whom he introduced to Bayreuth.

MOTTL, Felix, 1856–1911, Austrian conductor and composer. In 1876 he conducted the stage music at Bayreuth. From 1903 he was a director at Munich. In spite of his attachment to Cosima's Bayreuth he had very wide tastes in music, among them Berlioz.

NEUMANN, Angelo, 1838–1910, Austrian baritone and impresario who toured with the 1876 Bayreuth *Ring*, bringing it to London in 1882.

NIEMANN, Albert, 1831–1917, German tenor who sang in Berlin and was chosen by Wagner for the part of Siegmund in the Bayreuth *Ring* of 1876. He sang Tannhäuser in Paris in 1861.

PARRY, Charles Hubert Hastings, 1848–1918, English composer and writer on music: he held numerous academic posts and wrote a large amount of music including an opera. Knighted 1898.

PFITZNER, Hans, 1869–1949, German conductor and composer and advocate of the Romantic ideal. His opera *Palestrina* was first given at Munich in 1917.

PLÜDDERMANN, Martin, 1854–1897, German composer of ballads, generally regarded as the successor to Loewe in this genre. He became a member of the Wahnfried circle in the late 1870s.

PORGES, Heinrich, 1837–1900, German pianist, teacher and writer on music of Bohemian origin. He was active in Munich in the 1860s and became a champion for the cause of Wagner.

PUCCINI, Giacomo, 1858–1924, Italian composer of operas. He came from a long line of church composers; achieved great success and considerable wealth with his *verismo* style of opera.

RACHMANINOV, Sergei Vassilievich, 1873–1943, Russian pianist and composer, member of a noble family (related to the Czars) which fell on hard times in his early years. He left Russia in 1917, lived for a while in Paris, spent the rest of his life in America and on long concert tours.

RAFF, Joseph Joachim, 1822–1882, Swiss composer who studied with Mendelssohn and Liszt, orchestrating some of the latter's works. He became director of the Conservatoire in Frankfurt.

RANDEGGER, Alberto, 1832–1911, Italian singing teacher and composer who settled in London in the 1850s and became professor at the Royal Academy in 1868.

REGER, Max, 1873–1916, German composer and organist, seen as a conservative in the guise of a progressive, he held posts at Meiningen, Leipzig and Jena. By nineteenth century standards his output was vast.

DE RESZKE, Jean, 1850–1925, Polish tenor who studied in Italy and sang frequently in London before retiring in 1902.

REYER, Ernest, 1823–1909, French composer and critic, champion of Wagner and to the forefront of the French school that accepted his influence. Chiefly remembered on account of his opera *Sigurd*.

RICHTER, Hans, 1843–1916, Austro-Hungarian conductor who began his career playing the horn in Vienna. He was chosen by Wagner to conduct the *Ring* at the first Bayreuth Festival in 1876. Active in London between 1877 and 1910, he also conducted the Hallé Orchestra from 1900 to 1911.

RICHTER, Jean Paul, 1763–1825, German novelist who lived in Bayreuth. Born at nearby Wunsiedel his peasant origins led him to exploit a type of countryside romanticism.

RISLER, Edouard, 1873–1929, French pianist of German descent who studied with Karl Klindworth and became one of the group of remarkable musicians gathered by Cosima to work at Bayreuth. He later gained a reputation for his playing of Beethoven.

RUBINSTEIN, Anton Grigorievich, 1829–1924, Russian pianist and composer who founded the St Petersburg Conservatoire in 1862. Brother of Nikolai.

RUBINSTEIN, Nikolai, 1835–1881, who founded the Conservatoire in Moscow in 1864, inviting Tchaikovsky to take a post as Professor there.

RUBINSTEIN, Josef, 1847–1884, Russian pianist who wrote to Wagner in 1872 asking to work with him. He obtained a job as musical assistant at Bayreuth where he was unpopular when he tried to monopolise Wagner, to whom he developed a dog-like devotion. He took his own life in despair after the death of Wagner.

SAINT-SAËNS, Charles Camille, 1835–1921, French composer and pianist. His output was immense and included a dozen operas.

SCARIA, Emil, 1838–1886, Austrian bass who studied in Vienna. He was to have sung the role of Wotan in the first *Ring* in 1876 but dropped out at the last minute. He was the first to take the part of Gurnemanz in *Parsifal* in 1882.

SCHEIDEMANTEL, Karl, 1859–1923, German baritone whose fame rests on his assumption of Wagnerian roles, he sang at Bayreuth from 1886 onwards. In 1920 he became director of the Dresden Opera. He wrote two books on singing.

SCHJELDERUP, Gerhard, 1859–1933, Norwegian composer. He wrote a history of Norwegian music and biographies of his friend Grieg and of Wagner.

SCHNORR VON CAROLSFELD, Ludwig, 1836–1865, German tenor who sang the first Tristan at Munich in 1865 (his wife Malvina was the Isolde) – his death soon after this event gave rise to much superstition about the effects of the Wagner roles on those who sang them.

SCHRÖDER-DEVRIENT, Wilhelmine, 1804–1860, German soprano and dramatic actress, she had pleased Beethoven with her playing of his Leonore and greatly impressed the young Wagner in Dresden – perhaps with her in mind he created his heroines, even if her like never appeared to take the parts.

SCHUMANN-HEINK, Ernestine, 1861–1936, Czech-German contralto who first appeared at Bayreuth in 1896. After settling in America in 1898 she continued to sing in Europe.

SEMPER, Gottfried, 1803–1879, German architect and writer on the arts – associated with Wagner in Dresden, Zürich and Munich. He worked on designs for a Wagner Theatre in that last city, and also on the South Kensington Museums in London.

SHAW, (George) Bernard, 1856–1950, Irish dramatist, novelist and critic. He settled in London early in his career and wrote musical criticism with a pungent wit that all but disguises his passionate seriousness about music and opera. He insisted his plays were composed like operas without the music.

SIBELIUS, Jean, 1865–1957, Finnish composer who studied in Germany and Austria, was given an income by his government to enable him to compose, and became a national hero as a result of his international acclaim.

SMYTH, Ethel Mary, 1858–1944, English composer who studied and lived in Germany for many years. Later she took up the cause of women's suffrage; in 1922 she was made DBE. Her music received scant attention – she considered this was due to her being a woman.

SOOMER, Walter, 1878–1955, German bass-baritone active at Bayreuth from 1908 to 1925, later teacher and producer.

STANFORD, Charles Villiers, 1852–1924, Irish composer who held several academic posts in England. His extensive output includes seven operas. Knighted 1901.

STRAUSS, Richard Georg, 1864–1949, German composer and conductor whose early leanings towards Wagner led to his being hailed as 'Richard the Second'. The greater part of his output consists of operas; the range of subjects is wide. He was an active campaigner for the rights of composers and musicians.

STRAVINSKY, Igor Feodorovich, 1882–1971, Russian composer who spent most of his mature years in France and America. He wrote a large and varied quantity of music which embraces many styles, one or two of them being his own.

SUCHER, Rosa, 1849–1927, German soprano who took the part of Isolde in the first Bayreuth production in 1886.

SULLIVAN, Arthur Seymour, 1842–1900, English composer chiefly known for the operettas he composed to words by W. S. Gilbert but also the author of many 'serious' compositions which he considered his true metier. Knighted in 1883.

TCHAIKOVSKY, Peter Ilyich, 1840–1893, Russian composer whose list of compositions includes eight completed operas as well as three fragments of early attempts at the genre.

TWAIN, Mark (Samuel Langhorne Clemens), 1835–1910, American popular novelist and travel writer.

UHLIG, Theodor, 1822–1853, composer and writer who played the violin in the Dresden Opera orchestra and shared Wagner's revolutionary political views. They corresponded a great deal during Wagner's exile of 1849–52. Cosima later obtained copies of the letters from Uhiig's daughter Elsa and edited them to her own taste – the originals, however, are in the Burrell Collection.

UNGER, Georg, 1837–1887, German tenor who studied theology but took up singing and was the first Siegfried in 1876.

VAUGHAN WILLIAMS, Ralph, 1872–1958, English composer who studied with Max Bruch and Ravel; he was active in the collection of English folk songs and his works include five operas.

VOLKMANN, Robert, 1815–1883, German composer who held teaching posts in Budapest and Vienna.

WAGNER, Cosima, 1837–1930, daughter of Liszt and wife of Hans von Bülow, she married Wagner in 1870 and after his death in 1883 ran the Bayreuth Festival until 1909. She was as responsible as anyone for the living tradition there – with its good features and bad.

WAGNER, Siegfried, 1869–1930, German composer and conductor who intended to become an architect but was expected to continue his father's work. He took over the running of the Bayreuth Festivals in 1909 and continued until his death, which cast a shadow over the 1930 Festival. He was a pleasant and popular figure and much liked by those who worked with him.

WEBERN, Anton, 1883–1945, Austrian composer, pupil of Arnold Schoenberg and advocate of the twelve-tone system. He was accidentally shot by an American soldier at the end of the war.

WEGELIUS, Martin, 1846–1906, Finnish composer and teacher who studied in Germany but returned to his native land and there took an active part in musical life as critic and lecturer.

WILHELMJ, August, 1845–1908, German virtuoso violinist who led the Bayreuth orchestra in 1876. He settled in London and became professor at the Guildhall School of Music in 1894.

WOLF, Hugo, 1860–1903, Austrian composer known chiefly for a remarkable output of masterly songs. He studied for a time in Vienna but preferred to teach himself. He was, for a period, a music critic and led the counter-attack on Brahms. Wolf had a tragic end in a mental asylum.

WOLZOGEN, Hans von, 1848–1938, German musicologist who compiled thematic catalogues of Wagner's music and edited the *Bayreuther Blätter* for Wagner from 1877 onwards.

WOOD, Charles, 1866–1926, Irish musical scholar, teacher and composer. He occupied the chair of Music at Cambridge after Stanford; Beecham studied with him for a short time.

WOOD, Henry Joseph, 1869–1944, English conductor and founder of the Promenade Concerts which he directed for fifty years. He gave the first London performances of most of the important music of his day. Knighted 1911.

WOOLF, Virginia, 1882–1941, English writer and central figure of the 'Bloomsbury group' who is chiefly known for her novels. A sensitive nature caused her to suffer prolonged bouts of depression. The finest flower of the English aesthetic movement: depressed by the war, she took her life in 1941. She married Leonard Woolf in 1912.

APPENDIX II

Statistics
1876–1914

Works performed at Bayreuth 1876–1914. (The number of performances is shown in brackets)

1876 – *Ring* (3)
1882 – *Parsifal* (16)
1883 – *Parsifal* (12)
1884 – *Parsifal* (10)
1886 – *Parsifal* (9)
    – *Tristan und Isolde* (8)
1888 – *Parsifal* (9)
    – *Die Meistersinger* (8)
1889 – *Parsifal* (9)
    – *Tristan und Isolde* (4)
    – *Die Meistersinger* (5)
1891 – *Parsifal* (10)
    – *Tristan und Isolde* (3)
    – *Tannhäuser* (7)
1892 – *Parsifal* (8)
    – *Tristan und Isolde* (4)
    – *Die Meistersinger* (4)
    – *Tannhäuser* (4)
1894 – *Parsifal* (9)
    – *Tannhäuser* (5)
    – *Lohengrin* (6)
1896 – *Ring* (5)
1897 – *Ring* (3)
    – *Parsifal* (8)
1899 – *Ring* (2)
    – *Parsifal* (7)
    – *Die Meistersinger* (5)

1901 – *Ring* (2)
    – *Parsifal* (7)
    – *Der fliegende Holländer* (5)
1902 – *Ring* (2)
    – *Parsifal* (7)
    – *Der fliegende Holländer* (5)
1904 – *Ring* (2)
    – *Parsifal* (7)
    – *Tannhäuser* (5)
1906 – *Ring* (2)
    – *Parsifal* (7)
    – *Tristan und Isolde* (5)
1908 – *Ring* (2)
    – *Parsifal* (7)
    – *Lohengrin* (5)
1909 – *Ring* (2)
    – *Parsifal* (7)
1911 – *Ring* (2)
    – *Parsifal* (7)
    – *Die Meistersinger* (5)
1912 – *Ring* (2)
    – *Parsifal* (7)
    – *Die Meistersinger* (5)
1914 – *Ring* (1)
    – *Parsifal* (2)
    – *Der fliegende Holländer* (2)

The total number of performances of each work at the Bayreuth Festivals for the years 1876–1914 is as follows

Das Rheingold	30	*Die Meistersinger*	32
Die Walküre	30	*Tannhäuser*	21
Siegfried	30	*Lohengrin*	16
Die Götterdämmerung	30	*Der fliegende Holländer*	12
Parsifal	156		
Tristan und Isolde	24		381

Conductors at Bayreuth, 1876–1914

1876 – Hans Richter (*Ring*)
1882 – Franz Fischer (*Parsifal*)
     – Hermann Levi (*Parsifal*)
1883 – Franz Fischer (*Parsifal*)
     – Hermann Levi (*Parsifal*)
1884 – Franz Fischer (*Parsifal*)
     – Hermann Levi (*Parsifal*)
1886 – Hermann Levi (*Parsifal*)
     – Felix Mottl (*Tristan und Isolde*)
1888 – Felix Mottl (*Parsifal*)
     – Hans Richter (*Meistersinger*)
1889 – Hermann Levi (*Parsifal*)
     – Felix Mottl (*Tristan und Isolde*)
     – Hans Richter (*Meistersinger*)
1891 – Hermann Levi (*Parsifal*)
     – Felix Mottl (*Tristan und Isolde,
       Tannhäuser*)
1892 – Hermann Levi (*Parsifal*)
     – Felix Mottl (*Tristan und Isolde,
       Tannhäuser, Meistersinger*)
     – Hans Richter (*Meistersinger*)
1894 – Hermann Levi (*Parsifal*)
     – Felix Mottl (*Lohengrin*)
     – Richard Strauss (*Tannhäuser*)
1896 – Felix Mottl (*Ring*)
     – Hans Richter (*Ring*)
     – Siegfried Wagner (*Ring*)
1897 – Felix Mottl (*Parsifal*)
     – Hans Richter (*Ring*)
     – Anton Seidl (*Parsifal*)
     – Siegfried Wagner (*Ring*)
1899 – Franz Fischer (*Parsifal*)
     – Hans Richter (*Meistersinger*)
     – Siegfried Wagner (*Ring*)
1901 – Felix Mottl (*Der fliegende Holländer*)
     – Karl Muck (*Parsifal*)

     – Hans Richter (*Ring*)
     – Siegfried Wagner (*Ring*)
1902 – Felix Mottl (*Der fliegende Holländer*)
     – Karl Muck (*Parsifal*)
     – Hans Richter (*Ring*)
     – Siegfried Wagner (*Ring*)
1904 – Michael Balling (*Parsifal*)
     – Franz Beidler (*Ring*)
     – Karl Muck (*Parsifal*)
     – Hans Richter (*Ring*)
     – Siegfried Wagner (*Tannhäuser*)
1906 – Michael Balling (*Parsifal, Tristan und
       Isolde*)
     – Franz Beidler (*Parsifal*)
     – Felix Mottl (*Tristan und Isolde*)
     – Karl Muck (*Parsifal*)
     – Hans Richter (*Ring*)
     – Siegfried Wagner (*Ring*)
1908 – Michael Balling (*Parsifal*)
     – Karl Muck (*Parsifal*)
     – Hans Richter (*Ring*)
     – Siegfried Wagner (*Lohengrin*)
1909 – Michael Balling (*Ring*)
     – Karl Muck (*Parsifal, Lohengrin*)
     – Siegfried Wagner (*Parsifal. Lohengrin*)
1911 – Michael Balling (*Ring, Parsifal*)
     – Karl Muck (*Parsifal*)
     – Hans Richter (*Meistersinger*)
     – Siegfried Wagner (*Ring*)
1912 – Michael Balling (*Ring, Parsifal*)
     – Karl Muck (*Parsifal*)
     – Hans Richter (*Meistersinger*)
     – Siegfried Wagner (*Ring*)
1914 – Michael Balling (*Ring*)
     – Karl Muck (*Parsifal*)
     – Siegfried Wagner (*Der fliegende
       Holländer*)

The time taken by the various conductors for the works given at the Bayreuth Festivals was entered on their scores by the orchestral players. A representative selection is given here, the figures showing the number of minutes taken.

Das Rheingold
1876 – Hans Richter 151
1896 – Felix Mottl 152
    – Siegfried Wagner 141
1904 – Franz Beidler 143
1909 – Michael Balling 141
Die Walküre
1876 – Hans Richter 62–87–70
1896 – Felix Mottl 66–92–70
    – Siegfried Wagner 67–90–67
1904 – Franz Beidler 62–88–66
1909 – Michael Balling 65–87–67
Siegfried
1876 – Hans Richter 83–77–80
1896 – Felix Mottl 81–74–81
    – Siegfried Wagner 81–73–80
1904 – Franz Beidler 81–76–81
1909 – Michael Balling 79–75–80
Die Götterdämmerung
1876 – Hans Richter 117–64–78
1896 – Felix Mottl 116–62–76
    – Siegfried Wagner 117–65–73
1904 – Franz Beidler 131–66–81
1909 – Michael Balling 118–67–79
Parsifal
1882 – Hermann Levi 107–62–75

    – Franz Fischer 110–70–83
1888 – Felix Mottl 106–67–82
1897 – Anton Seidl 108–64–87
1901 – Karl Muck 116–67–83
1904 – Michael Balling 106–63–79
1906 – Franz Beidler 108–65–78
1909 – Siegfried Wagner 109–69–85
Tristan und Isolde
1886 – Felix Mottl 80–75–75
1906 – Michael Balling 86–81–78
Die Meistersinger von Nürnberg
1888 – Hans Richter 83–61–120
1892 – Felix Mottl 82–59–115
Lohengrin
1894 – Felix Mottl 70–82–69
1908 – Siegfried Wagner 69–83–68
Tannhäuser
1891 – Felix Mottl 70–67–60
1894 – Richard Strauss 74–68–61
1904 – Siegfried Wagner 76–72–60
Der fliegende Holländer
(This being given as Wagner intended, without an interval between the acts)
1901 – Felix Mottl 147
1914 – Siegfried Wagner 143

APPENDIX III

Chronology

A brief calendar of the events in Richard Wagner's life based on the work of Otto Strobel. The figures in brackets indicate the age of the person concerned.

1813 Wilhelm Richard Wagner born 22 May, in Leipzig. Son of Karl Friedrich Wilhelm Wagner (43) a police clerk, and Johanna Pätz Wagner (34). Father dies 23 November.

1814 The Wagner family moves to Dresden; widow marries Ludwig Geyer (33), a painter and actor.

1821 Death of Ludwig Geyer (41) on 30 September; his brother at Eisleben supervises RW's education.

1822 RW (9) returns to Dresden; enters Kreuzschule.

1823 RW enthusiastically studies the Greek tragedies.

1824 RW (11) begins study of piano with Humann but is more interested in opera; develops an enthusiasm for Weber (with whom his mother is acquainted); his sisters Clara and Rosalie make their debuts as opera singers.

1825 RW (12) commemorates the death of a schoolfellow with a poem; it wins him a prize.

1826 Wagner family moves to Prague; RW stays behind in Dresden and neglects studies; begins the writing of a long gruesome tragedy, *Leubold*.

1827 RW (14) rejoins family, now in Leipzig.

1828 Enters the St Nicholas school in Leipzig; completes his tragedy and hears, for the first time, the symphonies of Beethoven at the Gewandhaus; stimulated to attempt to compose for his tragedy.

1829 Studies violin and theory; hears Wilhelmine Schröder-Devrient in *Fidelio*; attracts the interest of Dorn, conductor at the newly-opened theatre in Leipzig.

1830 RW (17) passionately interested in the July Revolution in Paris, takes part in the Leipzig Revolution; makes a piano arrangement of Beethoven's Ninth Symphony. Dorn performs his Overture in B flat major which is ridiculed.

1831 Studies harmony and counterpoint with Weinlig and enters the University; composes an Overture in D minor and other works.

1832 RW (19) ends study with Weinlig; composes C major symphony, two overtures and shorter pieces; visits Vienna and Prague where students play his symphony; writes text and begins to compose an opera, *Die Hochzeit* (his sister Rosalie advises him to abandon it and he does so); drafts the text for another opera, *Die Feen*.

1833 C major symphony is played at a Gewandhaus concert (where Clara Wieck (14) also plays); RW (20) is appointed chorus-master at Würzburg; work on *Die Feen* proceeds.

1834 *Die Feen* is completed but plans for a production at Leipzig fall through; RW (21) joins, as conductor, the company that includes Minna Planer (25) and goes to Magdeburg with them; begins *Das Liebesverbot*; onset of erysipelas.

1835 *Columbus* Overture performed at Magdeburg.

1836 *Das Liebesverbot* produced at Magdeburg 29 March but has to be withdrawn after only two performances; RW (23) marries Minna (27) on 24 November; text of an opera, *Die hohe Braut*, is begun, offered to Scribe for translation and then abandoned.

1837 RW begins and subsequently abandons the text of *Die glückliche Bärenfamilie*; becomes conductor at the Königsberg theatre where Minna is acting; *Rule Britannia* Overture written and performed; Minna leaves him; he stays with his sister Ottolie Brockhaus in Dresden, conceives the idea of *Rienzi* there; appointed conductor at Riga; Minna returns to him; start of lifelong troubles with creditors.

1838 RW absorbed in work on *Rienzi*.

1839 RW makes stormy journey from Riga, via Norwegian coast and London, to Paris; meets Meyerbeer at Boulogne; finds only vain promises and no encouragement in Paris; hears Habeneck conduct Beethoven's Ninth Symphony; inspired to compose *Faust* Overture in November.

1840 A winter of hardship and suffering; RW engaged in hack work, arrangements and writing of articles; abortive attempt to have *Das Liebesverbot* produced; writes text of one-act opera on the subject of the Flying Dutchman; finishes *Rienzi*.

1841 Text of opera sold for 500 francs which allows RW to expand it into full-length opera for Germany, *Der fliegende Holländer*, completed by November; *Rienzi* accepted for eventual production at Dresden; hardships continue.

1842 RW and Minna return to Dresden; *Holländer* accepted by Berlin; *Tannhäuser* sketched; *Rienzi* performed at Dresden on 20 October; RW appointed second conductor there.

1843 *Holländer* produced at Dresden on 2 January; composition of the choral work, *Das Liebesmahl der Apostel*, June.

1844 RW composes funeral music for Weber and an ode to welcome the King of Saxony.

1845 *Tannhäuser* completed; produced at Dresden 19 October; sketches made for *Lohengrin* and *Die Meistersinger*.

1846 RW suggests changes in the court theatre; conducts Beethoven's Ninth Symphony; meets von Bülow (16) and begins the score of *Lohengrin*.

1847 *Lohengrin* completed in short score; *Rienzi* is produced at Berlin on 24 October but is not well received there.

1848 RW (35) completes the text of *Siegfried's Tod*; works on text of *Jesus von Nazareth* (uncompleted); joins the radical *Vaterlansverein*; begins friendship with Liszt.

1849 RW takes up the revolutionary cause but is forced to flee, first to Liszt at Weimar, then to Paris; settles in Zürich where Minna joins him; writes 'Art and Revolution' and 'The Art Work of the Future'.

1850 RW returns to Paris; plans to elope with Jessie Laussot whom he visits in Bordeaux; she changes her mind and he returns to Minna in Zürich; *Lohengrin* performed in Weimar on 28 August under the direction of Liszt.

1851 RW given an annuity by Julie Ritter; completes 'Opera and Drama'; completes text of *Junge Siegfried* and decides to expand the two dramas into a *Nibelungen* cycle.

1852 Text of *Die Walküre* and of *Das Rheingold* completed; others refashioned as *Siegfried* and *Die Götterdämmerung*.

1853 RW (40) meets Cosima Liszt (16) in Paris; writes piano sonata for Mathilde Wesendonck (25).

1854 *Das Rheingold* completed at Zürich; *Die Walküre* is begun; Minna absent in Germany and RW forms a relationship with Mathilde Wesendonck; idea of *Tristan und Isolde*.

1855 RW visits London; conducts eight concerts for the Philharmonic Society, press hostile; meets Berlioz (52) who is directing a rival orchestra.

1856 *Die Walküre* completed end of March; sketches for *Die Sieger* (subsequently abandoned); *Siegfried* is begun.

1857 RW conceives and sketches *Parsifal*; takes up residence with Minna at the Asyl on the Wesendonck estate; writes the text of *Tristan* and composes the music for the first act; visited by von Bülow and Cosima; sets poems of Mathilde Wesendonck.

1858 RW (45) revisits Paris; sets more poems by Mathilde Wesendonck; affair with her causes Minna to depart for Germany; RW goes to Venice and continues work on *Tristan*.

1859 RW living in Lucerne; *Tristan* completed there; in Paris, joined by Minna who has tried to obtain amnesty for him.

1860 Successful concert in Paris; revises *Tannhäuser* for Opéra but refuses to include a ballet; RW receives permission to return to Germany – but not to the Kingdom of Saxony.

1861 *Tannhäuser* performed in Paris 13 March; later performances are disturbed by demonstrations and it is withdrawn; RW hears *Lohengrin* for the first time, in Vienna; makes a trip to Venice to visit the Wesendoncks there; returns to work on *Die Meistersinger*.

1862 Completion of the text of *Die Meistersinger*; work on the musical score begun at Biebrich am Rhein; amnesty extended to allow RW to return to his native Saxony; concerts of his works in Leipzig and Vienna; feminine influences provided by Mathilde Maier and Frederike Meyer.

1863 RW (50) makes a concert tour to various cities including St Petersburg and Moscow but remains more than ever in debt.

1864 RW, plagued by debts and on the run from creditors, is sought out and befriended by King Ludwig II of Bavaria; plans to produce his works in Munich under von Bülow; involvement with Cosima; *Huldigungsmarsch* written for the King; scheme for a theatre to be built in Munich; start of intrigues against RW by the influential members of the court circles.

1865 *Tristan und Isolde* produced in Munich on 10 June; political intrigue causes RW to leave for sojourn in Geneva at the request of the King. Start of *Mein Leben*.

1866 First two acts of *Die Meistersinger* completed; Cosima (29) joins RW and they set up house together at Tribschen on Lake Lucerne; Hans Richter (23) engaged as assistant; RW dictates *Mein Leben* to Cosima.

1867 *Die Meistersinger* finished in short score; Cosima temporarily returns to von Bülow who is preparing the production of *Lohengrin* in Munich.

1868 *Die Meistersinger von Nürnberg* produced at Munich on 21 June; Cosima returns to Tribschen; RW (55) in Leipzig and meets Nietzsche (24); work on *Siegfried* resumed.

1869 Birth of son, Siegfried, 6 June; visit to Tribschen by Catulle Mendès and Judith Gautier; *Das Rheingold* produced in Munich on 22 September, against RW's wishes.

1870 RW begins the composition of *Götterdämmerung*; Cosima is divorced from von Bülow and marries RW on 25 August; first plans for a Festival at Bayreuth formed; composition of the *Siegfried Idyll* and performance on the staircase at Tribschen on 25 December, Cosima's birthday.

1871 RW completes the score of *Siegfried*; the *Kaisermarsch* composed to celebrate the Prussian victory; RW makes an incognito visit to Bayreuth and decides on the location of his Festival Theatre; visits to Berlin and Leipzig.

1872 Foundation stone of Theatre is laid on RW's fifty-ninth birthday; venture attacked by the press; departure from Tribschen for Bayreuth; successful visit to Vienna; start of tours to look for artists and raise money for Bayreuth project; short score of *Götterdämmerung* completed; foundation of the Wagner Societies in Germany.

1873 More concerts given to raise money for the Festival; project in danger of collapsing, publicity is increased; Theatre completed as far as *Richtfest*; full score of the first act of *Götterdämmerung* completed, 24 December.

1874 Bayreuth scheme saved by Ludwig II; Wagners move to Wahnfried; completion of *Götterdämmerung*, 21 November. Richter (31) and Seidl (24) begin to prepare the *Ring* cycle.

1875 RW gives concerts in Vienna, Budapest and Berlin; the preliminary rehearsals of the *Ring*, with some of the singers, begin in May; stage rehearsals take place in August; Vienna puts on the Paris version of *Tannhäuser* and Wagner is sought out, in that city, by Hugo Wolf (15) who idolises him.

1876 Festival still in jeopardy, aided by RW composing *American Centennial March* for 5,000 dollars; Felix Mottl (20) joins the Bayreuth staff; *Der Ring des Nibelungen* given, in three complete cycles, as the first Bayreuth Festival, beginning 13 August; resultant deficit leaves RW exhausted and in distress; Wagner family go to Italy to rest, September.

1877 RW elaborates the early sketches for *Parsifal*; eight concerts given in London; cure taken at Bad Ems; composition of *Parsifal* begun; onset of RW's heart trouble.

1878 *Bayreuther Blätter* appears; RW (65) suffering from heart trouble and rheumatism continues work on *Parsifal*; the complete *Ring* cycle is performed for the first time outside Bayreuth – at Leipzig, in April; the *Parsifal* prelude is scored and performed for Cosima's forty-first birthday.

1879 *Parsifal* completed in short score; RW still plagued by the Bayreuth Festival deficit appeals for funds; suffers from erysipelas once again.

1880 RW seeks relief from ailments in Italy; Humperdinck (26) begins his association with him; orchestration of *Parsifal* under way; visits to Venice and Munich; Angelo Neumann asks RW's permission to take the *Ring* on a tour of major cities.

1881 First two acts of *Parsifal* completed; RW (68) suffers a heart attack during an ovation after the *Ring* performance in Berlin; Wagner family goes to Palermo for the winter.

1882 RW completes *Parsifal* at Palermo on 13 January; rehearsals begin at Bayreuth; first performance on 26 July reserved for patrons, sixteen performances given, conducted by Levi; RW takes over last act of last performance; RW in poor health goes to Venice with family; frequent heart attacks.

1883 RW declares his interest in writing a symphony; deterioration in health and depression; RW dies of heart failure at Venice on 13 February.

Early Influences

A list of the stage works and operas which Wagner conducted, or was otherwise involved with, between 1833 and 1839 (his period at Königsberg in 1837 is not documented).

Würzburg, January 1833 to January 1834

Camilla (Paer, 1799)
Les Deux Journées (Cherubini, 1800)
Fidelio (Beethoven, 1805)
Fra Diavolo (Auber, 1830)
Der Freischütz (Weber), 1821)
Hans Heiling (Marschner, 1833)

La Muette de Portici (Auber, 1828)
Oberon (Weber, 1826)
Robert le Diable (Meyerbeer, 1831)
Tancredi (Rossini, 1813)
Der Vampyr (Marschner, 1831)
Zampa (Hérold, 1831)

Magdeburg, July 1834 to March 1836

Des Adlers Horst (Glaser, 1832)
Il Barbiere di Siviglia (Rossini, 1816)
I Capuleti ed i Montecchi (Bellini, 1830)
La Dame Blanche (Boieldieu, 1825)
Les Deux Journées
Don Giovanni (Mozart, 1787)
Der Dorfbarbier (Schenk, 1796)
Der Freischütz
Fra Diavolo
Jessonda (Spohr, 1823)
Lestocq (Auber, 1834)
Das Liebesverbot (Wagner, 1836), first
  performance

Maurer und Schlosser (Auber, 1825)
La Molinara (Paisiello, 1788)
La Muette de Portici
Oberon
Otello (Rossini, 1816)
Preziosa (Weber, 1820) incidental music to
  Wolff's drama
Die Schweizerfamilie (Weigl, 1809)
Le Secret (Solié, 1796)
La Straniera (Bellini, 1829)
Tancredi
Der Templar und die Jüdin (Marschner, 1829)
Zampa

Riga, August 1837 to August 1839 (The number of performances is given in brackets)

Il Barbiere di Siviglia (5)
I Capuleti ed i Montecchi (14)
La Dame Blanche (6)
Les Deux Journées (2)
Don Giovanni (6)
Fra Diavolo (6)
Der Freischütz (15)
Jessonda (3)
Joseph (Méhul, 1807) (5)
Maurer und Schlosser (2)
La Muette de Portici (5)

Norma (Bellini, 1831) (8)
Le Nozze de Figaro (Mozart, 1786) (6)
Oberon (2)
Le Postillon de Longjumeau (Adam, 1836)
  (14)
Preziosa (3)
Die Schweizerfamilie (6)
Das unterbrochene Opferfest (Winter, 1796)
  (7)
Zampa (6)
Die Zauberflöte (Mozart, 1791) (5)

NOTES ON SOURCES

Full titles of the works quoted or referred to are given in the Book List on page 275.

RW = Richard Wagner

page
15 RW on Schröder-Devrient: R W, *Mein Leben.*
17 RW, 'A German National Theatre' in *Prose Works of R W*, ed. Ashton Ellis, Vol. VII.
17 RW's revolutionary activities in Dresden: 'The Revolution', *Volksblätter* February 1849, ibid., Vol. VIII.
18 RW, 'The Abolition of the Monarchy', paper read to the *Vaterlandsverein*, ibid., Vol. IV.
18 RW, 'The Artwork of the Future', 'A Communication to my Friends', etc. ibid., Vol. I.
18 RW to Heine 1850: *R W's Letters to his Dresden Friends.*
18 RW to Uhlig 1850: ibid.
19 RW to Liszt 1852: *Correspondence of R W and Liszt.*
24 Cosima Wagner on Bayreuth: Cosima Wagner, *Tagebücher*, Vol. I.
24 RW to Feustel 1871: RW, *Bayreuther Briefe* (ed. Glasenapp) and *Letters of R W* (ed. Altmann, trans. Ashton Ellis) Vol. II.
25 RW, 'Bayreuth', *Prose Works* op. cit., Vol. V.
26 Nietzsche, 'Richard Wagner in Bayreuth', *Complete Works*, Vol. I.
31 RW to Feustel 1872: *Bayreuther Briefe* and *Letters of R W*, op. cit.
32 RW to Hoffman 1873: ibid.
33 RW to Feustel 1875: ibid.
37 Financing of the Festival: von Kraft, *Das Festspielhaus in Bayreuth.*
45 Lilli Lehmann, *Mein Weg.*
52 RW to Feustel 1875: *Bayreuther Briefe* and *Letters of R W*, op. cit.
52 Modeste Tchaikovsky, *Life and Letters of Peter Ilyitch Tchaikovsky.*
57 Saint-Saëns, *Harmonie et Mélodie.*
61 Grieg: *Bergensposten*, August and September 1876.
70 Neumann, *Recollections.*
72 Hanslick, *Musical Criticisms.*
85 Clemens Brockhaus's letter: private source.
87 Bennett, *Letters from Bayreuth.*
94 *Manchester Guardian*, August 1876.
97 Davison: *The Times*, 9–29 August, 1876.
104 Stanford, *Pages from an Unwritten Diary, Records and Reflections.*
107 *The Times*, 22 August 1876.
112 RW to Feustel 1881: *Bayreuther Briefe* and *Letters of R W* op. cit.
113 Humperdinck: *Völkischer Beobachter*, 17 August 1932.
119 Neumann, *Recollections.*
121 Hanslick, *Musical Criticisms.*
129 Weingartner, *Buffets and Rewards.*
137 Wood, *My Life of Music.*

138 Graves, *Life of Sir George Grove*.

139 Shaw: *The Hawk*, 13 August 1889.

143 —— *English Illustrated Magazine*, October 1889.

147 —— *The World*, 25 February 1891.

147 —— *Collected Letters*, Vol. I.

147 —— *The World*, 16 September 1891.

149 Mark Twain, 'At the Shrine of St Wagner' in *What is Man? and other Essays*.

156 Richard Strauss, '*Tannhäuser* at Bayreuth', *Bayreuther Blätter*, 1892, in *Recollections and Reflections* (ed. Schuh, trans. Lawrence).

160 Strauss, 'On the *Parsifal* Copyright', *Hamburger Fremdenblatt*, 1912. ibid.

161 Shaw: *The World*, 25 March 1891.

162 Strauss, 'Remarks on Wagner and Bayreuth' (1940), *Recollections and Reflections*, op. cit.

164 Shaw, *Collected Letters*, Vol. I.

165 Shaw: *The World*, 1 and 8 August 1894.

169 Crane, *An Artist's Reminiscences*.

173 Bülow, 'Bruckner, Wolf und Reger in Bayreuth', *Bayreuther Festspielführer*, 1934;

175 Hausswald, 'Musiker im Banne von Bayreuth', *Bayreuther Festspielbuch*, 1952;

178 Alma Mahler, *Gustav Mahler: Memories and Letters*.

180 Alban Berg, *Letters to his Wife*.

185 Emile de Saint-Auban, *Un pèlerinage à Bayreuth* quoted in Lockspeiser, *Debussy: his Life and Mind*, Vol. I.

189 Graves, *Hubert Parry: his Life and Works*, Vol. I.

191 Delius: Redwood (ed.), *A Delius Companion*.

192 Ethel Smyth, *As Time Went on . . .*

193 Tawastsjerna, *Sibelius*, Vol. I.

194 Carner, *Puccini*.

199 Lavignac, *Le voyage artistique à Bayreuth*, published in English as *The Music Dramas of Richard Wagner*.

212 Lilli Lehmann, *Mein Weg*.

218 Romain Rolland: 'Vier Tage in Bayreuth' given to the author in an uncredited German version; the original has proved impossible to locate. The authenticity is confirmed by parallel comments of Rolland concerning *Götterdämmerung* in his book *Musicians of Today*.

223 Fauré: *Bayreuther Festspielführer*, 1938.

223 Shaw: *The Star*, July 1896.

235 Shaw to Beatrice Webb: *Collected Letters*, Vol. I. Shaw, 'Prefaces' and 'Postscripts' to *The Perfect Wagnerite*, 4th edition, 1922.

238 Sullivan, *Letter and Diaries*.

239 Sir Charles Tennyson, radio broadcast, BBC Radio 3, April 1976.

243 Beecham, *A Mingled Chime*.

245 Bartók, *Letters*.

245 Shaw, *Collected Letters*, Vol. II.

247 Virginia Woolf, 'Impressions at Bayreuth' from *The Times*, 21 August 1909.

251 Boult, *My Own Trumpet*.

251 Stravinsky, *Chronicle of My Life*.

253 'The Gradual Change', *The Times*, 31 January 1914.

BOOK LIST

A list of the books and articles consulted, published in London unless otherwise stated. The asterisk indicates those from which an extended extract is printed.

ABRAHAM, Gerald: *A Hundred Years of Music* (4th edition, 1974)

ANDERTON, Howard O.: *Granville Bantock* (1915)

Baedeker's Southern Germany and Austria (Leipzig, 1873)

BARTH, Herbert *et al*: *Wagner: a Documentary Study* (1975)

*BARTÓK, Béla: *Béla Bartók Letters*, ed. Janos Démény (1971)

BAUER, Oswald Georg and MACK, Dietrich: *Bayreuther Festspiele: Die Idee, Der Bau, Die Aufführungen* (7th edition, Bayreuth, 1979)

BEAUFILS, Marcel: *Wagner et le Wagnérisme* (Paris, 1947)

*BEECHAM, Sir Thomas: *A Mingled Chime* (1944)

*BENNETT, Joseph: *Letters from Bayreuth Descriptive and Critical of Wagner's 'Der Ring des Nibelungen', etc.* (1877)

BERG, Alban: *Alban Berg, Letters to His Wife*, ed., trans. and annotated by Bernard Grun (1971)

BLUNT, Wilfred: *The Dream King: Ludwig II of Bavaria* (1970)

BÜLOW, Paul: 'Bruckner, Wolf und Reger in Bayreuth' *Bayreuther Festspielführer* (Bayreuth, 1934)

CARDUS, Neville: *Ten Composers* (1945)

CARNER, Mosco: *Puccini* (1958)

CHAMBERLAIN, Houston Stewart: *Richard Wagner*, trans. G. A. Hight (1897)

COOPER, Martin: *French Music from the death of Berlioz to the death of Fauré* (1951)

CRANE, Walter: *An Artist's Reminiscences* (1907)

CUTHELL, Edith E.: *Wilhemina, Margravine of Baireuth*, 2 vols (1905)

DAVIES, Laurence: *The Gallic Muse* (1967)

—— *César Franck and His Circle* (1970)

DEMUTH, Norman: *César Franck* (1949)

—— *Vincent d'Indy: Champion of Classicism* (1951)

DENT, Edward J.: *Feruccio Busoni* (1933, reprinted 1974)

FESCHOTTE, Jacques: 'Alfred Cortot und Bayreuth' *Festspiele Nachrichten* (Bayreuth, 1957)

FISCHER-DIESKAU, Dietrich: *Wagner and Nietzsche*, trans. Joachim Neugroschel (1976)

GAL, Hans: *Richard Wagner*, trans. Hans-Hubert Schönzeler (1976)

GLASENAPP, Carl Friedrich: *Das Leben Richard Wagners*, 6 vols, (Leipzig, 1894–1911) translated into English by William Ashton Ellis as *The Life of Richard Wagner*, 6 vols, (1902–8) of which the last two volumes are written by Ellis, independently of Glasenapp

DE LA GRANGE, Henri-Louis: *Mahler* (1974)

*GRAVES, Charles L.: *Life of Sir George Grove* (1903)

—— *Hubert Parry: his Life and Works*, 2 vols (1926)

*HANSLICK, Eduard: *Musical Criticisms 1846–99*, trans. Henry Pleasants (1951)

HARDING, James: *Saint-Saëns and His Circle* (1965)

HARMAN, Alec and MELLORS, Wilfred: *Man and his Music* (1962)

HAUSSWALD, Gunther: 'Musiker im Banne von Bayreuth' *Bayreuther Festspielbuch* (Bayreuth, 1952)

HIGHT, George Ainslie: *Richard Wagner: a Critical Biography*, 2 vols (1925)

*HUMPERDINCK, Engelbert: 'Persönliche Parsifal-Errinerungen und die erste Aufführungen des Bühnenweihfestspieles am 26 Juli 1882', *Bayreuther Festspielführer* (1927) and *Völkischer Beobachter* (1932)

HUNEKER, James: *Mezzotints in Modern Music* (1899)

JACOBS, Robert L.: *Wagner* (1935, revised 1974)

JEFFERSON, Alan: *Delius* (1972)

—— *Life of Richard Strauss* (1973)

KENNEDY, Michael: *Portrait of Elgar* (1968)

KRAFT, Zdenko von: *Das Festspielhaus in Bayreuth* (Bayreuth, 1969)

*LAVIGNAC, Albert: *The Music Dramas of Richard Wagner and his Festival Theatre at Bayreuth* (New York, 1898)

*LEHMANN, Lilli: *Mein Weg* (Leipzig, 1913)

LEVAS, Santeri: *Sibelius, a personal portrait* (1972)

LIPPERT, Woldemar: *Wagner in Exile 1849–62*, trans. Paul England (1930)

LOCKSPEISER, Edward: *Debussy, His Life and Mind*, 2 vols (1962)

MAHLER, Alma: *Gustav Mahler: Memories and Letters*, 2 vols (1968, 1973)

MANN, Thomas: *Essays of Three Decades*, trans. H. T. Lowe-Porter (1947)

DEL MAR, Norman: *Richard Strauss*, 3 vols (1962–72)

MAREK, George: *Richard Strauss* (1967)

MAYER, Hans: *Richard Wagner in Bayreuth*, trans. Jack Zipes (1976)

MOULIN-ECKART, Count Richard du: *Cosima Wagner*, trans. Catherine Allison, 2 vols (1930)

MYERS, Rollo: *Emmanuel Chabrier and His Circle* (1969)

*NEUMANN, Angelo: *Personal Recollections of Richard Wagner* (1909)

NEUPERT, Käte: *Die Besetzung der Bayreuther Festspiele 1876–1960* (Bayreuth, 1961)

NEWMAN, Ernest: *The Life of Richard Wagner*, 4 vols (1933–47)

—— *A Study of Wagner* (1890)

—— *Wagner as Man and Artist* (1914, reprinted 1963)

—— *Wagner Nights* (1949)

—— *Hugo Wolf* (1907, reprinted 1968 with Introduction by Walter Legge)

*NIETZSCHE, Friedrich: *Complete Works*, trans. A. M. Ludovici (1909)

PANOFSKY, Walter: *Wagner: a Pictorial Biography*, trans. Richard Rickett (1963)

PASLEY, Malcolm (ed.): *A Companion to German Studies* (1972)

REDWOOD, Christopher (ed.): *A Delius Companion* (1976)

ROLLAND, Romain: *Musicians of Today*, trans. Mary Blaiklock (1915)

*SAINT-SAËNS, Camille: *Harmonie et Mélodie* (Paris, 1885)

SCHÖNZELER, Hans Hubert: *Bruckner* (1978)

SCOTT-SUTHERLAND, Colin: *Arnold Bax* (1975)

*SHAW, Bernard: *How to become a Musical Critic*, ed. Dan H. Laurence (1960)

—— *The Perfect Wagnerite* (4th edition, 1922)

—— *Collected Letters 1874–97*, ed. Dan H. Laurence (1965)

—— *Collected Letters 1898–1910*, ed. Dan H. Laurence (1972)

SMYTH, Ethel: *As Time Went on . . .* (1936)

SOKOLOFF, Alice Hunt: *Cosima Wagner: a Biography* (1969)

*STANFORD, Sir Charles Villiers: *Pages from an Unwritten Diary* (1914)

—— *Records and Reflections* (1922)

STEIN, Jack M.: *Richard Wagner and the Synthesis of the Arts* (Detroit, 1960)

*Strauss, Richard: *Recollections and Reflections*, ed. Willi Schuh, trans. L. J. Lawrence (1953)

*Stravinsky, Igor: *Chronicle of my Life* (1936) reprinted as *An Autobiography* (1973)

Strobel, Otto: *Richard Wagner, Leben und Schaffen: Eine Zeittafel* (Bayreuth, 1952)

*Sullivan, Sir Arthur Seymour: *Letter and Diaries* (n.d.)

Sutherland, Douglas: *Twilight of the Swans* (1974)

Tawastsjerna, Erik: *Sibelius*, Vol. I, 1865–1905, trans. Robert Layton (1976)

Taylor, Ronald: *Richard Wagner: His Life, Art and Thought* (1979)

*Tchaikovsky, Modeste: *The Life and Letters of Peter Ilyich Tchaikovsky* (1906)

*Twain, Mark (Samuel Langhorne Clemens): 'At the Shrine of St Wagner', *What is Man? and other Essays* (1917)

Vaughan Williams, Ursula: *RVW: a Biography of Ralph Vaughan Williams* (1964)

Wagner, Cosima: *Die Tagebücher*, ed. Martin Gregor-Dellin and Dietrich Mack, Band I, 1869–77 (Munich, 1976), Band II, 1878–83 (1977)

*Wagner, Richard: *Richard Wagner's Letters to his Dresden Friends, Theodor Uhlig, Wilhelm Fischer, Ferdinand Heine*, trans. J. S. Shedlock (1890)

—— *Richard Wagner's Letters to Emil Heckel*, trans. William Ashton Ellis (1897)

—— *Letters to Auguste Röckel*, trans. E. C. Sellar (1897)

—— and Liszt, Franz: *Correspondence of Wagner and Liszt*, trans. Francis Hueffer, 2 vols (1897)

—— *The Prose Works of Richard Wagner*, trans. William Ashton Ellis, 8 vols (1895–99) in particular 'The Artwork of the Future' and 'A Communication to my Friends' (Vol. I); 'Opera and Drama' (Vol. II); 'Bayreuth' (Vol. V); '*Parsifal* at Bayreuth' (Vol. VI)

—— *Bayreuther Briefe von Richard Wagner, 1871–1883*, ed. Carl Friedrich Glasenapp (Berlin and Leipzig, 1907)

—— *Richard Wagner an seine Künstler*, ed. Erich Kloss (Berlin, 1908)

—— *Richard Wagner an Ferdinand Praeger*, ed. Houston Stewart Chamberlain (Berlin and Leipzig, 1908)

—— *Richard Wagner an Freunde und Zeitgenossen*, ed. Erich Kloss (Berlin 1909)

—— *The Family Letters of Richard Wagner*, trans. William Ashton Ellis (1911)

—— *My Life*, 2 vols (1911)

—— and Nietzsche, Friedrich: *The Nietzsche-Wagner Correspondence*, ed. Elisabeth Förster-Nietzsche, trans. C. V. Kerr (1922)

—— *Letters of Richard Wagner*, selected and edited by Wilhelm Altman, trans. William Ashton Ellis, 2 vols (1927)

—— *Letters of Richard Wagner: the Burrell Collection*, edited with notes by John N. Burk (1951)

Walker, Frank: *Hugo Wolf* (1968)

Wallace, William, *Richard Wagner as He Lived* (1925)

—— *Liszt, Wagner and the Princess* (1927)

Watson, Derek: *Bruckner* (1975)

*Weingartner, Felix: *Buffets and Rewards*, trans. Marguerite Wolff (1937)

Westernhagen, Curt von: *Wagner: A Biography*, trans. Mary Whittall, 2 vols (1978)

*Wood, Sir Henry J.: *My Life of Music* (1938)

Woolf, Virginia: *The Flight of the Mind*, Letters of Virginia Woolf (Stephen) Vol. I, 1888–1912, ed. Nigel Nicolson (1975)

—— *Books and Portraits*, ed. Mary Lyon (1977)

Young, Percy: *Elgar, O. M.: a Study of a Musician* (1955)

ZUCKERMAN, Elliott: *The First Hundred Years of Wagner's Tristan* (New York, 1964)

Grove's Dictionary of Music and Musicians (5th edition, 1954)
Dictionary of National Biography and Supplements
Oxford Companion to German Literature, ed. Henry and Mary Garland (1976)

GENERAL INDEX

INDEX OF RICHARD WAGNER'S WORKS